Kellogg *on* Technology & Innovation

Kellogg *on* Technology & Innovation

EDITED BY

RANJAY GULATI

MOHANBIR SAWHNEY

AND ANTHONY PAONI

John Wiley & Sons, Inc.

Published by John Wiley & Sons, Inc., Hoboken, New Jersey.
Published simultaneously in Canada.

For general information on our other products and services please contact our Customer Care Department within the U.S. at (800) 762-2974, outside the United States at (317) 572-3993 or fax (317) 572-4002.

Wiley also publishes its books in a variety of electronic formats. Some content that appears in print may not be available in electronic books.

Library of Congress Cataloging-in-Publication Data:

Gulati, Ranjay.
  Kellogg on technology & innovation / Ranjay Gulati, Mohanbir Sawhney, Anthony Paoni.
       p.   cm.
Includes bibliographical references and index.
    ISBN 0-471-23592-X (alk. Paper)
    1. Technological innovations—Economic aspects.   I. Title: Kellogg on technology and innovation.   II. J.L. Kellogg Graduate School of Management.   III. Sawhney, Mohanbir S.   IV. Paoni, Anthony.   V. Title.
  HC79.T4   G85   2002
  338'.064—dc21

                                                                2002011427

Printed in the United States of America.

10   9   8   7   6   5   4   3   2   1

To Donald P. Jacobs, Dean Emeritus
of the Kellogg School of Management,
who served as Dean from 1975 to 2001.
Dean Jacobs fostered a culture of collaboration,
teamwork, and entrepreneurship.
Without his support for our TechVenture course,
this book would not have been possible.

CONTENTS

Preface   ix

Section I
ENABLING TECHNOLOGIES AND INFRASTRUCTURE

Chapter 1
The Future of Semiconductor Technology   3
  *Hagai Bar-Lev, Paul W. F. Rutten, Avner M. I. Sonnino, and
  Michal Tauman*

Chapter 2
Optical Networking   38
  *Mike Doheny, Jennifer Ann Glaspie, B. Jason Koval,
  Nicholas L. Leeming, and Eric M. Smyth*

Chapter 3
The Wireless Value Chain and Infrastructure   79
  *Jennifer L. Eselius, Deepak Garg, Greg Hughes, Jeff Kelly,
  Ian R. Lacy, Daniel A. Levine, Nelson Francisco Molina,
  Manish Panjwani, Donaldson C. Pillsbury, Andrew I. Quarles,
  Charity C. C. Rivera, Tom Stokes, Shyam V. P. Sharma,
  Lori S. Tabuchi, Christopher Thun, Karthik Vasudevan,
  Vivian Yang, and Rich Yeh*

Section II
BUSINESS MODELS AND MARKETS

Chapter 4
Interactive Television   155
  Marc P. Adams, Parul Anand, and Sebastien M. Fox

vii

Chapter 5

Wireless Applications   193

*Albert V. Fratini, Deepak Garg, Daniel C. Grace, Esteban
Greenberg, Christina N. Goletz, Jonathon D. Lewis,
Laura J. Lewis, James E. Lutz, Rodrigo Manzano, Armoghan
Mohammed, Evan M. Norton, Ian M. Norton, Manish Panjwani,
Daniel B. Rosenbloom, Lisa S. Roth, Shyam V. P. Sharma,
Sonia A. De La Torre, Karthik Vasudevan, and Rich Yeh*

Section III
EMERGING TECHNOLOGIES

Chapter 6

Recent Trends in Nanotechnology   261

*Puneet Gupta, Rajit Malhotra, Michael A. Segal, and
Marc Y. F. J. Verhaeren*

Chapter 7

Peer-to-Peer Computing   284

Alanso Quintana, Jayesh Ramsinghani, and Timothy Walls

Chapter 8

A Framework for the Biotechnology Industry   312

*Katie Arnold, Thomas H. Fuchs, Scott T. Saywell,
Wallace Saunders, and David M. Scalzo*

Index   343

PREFACE

Genius is one percent inspiration and ninety-nine percent perspiration.
—Thomas Edison

Edison reminds us that successful innovation requires more than just a good idea. Given the current state of the technology sector in 2002, which has witnessed dramatic drops in stock prices, tens of thousands of layoffs, and the demise of many start-ups, Edison's quote seems particularly relevant. After all, couldn't we argue that many technology companies started out with good ideas and have been working hard? Perhaps they were working hard, but not necessarily working smart. Or perhaps some good old-fashioned luck is needed in addition to inspiration and perspiration, given the rapidly changing market and business conditions. Or maybe there were just too many players competing for the same pie.

All of these observations have some truth. Early in the development of an industry, more inspiration may be required. While for mature industries, more perspiration may be required. Regardless, successful business practice is about positioning a company well to beat the odds and executing relentlessly to capitalize on the position. To create positions of advantage, business decision makers need information that can help them understand the trends in their markets so they can place their strategic bets intelligently.

The past decade has witnessed unprecedented advances across a variety of technological frontiers. The pace of change is compounded by the convergence of some of these frontiers. Many promises have been made about the value creation potential of some of these developments, only to fizzle out later on. The list is long—e-retailing, business-to-business market-places, satellite phones, HDTV, wireless data, optical networking, genomics, broadband, third-generation wireless technology, interactive TV, home networking, and so on. Skeptics have looked back and pointed to a pattern of hype surrounding new technological developments and have become dismissive of any new claims because of their poor track record.

We believe that at least part of the reason we see this "boom-and-bust" pendulum in technology industries is because much of the early discussion of new technologies is about the *technical merits* of the new technologies. Very seldom does the discussion focus on the *business value* of the technology and the business models that need to be developed to capture value from the technology. Too often, business-model and customer-value-proposition discussions are conducted as a postmortem, when entire technology sectors flame out, and journalists and academics build retrospective accounts of why things did not turn out the way people thought they would. Unless we change the nature of the conversation about new technologies, we may not be able to break free from this vicious cycle.

THE PURPOSE OF THIS BOOK

This book is an attempt to view emerging frontiers in technology through the clear lenses of business instead of the rose-tinted glasses of technologists. Our goal is to help managers and investors gain an intelligent understanding of some of the most-promising new technologies and develop an informed opinion of the business prospects of these technologies. In discussing a technology frontier, we provide enough details for the reader to develop strategic fluency with the technology, and then we quickly turn to the business challenges in commercializing it. We also present likely alternative scenarios that paint a picture of how the markets for each technology might develop and identify some of the key players and plays that are likely to capture a dominant role in each domain. The primary audience for this book is managers who are intrigued by these exciting frontiers and have a feeling that some of these developments will have an impact on their industries but are not sure how. Given our business-focused stance, this book makes no attempt to provide complete coverage of the various technologies. Technology is discussed only as necessary to understand the key drivers and trends in the industries. Our main focus is to help the reader in understanding the value chains in these industries, the business impact of technological innovations, the competitive landscape in the industries, and the battle for standards and control of value-capture points in these arenas.

HOW THIS BOOK WAS WRITTEN

This book is the outcome of a unique collaborative effort that is the hallmark of the Kellogg culture. The insight that motivated it is simple, yet powerful: *Students don't merely consume knowledge, they co-create knowledge.* As Kellogg faculty charged with the impossible task of keeping pace with developments across the diverse frontiers of technology, we quickly realized that this was a task we could not do justice to by ourselves. Instead, we harnessed the collective energies of our students. We jointly teach a course called Kellogg TechVenture. TechVenture is an action learning course that exposes students to the latest developments in technology, and it includes a field trip to Silicon Valley to meet with representatives of the companies that are leading the charge in various technology sectors. As part of this course, we encourage students to pick a technology frontier that excites them the most and to work with one of us to develop an insightful and rigorously researched paper on the subject. We serve as guides and mentors in the process, and the students do the research and writing. Students conduct secondary research, and every team also conducts a number of interviews with executives and industry experts during their field visit. The collection of papers formed the raw material for this book. We selected the best papers, designed the overall architecture for the book, reorganized the content of the papers to create a logical flow and sequence, and edited the papers to create chapters. This book is the final result of that process.

THE ORGANIZATION OF THIS BOOK

Each chapter focuses on a specific technology arena or a specific set of business models within a technology arena. All chapters begin with an introduction to the technology and then survey the landscape of the sector to highlight the forces driving the development of the sector. Each chapter then offers conceptual and analytical frameworks that illuminate the dynamics within the industries. We take a forward-looking approach and attempt to paint a picture of the future of these industries on the basis of important trends and forces. The book is organized into three sections:

I. *Enabling Technologies and Infrastructure.* The book begins with three chapters that familiarize readers with the key technologies that are driving the evolution of the computing and communications markets: wireless networking, optical networking, and challenges in semiconductor development.

Chapter 1, titled "The Future of Semiconductor Technology," analyzes the semiconductor industry. In particular, it develops an economic analysis of Moore's law and looks not just at whether the semiconductor industry will be able to keep up the trend of increasing computing power, but also at various potential future scenarios and strategies for dealing with the uncertainty facing the semiconductor companies.

Chapter 2, titled "Optical Networking," covers the optical-networking industry and how value is created and captured in the long-haul, metro, and last-mile segments of that industry. The future prospects of the players are examined as the industry matures.

Chapter 3, titled "The Wireless Value Chain and Infrastructure," considers the dynamics in the wireless value chain and foundations of the wireless infrastructure including Bluetooth and Infrared technology.

II. *Business Models and Markets.* In this section, the emphasis is on the evolution of selected industries and interesting areas of emerging opportunity. We discuss interactive TV and wireless applictions.

Chapter 4, titled "Interactive Television," discusses an emergent consumer technology—interactive television. It places particular emphasis on emerging business models and the complex and dynamic value chain in the interactive TV business, which includes a look at expected industry patterns that will change the competitive landscape and cause value to migrate in the value chain.

Chapter 5, titled "Wireless Applications," focuses on the future of wireless applications. Although the adoption of wireless phones, personal digital assistants (PDAs), and two-way pagers has been rapid, the adoption of the wireless Internet and mobile data services in general has been less remarkable. This chapter offers a framework for segmenting various types of wireless applications and examines each type in detail.

III. *Emerging Technologies.* In the final section, we look at futuristic technologies and nascent markets that are not yet well defined. Three of the more-recent hot areas of technology investment, nanotechnology, peer-to-peer computing, and biotechnology, are investigated in the next three chapters.

Chapter 6, titled "Recent Trends in Nanotechnology," covers future applications for nanotechnology and likely areas of success.

Chapter 7, titled "Peer-to-Peer Computing," discusses a technology that would benefit from the widespread availability of digital bandwidth and the players and future prospects of various business models for this market.

Finally, Chapter 8, titled "A Framework for the Biotechnology Industry," discusses the evolution and dynamics of the value chain in biotechnology and reveals the implications for future competition and value capture.

Taken together, these chapters offer insights and frameworks that will help the reader make sense of the confusing world of technology and the even more confusing business prospects of the many new technologies that are breathlessly hyped in the media. We hope that we have been able to balance our optimism about the promise of technology to change the way we work and live with the hard-nosed pragmatism about the ability of these technologies to create sustainable and profitable businesses. As most readers will acknowledge, there is a big gulf between a hot technology and a profitable business. We hope this book will help you understand this gulf and find ways of bridging it.

We would like to thank a number of individuals who helped in important ways to complete this book. First, we would like to thank our Dean Emeritus Donald Jacobs to whom this book is dedicated for making this course possible. His encouragement and support for innovative courses like this one made this book possible. Our new dean, Dipak Jain, was formerly the associate dean. He played an instrumental role not only in the creation of the course but also in guiding us to publish it as a book. We would also like to thank editors Martha J. Crowe and Richard Yeh who assisted with the careful editing and updating of the chapters included in this book. Crucial administrative support in assembling all the materials together was provided by Rahi Gurung, Sarah Huffman, and James B. Oldroyd. Finally, we would like to thank Matt Holt at Wiley & Sons, who patiently ushered this book through the publication process.

RANJAY GULATI
MOHANBIR SAWHNEY
ANTHONY PAONI

Evanston
August 2002

SECTION I

ENABLING TECHNOLOGIES AND INFRASTRUCTURE

CHAPTER 1

THE FUTURE OF SEMICONDUCTOR TECHNOLOGY

Those that go up against Moore usually lose.
—Dan Hutcheson, VLSI Research

Moore's law essentially predicts that the cost of computing power will be cut in half every 18 months. This forecast has held for five years because the industry has constantly discovered new ways to miniaturize transistors. Increased computing power has benefited consumers, scientists, and business immensely, but the question is whether this bonanza will continue. Economists, technologists, philosophers, and businesspeople disagree on virtually every major answer to that question. Perhaps the rate in Moore's law will slow down in tandem with other sectors of the economy. Perhaps Moore's law will cease to be valid, *and,* more surprisingly, we will still have a computing revolution ahead of us. Perhaps Moore's law will continue to be in force, but we will not need the increased computing power.

If anything, people in the industry believe that many surprises are in store. In this chapter, beyond exploring the limits to Moore's law, both physical and economic, we also ask if Moore's law is the right law to study. Finally, we try to look ahead to what may happen after 2010.

THE HISTORY OF MOORE'S LAW

In 1965, Gordon Moore, an engineer at Fairchild Semiconductor, stated his famous prediction, now known as Moore's law: The number of transistors that can be packed onto a sliver of silicon will double every 12 months (this was amended to 24 months in the 1970s). A corollary to Moore's law is that the speed of microprocessors, at a constant cost, also doubles every 18 to 24

3

months. Thus, the speed of microprocessors actually increases faster than the number of transistors on a chip. In the words of Moore: "By making things smaller, everything gets better simultaneously. There is little need for trade-offs. The speed of our products goes up; the power consumption goes down; system reliability, as we put more of the system on a chip, improves by leaps and bounds; but especially the cost of doing things electronically drops as a result of the technology." The semiconductor industry had essentially only one direction to go: smaller.

That Moore's law has prevailed for more than 35 years is primarily a classic result of extrapolative thinking: The industry conformed to its prediction. As Moore explains: "Moore's law has become a self-fulfilling prophecy. Chipmakers know they have to stay on that curve to remain competitive, so they put in the effort to make it happen." The first chip appeared on the market in 1961 with one transistor. By 1964 some chips had as many as 32 transistors; in 1965 this number had doubled to 64; and today, Intel's Pentium 4 has 42 million transistors (Figure 1.1). Meanwhile, Moore's law has helped to build and destroy industry after industry, fueling the New Economy and creating enormous wealth.

Shona Brown calls this the "time pacing of technology": "Intel has created a treadmill of new-product introductions that have set a blistering pace

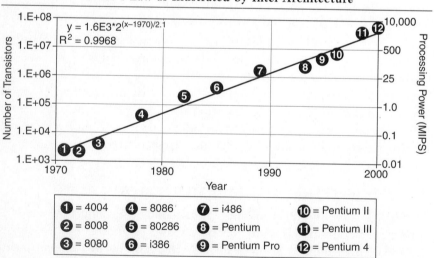

Figure 1.1
Moore's Law as Illustrated by Intel Architecture

$$y = 1.6E3 * 2^{(x-1970)/2.1}$$
$$R^2 = 0.9968$$

1 = 4004	**4** = 8086	**7** = i486	**10** = Pentium II
2 = 8008	**5** = 80286	**8** = Pentium	**11** = Pentium III
3 = 8080	**6** = i386	**9** = Pentium Pro	**12** = Pentium 4

Source: Intel. Note that the secondary axis, expressed in Millions of Instructions per Second (MIPS) is not exact, and actually increases faster than the number of transistors on a chip.

in its industry." On a continuous cycle, Moore's law determines the introduction of new products and facilities (Figure 1.2). This cycle is partly responsible for Intel's frenetic drive to move down the learning curve. Over and over again, the industry has proven to itself that miniaturization is the way to go. Miniaturization has become the lifeblood of the industry.

Many extrapolations of Moore's law were considered ridiculous at first, but the industry overcame all the barriers. Moore has reflected on the course of events: "In one of these early talks I gave in the early days of Moore's law . . . I extrapolated wafer size. This would have been in the mid-1960s [when wafer size had just dramatically increased to two inches], and I extrapolated wafer size to the year 2000 and came up with a fifty-six-inch wafer. I had a cardboard model of one these cut out and painted black and had one of the operators standing there holding it for a slide. I wish I still had that slide. We didn't get to fifty-six, but getting to twelve was a lot closer than I ever thought we were going to get. I was really using that . . . as an example of how ridiculous some of these exponential extrapolations could be if you really carried them out long enough."

Continuously increasing computing power is the single most important facet of the semiconductor industry. The business model of all players is

Figure 1.2
The Pentium III and Willamette Architecture Processor Shipments

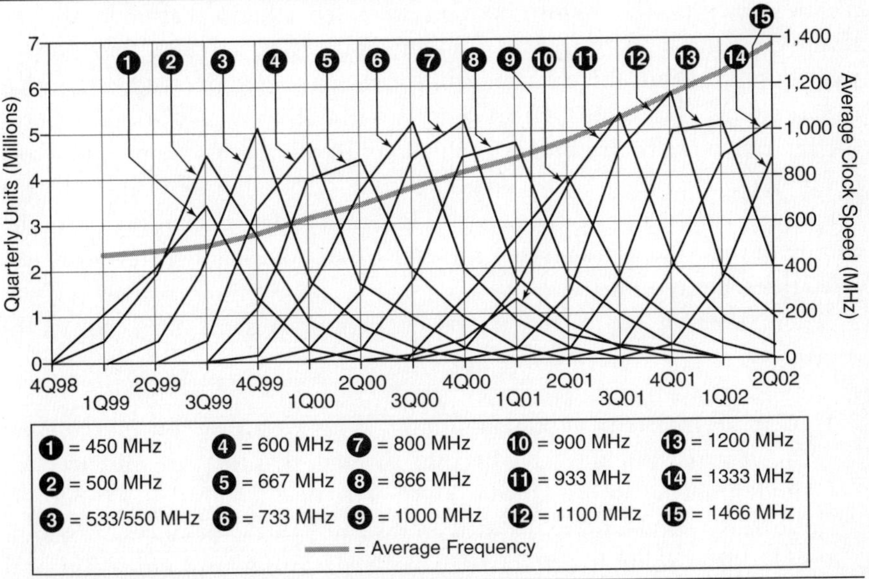

Source: Gwennap, 2000.

based on that objective. The question therefore arises whether it is the right objective for the future. In this chapter, we first ask whether it is physically possible to increase computing power. Next, how do the costs of developing more computing power influence the industry structure? Third, do the revenues outweigh the costs, or more fundamentally, does increased computing power offer enough marginal utility to offset the capital costs? Fourth, are there ways to cheat the laws of physics? Fifth, we try to develop a strategic framework for a semiconductor firm. Finally, we reflect on the knowledge gained from this exercise.

THE FIRST TEN YEARS: DO WE HIT PHYSICAL LIMITS?

Technological Challenges

The death of Moore's law has been predicted so many times that rumors of its demise have become an industry joke. The current alarms, however, may be different. Squeezing more and more devices onto a chip means fabricating smaller and smaller features. The industry's newest chip has pitches as small as 130 to 150 nanometers (billionths of a meter; a human hair is about 500 times as thick). A recent industry road map points out that the pitches must shrink to 100nm by 2005 to meet Moore's law. Some scenarios even place the 100nm node in 2003. To achieve that node, the industry will have to overcome fundamental problems with "no known solutions" for about three quarters of the technologies involved, a task that is as ominous as it sounds. Because areas without known solutions are colored in red in the International Technology Road Map for Semiconductors (ITRS), the challenge has become known as "the red brick wall." The red brick wall is a recurring theme in ITRS road maps, but worryingly, the timing of these issues has shifted forward by approximately three years relative to earlier road maps.

There are four key technological challenges to decreasing the size of transistors:

1. *CMOS transistor gate oxide limits.* The gates that control the flow of electrons in chips have become so small that they are prey to odd, undesirable quantum effects. The beauty of silicon is that it functions both as a conductor (Si) and as an insulator (SiO_2, or silicon dioxide). The gate oxide is one of the smallest features in a chip. But at a very small scale, tunneling-induced leaking currents and dielectric

breakdown (essentially a short circuit) will lead to unacceptable device performance.

2. *A maximum limit to the use of dopants.* Dopants are impurities, such as boron, that are mixed into silicon to alter its electrical properties (e.g., to increase its ability to hold localized electric charges). Although transistors can shrink in size, the smaller devices still need to maintain the same charge. To do that, the silicon has to have a higher concentration of dopant atoms. Above a certain limit, however, the dopant atoms begin to clump together, forming clusters that are not electronically active. It is impossible to increase the concentration of a dopant since all the extras simply go into the clusters. Today's level of dopants in chips is close to the theoretical maximum.

3. *Interconnect crisis.* Chips today already need more than 20 layers to connect all the elements. As chips become larger, it becomes progressively more difficult to connect all the transistors. Furthermore, these modern chips are so complex that it is impossible, as a practical matter, to test them exhaustively. Increasingly, chipmakers rely on incomplete testing combined with statistical analysis. At the present rate of improvement in test equipment, the factory yield of good chips would plummet from 90 percent in 1998 to an unacceptable 52 percent in 2012.

4. *Lithography limits.* Feature sizes are now smaller than the wavelength of visible light. Because the ability to create the smallest feature on a chip is determined by the wavelength of the light used (Rayleigh's law), chip manufacturers are looking for new lithographic methods. The latest optical-lithography technology, using all calcium fluoride optics and deep ultraviolet light, promises to enable pitches of 70 nanometers by 2005 or sooner. However, challenges are mounting to further decrease feature sizes with the same manufacturing paradigm.

Technological Solutions

It is easy to understand why researchers talk about a red brick wall; however, two historical examples can help put this dilemma into perspective. Because the resistance of connection lines increases as they shrink, the prediction was that the aluminum traditionally used in chips would be an insurmountable roadblock. Copper, a better conductor, was considered virtually impossible to use. But in 1997, IBM overcame this roadblock, and in 1998 the technology was first used in commercial chips. In another instance, Intel has announced that heat should be added to the preceding list of insurmountable roadblocks. A Pentium 4 already generates around 40 watts of heat (equivalent to a lightbulb), but in 10 years, the silicon could hypothetically reach a temperature comparable, in proportion to size, to that of a nuclear reactor. In Moore's original paper, he predicted that heat would be a barrier. In other words, it is not the first time that the industry faces predictions that a real physical barrier will prevent Moore's law from continuing. All previous "impregnable barriers" have succumbed to human ingenuity. Research by psychologists points out that this is a common phenomenon: People are more confident about their own abilities if they predict something far out in the future but less confident when predicting their ability in the short term. Hutcheson goes even further and formulates the industry's ability to find solutions as follows: "Forecasts of failures are self-unfulfilling prophecies. The industry has benefited enormously from forecasting failure since it makes a problem a visible target."

Given the industry's history, experts are comfortable extrapolating the current rate of change to 2012 for the pessimists and 2020 for the optimists. This magical boundary was 10 years out when Moore first formulated his law and has remained about 10 to 15 years in the future ever since. This time around, however, features on silicon chips will have to become the size of a few atoms, and further miniaturization will not be possible. This situation has led to an expansive research field that explores new paradigms.

All computer chips now have exactly one active switching layer of silicon. This was the essence of the revolution of the integrated circuit: No longer was it necessary to make a bulky 3-D device looking like a resistor because printing techniques (i.e., lithography) could be applied to a planar, or 2-D device. If there were a way to stack a second layer on the first one, the number of transistors could be doubled. Currently, that technique is highly impractical because it faces the interconnection problems mentioned earlier. But this technologically radical change could be a sustaining innovation for silicon-based computers.

Other researchers propose to leave silicon for what it is and search for technologies based on other materials that can overcome the barriers of silicon. DNA computing, quantum computing, and nanotubes have been proposed to surmount this barrier. Although each of these technologies is now less developed than integrated circuits were when Moore made his prediction, scientists hope that they can remove the barrier.

The point is that engineers and scientists will find a way to defeat the red brick wall. They can jump over it, go around it, or tunnel under it, but they will get to the other side. Doing that, however, comes at a cost, and consumers will be willing to pay that cost only if the increased computing power brings enough value. If new applications will bring in enough revenue or utility, people will pay for better PCs.

COSTS OF MOORE'S LAW AND MARKET DYNAMICS

Moore's Second Law

Industry experts agree that although many problems with the technology will one day be solvable, the technical requirements will make manufacturing facilities ever more expensive. This fact is known as Moore's second law—the increasing cost of manufacturing chips doubles with every new generation of chips, roughly every four years. Therefore, financial realities might constrain the rate of technological progress.

Growth in revenues must cover the increasing capital costs of producing chips. Drawn by rapidly improving products at rapidly falling prices, U.S. spending on computers has risen for the past 40 years at an average annual rate of 24 percent. However, revenue growth is slowing, and in many years capital spending has arguably outgrown revenues. When Intel was founded in 1968, the equipment to make chips cost roughly $12,000 per machine; today, the equipment costs tens of millions of dollars per machine. Firms must pay more for the exotic tools (fabs) needed to etch finer and finer lines on the chip. In today's dollars, the tab for a fab has risen from $14 million in 1966 to $1 billion in 1995 to $2.7 billion in 1997. The fab Intel will begin building in Israel for its Pentium 4 costs $3.5 billion. In effect, the costs are doubling every four and a half years.

Market Dynamics

The effects of these rising costs are manifold and have determined the industry structure. First, the huge investments in equipment have caused a jump in manufacturing joint ventures. Among the companies pairing up are Texas Instruments and Hitachi, AMD and Fujitsu, and Motorola and Toshiba.

Second, the high-end microprocessors for personal computers and servers that are Intel's forte are best characterized as a natural monopoly. About 75 percent of Intel's revenues is derived from products for PCs and servers, where it holds about 82 percent of the market share. This is a direct consequence of the massive entry barrier Intel has created: the need to invest in a multibillion-dollar fab every nine months (cf. the enormous speed of product introductions illustrated in Figure 1.2). Then it takes an immense effort to quickly move down the learning curve.

Third, rising capital costs have also driven the industry to consolidate R&D. Originally a purely American initiative, the semiconductor industry association Sematech has successfully expanded its road map activity to an international level. In effect, this has led to a different kind of natural monopoly on the supply side of R&D in the industry. It is noteworthy that Japanese firms that opted out of the Sematech consortium have performed badly. Working together with vicious competitors has been a critical success factor for chip manufacturers in the recent past and might be in the future.

On the other hand, there can also be considerable negative consequences if ITRS's road map points to the wrong road. A report by the Institute of Electrical and Electronic Engineers (IEEE) notes that the semiconductor industry's internal R&D investments are already 13 percent of sales per year but are focused only on developing the next generation (two to three years out). There is little government support, and what little there is has not doubled according to Moore's second law but has remained constant. Although an epiphany by a small group of people might produce a scientific or theoretical breakthrough, scaling up an engineering technology from a single switch to a system that produces millions or even billions of switches per computing unit requires an effort of a totally different order: It takes many work hours of dedicated engineers. Irrespective of theoretical or experimental breakthroughs in young fields like quantum and nanotechnologies, it is hard to visualize a breakthrough that could produce a manufacturable technology rivaling the industrial complex of the semiconductor industry. This is particularly worrisome because the transistor would not have been invented in 1947 without the Shockley's insight into quantum mechanics, which at that time was a profoundly theoretical and impractical theory.

Ordinarily, a competitive market would solve the dilemma because multiple firms make multiple bets. Since the market is a natural monopoly, however, it is unlikely that ordinary market forces will be efficient enough to choose the right road. Also, since semiconductor firms have to decide almost five years in advance which direction to pursue, with no guarantee of success, the level of risk is much greater than it would be with a shorter research and development cycle. If the capital-spending trend continues, by 2005 the cost of a single fab will pass $10 billion. In 2015, some experts predict this cost will be $200 billion (approximately the same as Intel's current net worth). Though it is hard to measure, each new generation of chips has seemingly produced a smaller return on capital. It might be possible to put more transistors on a chip, but there will be no reason to do so, as computer buyers will not be enthusiastic about buying more expensive chips that surpass their needs.

Not only are fixed costs rising, but yields are decreasing for several reasons. Larger chips mean fewer chips per wafer; larger surface areas mean more likelihood of an error in any one of the chips; and, finally, incomplete testing tools combined with statistical analysis could dramatically decrease factory yields. All these factors make chips more expensive and erode producers' abilities to efficiently reduce production costs. The costs of manufacturing a chip have risen consistently more than 20 percent per year from 1990 through 1998. Analysts estimate that the variable costs of a Pentium 4 will eventually be around $80 to $90, more than double the $40 manufacturing costs of a Pentium III. Owing to the transition to larger wafers, Intel got a one-time relief in 2002 of about 10 percent to 20 percent per chip, but experts are bearish about these costs. The increasing rate of technological change may therefore lead to a worsening of industry economics, giving each new generation of chips not only a lower return on capital, but also an inherently higher risk.

The picture sketched here might be bleaker than reality. Hutcheson and Hutcheson (2001), as well as Grove (2001), point out that the industry has seen this analysis of lower returns on investments and has adapted itself. Furthermore, the cost per transistor is still dropping, although production of those chips requires an ever-greater investment. Even if consumers do not want to buy more powerful chips, it might be economical to build a bigger plant; despite many generations of exponential growth, there are still economies of scale. New technology still enables cheaper computing power.

The recognition of exploding capital costs must be painfully familiar to anyone associated with supersonic planes, mag-lev trains, high-speed mass transit, large-scale particle accelerators, and other technological marvels that were strangled by high costs. In the past hundred years, engineers and scientists have repeatedly shown how human ingenuity can make an end run around the difficulties posed by the laws of nature, but they have been much less successful in cheating the laws of economics.

The relevant law of economics is the law of diminishing returns, which says that the productivity increase for any single individual is necessarily limited by the person's supply of time. Becker's theory of the allocation of time (1965) states that a fully rational treatment of consumption of a product should include time in the price (e.g., the more time an activity costs, the more expensive it is). Economists express productivity and consumption in numbers like costs and revenues. Since household consumption and production are limited by the available time, there is a fundamental limit on the ability of exponential increases in computer speed to create commensurate increases in productivity.

Seeing Ahead by Looking Back

Consider the airline industry. From early 1900 until 1965, airplane productivity steadily increased. Planes generated ever more revenues, and the cost per passenger kept dropping. According to Gordon (1991), however, the value of time saved is by far the most important output of airlines. His calculations show that this output accounts for roughly 3.5 percent of GDP, or 400 percent of airline revenues. With each new model, planes became faster, bigger, and cheaper. The pinnacle of the evolution in size was the Boeing 747, and in speed, the Concorde. Although larger and faster planes could be built, there was no longer an economic reason for further evolution. The development of a larger or faster plane was therefore not limited by physical limits, but by the laws of economics.

After 747s were introduced, the structure of the airline industry changed. No longer did it keep replacing planes with larger ones; the planes remained longer in operation, and operating costs over the long term became more important than performance. In a sense, air travel has been commoditized, both for airplane producers and for airlines. Ever since, the manufacturers have tried to differentiate in other directions, as have the airlines. Although manufacturers have looked at fly by wire, telephones and screens in the backs of chairs, the single most important factor is still cost per passenger mile—a factor that has not diminished over the years. Introducing airline meals of different quality did not help much. Air miles were another attempt to induce customer loyalty. However, price wars and the success of a low-cost airline like Southwest prove that consumers place limited value on this differentiation. Price and time are the most important attributes of different travel methods. Even now, as Airbus and Boeing develop new planes focused on improvements in size and speed respectively, experts seriously doubt that enhanced productivity of air travel can match the enormous fixed costs of developing faster and bigger planes. Gordon (1991) expresses this concept as follows: "It makes sense to reduce a railroad trip of weeks to days and a trip of a week to a day. However, what is the marginal benefit of reducing a trip between two cities by another hour? $10 per hour per person? $20 per hour? The answer is that it is a lot less valuable than the first step."

The lesson from the airline industry is that the performance character-istic will change. Boeing 747s have been used for decades though older planes have been disappearing much more quickly. In addition to the cost per passenger mile, long-term operating costs also have been important.

Arguably, word processors and spreadsheets (and other applications) have gone through this same development (Figure 1.3). One of the largest ben-efits of computers was the timesaving achieved by a word processor over a typewriter. After that, using Word for Windows instead of WordPerfect was another big, though smaller step. Word for Windows 2000 hardly adds any productivity. The improvements did not demand a further enormous increase in computing power and therefore offered diminishing returns to consumers. Computer productivity is also limited by its inability to replace certain human services. No matter how powerful the word processor, it

Figure 1.3
Total and Marginal Utility Curve for Word Processing

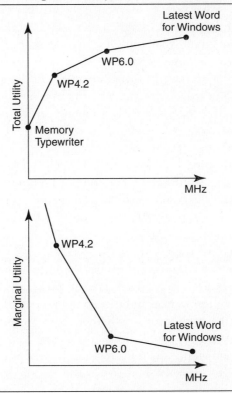

Source: Gordon, 2000.

still needs human input to work. The argument is most succinctly summarized by an epigram attributed to Robert Solow: "We see computers everywhere but in the productivity statistics."

There is no physical reason why computers could not be used for several years (apart from the more fragile mobile devices). However, the productivity of products is meaningful only with respect to money and time. New applications are a great example of ways to increase utility although they do not increase productivity. Consequently, the argument of diminishing returns is not appropriate to the invention of new applications that enhance the value of time. Economists blissfully ignore new and cheaper entertainment applications. The greater variety represents more value to the consumer, but that value does not show up in productivity statistics.

UTILITY OF INCREASED COMPUTING POWER

The real question, therefore, is not whether new applications save enough costs or time, but rather how to maximize the utility of computing power. Theoretically there is always a marginal user who benefits from more computing power. But given that capital costs are rising, it is questionable whether a significantly large group of people are interested in it.

Technology products have a distinct life cycle. Early on, users have to be familiarized, or "pushed," with the benefits of a new technology. At the beginning of the life cycle, the early adopters can determine the success of technology, and their enthusiasm drives initial use. Later, the majority of consumers see the benefits of the technology. This cycle is evident in the history of PCs. Initially, hobbyists used the PC, but later there was a remarkable history of consumer pull for computing power. Some argue that consumers have become conditioned to expect more computing power for a lower price every few years. In this sense, the PC industry has created both a growth bonanza and growth trap. Each new generation of more powerful chips goes through a similar life cycle.

New generations of computer chips have repeatedly been hailed as great and valuable innovations. Some hackers even proclaim that Intel has purposely slowed down innovation and that computers should be faster. Lately, however, skeptics have questioned whether more powerful computers are still in demand: Will new applications create sufficient pull or return the PC to a push market? Since utility is inherently a subjective measure, both low utility and high utility of increases in computing power have vociferous supporters.

Proponents of Low Utility of Computing Power

Are new applications really showing decreasing marginal utility? An old industry maxim quips, "What Intel giveth, Microsoft taketh away." Or in the words of another industry expert: "While computing power and number of lines of code are increasing exponentially, functionality is constant." If new technology does not offer more functionality, consumers will question buying a new computer.

There are several indicators that the demand for more computing power might be decreasing. The growth of PC sales in the United States in the second half of 2000 was down, which *The Economist* attributes to the fact that "most consumers already have as fast and powerful a computer as they need for most applications. Other, generally less expensive high-tech gear offers more value." Furthermore, skeptics say that the newest high-end chip by Intel, the P4, offers computing power few people really need. These two pieces of data are simply point estimates, but they concur with predictions of industry experts over the past two years. Even more interesting is that there does not seem to be a convinced group of early adopters. This fact is particularly worrying for Intel, since it has traditionally relied on a relatively large group of early adopters to subsidize part of the learning curve. Gordon (2000) and Gwennap (2000) formulate it differently: The proposed new applications might not bring enough business-productivity applications to justify further investments in PCs, meaning that the replacement rate of PCs might slow down, as we have seen happen in the airline industry with investments in planes.

In this scenario, an early sign would be that value PCs (defined as prices less than $1,000) might become a larger percentage of PC shipments. Previously, the introduction of sub-$1,000 PCs was a real revolution in the PC segment, but only because consumers that did not derive enough benefit from a high-performance PC were now able to buy a cheap PC. However, if business users and consumers derive less value from a PC, this segment should be growing. Increased reliance on this segment would make it harder for PC manufacturers to sustain revenue growth. Worse, these actions would reduce margins, which might prevent a semiconductor firm from developing high-performance devices. Data do not yet clearly show this trend, but the value segment is an important industry indicator.

Another argument against the need for more computing power is that it is used as a panacea for problems such as information overload. It is a trap to use increasingly more computer power to solve problems, which Brown, Seely, and Duguid (2000) call "Moore's law solutions." They argue that

Moore's law solutions take it on faith that more power will solve the very problems it helped to create. Instead of thinking more, consumers are encouraged to "embrace dumb power." Adding 1,000 more hits on a search engine, however, will not make the user wiser.

If the market leader focuses on a single performance metric, but the market is not demanding that particular performance, it would offer opportunities for disruptive technologies. A disruptive technology is one that offers less performance than the leading technology, but more on a different and new dimension. Since industry leaders frequently ignore the "ill-performing product," they are often surprised when the product becomes better over time and significantly disrupts the industry. We all know what the PC did to the mainframe.

This is part of Transmeta's strategy. Transmeta produces "Crusoe," a CPU that is not optimized for computing power and consumes up to a fifth of the power used by a Pentium III. Crusoe was originally thought by industry analysts to be perfect for laptops, where battery power is a key bottleneck. In a surprise move, a couple smaller companies (e.g., RLX Technologies and Amphus) fitted Crusoe into Web servers. Web servers are typically located in server racks in data centers, where real estate is expensive, given all the provisions necessary (fire protection, security, anti-flooding measures, etc.). However, servers in racks cannot be placed close together because they produce too much heat. Transmeta's chip uses much less power and thus produces much less heat, so several Crusoe Web servers can be placed in a single rack spot. Although it remains to be seen whether Transmeta can survive under the recently difficult economic conditions, it is obvious that computing power is not the single metric that it used to be. Even if Transmeta, the company, does not survive, its technology will.

There is also a second category of disruptive technologies, for which revenues are already significantly higher: new devices. Palm Pilots, Pocket PCs, and Web-enabled mobile phones are fast-growing examples of this category, but its proponents are much more ambitious. Michael Dertouzos, who was the director of MIT's Media Lab, called the developers to arms to "kill the PC." Dertouzos's setup project, Oxygen, aims to develop a new platform using a constellation of devices that hear, see, and respond to the user's every need. There is a strong feeling among computer gurus that there is room for a new "device world," in which ever-increasing bandwidth connects all kinds of devices. In that world, it is no longer high-performance, high-computing power that is valuable, but the constellation of devices.

Assuming increased computing power indeed has only low utility, this issue might be solvable if the semiconductor industry can increase a chip generation's life and continue to milk existing generations of chips. That will increase the life cycle of computers, giving software developers more time to come up with new applications. Investments in next-generation technology will then again be fueled by the demand for new applications that need more computing power. Delaying innovation is a risky strategy in an industry where leadership traditionally has been defined as "the most powerful chip." Thus, if the trends persist, investments in research and development will become riskier (as confirmed by the industry), and the processes of Moore's law will necessarily, but not voluntarily, slow down.

This has enormous consequences: Bandwidth shifts the place where value of technology for a user resides. Intelligence no longer resides in a single location, nor in a hub, but at the edges of a network, wherever we can connect intelligence to the network (Sawhney, 2001).

The logical consequence could be that more computing power on the user's desk would become less relevant if bandwidth were to become ubiquitous. High bandwidth could reduce the need for more computing power at the end user since it could be delivered from "hubs" within the network. A good analogy is a central furnace in the basement that provides heat and warm water to the whole building. The central location would need a large amount of computing power, but the needed power should be deliverable by using high-powered servers and parallel computing, technologies not far beyond current technological capabilities.

Peer-to-peer (P2P) technology could further commoditize computing power. P2P is the ability of computers and devices to talk directly to each other—to exchange information but also to give commands, creating numerous "DPUs" or distributed processing units. P2P applications can be divided into two primary uses—the ability to share files of all types (i.e., text, audio, video) and the ability to share geographically disparate resources (i.e., CPU cycles, disk space). A relevant example is using the computing power of other computers, as in the Seti@home project, in which computing power of up to millions of PCs all over the world is used to search for extraterrestrial radio signals. Seti@home has now been followed by numerous other initiatives. In research, folding@home studies protein folding. Intel's United Devices has started to harness its own PCs to study hard chip design and test problems in a technology called Netbatch. Intel claims that it has saved $500 million cumulatively over 10 years by "leveraging the power of its worldwide network of PCs." Companies like Parabon, Porivo, Popular Power, Infrasearch and Centrata promise to sell a user's computing power thus making "supercomputing power" easily accessible for other companies. One of the applications developed by

Case Study: Bandwidth Abundance

Bandwidth might make increased computing power less valuable. The recent explosion of bandwidth supports the people who argue that more computing power has low utility. According to George Gilder (2000), an economic age is defined by the most abundant good. Processing power might have been the defining metric in the past, but bandwidth is the new horizon. In the past, users needed more power on their PCs to run their applications. However, computing power is a substitute for bandwidth. Bandwidth is a substitute for storage capacity. Storage capacity is a substitute for computing power. Storage capacity has increased faster than Moore's law in the past few years, doubling every month. Even more amazing is that the cost of bandwidth decreases by half every 9 months.

The Performance of Several Complementary Technologies to Computing Power Is Improving Performance Faster than Moore's Law

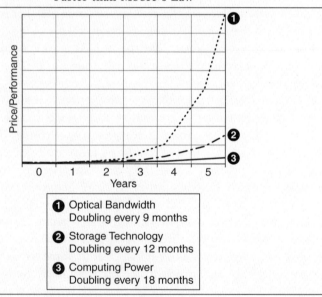

1 Optical Bandwidth
  Doubling every 9 months

2 Storage Technology
  Doubling every 12 months

3 Computing Power
  Doubling every 18 months

Source: Khosla, 2000.

Infrasearch is using this power for a fully distributed search engine. This search engine not only is fully up to date all the time (ordinary search engines take at least 24 hours to update their data) but also covers all kinds of files other than html.

The vision by Dertouzos nicely dovetails with this vision: Dumber and smaller terminal devices will use the available cheap bandwidth to access any computing power they need. This will reduce the demand for computing power compared with a PC-centered world.

In a device-to-device (D2D) model, no major central server is necessary to do heavy calculations. Instead, everybody will use network-enabled devices. Ultimately, some people predict, computing power may become analogous to electricity: Users will be able to plug into the network anywhere and instantaneously get as much as they need. Project Oxygen at MIT's Media Lab consists of two major hardware components, a small handheld device, christened the Handy21, and a stationary computer in the walls of a room, the Enviro21. Network 21 is a set of protocols that connects these devices and shows the same user interface, no matter where the user is. Furthermore, the semiconductor architecture in the H21 is fundamentally different from the current microprocessor. The Intel architecture is a complex amalgam of processing units, memory, and other functions that were previously done in specialized devices on the motherboard. Furthermore, a computer still contains other specialized computer chips—for example, in a 3D graphics card—that are optimized for that function. For any single operation, Intel-architecture chips use only a part of all the logic gates on a chip. The "Raw" architecture proposed by Project Oxygen is fundamentally different. This new model of computation is called Raw because it exposes the raw hardware on a chip—including the wires—to the software. By using the free logic gates to direct and store the signals that run through the chip's wires, the compiler customizes the wiring for each application. This is a radical departure from existing architectures, in which software controls the chip's logic operations—basic functions such as ADD and SUBTRACT—but not the chip's wiring. In contrast, Raw allows the software to program the wires, the microchip's most valuable resource. To illustrate the power of this approach, consider the following hypothetical situation. A user would be able to tell the Handy 21, "Hey, turn yourself into a cell phone." The device would then locate the appropriate configuration software, download it and configure the wires of the Raw chip inside to give it the characteristics of a cell phone—or a beeper, a personal digital assistant (PDA), or any other configuration the user might want. Again, researchers are thinking about a world in which increased bandwidth might make computing power a less relevant measure, confirming that more centralized computing power might not have high utility.

Proponents of High Utility of Computing Power

Although the skeptics' view has all the attention in the current economic climate, there are at least as many optimists among the experts. First there is the view proposed by Ray Kurzweil (2001), who predicts that the demand for computing power is infinite. He believes that the current user interface is slow and ineffective compared with that of a future computer. Speech recognition, virtual reality, and personal intelligent assistants (and other agent-type technology) will make interacting with a computer more like interacting with a human. Kurzweil argues that these applications are only a few years away.

Furthermore, the view is that previous software innovations have been one-dimensional: focused on speed. Word processing might run faster, but the intelligence in Word is extremely awkward (e.g., its error-correction efforts). That is to say, real intelligent-user interfaces do not exist. In the words of Dertouzos: [Computing power may increase exponentially] "but transistors and the systems made with them are used by people. And that's where exponential change stops! Has word-processing software, running on millions of transistors, empowered humans to contribute better writings than Socrates, Descartes, or Lao Tzu?"

The computer is a human-machine system. Using manufacturing as an analogy, from a theory-of-constraints (TOC) view, system throughput is determined by the constraint with the smallest throughput in the system; the bottleneck determines the system throughput. The theory of constraint prescribes optimizing bottleneck throughput to increase the system throughput. It is important to realize that every single constraint before the bottleneck has overcapacity—after all, it produces more than the bottleneck can handle. This overcapacity should be used to alleviate demands on the bottleneck. For example, in manufacturing, overcapacity can be used to preprocess materials.

Moving from CPU cycles to a viewpoint focusing on the value add to humans, the first constraint is that the CPU needs to communicate with other, but slower, hardware devices like random-access memory. On a higher level, the interaction between human and machine (currently a keyboard and a screen) is a constraint. At the highest level, there is the intelligence added to human commands by the system. Finally, there are constraints in the data-processing capabilities of a human. From a TOC perspective, any of these can be the critical constraint that determines system throughput. Some of these constraints can be removed by using the overcapacity of computing power.

The lower-level interactions do not require much computing power. Many of them have been solved. However, higher level problems like usability and natural interfaces have not been solved. The applications that can handle these problems most likely require significant computing power. The human barrier is probably the limit that is the most difficult to overcome (humans can process information at about 55 bits per second).

Even taking both CPU performance and the application features to an extreme, no matter how powerful the computer hardware and how user-friendly the software, most functionalities provided by personal computers, including word processing, spreadsheets, and database management, require hands-on human contact to be productive. That need for human contact creates diminishing returns for the productivity impact of the computer. Proponents of high utility of computing power argue that this means we need real intelligence in our computers.

Dertouzos (2001) provides a road map to produce "the steering wheel and gas pedal" of computing. In his terms, the computer should be human-centered. Or, in other terms: The human-computer interface is the bottleneck, and all effort should therefore be directed at alleviating demands on the bottleneck. Dertouzos points to five key forces to do this: speech understanding, automation, individualized information access, collaboration, and customization. These five forces are fundamental because they focus on the only possible categories of interaction between humans and machines.

A longer term (25-year) answer may be artificial intelligence. Kurzweil is confident that artificial-intelligence systems will bring enormous benefits. Artificial intelligence that is valuable is a quantum jump from today's state of technology, but it might just provide the drive to continue building more powerful computers well into this century.

An argument focusing on the short term says that nonproductivity applications like gaming and entertainment will drive demand. Virtually every PC made before 1980 was next to useless. The makers and the buyers thought of them as electronic toys. The argument is that basically we do not know what any new technology will be used for, but games and entertainment are likely to help us understand the medium's possibilities. Playing is vital for development, as Negroponte (1998) states: "When people play, they have their best ideas, and they make their best connections with their best friends. In playing a game, the learning and exercise come for free. Playing produces some of the most special times and most valuable lessons in life." Games and entertainment are among the most processor-hungry applications. Audio and video compression and the rendering of 3-D environments are high-growth areas for computing applications.

It is no surprise that both Intel and Microsoft are making considerable strategic efforts in these areas. Intel is researching applications like speech recognition, video technology, and games. It was an instrumental player in developing RealPlayer and is selling the Pentium 4 as a vehicle for multi-media. Microsoft has a strong relationship with Lernout & Hauspie, the troubled speech-recognition firm to whom Kurzweil sold his firm, and has developed the X-box (a gaming computer that competes with Sony Play-station and Nintendo).

Despite its being a classic case of strategy under extreme uncertainty, the industry response has been extremely optimistic to the question of what will need that much computational power. Former Microsoft executive Myhrvold stated: "Everything will. At every point in the history of this technology, people have argued that we don't need that kind of power. And every single time, they have been dead wrong. There's no feedback mechanism yet for people to stop asking that question, despite the fact that it has such a miserable track record."

TEN YEARS OUT: NEW PARADIGMS THAT MIGHT DISRUPT THE SILICON EMPIRE

If silicon cannot double its processing speed every 18 months, another technology might be able to take over. Scientists and technology enthusiasts have been pointing in numerous directions, but three approaches are considered particularly powerful: quantum computing, DNA computing, and nanotube-based computers. All these approaches are highly experimental but have known early successes, such as creating elementary transistors and memory cells, or solving a scaled version of a hard mathematical problem. Still, bringing engineering procedures used in experiments to a mass-production environment may pose greater challenges for these technologies than silicon faced in its 30 years of improving performance. At best, most methods suffer from not being as general purpose as silicon computing. In some of these areas, however, the new technologies outpower silicon-based methods by far. They may start out in a niche, like any disruptive technology, so these are trends to watch.

Quantum Computing

Quantum computing is not based on ordinary bits, but on quantum bits, or *qu-bits*. Qu-bits have the extraordinary property that they can be both zero and one at the same time. If we could string several qu-bits together in a so-called quantum-coherent manner, we could perform calculations on all potential states at the same time. Or, alternatively, we could use the calculation as a sieve: Start with all potential states and end up with only one (similar to searching for a single element in a large collection). Research has shown that in special classes of problems, quantum computing offers solutions that would take ordinary computers an impractical amount of time. An example would be breaking current-day encryption systems. Fortunately, quantum encryption (an unrelated technique also based on quantum principles like coherence) offers an unbreakable alternative. In theory, a quantum computer could search a database quickly and efficiently.

Scientists have not yet shown how qu-bits could form the basis of a general-purpose computer that is faster than ordinary computers, but there is no theoretical barrier. Furthermore, to be practical, a computer would need to consist of hundreds of qu-bits in quantum coherence. This poses extraordinary engineering challenges, as quantum coherence is a property that is almost always lost in larger systems. That is a lucky situation for us because it means that we live in a classical, relatively predictable world, and not a fuzzy, extremely probabilistic place. The fact, however, that even under a microscope we never encounter quantum phenomena like coherence in the real world indicates how hard it is to scale these systems. So far, scientists have not produced coherent systems with more than seven qu-bits in a system of trapped ion atoms in a vacuum. Experts estimate that it will take at least a decade, if not multiple decades, for quantum computing to become practical.

Of the three technologies, however, quantum computing may be the most promising, for some researchers are making qu-bits using ordinary lithographic methods, meaning that Moore's law might apply to quantum computers.

DNA Computing

DNA is essentially the biological equivalent of information. Biotechnology is sometimes called the marriage of biology and information technology. Therefore, DNA can be used as information storage. Since biological agents can manipulate DNA, DNA can be seen as a kind of computer—much like the famous ribbon-based Turing machine. A Turing machine is a theoretical construct: Imagine a machine that processes a long ribbon of instructions and then either writes an output or not and moves to the next instruction on the ribbon. Turing showed that any computable problem could be solved by a machine with these simple functions.

DNA computing is particularly suited for combinatorial problems like the traveling salesman problem, a particularly hard-to-solve optimization problem that deals with finding the shortest route to visit some number of cities. When Adleman (1994) showed how to solve the problem for seven cities using DNA sequences, DNA computing got a big boost. The largest challenge for a DNA computer is that most calculations take place in a fluid phase by adding chemicals. This introduces hairy engineering problems, particularly if the results of the DNA computer are to feed into an ordinary silicon-based environment. In short, water and electricity don't mix. Furthermore, the DNA computer is not errorless. Thus, for particularly difficult problems, it might be worth the effort to set up a DNA computer in a wet lab, but for now this method seems ill suited for a desktop model. Perhaps, however, the application for a DNA computer will be more prosaic: to store genetic information without resorting to silicon. Adleman makes a similar point: "Whether or not DNA computers will ever become stand-alone competitors for electronics is besides the point. . . . I believe things like DNA computing, along with the other ways we are learning to use these wonderful tools, will eventually lead to a 'molecular revolution,' which ultimately will have a very dramatic effect on the world."

Nanotubes

After three professors shared the Nobel Prize in 1996 for discovering bucky-balls (soccer-ball-shaped molecules of carbon) in 1985, researchers discovered buckytubes, or nanotubes. These are molecular tubes of carbon molecules, comparable to a sheet of rolled-up graphite. They conduct electricity and, in a different configuration, act as a semiconductor, which is also a useful property of silicon and accounts for the enormous flexibility of the material.

Researchers have built an elementary transistor with nanotubes. Given that some tubes conduct, they might connect different parts of a chip. Since nanotubes are very small (only a few atoms in width), they could be used as a tiny building block of future circuits, thus allowing a silicon-like architecture to be built with smaller components. This means that nanotubes are a serious candidate for building a general-purpose computer. Nevertheless, because ordinary lithographic techniques are not possible with nano-tubes, some mechanism must manipulate them in the right place with accuracy equal to a few atoms. Although this has been accomplished for single nanotubes, it is not yet possible for the vast quantities needed to build even a small chip. Related fields explore other molecules as switches and auto-assembly, a nanotechnological area in which researchers try to find a way in which molecules automatically line themselves up on the right place.

Afterthought: The Empire Strikes Back

An enormous knowledge base has been built around silicon and its applications. It will take any of the previously mentioned technologies at least one, if not several, decades to come to full fruition. A sobering thought is that progress might well be linear to the number of researchers in a field. Even worse, there is a feeling among researchers that they were extremely lucky with silicon, one of the most abundant elements on earth. Grove (2001) has said: "The silicon–silicon dioxide system is one of the most stable compound systems available in nature. I don't think we'll find another one that will allows us to fabricate tens of millions of transistors that will live and work forever on a single chip like silicon–silicon dioxide allows us to do that. So, I think it is going to be modifications of silicon technology . . . working around the limitations, physical limitations imposed on the size shrinking below optical limits."

POTENTIAL STRATEGY FOR INTEL AND THE SEMICONDUCTOR INDUSTRY

Given the tremendous uncertainty facing semiconductor firms, particularly Intel, a real-options-based outlook is the most appropriate framework for strategy in the semiconductor industry. Following are four simplified scenarios based on Porter's five-forces analysis and then a discussion of the power of an options, or "strategic bets," framework—bets that Intel could place.

Scenario 1: Moore of the Same

The basis for this scenario is that Moore's law will continue to yield more and more computing power. The five-forces analysis shows that this in large part sustains the current industry structure. First of all, entry barriers will remain in place. Since innovations of ever-increasing complexity are necessary, capital costs for entry will continue to rise. At the same time, that will mean higher capital costs for suppliers, which will lead to consolidation among suppliers (e.g., the proposed merger of ASML and SVG into the world's leading photolithography firm, with about 45 percent market share). Although we do not expect supplier power to be an important force to deal with in the industry, complementary products are of prime importance. The foundation for this scenario is that the increased computing power will find applications. This idea is based primarily on a "build it and they will come" principle. The history of predictions of new applications is spotty, so it is appropriate to adopt Myhrvold's view: One of the few things we are sure of is that some people will find creative ways of using computing power. Implicitly, the assumption is that Microsoft or other software companies will see the extra computing power as an opportunity to make computers more effective at time saving, more valuable in terms of variety, and/or more usable. If the right complementary products are developed, customers will follow the applications. Rivalry will be much on the same basis as today: high capital expenditures and a fight for the top spot in MHz-performance rankings. This scenario is almost equal to the status quo.

Scenario 2: Vicious Circle

If Moore's law slows down, it will affect virtually all the five forces. Entry barriers might come down for two reasons: (1) Computing power is not the differentiating factor it used to be, enabling entrants like Transmeta; and (2) the technology used for production will be less cutting edge; Intel will have to focus less on research and development and more on manufacturing (e.g., high yields will become very important). This will erode the competitive advantage of Intel. A firm like AMD, which because of its lower margins has traditionally focused on being low cost, will be better positioned for this scenario. Again, supplier power will be marginal. Pressure on their margins might still lead to consolidation, but not on the scale of the first scenario. The remaining two forces are of particular importance here. First, the slowdown of Moore's law will result in much lower complementarity of Intel products with Windows. It will be natural for Microsoft to try to find other benefits for its customers (e.g., build out its Net strategy so that it is not dependent on advances in processing power, but on bandwidth). This will be particularly vicious for Intel since customers will no longer demand products that are complementary to more computing power. It will reduce revenues from people who want to replace their old PC with a faster one, and, in turn, there will be fewer revenues available for investment in faster systems. Taken together, these forces reinforce each other, which may lead to a vicious circle in demand for Intel products with ever-higher computing power.

Scenario 3: Business Will Use Less Processing Power

This scenario shares aspects of scenarios 1 and 2. The biggest performance drivers today are leading-edge 3-D games, digital photo, and audio editing. These applications require a lot of power, but they have little or no role in the business market, which buys the majority of PCs.

Business applications for PCs put demand mainly on Microsoft, and Intel has little influence there. Intel and Microsoft cooperate closely on the operating-systems side, but the same is certainly not true for applications. Office 2000 or Windows 2000 do not include significant increases in performance-intensive features like 3-D graphics or speech recognition. Windows XP is expected to need a Pentium III with 128 MB as a minimum, which does not sound like it is very processor hungry. Rather, beta-testers have pointed out that there is more value in installing more memory. In the words of Microsoft executive Allchin, "It will not require the most-advanced hardware available." Even more worryingly, Windows XP is positioned as having major benefits for consumers. It features more stability, always-on functionality, CD-burning software, and management of images and sound files. Microsoft analysts are downplaying the potential for speech technology, however: "*Star Trek* has set the standards too high for consumers to be easily satisfied."

Therefore, Moore's law will slow down in this third scenario, though not as radically as in scenario 2. This will still mean a major shock to the industry, as lessening demand for increased performance can be satisfied with the doubling of computer power every three or four years instead of every two. This is the most likely scenario for the future, but scenario 1 and 2 are contrasted in the following discussion.

Scenario 4 and Others: The PC Is Dead

This scenario was explored in the Case Study: Bandwidth Abundance. Although nobody foresees the PC disappearing in the short term, there is a distinct probability that other devices will become much more important and that the PC will shift more and more into certain productivity functions that are impossible on small screens or with low computing power. Bluetooth could have a significant impact on PC form (e.g., the monitor is on one side of the room and the ugly big box is somewhere under a couch). This might be the first step to a world where the big CPU becomes ever more invisible in the house. The result might be that computing power will be commoditized as it moves farther and farther away from the user (not just physically, but through better user interfaces).

Real Options

I returned and saw under the sun that the race is not to the swift, nor the battle to the strong, neither yet bread to the wise, nor yet riches to men of understanding, or yet favour to men of skill; but time and chance happeneth to them all.

—Ecclesiastes

There is a fundamental uncertainty in the semiconductor market that cannot be resolved until the future. Work by McKinsey & Company expresses a real-options theory that is particularly valuable in this environment. The McKinsey authors argue that growth should be stimulated by betting on multiple horses and then letting evolution take care of options that do not work out. The most robust strategy is betting on all scenarios (though at differing levels of capital intensity). Essentially, it is most promising if Intel continues its real-option approach to strategy (although the financial consequences of real options are not explored here).

Intel has successfully employed this strategy in the past. In previous years, there were four major contenders for the next lithography technology: optical lithography, electron-beam lithography, X-ray lithography, and Extreme UV (EUV) lithography. Intel has been a party to all the industry consortia that were developing these technologies. It has always been known that optical lithography, though useful for five years, would not be extendable because of physical limits. IBM announced that its E-beam effort would not be able to deliver, and X-ray lithography has proven to be very expensive. Extreme UV lithography, however, has shown promise, and an experimental system has been built. Intel has announced that EUV will be the final contender and has therefore aimed all its resources at this development. That is a dramatic choice, since EUV is capable of delivering resolution beyond the point where other physical limits are predicted to slow down Moore's law. What one can conclude is that Intel has successfully hedged its bets by investing in all these (expensive) technologies.

With respect to Moore's law, Intel faces uncertainty on "level 3: a range of futures," as defined by Courtney. Level 1 is a "clear enough" future, in which a single forecast is precise enough to plan a strategy. Although any prediction is inexact, the imprecision in the forecast is not large enough to effect a change in strategy. Level 2 is "alternate futures," in which two mutually exclusive events or discrete scenarios can be distinguished. Many regulatory changes are of this type. A range of variables define level 3, but the actual outcome may lie anywhere between the boundaries. As in level 2, some, if not all, elements of a strategy would change if the outcome were predictable. Level 3 uncertainty is best dealt with by using a range of scenarios for illustrative purposes, although discrete outcomes do not exist. A portfolio of actions can then be developed to fulfill the company's strategic intent (Figure 1.4). Level 4 is the rarest of uncertainties: "true ambiguity." In this case, even the range of potential outcomes cannot be defined.

Growth is managed across time horizons. The action one takes is dependent on the time and the corresponding uncertainty. "No regrets" moves (horizon 1) are short-term in focus and often tactical. "Big bets" often involve large capital investments or acquisitions that can result in both large profits and large losses. "Options" are relatively small investments with potentially high payoffs. Focusing on low-cost manufacturing is a clear no-regrets move. Intel announced in April 2001 that it would slash the price for the Pentium 4 by 50 percent, an unprecedented price cut probably due to

Figure 1.4
Concurrent Management of Growth across Three Time Horizons

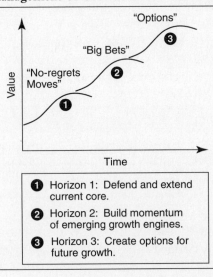

lack of demand. Nevertheless, the Pentium 4 is now produced with 180nm technology, which is relatively expensive. By switching to 300mm wafers and 130nm, the manufacturing cost of the Pentium 4 will fall dramatically.

For the purpose of this discussion, horizons 2 and 3 are more interesting. On horizon 2, Intel will have to make a big bet on further demand for computing power. Ordinarily, firms have a choice if they want to invest on horizon 2. This depends on the *strategic posture* of the firm: Is it a shaper, an adapter, or just reserving the right to play? Since Intel has such a commanding market share, it has no choice but to shape the market. Not investing would immediately lead to scenario 2 (vicious cycle) with its detrimental effects on industry evolution. This does not stop Intel from trying to create some reversibility in its decision. It could try to make its manufacturing capacity flexible, so that it could postpone the introduction of the next generation of chips after the Itanium (the Itanium is the heir to the Pentium 4).

Under level 3 uncertainty, most firms adopt a "reserving the right to play" posture. For a shaper like Intel, options on the third horizon are extremely important. The following list of recommended potential options is by no means exhaustive:

1. Intel should keep investing in infrastructure and software companies to help develop applications that require high-speed processors. Despite the lackluster performance of this strategy, it is an important option for Intel to keep open. Intel's Internet strategy is to be viewed in the same light.

2. Intel should try to develop strategic partnerships with people on the applications side of Microsoft. Traditionally, it has focused on the operating-systems side of the business. A key problem is that Intel is lacking a driver of demand for more computing power in business. Dertouzos (2001) predicts a 300 percent increase in PC productivity as a result of human-centered computing. It could be very advantageous to focus on this sector. Such a strategy might be the big bet of tomorrow.

3. The R&D strategy of Intel should be a portfolio of options.

4. Intel should create an option that allows it to switch from a capital-intensive, R&D-driven business to a more operations-driven company.

5. Intel should investigate the possibility of diversifying its PC offerings by emphasizing other performance factors, such as usability.

6. Investments in Bluetooth, the home PC, and maybe even a set-top box would be crucial in gaining a foothold in scenario 4.

Key Indicators of Change

This type of thinking should be done systematically within a firm. Following are proposed early warning conditions that could influence either the portfolio of options or the posture of a firm with respect to those options. These indicators essentially resolve uncertainty in the preceding scenarios:

1. The market share of economy/value and high-performance segments (apart from organic growth through new computer users).
2. The reaction of businesses to the next version of the Windows/Office platform.
3. PC replacement rates in businesses.
4. The speed of product introductions.

Given the uncertainty in which semiconductor firms operate, a systematic application of the preceding tools is vital for success. The approach outlined will help managers avoid dangerous binary views of uncertainty. It offers a discipline for thinking rigorously and systematically about uncertainty.

PERILS OF PREDICTION

It's tough to make predictions, especially about the future.

—Yogi Berra

Moore's law is not infinite. Fundamental equations, such as the Heisenberg uncertainty principle, the speed of light, and entropy laws, put real physical limits on the computational capacity of a computer with a mass of one kilogram and a volume of one liter. Fortunately, the theoretical limits to computing power are roughly 10^{40} times higher than a current laptop's performance. Long before we reach that limit, we will run into difficult engineering problems (e.g., it will take longer for a signal to travel from one side of the chip to the other than there is time between clock pulses—even at light speed). New concepts like the Raw architecture will need to evolve to solve these problems. It is hard to predict any fundamental economic limits to Moore's law, especially since these limits are as flexible as human ingenuity. For the sake of argument, one can safely assume that something like Moore's law will hold for at least another decade, be it a bit faster or slower than previously.

That realization might not be as valuable as it seems, however. Moore's law has been heavily criticized as inducing linear and extrapolative thinking and encouraging the use of computing power to solve every problem. A Zen master's response to "Is Moore's law infinite?" might be *mu* (roughly translatable as "un-ask the question"). Asking the right question might be fiendishly more difficult. Does value live in distributed devices? Is the human-computer interface the real constraint in the system? Would artificial intelligence increase productivity? Is exponential growth fundamental to technological advance, as argued by many authors (e.g., Kurzweil, Lucky, Gilder)? Two hypotheses illustrate these problems: (1) Any nonlinear growth is very difficult for people to grasp and (2) Moore's law has influenced our subjective experience of time.

Nonlinear Growth

Humans cannot cope easily with exponential growth. This age-old fact can be appreciated by recalling the fable of the emperor of China, the peasant, and the chessboard. The peasant has done a favor for the emperor and may choose his reward. He says that he would wish simply to be given a single grain of rice on the first square of his chessboard and then twice as many grains on each succeeding square. Since that sounds simple, the emperor agrees. At the beginning, the board requires very little rice. The rice on the first eighteen to twenty squares of the board can be stored easily in a small wastebasket. The next couple of squares need a large wastebasket. Squares 23 through 27 take an area of rice about the size of a large table. Squares 28 through 37 take up roughly a room. To get to the last square—the sixty-fourth—requires a number of grains represented by 2 followed by nineteen zeros—variously estimated at requiring the entire area of earth to produce, weighing 100 billion tons, or filling one million large ships or one billion swimming pools.

This is the way exponentials work. The first doublings are easy to grasp, but later they become overwhelming. Moore's law says there will be exponential progress in microelectronics and that doublings will occur every 18 months. Since the invention of the transistor, there have been about 32 doublings, as predicted by Moore—the first half of the chessboard. Should Moore's law continue, what overwhelming implications await as we begin covering the second half of the board? It is easy to extrapolate an exponential trend and get ridiculous results. But it is just as easy to underpredict the consequences of exponential growth.

The problem of predicting the consequences of growth is even more acute in systems that follow an S-type curve. Figure 1.5 shows a tendency

Figure 1.5
Overprediction and Underprediction in S-Curve Type Developments

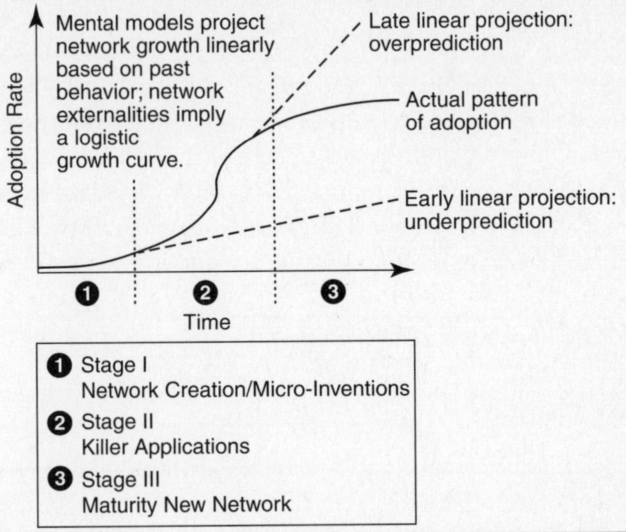

Source: Sawhney, 2001.

to underestimate technology that is in an exponential-growth phase and to overestimate it when it is actually slowing. Grove (2001) calls the point at which the one becomes the other the "strategic inflection point." As we develop scenarios, we must keep in mind that an error in prediction for exponential growth results in mistakes that are on the order of several magnitudes, rather than an error of the same or smaller order of magnitude.

This tendency is analogous to why several centuries went by before Newton realized that movements are proportional to the second time derivative of space, not the first, as Galileo postulated. Research has shown that our subconscious model of movement is linear: Something moves if we apply a force to it, and the harder we push, the faster something moves. This is Galileo's theory of physics. Newton, however, states that an object will keep moving at the same velocity unless a force is applied. His theory is obviously less related to our daily experience but has been proven right over and over again. Although we have been exposed for several centuries to Newtonian physics, the human mind's subconscious model remains based on Galileo's intuitive theory, not on Newton's classical mechanics. This is a consequence of evolution—when a human is facing a predator, it is of no use to compute a complex model. A simple first-order approximation is the lifesaver. Nonetheless, the hard wiring of the human mind for simple linear scenarios is dangerous for predicting a trend. Even though the hard-drive industry has known for years that low-performance, smaller hard drives could disrupt the basis for competition, it still linearly extrapolates their performance curve. The same holds for IBM and its mainframes, which were disrupted by minicomputers and DEC, which was in turn disrupted by the PC revolution. The lesson to apply when extrapolating Moore's law in the semiconductor industry is twofold: Our intuition is probably flawed, and a disruptive change to the industry is more likely than a smooth transition to a new era, even after exposure to the harsh lessons of the past.

Moore's Law and the Perception of Time

Moore's law is a fundamental rhythm to our time. Not only were semiconductors a major part of the growth of the economy in the past years, but they also inspired abundances in related technologies. Our lifetime is the most fundamental limit to our experience. Because Moore's law predicts the magnitude of change during that span, it is a fundamental driver of human experience and can have an enormous impact. Our subjective experience of time will be different as a consequence of Moore's law.

Kurzweil argues that this force is so fundamental that progress in technologies is not only exponential, but double exponential: The rate of progress is increasing over time. He offers compelling evidence in the fact that Moore's law is not the first computing paradigm, but rather the fifth, and that each of these paradigms has seen ever-increasing exponential returns. It is therefore not surprising to find Moore's law as a model in strategy—it is the theory of "time pacing." Most companies change in reaction to events such as moves by the competition, shifts in technology, or new customer demands. In fairly stable markets, such event pacing is an effective way to deal with change. But successful companies in rapidly changing, intensely competitive industries take a different approach: They change proactively through regular deadlines. There are two essentials of time-pacing: managing transitions such as the shift from one new-product-development project to the next and setting the right rhythm for change. Companies that march to the rhythm of time-pacing build momentum, and companies that effectively manage transitions sustain that momentum without missing important beats. Figure 1.2 is a compelling illustration of this concept.

Moore's law is an emblem of the powerful benefits of science. If it slows down, it will be one of the great disappointments of the modern age. The concept of ever-increasing power for the same price has continued to inspire enormous enthusiasm despite the recent economic downturn. Nobody has sufficient foresight to proclaim the end of Moore's law. The only way to know is to try it, or in other words, to exercise the option. Pushing the boundary is undoubtedly a costly and risky strategy. The semiconductor industry must bet on one of two horses: Moore's law will continue, or Moore's law will peter out—the fundamental quandary for the semiconductor industry. Although running down the same path as before may not necessarily be the best answer, that path has been vital in the past, and what we learn along the road will be vital in the future. Therefore: Moore's law is dead, long live Moore's law!

References

Adleman, Leonard. "Molecular Computation of Solutions to Combinatorial Problems." *Science* (November 11, 1994).

Baghai, Mehrdad, Stephen C. Coley, and David White with Charles Conn and Robert J. McLean. "Staircases to Growth." *McKinsey Quarterly* (1996).

Becker, Gary. "A Theory of the Allocation of Time." *Economic Journal* (1965).

Beinhocker, Eric D. "On the Origin of Strategies, or, Robust Adaptive Strategies." *McKinsey Quarterly* (1999).

Bower, Joseph, and Clayton Christensen. "Disruptive Technologies: Catching the Wave." In John Seely Brown (Ed.), *Seeing Differently: Insights on Innovation*. Harvard Business Review Book, 1997.

Brown, John Seely, and Paul Duguid. *The Social Life of Information*. Boston: Harvard Business School Press, 2000.

Brown, Shona. "McKinsey & Company." *Harvard Business Review* (March 1998).

Burgelman, Robert A., Dennis L. Carter, and Raymond S. Bamford. "Intel Corporation: The Evolution of an Adaptive Organization." *Stanford Graduate School of Business* (July 22, 1996).

Burgelman, Robert A., and Andrew S. Grove. "Strategic Dissonance." *California Management Review* (Winter 1996).

Courtney, Hugh, Jane Kirkland, and Patrick Viguerie. "Strategy under Uncertainty." *Harvard Business Review* (November/December 1997).

Demil, B., B. Leca, and P. Naccache. "Reconsidering Moore's Law." Les Cahiers de la recherche, Center lillois d'analyze et de recherche sur l'évolution d'entreprises (CLAREE), UPRES-A CNRS 8020.

Dertouzos, Michael L. *The Unfinished Revolution: Human-Centered Computers and What They Can Do for Us*. New York: HarperBusiness, 2001.

Devaney. "Breaking Moore's Law: R&D Policy for Emerging Computer Hardware Technologies." IEEE/WISE (2000).

Doyle, John R. "Serial, Parallel and Neural Computers: Technological Trajectories in the Future of Computing." *Futures* (July/August 1991).

Economist. "The PC Is Dead, Long Live the PC." (December 14, 2000).

Forbes, Nancy. "Biologically Inspired Computing." IEEE Computing Society, computer.org. In *Computing in Science & Engineering,* 2000.

Gelsinger, Pat. "Microprocessors for the New Millennium—Challenges, Opportunities and New Frontiers." At IEEE International Solid-State Circuits Conference. (February 5, 2001).

Gibbs, W. Wayt. Interview with Gordon E. Moore: "The Law of More." *Scientific American* (1998). "The Solid State Century" (January 2002).

Gilder, George F. *Telecosm: How Infinite Bandwidth Will Revolutionize Our World.* New York: The Free Press, 2000.

Goldratt, Eliyahyu, and Jeff Cox. *The Goal, a Process of Ongoing Improvement.* North River Press, 1984 (2d rev. ed., 1992).

Gordon, Robert J. *Productivity in the Transportation Sector.* National Bureau of Economic Research, Working Paper no. 3815 (1991).

————. "Does the New Economy Measure Up to the Great Inventions of the Past?" *Journal of Economic Perspectives* (Fall 2000).

Greenstein, Shance. "It Has Bugs, but the Games Are out of This World." *Microeconomics Department, IEEE Micro: Chips, Systems and Applications* (2001).

Grove, Andy. Interview by Michael Sweeney, Intel Corporation Technology & Manufacturing Group Training. "Moore's Law, an Intel Perspective." (2001).

Gwennap, Linley, and Kevin Krewell. "Intel Microprocessor Forecast; Product Road map, Volumes, Costs and Prices." Sunnyvale, CA: MicroDesign Resources, 2000.

Hibbard, Justin. "Transmeta's Chips Make the Journey to Servers. *Red Herring* (February 13, 2001).

Hutcheson, G., and Dan Hutcheson. Telephone interview (2001).

Hutcheson, G., and Dan Hutcheson, and Jerry D. Hutcheson. "Technology and Economics in the Semiconductor Industry." *Scientific American* (January 22, 1998).

Iijima, S. (1991), "Helical Microtubules of Graphitic Carbon." *Nature* (1991).

International Technology Road Map for Semiconductors (ITRS) 2000. Sematech, 2000.

Ito, Takashi, and Shinji Okazaki. "Pushing the Limits of Lithography." *Nature* (August 2000).

Khosla, Vinod. "Infrastructure—the Next Tsunami," Kleiner, Perkins, Caufield and Byers (July 2000).

Kiernan, Vincent. "DNA-based Computers Could Race Past Supercomputers, Researchers Predict." *Chronicle of Higher Education* (November 28, 1997).

Kingon, Angus I., Jonpaul Maria, and S. K. Streiffer. "Alternative Dielectrics to Silicon Dioxide for Memory and Logic Devices." *Nature,* vol. 406 (August 31, 2000).

Kurzweil, Ray. *The Age of Spiritual Machines: When Computers Exceed Human Intelligence.* New York: Penguin United States, 2000.

Kurzweil, Ray, and Michael Dertouzos. "Kurzweil versus Dertouzos." *MIT Technology Review* (January 1, 2001).

Lloyd, Seith. "Ultimate Limits to Computation." *Nature* (August 31, 2000).

Lucky, Robert. *Silicon Dreams: Information, Man, and Machine.* New York: St. Martin's Press, 1989.

_____. "Clock Speed." *IEEE Spectrum "Reflections"* (July 1998).

Macher, Jeffrey T., David Mowery, and David Hodges. "Semiconductors." In David Mowery (ed.), *U.S. Industry 2000: Studies in Competitive Performance.* Washington, DC: National Academy Press, 2000.

Meyer, David. "Sophisticated Quantum Search without Entanglement." *Physical Review Letters* (2000).

Mihocka, Darek. "Pentium 4 in Depth and How Intel Blew It." *Emulators Inc.* (2001).

Moore, Geoffrey A. "Crossing the Chasm: Marketing and Selling High-Tech Products to Mainstream Customers." New York: HarperBusiness, 1991.

Moore, Gordon E. "Cramming More Components onto Integrated Circuits." *Electronics* (1965).

_____. *IEDM Tech.* (1975). Dig., 11.

_____. "Lithography and the Future of Moore's Law." Paper presented to the Microlithography Symposium (February 20, 1995).

_____. Interview by Michael Sweeney, Intel Corporation, Technology & Manufacturing Group Training "Moore's Law, an Intel Perspective." (2001).

Negroponte, Nicholas. "Toys of Tomorrow." *Wired* (March 1, 1998).

Packan, Paul A. "Device Physics: Pushing the Limits." *Science* (September 24, 1999).

Peercy, Paul S. "The Drive to Miniaturization." *Nature* (August 2000).

Sawhney, Mohan. "Where Value Lives in Networks." India Internet World Keynote Speech, New Delhi (September 28, 2000).

_____. "Seeing Ahead by Looking Back: Lessons from Network Evolution and Implications for the Internet." Kellogg Graduate School of Management, Techventure class presentation (February 27, 2001).

Shor, Peter W. "Algorithms for Quantum Computation: Discrete Logarithms and Factoring." In Shafi Goldwasser (ed.), *Proceedings of the 35th Annual Symposium on Foundations of Computer Science.* IEEE Computer Society Press, 1994.

Tans, Sander J., et al. "Individual Single-Wall Carbon Nanotubes as Quantum Wires." *Nature* (1997).

Tans, Sander J., Alwin R. M. Verschueren, and Cees Dekker. "Room-Temperature Transistor Based on a Single Carbon Nanotube." *Nature* (1998).

Turing, Alan. "On Computable Numbers, with an Application to the Entscheidungsproblem." *Proceedings of the London Mathematical Society.* 1936. Reprinted in M. David (Ed.), *The Undecidable.* Hewlett, NY: Raven Press, 1965.

Williams, Moody. "Intel is Banking on Pentium 4 to Revive Sales." *Wall Street Journal* (February 15, 2000).

CHAPTER 2

OPTICAL NETWORKING

The Roman Empire had a lasting impact on history. The Romans constructed roads and cities throughout Europe, the Middle East, and North Africa. One of the technologies that permitted the development of vast and densely populated cities was the aqueduct—tunnels and pipes from rivers and aquifers with carefully designed gradients that allowed gravity to move the water. Complex manifolds underneath cities routed water to mains and eventually to homes and public works. In this way, Roman engineering enabled large numbers of people to live in proximity. Homeowners got their water through a nozzle and paid according to the size of the nozzle. Pipes into the homes were labeled with the subscriber's name, and freeloading was discouraged. Despite all this planning, however, urban sprawl and dense populations still caused water shortages.

Striking similarities exist between the demands on the water supply of Roman aqueducts and the increasing demand for data across existing networks in the United States and the rest of the world. The tunnels and their gradients are comparable to data-transmission lines (fiber optic, cable, or copper) and their capacity. Manifolds that direct water are much like the routers in today's network that direct data to the end user. Finally, the data of today is like water during the Roman Empire—it sustains both the populace and businesses.

Investors and the general public are coming to understand that optical networking means more and faster data transmission over existing lines. Few, however, know which companies and segments are the most promising. This chapter establishes a rationale for evaluating value creation across the industry. To begin this journey, we must first answer the question, Why fiber optics in the first place?

Speaking on the subject of communication delays, Frank Dzubek, the president of the network consulting firm Communications Network Architects, said that without optical networks, "We've got California on our

---

Wiring the Desert

"It's a winner all around!" exclaimed Mayor Jim Baca, of Albuquerque, New Mexico. What was he so excited about? Albuquerque had contracted with CityNet Telecom to install fiber-optic cable in sewer systems using a remotely operated vehicle. As an above-ground technician controlled the process, SAM, or Sewer Access Module, laid the fiber essential to downtown Albuquerque's broadband future. By contracting with CityNet, Albuquerque avoided ripping up streets and sidewalks to lay new wire.

Adapted from the *Arizona Republic* (March 25, 2001).

---

hands," referring to the recent electricity shortages in that state. Unquestionably, the need for data transmission is increasing significantly. The Internet can now support 250 million users worldwide. As the number of users is expected to grow to one billion in three or four years, capacity must grow in tandem. Today's networks would collapse if everybody in the world, or even in the United States, had a high-speed connection to the home. Each broadband connection, such as a cable or digital subscriber line (DSL) modem, increases the traffic on the network by 10 times, according to Larry Lang, a vice president with Cisco Systems. As the city expands, the current system of aqueducts will not supply the water we need.

Optical-networking technology has been under development for some time and is uniquely positioned to meet this explosion of demand. For long-haul data transmission, the adoption of optical networking to transmit data, especially nonvoice data, is nearly absolute. Legacy networks are unable to satisfy current service needs by using time-division multiplexing (TDM), which separates packets of *electrical* data along transmission lines by time. Optical networks evolved through research that allowed transmission of data by *light* through optical (glass) fiber. Further innovations

---

The increased capability to transmit data is tied to bandwidth-hungry applications. The two are locked in a virtual cycle that is unlikely to be broken in the near term. The success of optical networks in meeting the needs of existing Internet and other data-transmission sources may lead to greater demand rather than a point of equilibrium.

Figure 2.1
Year 2000 Carrier Spending on Optical Equipment

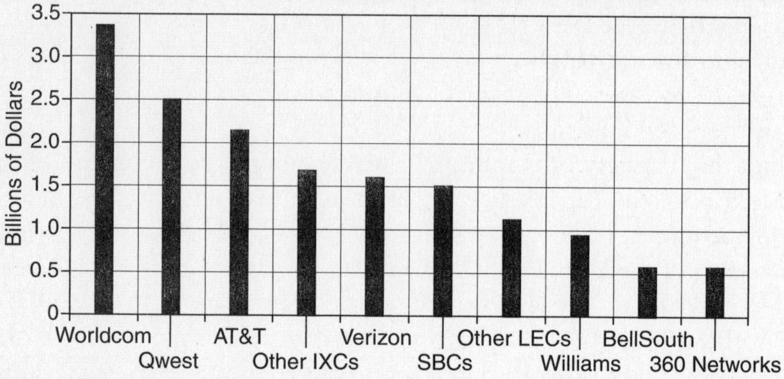

Source: Yankee Group.

have allowed for simultaneous transmission of data packets across the same fiber with multiple-wave-division multiplexing (MWDM). Thus, optical networks provide a two-dimensional increase in throughput in terms of time separation between data packets and the ability to send multiple data packets simultaneously. Network operators are investing significant amounts in optical equipment (Figure 2.1) and will continue to do so in the future.

This chapter broadly describes optical-networking technology to demonstrate how fiber optics helps service providers meet increasing bandwidth demands. It presents a normative approach to evaluating the industry from a broad perspective and then by each major market segment. A discussion of the value chain both now and in the future follows. Finally, we take a look at the future and predict what external industries are in a unique position to benefit from the optical revolution.

TECHNOLOGY PRIMER

The telecommunications industry looks to optical technology as the Holy Grail of high-speed communications.

—Naser Partovi

Optical networking is, quite simply, the networking of light. As copper wiring conducts electricity, optical networks use optical fiber to provide pathways for light. The fiber is made of glass wire and is surrounded by a series of coatings similar to those of other wires. Initial optical networks were point-to-point systems. They consisted of a laser that generated data as infrared light, the fiber it traveled on, and a laser regenerator at specified distances in the network that ensured that the light had sufficient strength to reach the receiver. The receiver translated the light into data for the device at the receiving end.

Since the first networks appeared, several innovations in equipment have increased both the capabilities and uses of optical networking. First, the development of an erbium-doped fiber amplifier (EDFA) increased the signal strength of the laser and did not require a conversion of the laser signal to electricity, thus decreasing the need for amplifiers. In addition, the EDFA allowed for the simultaneous transmission of signals on the same fiber. These innovations in light-based data transmission greatly reduced both the fixed costs of required equipment and the variable costs of the fiber by increasing its capacity.

Next, the development of dense-wave-division multiplexing (DWDM) capitalized on the new capabilities introduced by the EDFA. DWDM enabled the simultaneous transmission of multiple wavelengths of light, that is, packets of light data at the same time on the same fiber. Prior to the development of DWDM, all networks had to employ some form of TDM, which separated packets of information by time. For the first time, data could be aggregated on the same fiber. Initial wave-division multiplexing (WDM) combined two to five wavelengths. Today, aggregations of a hundred or more wavelengths on a single fiber are commonplace.

The difference in the cost of transporting data using optical networking as opposed to a traditional TDM network is profound. The variable costs of data transport over a DWDM network are $\frac{1}{100}$ of the TDM network costs. Although these technologies are partially responsible for the adoption of optical networking, there are further enablers. John Dexheimer (2000), the President of Lightwave Advisors, Inc., sums up the situation: "Long-term demands, technologies, and capital are ideally aligned to create a massive ramp of the optics industry."

The following discussion of the optical-networking industry uncovers the source of value in these complicated networks of light, fiber, and technology.

VALUE ANALYSIS

The demand for greater bandwidth is accelerating. Optical networking already dominates the long-distance transportation of data, but other solutions, including DSL, cable, and phone lines, are positioned at the ends of the network. Because of the capability to maximize bandwidth in the middle of the network, one can easily predict a traffic jam of data. The value chain provides a way to analyze the effects of these trends (see Figure 2.2).

There are four components in the value chain:

1. *End customer.* Value has a tendency to migrate to the edges in any network or connected system. The backbone of a network is typically a simple data-transmission conduit. Here, differentiation (and therefore value) tends to migrate to the core or the edges. This trend will form the future of optical networking. Customers demand and receive higher quality, speed, savings, and reliability from their network operator and service providers.

2. *Network operator.* Network operators will capture very little of the value that optical networking creates. They work in a crowded and competitive space, where it is difficult to differentiate. In short, they sell bandwidth, a commodity product.

3. *Solutions provider.* In this context, the term solutions providers refers to equipment vendors who offer an end-to-end solution and a full suite of services. Because the technology is evolving, especially outside the long-haul segment, solutions providers are able to differentiate their product and services. Sales for solutions providers are also quite sticky. Once providers have installed equipment within a network, prohibitive switching costs develop. Although companies are fiercely vying for dominance, these entities are still more concentrated than network operators, and the potential to earn substantial economic rents remains.

4. *Component manufacturers.* Pioneer Consulting predicts that the optical access–equipment market will grow from $1 billion (in 2001) to

Figure 2.2
Components of the Value Chain

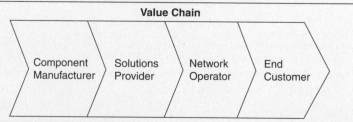

$2.4 billion in 2004 (a 34 percent CAGR). However, not everyone is going to profit from that growth. Although the technology is evolving, there are many manufacturers in the market. For example, there are large numbers of DWDM manufacturers that offer comparable channels on a fiber. Firms could develop innovative and proprietary technology, but such shooting stars will be rare. Also, component manufacturers do not enjoy the benefits of high switching costs like their larger counterparts (the solutions providers). Manufacturers will differentiate themselves on the scalability and interoperability of their equipment.

Optical networking is an exciting and emerging market. The consumer will garner extraordinary benefits and capabilities at the home and office, but different segments are likely to reap economic rents at different times. Of all the players in the market, the equipment vendors (both solutions providers and component manufacturers) are most likely to achieve superior results in the long-haul and metro markets. Therefore, the discussion of value focuses on these two portions of the value chain in the long-haul and metro markets and concentrates on the end consumer in the last mile.

Ends of the Network

Thomas Weisel Partners, a San Francisco-based merchant-banking firm, is ecstatic about LuxN.* "LuxN brings together enterprises that need gigabit access speeds with service providers that are carrying dark fiber and makes the termination and management of optical networks easy and economical," states company literature.

Where is LuxN in the network? LuxN's full-service solutions allow carriers to offer optical virtual private networks, full optical Internet access, and storage-area networks at affordable prices. The company also provides high-speed Ethernet connections at prices five times lower than those of Synchronous Optical Network (SONET).

---

*LuxN is a middleman positioned at the end of the network. The company combines hardware and software to provide more value to the end user and helps service providers differentiate themselves from their competition.

Source: Dreaderman's Internet Research Trends.

Normative Framework

As equipment manufacturers possess tremendous value in optical networking, they are most likely to dominate the space. Two criteria are critical to a network operator when selecting equipment vendors: the total installed cost of equipment and previous relationships.

The total installed cost incorporates many elements of a vendor's offering and provides a measure of technological advancement. More advanced technologies provide higher capacity in smaller boxes with simpler maintenance needs and the ability to add capacity as required.

Previous vendor relationships are also critical. Dave Shipley, the CEO of Rye Telephone, states, "Ninety percent of my purchase decision is based on previous experience with a vendor." Network operators must make trade-offs along these two dimensions. The vendors that are best positioned on these dimensions will become the ultimate winners.

Figure 2.3 illustrates the dynamics in the equipment-manufacturers' space. Cherry performers will be those firms that possess strong existing

Figure 2.3
Players in the Equipment-Manufacturing Space

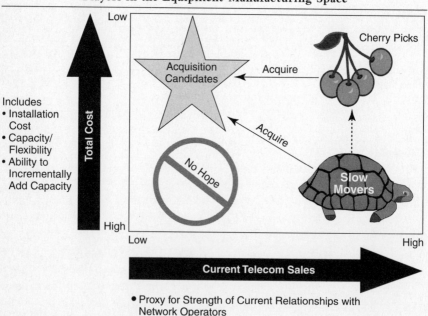

relationships and provide low-cost solutions through cutting-edge technology. These firms, however, are by no means safe from the vagaries of a competitive market. Nipping at their heels are the occupants of the southeast quadrant, those that have been slow to move to the technology frontier. Lucent is an excellent example of a slow mover, at least in the metro market. However, these slow movers can bolster their offerings through acquisitions. The companies in the northwest quadrant are excellent innovators. Their position is not viable in the long term, however, and they will likely be acquired. Finally, there are the duds in the southwest quadrant, those companies that lack an existing customer base and own subpar technology. The competitive optical industry will naturally select these companies out, and they will become obsolete. This framework will be used to assess the chances of various players in the long-haul, metro, and fiber-to-the-home (FTTH) markets.

Long-Haul Winners. In the long-haul segment, component manufacturers and systems providers are best positioned to earn economic rents. Demand for their products, although potentially soft in the short term, will grow rapidly as network operators seek complete solutions for their fiber-optic needs. Purchase criteria will focus on products with the highest quality, scalability, and reliability, leaving price to be the least important driver. Component manufacturers will also do well by developing technology that large systems providers in turn will acquire. The position of network operators will remain dismal until they learn to control the end user (as metro and last-mile systems are implemented). In the meantime, they have little choice but to invest in fiber while lacking the differentiation to price their products at a premium and concurrently build out demand.

Metro-Market Winners. The metro-area network is the most significant bottleneck in optical networking. Businesses and the government largely connect to long-haul optical fiber through the SONET network. Despite the cost savings and added benefits of metro optical networks (MONs), their adoption will take two paths. First, MON vendors will have to satisfy incumbent local-exchange carriers (ILECs), who, because of their legacy networks, will want evolutionary rather than revolutionary equipment. Second, MON vendors will have to satisfy competitive local-exchange carriers (CLECs), who will favor a revolutionary approach because they are not tied to significant existing infrastructure. In any event, the cost of installation in an urban environment is high. For that reason, MONs must provide easily scalable equipment with high quality of service (QoS) if they want to capture value in the metro segment. Two winners will emerge in this category—Ciena and Nortel.

Last-Mile Winners.   There are no clear overall winners in today's FTTH market (see Figure 2.17). Optical Solutions, Inc., is positioned in the star quadrant because it is flexible and technologically adaptive to the changing last-mile landscape. Daniel Island Media and Rye Telephone Company, located in the tortoise quadrant, are distinguished from Optical Solutions by their lack of adaptability yet superior scalability. The area of greatest value—the cherry or area of high scalability and technological flexibility—is conspicuously vacant. Players in this quadrant will need to scale rapidly to capture market share and control customers. They must be flexible enough to implement new technologies as they are developed. Within this quadrant, true value players will emerge.

The needs of network operators and end customers vary by market segment. Total-cost considerations and relationship-building requirements have different components and levels of importance in each sector. This chapter therefore turns next to a normative analysis of the three major market segments: long-haul, metro, and FTTH.

Long-Haul Segment

Long haul refers to wide-area networks (WANs), in which long distances separate major areas, much like an interstate highway system. WANs consist of a fiber backbone owned by large interexchange carriers such as AT&T, WorldCom, and Sprint, and by overbuilders such as Level 3, Qwest, Global Crossing, and Williams. These companies have paid prodigious amounts to light their fiber to meet global bandwidth demand created by the Internet, but none have truly figured out how to capture the value they have created through spending on their networks. One thing seems certain: As supply has caught up to, and even outpaced, demand over the past 12 months, we have witnessed increased price competition by providers of bandwidth services and reduced component spending in the near term.

Though great for the consumer, this has increased pressure on long-haul companies to rethink how they will turn their investments into profits. Traditional carriers like AT&T, WorldCom, and Sprint have the unfortunate task of upgrading a huge installed base of legacy equipment to compete with overbuilders in the search for controlling the bandwidth market. J.P. Morgan's telecommunications-equipment analyst Greg Geiling (2000) estimates that once service providers have deployed their next-generation-backbone networks, they will see savings on the order of 40 percent to 50 percent in capital costs and up to 20 percent in operational costs over traditional networks. To compete over the long term, they have little choice but to focus on enhancing their optical capabilities both to achieve cost savings for current services and to possess the infrastructure to meet future customer demands.

Nowhere else is bandwidth devoured as quickly as in the long-haul network. Spanning thousands of miles in many cases, these networks differ from other markets in two important ways: long spans between nodes and extremely high bandwidth requirements. Long-haul networks were the first to deploy optical amplifiers and wideband/WDM systems, mainly to reduce cost. Optical amplifiers are a cheaper alternative to a large number of electrical regenerators in a span. In addition, interexchange carriers increased the fiber capacity by using WDM, avoiding the large expenditures of installing new fiber.

Most long-haul fiber is already lit, but new products with longer distance capabilities, higher speed, and higher quality are developed every day. Bill Rabin, a networking analyst at J.P. Morgan, estimates that router prices and performance double every 18 months, which will help maintain sales (through upgrades) in the U.S. long-haul market in the long term at 40 percent to 50 percent growth per annum. Service providers will periodically upgrade to increased-channel-count WDMs with higher transmission rates, focus more on ultra-long-haul transmission, and use optical cross-connects that lead to all-optical networks. Service providers, both old and new, focused first on the low-hanging fruit of long haul because it was the most available revenue stream for them: long-haul wholesale and point-to-point.

Intelligent optical-networking hardware that makes it easier to control networks by automating network functions should also be considered. Intelligent hardware currently represents 15 percent to 20 percent of the overall market for optical-networking equipment, with particularly strong demand for long-haul applications (Figure 2.4). Although most intelligent products are now designed for long-haul applications, that will change as the backbone gets faster and the network edge and access portions shift to take advantage of greater bandwidth. Michael Howard, of Infonetics, states, "Expect a lot of growth in the metro edge, metro core/regional, and last-mile-access parts of the network." Some of the companies focusing on intelligent products are Ciena, Nortel, Corvis, and Sycamore, and the market is expected to grow by more than 50 percent this year.

Figure 2.4
Intelligent Optical Network Hardware Market, Year 2000

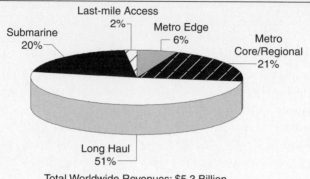

Total Worldwide Revenues: $5.3 Billion

Source: Infonetics Research, Inc.

The ultra-long-haul market is also becoming increasingly important (Figure 2.5). This segment could further reduce costs for providers by removing the need for the expensive regenerating equipment currently used in the long-haul market. During the StarTrax2000 conference, it was estimated that coast-to-coast traffic passes through 30 SONET devices. This could be reduced to one or two devices that have 10 times the signal strength. The major challenge faced by ultra-long-haul component manufacturers is further reducing costs for providers by increasing capacity through tighter wavelength spacing extended over a broader spectrum.

Figure 2.5
Ultra-Long-Haul DWDM Market

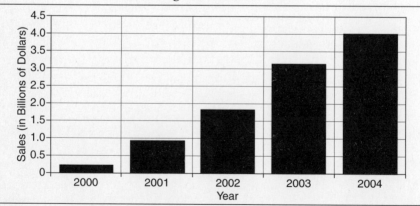

Component manufacturers in this space are likely to be Ciena, Sycamore, Alcatel, Corvis, Nortel, and Marconi, all probably introducing products in the upcoming 12 months.

Long-Haul Value Chain

To grasp where value will be captured, it is important to understand the value chain for the long-haul market. As discussed earlier, equipment vendors will capture most of the value, and service providers will be left with a commodified product facing serious price competition. The following discussion examines each part of the value chain, how it affects the size of the total market, and which equipment vendors will dominate the space (see Figure 2.6).

End Customer.   The end customer in the long run will be the corporations, government entities, and residential consumers who use the backbone to send applications or data. Intermediaries will still serve these markets but must differentiate themselves by controlling end users. Still early in the development of a full optical solution for end users, long-haul players lack appropriate technology. These companies own the fiber to transmit huge quantities of information at low prices. Metro-market and

Figure 2.6
Value Chain for the Long-Haul Market

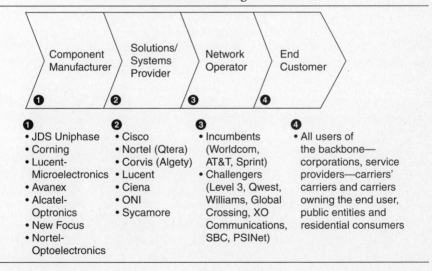

❶	❷	❸	❹
• JDS Uniphase	• Cisco	• Incumbents	• All users of
• Corning	• Nortel (Qtera)	(Worldcom,	the backbone—
• Lucent-	• Corvis (Algety)	AT&T, Sprint)	corporations, service
Microelectronics	• Lucent	• Challengers	providers—carriers'
• Avanex	• Ciena	(Level 3, Qwest,	carriers and carriers
• Alcatel-	• ONI	Williams, Global	owning the end user,
Optronics	• Sycamore	Crossing, XO	public entities and
• New Focus		Communications,	residential consumers
• Nortel-		SBC, PSINet)	
Optoelectronics			

last-mile players are far behind, for although the highways have been paved, there are few off-ramps to get to the final destination. Network operators will have to gain control of this end market. The buildout of the metro-market and last-mile networks will create huge opportunities for both equipment manufacturers and the solutions providers.

Network Provider.   Most network providers have lit a substantial portion of their fiber. Ultra-long-haul data transmission has forced networks to search for systems providers that are capable of providing end-to-end solutions. Purchase decisions are made on the basis of a vendor's position on the learning curve and the sophistication of proprietary equipment. Top providers such as Nortel and Ciena are often the first to market with their new technologies and can easily upgrade as they unveil these technologies. Systems providers have been willing to practically give away their early-stage equipment in hopes of building the relationships that are so valuable for ensuring future purchases.

Equipment costs have not been a detriment to sales until recently, as more and more sales were made with special financing, and production capacity has started to meet demand. Long-haul network operators now have vast quantities of bandwidth that is not used because of limitations at the peripheries.

Level 3 seeks to become the low-cost provider in this declining-price environment. The company plans on accomplishing its goal by employing a horizontal business model to sustain its cost advantage. The technologies that enable growth in fiber capabilities are supplying bandwidth at a rate that may have surpassed the level of demand that has come onstream. Price reductions created by improvements in performance have helped spur demand, but at a rate insufficient to match the rapid rollout of these long-haul DWDMs. This in turn has reduced the company's short-term outlook. So powerful is their low-price selling strategy that competitors such as Global Crossing, Qwest, and Williams have named it the "Level 3 effect." On the positive side, Level 3 is able to sell more bandwidth as it rolls it out. However, the company is selling bandwidth at reduced prices, a problem that will only become exacerbated over the next few years as better technology provides greater capacity. Large providers such as Level 3 have invested so much in the networks that it is important to secure high-capacity use rates, which will further deteriorate margins.

This truth illuminates the company's strategy: If you build it, they will come. The goal is to build something the world doesn't yet have but will truly need as new content is developed. Increased capabilities will create demand as services and new products are provided to end users (such as movies on demand and other applications). Last-mile data-transmission constraints have isolated end users from the benefits of backbone bandwidth improvements. Component manufacturers are beginning to focus their efforts on the last-mile market, as this segment could yield revenue opportunities that dwarf recent long-haul spending. Level 3 owns over 15,000 fiber-optic miles in the United States and almost 4,000 miles in Europe.

Qwest recognizes that as price competition is likely to remain strong, bandwidth sales will not be sufficient to effectively differentiate network providers in today's fiber-optic market. Companies in this space will need to bundle voice and video products with bandwidth to make their offerings more attractive. Qwest's Web site states: "Anyone can put fiber in the ground. A few can light it. Some can operate it. But only one can be the preeminent provider of applications built into the network. Qwest is that one. Through partnerships with some of the world's most-advanced companies, Qwest removes costs and complications from our customers' Internet activities."

Qwest has also formed alliances with other companies to become the industry's largest enterprise application-service provider. It is the only company that offers a single source to manage and integrate a complete menu of Internet uses, beginning with connectivity and moving through security, hosting, application services, and content—all supported by "best-in-class" network performance.

Global Crossing, another major competitor in this market, projected the control of over 100,000 fiber-optic miles by the end of 2001. The company serves many of the world's largest corporations, providing a full range of managed-data/voice products. Global Crossing operates throughout the Americas, Europe, and the Asia/Pacific region and provides services in Asia through its subsidiary, Asia Global Crossing. The Global Crossing Network and its telecommunications and Internet product offerings will be available to more than 80 percent of the world's international communications traffic.

The company is implementing more than 80 Global Crossing Networks. These networks consist of citywide rings that provide fiber-optic connectivity to individual buildings. These technologically advanced networks do not rely on standard telephone lines for data transmission, but instead on updated equipment designed to handle the vast demands of the new Internet era. The network is constructed with the latest DWDM technology, allowing for easy expandability. Self-healing ring structures, erbium-doped fiber amplifier repeaters, and the use of redundant capacity ensure outstanding reliability and service.

Systems Provider.   Long-haul systems providers are seeking to create competitive advantages by combining forces with component manufacturers. In so doing, systems providers will provide complete and fully integrated product lines for network operators. It is imperative, however, that systems providers continue to focus on their core strengths, including the distribution and marketing of next-generation equipment. Component suppliers will continue to provide integrated optical modules and subsystems. These trends are especially evident in the metro space, where companies are focusing more on software, billing, quality of service and prioritization, redundancy, and other solutions for their customers.

Nortel specializes in complete optical-solutions strategies for network operators. It is seeking growth in different parts of the world and is targeting the fast-growing regions of Europe, Asia, and Latin America. Through these efforts, it hopes to compensate for softness in U.S. technology markets. With a 43 percent share of the global optical-transport market, Nortel commands over 60 percent of the DWDM long-haul market and continues to increase its share through a mix of market-leading optical systems and component technology; a powerful, next-generation product portfolio; and complete customer-fulfillment services. "Our leadership reflects an absolute focus on global customers and ensures the lowest costs per managed bit," says Greg Mumford, the president of Optical Internet, Nortel Networks. "We expect to expand this focus with the introduction of new optical and photonic switching, increased network intelligence, and eighty-gigabit-per-second networks."

Ciena has successfully transitioned from a component manufacturer to a full-service data-transmission provider. Traditionally, the company has relied on the business of a few key long-haul customers, including World-Com and Williams. More recently, Ciena has emerged as a strong next-generation component producer for the long-haul market and has begun to win contracts. Its latest success involved Core Director, a switching product that accounted for 10 percent of sales in the past quarter. This and other optical cross-connect products have reduced the company's dependence on DWDM technologies. Finally, Ciena recently acquired Cyras to better target the rapidly growing metro market.

Lucent, despite an enviable installed base in the long-haul market, has been slow to develop innovative solutions for its customers and has placed many unsuccessful technology bets. The company's greatest assets are its strong customer relationships, abundant R&D talent, and a wide-reaching installed base of proprietary equipment. If Lucent can leverage these resources and successfully cut costs and restructure, it will be poised to capture significant value in the near future.

There are also financial challenges for Lucent. The company has amassed $7 billion in equipment-financing commitments in a desperate attempt to meet Wall Street's expectations. However, many of the service providers associated with those commitments will be unable to meet their obligations. Also, the downturn in technology markets has made capital-raising activities more costly. Tough market conditions have reduced investor interest, corporate valuations, and short-term sales forecasts for systems providers.

Despite Lucent's present difficulties, its long-term outlook is favorable. The company's recent purchase of Chromatis Networks for $4 billion is evidence of its belief in the viability of the metro market. Richard Wong, the head of Lucent's Strategic Development Group, stated that the company will focus on providing complete optical solutions rather than just on manufacturing optical components.

JDS-Uniphase, traditionally a component manufacturer of pumps and lasers, has recently completed aggressive acquisitions in the systems-solutions market. It has bet on increased outsourcing of optical-component manufacturing and used its stock to acquire companies that can improve its product line. In this way, the company will provide complete solutions to vendors and can begin consolidation of this fragmented industry. Because JDSU sells optical-networking systems to Nortel, Lucent, and others, it has encountered difficulties as systems providers begin to manufacture their own products. Recent acquisitions (including ETEK and SDLI) have allowed JDSU to become a dominant force in component production and a beneficiary of increased technology revenues as bandwidth demands increase (see Figure 2.7).

Summary

From network providers to systems providers, market conditions have negatively affected the near-term outlook for all players in the long-haul space. A dearth of capital has spurred a vicious cycle: As carriers issued lackluster forecasts, doubts about profitability began to take over the market. Large carriers started to redo aggressive growth plans, and emerging carriers started to run out of money while missing sales targets on high-margin broadband services. These carriers then reduced spending, and systems providers witnessed a loss of projected sales. Component manufacturers, whose stock rose to improbable valuations in spring 2000, were punished as capex forecasts were reduced. It was a trying year for companies with inflated valuations.

Given the cash-poor state of their major customers, long-haul equipment manufacturers are in for a difficult period. Lighting fiber and

Figure 2.7
Cost versus Telecom Sales

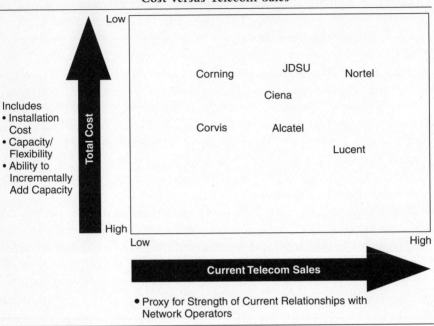

• Proxy for Strength of Current Relationships with Network Operators

upgrading optical equipment will be crucial to remaining competitive. Intelligent all-optical networking in Europe and other leading markets lags that of the United States; this will increase equipment purchases and help reduce the effects of a soft American market. As growth forecasts range from 30 percent to 40 percent over the next four years, component and systems manufacturers are sure to reap substantial benefits. Network providers, on the other hand, will realize value only if they are better able to control end users (see Table 2.1).

METRO-AREA NETWORKS

Metro networks comprise the most significant bottleneck in telecommunications. Sandwiched between the bandwidth-rich long-haul network and the bandwidth-hungry access market, the metro network is under significant pressure to increase bandwidth capacity (see Figure 2.8).

Metro networks have lagged in bandwidth improvement because of the unique engineering challenges in this segment. The metro network

Table 2.1
Telecom Vendor and Infrastructure Investment

Vendor	Financing Commitment	Amount Drawn Down	Notes
Alcatel	$1.5 billion	Unknown	• Source: Company data, research from Commerzbank AG. • Acatel's vendor-financing commitments amount to about 6% of its sales.
Cisco	$2.5 billion	$625 million	• Source: SEC filings, published reports. • Cisco's financing transactions will sustain about 9 to 10% of its revenues over the coming year, according to a September 2000 report by Morgan Stanley Dean Witter analyst Chris Stix. • About two-thirds of Cisco's financing is reserved for Tier 1 service providers, while the rest is set for structured loans offered to higher-risk service providers.
Norel	$2.1 billion	$1.4 billion	• Source: SEC filings, published reports. • Analysts predict Nortel's financing commitments will grow to between $3 billion and $3.5 billion in 2001.
Lucent	$7 billion	$1.6 billion	• Source SEC filings, published reports. • Five percent of Lucient's sales last year came from deals it financed. • From 3Q 2000 to 4Q 2000, Lucent decreased its overall vendor-financing commitments from $7.7 billion to $7 billion. • Lucent had only $2.3 billion in vendor-financing commitments in 1998, according to the *Wall Street Journal*.

distributes voice and data traffic throughout the region and also connects to the long-haul network. Both enterprise and private customers in access networks require a large range of protocols and these drive complexity. The access market includes IP Protocol, ATM, SONET/SDH (Synchronous Optical Network/Synchronous Digital Hierarchy), Ethernet, multiplexed TDM voice, digital video, and other more specific protocols such as fiber-distributed data interface (FDDI), enterprise-system connectivity

Figure 2.8
Model of a Metro-Area Network

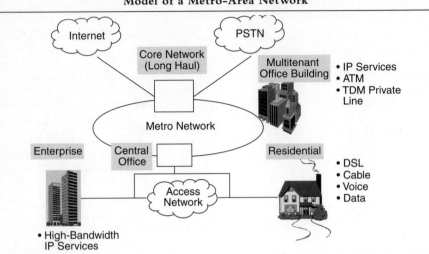

(ESCON), and fiber channel. The infrastructure in the metro network is predominantly SONET/SDH—legacy equipment that is significantly lacking; it is not capable of dealing with the multiple protocols just mentioned. SONET was originally developed to transport limited traffic types, mainly multiplexed voice and private-line services (e.g., DS-1, D-3, T-1, T-3). Thus, the current architecture is inefficient and insufficient for next-generation networks.

The metro network is in dire need of an updated solution with higher capacity and higher flexibility. Advances in optical technology have largely met those needs. Many service providers are already implementing MONs. Many others wonder when, not if, the technologies will be implemented. The MON is a dynamic and exciting market. But the question is where value will be created and who is best positioned to capture that value.

Metro-Market Value Chain

Analysis of the metro-market value chain demonstrates that equipment vendors will reap the greatest benefits. The following discussion examines each part of the value chain and studies its impact on the total market (see Figure 2.9).

End Customer. The end customer has an insatiable appetite for bandwidth. This growth will continue as applications become more bandwidth

Figure 2.9
Value Chain for the Metro Market

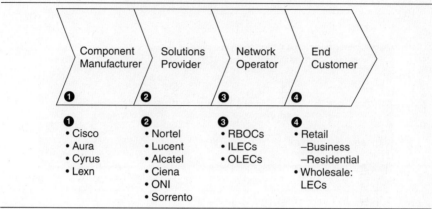

❶ Component Manufacturer	❷ Solutions Provider	❸ Network Operator	❹ End Customer
❶ • Cisco • Aura • Cyrus • Lexn	**❷** • Nortel • Lucent • Alcatel • Ciena • ONI • Sorrento	**❸** • RBOCs • ILECs • OLECs	**❹** • Retail –Business –Residential • Wholesale: LECs

intensive and consumers adopt cable, DSL, voice, and data services. Over the next several years, we can expect continued expansion of end-user applications. Enterprise consumers, unlike their residential counterparts, use IP services, private lines, and high-bandwidth IP services. The proliferation of storage-area networks and Internet data storage will add to this rapid growth. Like the residential market, new enterprise applications will continually be more bandwidth intensive.

Network Operator. To understand the market dynamics and potential of different technologies, it is imperative to study the value proposition from the viewpoint of the service provider. Network operators must upgrade their metro networks to fully optical systems, but there remains the question of *how* and *when* to best implement the changes. Many metro service providers are already deploying or are considering WDM. These companies include Ameritech, Sprint, MCI WorldCom local, AT&T Local Services, GST, Williams local, Level 3, and Regional Bell Operating Companies (RBOCs), such as Bell Atlantic/Verizon, Bell South, USWest/Qwest, and SBC.

It is important to consider this market by segment, as ILECs and CLECs will undoubtedly have different approaches to investing in optical-networking equipment. Heavy investment in legacy equipment will force ILECs to follow an evolutionary rather than revolutionary approach. As a result, ILECs will continue to install SONET equipment and require backward compatibility with new optical systems when they upgrade. As can be seen from Figure 2.10, SONET equipment expenditures will still outweigh optical expenditures in 2003. ILECs, however, will continue to play

Figure 2.10
Split of Spending Worldwide

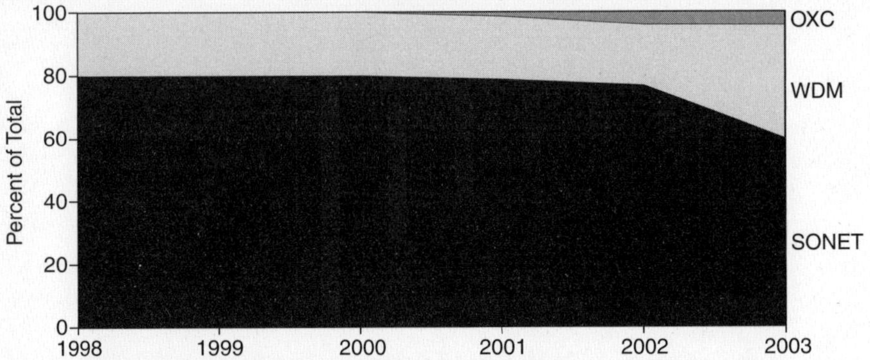

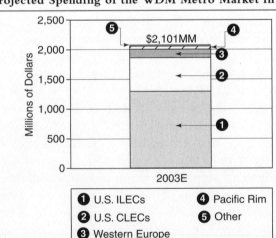

Sources: RHK, Dell'Oro, and Salomon Smith Barney.

a significant role in the emerging WDM metro market. Figure 2.11 shows that ILECs are expected to initiate half the total spending of the WDM metro market in 2003.

New and established network operators have basic requirements in choosing MON vendors: they must deliver exceptional quality of service and equipment must be "future proof" in that the systems must be useful for many years. Other requirements include multiple-protocol support (the

Figure 2.11
Projected Spending of the WDM Metro Market in 2003

ability to interact with multiple-access protocols) and quick provisioning time (simple and rapid capacity upgrades). These requirements constitute the entry fee for equipment vendors.

Solutions Provider/Equipment Manufacturer. As service providers scurry to relieve the bandwidth crunch, revenues from MON equipment are expected to grow at an astonishing rate. In 1999, the metro market represented a mere 3 percent of total shipments of WDM and Optical Switches (OXC) equipment. Total metro-market spending is forecasted to grow at 106 percent per year (Figure 2.12). While industry experts predict a wide range of optical spending, all sources agree that significant growth potential exists in the metro segment.

Many equipment vendors operate in the metro-market space. A snapshot of the WDM metro market in the second quarter of 2000 (Figure 2.13) portrays a fairly concentrated market. This picture has been far from stable, however. From start-ups to entrenched telecom vendors, many firms are scrambling to gain a foothold in the dynamic, rapidly growing metro segment.

The normative framework determines the winners in this industry and shows how the market will be divided over a period of five years (Figure 2.14). Not surprisingly, traditional-equipment vendors occupy

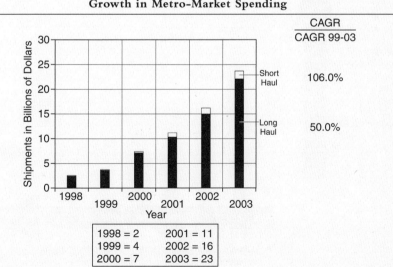

Figure 2.12
Growth in Metro-Market Spending

Figure 2.13
WDM Metro Market in 2Q 2000

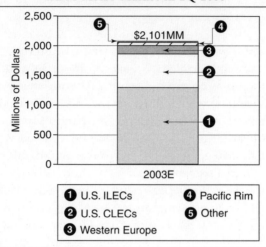

① U.S. ILECs   ④ Pacific Rim
② U.S. CLECs   ⑤ Other
③ Western Europe

Figure 2.14
The Metro Market in Five Years

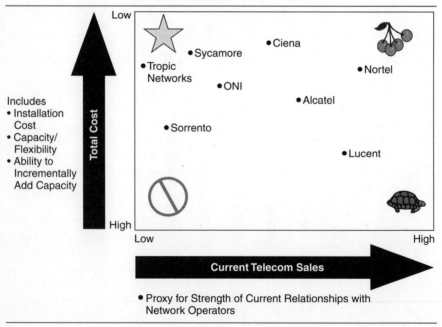

the right side of the framework. These companies have supplied legacy equipment to incumbent carriers and therefore possess substantial credibility and understanding of the service-provider network. Vendors to the right of the framework will certainly benefit from the substantial switching costs involved in moving from one supplier to another. On the northwest side of the framework are the smaller, newer companies that have emerged solely on the basis of their successful technology. Although these companies possess advanced equipment, they have neither the experience nor the relationships of their more established counterparts. The companies in this segment will likely follow one of two strategies: They will either try to carve out a small niche, potentially going after greenfield operators such as optical local-exchange carriers (OLECs), or they will sell themselves to one of their entrenched counterparts. Though this segment will find it difficult to do the latter, it will not be impossible. Nevertheless, by examining Ciena and ONI, we see that it is possible to become a viable stand-alone player in the metro optical-networking market. Ciena, founded in 1992, gained significant exposure in 1996 because of its advanced optical-networking equipment and has since become the second-largest company in the metro market, rapidly approaching the status of Nortel.

The opportunity for such fantastic gains in market share has long since passed. Ciena was one of the first entities to offer optical equipment to the

---

Ciena Case Study

Ciena is the best positioned company in the metro space. Practically non-existent in 1996, it was able to bolster sales and continuously steal market share from entrenched telecom-equipment manufacturers such as Nortel, Alcatel, and Lucent. It is focusing on next-generation optical equipment, a unique position in today's market. Competitors must continuously upgrade legacy equipment to avoid cannibalizing sales. Outdated legacy equipment does not hinder Ciena, and therefore it can develop the most cost-effective, technologically advanced equipment available.

Ciena occupies an exceptional cost position. The company offers a complete solution and has the capabilities to fully implement major system installations. In addition, its focus on next-generation fiber optics should keep it ahead of competitors. Ciena is also adding customers at a faster pace than anyone else. Clients have included Bell South, Sprint, WorldCom, and Japan Telecom, to name a few.

metro market. Not long ago, network operators had few choices among equipment vendors and manufacturers. Although other equipment vendors will develop similar technologies, network operators are likely to purchase according to established relationships.

Summary

The metro market will experience continued sales growth that will outpace the expansion of those companies in the northeast corner of the diagram, Nortel, Alcatel, and Lucent. Ciena will continue to move to the right and capture increasing market share. The landscape of the metro market will undergo significant change, and consolidation will occur—established companies will likely purchase smaller companies such as Sorrento and Tropic Networks.

THE LAST MILE

The advertisement for Harbor Hills, a new housing community on the Oregon coast, promises all one could want, with spectacular views, peaceful surroundings, and . . . "ultimate bandwidth?" With the phrase liberally sprinkled in its promotional literature, the community is touting the fact that all its houses are being built with fiber-optic cables to link them to high-bandwidth servers, providing optical communications directly into the home at rates up to 1.8 Gbps.

—Jennifer Niemela, Optical Solutions, Inc.

Fiber to the home (FTTH) is rapidly becoming the most exciting and promising aspect of optical networking. Though less than 5 percent of homes and offices possess fiber connectivity today, residential fiber deployment is estimated to grow to more than nine million lines in less than four years. Last-mile demand is being driven by the increased bandwidth requirements of online video, music, and data applications. The most powerful drivers of last-mile fiber, however, are the impending ultra-high-bandwidth requirements of high-definition television (HDTV); on-demand, full-length video; teleconferencing; 3-D holography; interactive gaming; smart home; and other soon-to-be-available technologies. Bandwidth demands will grow even more as consumers move toward the flexibility and ease of online computing applications.

Traditionally, these exciting applications were separated from consumers by logistic, technical, and financial constraints. Logistic difficulties involved trenching fiber from local loops to residences, the lack of standardized protocols for fiber networks, the intricacy of establishing passive optical networks (PONs), and the unattractive prospect of replacing existing DSL and cable-modem systems. The technical barriers to FTTH adoption included optical-to-electrical conversion (O/E) problems and the need to split and route optical signals among many subscribers and data providers. The greatest obstacle, however, was financing. The high costs of laying fiber (up to $30,000 per mile in urban areas), O/E conversion equipment, and usage fees have retarded the acceptance of last-mile optical solutions.

Now, however, the barriers have largely been surmounted, and FTTH solutions are now being implemented from Tokyo to Dallas and from Wyoming to Sweden. They are not test projects, but fully working last-mile fiber-optic systems. The systems have demonstrated the viability of the FTTH model and will spearhead the acceptance of the technologies. Evidence of PON growth is shown in Figure 2.15.

To better appreciate the awesome capabilities of these nascent systems, one must understand the leading alternative technological solutions. FTTH competes in a crowded and competitive market comprising cable modems and digital subscriber lines. Because DSL uses standard twisted-pair copper phone lines for data transmission, it has enjoyed rapid and expansive penetration in residential areas. Installation has been relatively inexpensive and rapid. However, DSL suffers from many failings and limitations: Twisted-pair

Figure 2.15
PON Revenue Growth

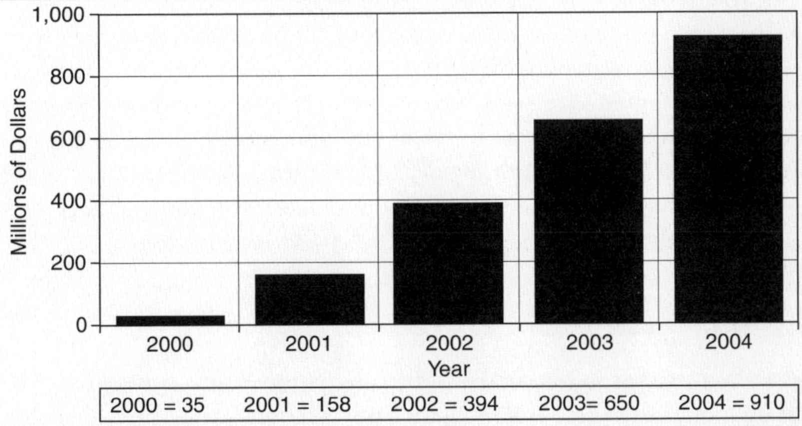

| 2000 = 35 | 2001 = 158 | 2002 = 394 | 2003= 650 | 2004 = 910 |

Source: Yankee Group.

copper is subject to maintenance concerns, transmission distances from central offices are limited, and bandwidth is inadequate to meet the increasing demands of newer applications. The newest DSL development, xDSL, though capable of carrying greater bandwidth, is relatively limited in offering areas. Even this newer technology pales in comparison to the bandwidth capabilities of fiber optics. Cable-modem technologies have been widely accepted as well. Like DSL, the prevalence of installed coaxial cable has enabled low setup and data-transmission costs. However, cable-modem technology is close to its maximum theoretical downstream capacity. More important, upstream data transmission, such as e-mail, is limited to a fraction of the downstream rate. Finally, cable-modem systems are often shared by multiple subscribers and are thus subject to reduced transmission speeds and environmental RF-noise issues, resulting in a lower quality of service.

FTTH technologies suffer from few of these disadvantages and offer a plethora of additional benefits. Because of these tremendous advantages, last-mile fiber will take market share from DSL and cable-modem technologies, and the installed base for fiber will rapidly increase:

1. *Bundled services.* Customers will soon demand the ease and cost savings of voice, video, and data-service integration.
2. *Data-transmission speeds of 10Gbps (up to 100Gbps soon).* These speeds will be required to handle new, data-intensive applications.
3. *"Future-proofed" technology.* DSL and cable-modem technologies will not be able to handle high-bandwidth applications.
4. *Universal protocols.* Incompatible technologies often hinder DSL and cable-modem systems.
5. *Flexibility and scalability.* Changing technological demands will require these characteristics.
6. *Elimination of electrical components.* Optical systems do not rely on maintenance-intensive electrical components.
7. *Customer retention and loyalty.* As consumers increase their usage of high-bandwidth applications and demand the highest quality of service, they will become wedded to FTTH technologies.

Last-Mile Value Chain

The following discussion analyzes the components and companies within each segment of the last-mile value chain (Figure 2.16).

Figure 2.16
Value Chain for the Last Mile

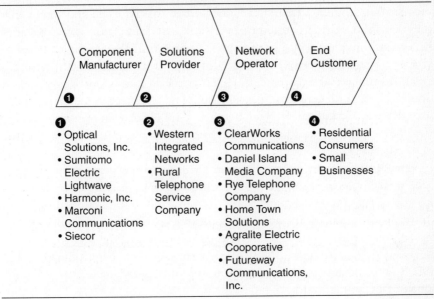

Component Manufacturer ❶	Solutions Provider ❷	Network Operator ❸	End Customer ❹
❶ • Optical Solutions, Inc. • Sumitomo Electric Lightwave • Harmonic, Inc. • Marconi Communications • Siecor	**❷** • Western Integrated Networks • Rural Telephone Service Company	**❸** • ClearWorks Communications • Daniel Island Media Company • Rye Telephone Company • Home Town Solutions • Agralite Electric Cooporative • Futureway Communications, Inc.	**❹** • Residential Consumers • Small Businesses

End Customer. Residential consumers and small businesses stand to reap tremendous rewards as competition and technological advances reduce fiber-installation and access costs. An interesting parallel can be drawn between the adoption and cost trends of personal computers and that of FTTH: Customers will demand faster, more reliable, and cheaper fiber solutions as time progresses, and market entry and competition will seek to meet these demands and therefore lower costs. The residential market is the last ripe fruit on the optical tree. The following sections describe forward-seeing arborists—modern-day harvesters of low-hanging fruit.

Network Operator. FTTH equipment is being purchased, installed, and run by a handful of daring entrepreneurs. So far, only a few CLECs and ISP/media companies have installed last-mile fiber-optic systems. One of these operators is the Daniel Island Media Company (DIMC) of Charleston, South Carolina. The company was established to provide voice, video, and data services to the Daniel Island community, a 4,000-acre development consisting of 5,000 homes, 2,000,000 square feet of office space, a high school, and various hotels and restaurants. Bob Pinckney, the president of

DIMC, was charged with finding a flexible, economical technology that could meet the expanding bandwidth requirements of the Daniel Island residents: "We studied VDSL and hybrid-fiber coaxial cable and found that they fell short of fiber-optic capabilities. VDSL had transmission-distance issues, and, besides, why install copper (which will have to be replaced in seven years and has severe bandwidth limitations), when I can simply install fiber from the start? Hybrid Fiber-Coax (HFC) was not an option. It doesn't allow for return-path transmissions and is subject to radio-frequency interference. We looked at the end-to-end FTTH solution provided by Optical Solutions, Inc. (a leading FTTH component manufacturer), and the choice became easy."

One of the primary motivations for a fiber solution is the ability to provide smart-home features to tenants. Offerings such as closed-circuit monitoring of the nursery, online recipe retrieval in the kitchen, and different music in different rooms are very appealing to new homeowners. Traditionally, last-mile bottlenecks have stood in the way of the high-bandwidth needs of the smart house. Now those concerns have been obviated, and DIMC will be able to offer increasingly sophisticated applications to tenants of fiber-enhanced homes.

Another network operator is Rye Telephone Company, of Denver, Colorado, which serves 2,300 lines about 140 miles south of Denver. Its customers are scattered around a 125-square-mile area encompassing the cities of Rye, San Isabel, Colorado City, and Kim. A local developer purchased a 30,000-acre parcel between Pueblo and Colorado City and divided it into approximately 650, 40-to-200-acre lots. The company suggested using fiber, not copper, to connect the new homes to the local distribution point, 8.5 miles from the serving central office. Jeff Starcer, of Rye Telephone, states, "I didn't see going in there and feeding a digital-loop carrier and then distributing copper to each of the homes. Using FTTH will cost us about an additional $600 per subscriber, but unlike copper, we won't have to replace it within seven years." So far, Rye is delivering basic telephony to 18 new homes in the development. Soon television programming and high-speed Internet access will join these services. Although it costs the company about $3,200 per subscriber to install the FTTH PON, it estimates that future revenues will rapidly recover the high installation costs.

In a telephone interview, Dave Shipley, the president of Rye Telephone, shared his predictions for the future of last-mile fiber: "One of the greatest problems that we are facing is the unbelievable cost of leasing fiber. At nearly $2,000 per mile, the need for company-owned fiber is obvious. Many operators are now buying the right-of-way from railroad companies so they can lay fiber along tracks. This is still very expensive. In the near future operators will need to merge to share the costs of leasing or installing fiber. Expenses will be the leading driver of consolidation in the FTTH market."

Another company, ClearWorks Communications, founded in 1998 and based in Houston, provides proprietary bundled digital services (BDS) to both residences and small businesses. These services include high-speed Internet connectivity, dial tone, digital multichannel video, on-demand video rental, and a community intranet. Carefully tested in the field, its equipment and services have been well received by developers and telcos.

ClearWorks has provided bundled digital services to the prestigious communities of Rock Creek and Stonegate, in central Texas. The fiber network will allow the connection of 5,500 subscribers and provide for access to other communities in the area. The president of ClearWorks Communications states: "Adding subscribers is our main focus, and our fiber network will increase the speed at which we can do so. We are currently adding subscribers in Rock Creek and Stonegate, two of our BDS communities, and we anticipate adding subscribers in several other communities over the next thirty days. Now that we have the physical facilities complete, we can quickly address the backlog of communities that are waiting for our service."

The company has also been working with Texas Instruments to expand its fiber-optic network and install additional capacity for voice, data, and video capability. As the president of ClearWorks, states: "Working with Texas Instruments to build out this fiber is a great opportunity for us. We hope to continue to expand our relationship with TI and become a key part of its internal deployment strategy. Our goal is to deploy the fiber safely and within budget while meeting all OSHA and Texas Instruments safety requirements. Our outside fiber-plant team is very efficient and has largely been deploying fiber on bundled-digital-service projects. In that capacity we have deployed approximately 300 miles of fiber-optic cabling for our fiber-to-the-home communities."

Solutions Provider/Equipment Manufacturer. Although many companies are entering the FTTH space, few have developed the actual last-mile components that are facilitating the revolution. The vanguard of this segment is Optical Solutions, Inc. As Daryl Ponder, the CEO of Optical Solutions, says: "FiberPath is superior to DSL and HFC solutions because its bandwidth is virtually limitless. Traditional copper and coaxial cable can be leveraged only so far, and DSL and HFC are already testing the outer limits. Of course, many in the industry still believe fiber is cost prohibitive,

---

Optical Solutions, Inc.

Optical Solutions, Inc., founded in 1994 and based in Minneapolis, Minnesota, designs, manufactures, and markets FTTH passive optical networks. The company offers its equipment and expertise to CLECs and network operators worldwide. Optical Solutions has developed the FiberPath family of products that can deliver scalable bundled services over the same network. Located at the subscriber's premises, Optical Solutions' patented network-interface device, the Home Universal Demarcation Point, delivers up to four telephone lines, two-way analog/digital video, and scalable high-speed data. With FiberPath FTTH, service providers can preempt competition, diversify, increase revenue streams, minimize expenses (the use of a PON minimizes maintenance expenses and on-site service calls), and future-proof its networks.

---

but that's not the case anymore. Increased demand for fiber has driven the price down to reasonable levels. Moreover, in using a passive optical network versus an active electronic network, fewer amplifiers and less maintenance are required—that also saves money."

Normative-Framework Conclusions

In comparing the cost of fiber to the value that it provides, there is no question that FTTH is the right decision for today. It has the bandwidth to provide today's and tomorrow's services, it protects and enhances future revenue streams and preserves customer loyalty, and it costs virtually the same to deploy today as less-robust, alternative technologies. For carriers and their customers, it's a no-brainer: those that get FTTH first, win.

—Daryl Ponder, Optical Solutions, Inc.

The lack of high-bandwidth applications, prohibitive installation and equipment costs, and the current adequacy of DSL and cable-modem services have all conspired to impede the acceptance of last-mile fiber technologies. These barriers are now eroding with startling rapidity: New applications such as HDTV, on-demand video, and teleconferencing require the capabilities of fiber optics. Innovative and inexpensive products such as FiberPath and Home Universal Demarcation Point have brought costs in line with residential budgets, and projects in Wyoming and Texas have demonstrated that the wait is finally over: Fiber to the home is now a reality.

We are witnessing the birth of a new market, the edge of an adoption wave. Companies such as Optical Solutions and Rye Telephone are leading this revolution to the battle cry of faster, better, and cheaper: The demands of end users will shape this industry. Demand for applications will lead to increased adoption, increased adoption will lead to demand for bandwidth, and increasing ubiquity will lead to more applications. This virtuous cycle will yield tremendous profits for FTTH operators and will radically erode the installed base of DSL and cable-modem systems. Their capacity having reached its theoretical limits, these systems will be replaced as the twin forces of inexpensive fiber and mega-bandwidth applications drive alternative systems to their nadir. As a result, last-mile fiber will reach its zenith with startling rapidity.

Figure 2.17 illustrates the relative value position of those companies in the last-mile sector. The intersection of scalability (on the x-axis) and technological flexibility/adaptability/innovative capacity (on the y-axis) characterizes value capture.

Figure 2.17
Relative Value Position of Companies in the Last-Mile Sector

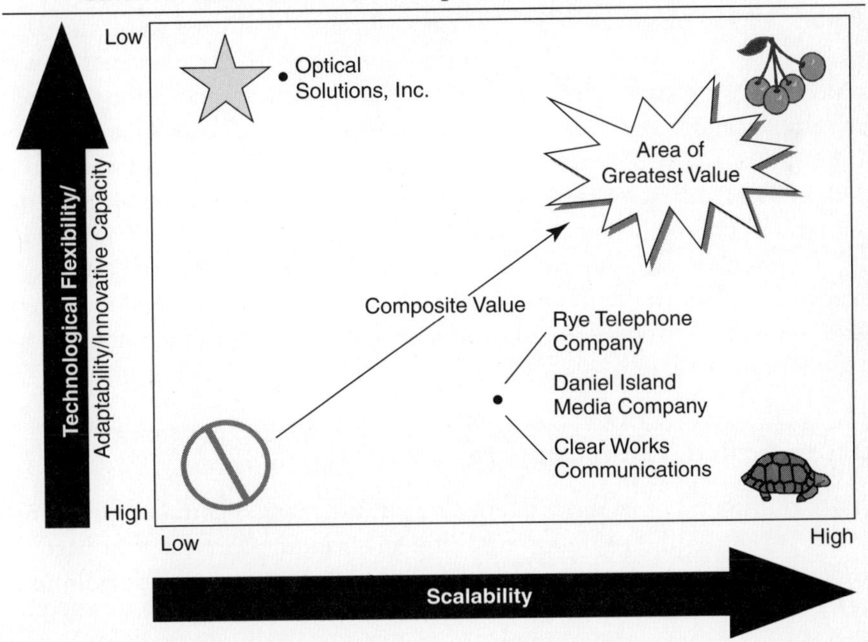

Operating in a nascent market, companies must rapidly and effectively scale their operations. We are, in effect, at the beginning of a massive land-grab: As equipment prices fall and high-bandwidth applications proliferate, companies will need to move rapidly to capture market share. Rye Telephone Company, Daniel Island Media, and ClearWorks Communications remain somewhat flexible in technological adaptability—as new products are developed, they can purchase and install them. They are not, however, developing those products and therefore lack innovative flexibility. Being small regional operators, it is unlikely that they will be able to scale their operations nationally to capture a sizable portion of the last-mile market.

Flexibility and adaptability are required in a market characterized by sudden changes in technology, the need to think rapidly and take risks to capture market share, and the ability to lead the last-mile optical revolution with newer, cheaper products. Optical Solutions, the only provider of end-to-end last-mile equipment, dominates this segment. Although it is innovative, it is not clear that Optical Solutions will be able to scale its production quickly enough to meet the explosion in demand that is destined to occur. For that reason it scores low on scalability.

The area of greatest value, the intersection of high scalability and advanced technological adaptability, is conspicuously vacant. The cherry in Figure 2.17 represents this area. Large companies will need to occupy this space if they are to successfully capture value in the FTTH market. The star represents the area of high technological adaptability/innovation and low scalability, and is the domain of ideal acquisition candidates such as Optical Solutions. The southeastern quadrant, occupied by the tortoise, is the area of high scalability yet low technological flexibility. Companies in this sector will rapidly be left behind as faster, cheaper, and more reliable technologies replace old systems. The bottom left-hand sector represents those companies that offer neither scalability nor technological adaptability. Few companies will last very long in this area and, not surprisingly, none operate there today.

Time-Scaled Value Capture

Value capture becomes more interesting with the introduction of time (Figure 2.18). Over the coming years, an ever-changing succession of participants will capture value within the FTTH market. Today, Optical Solutions is the only affordable last-mile, end-to-end, fiber-optic-component manufacturer in existence. Thus, the company enjoys a large portion of the total

Figure 2.18
Change in Value Capture

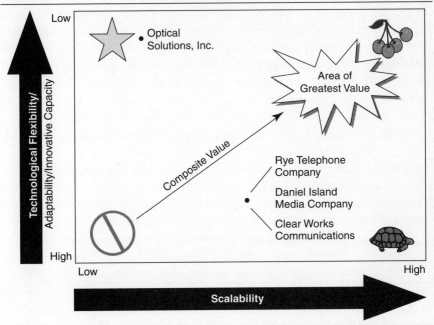

value in this sector—without its Home Universal Demarcation Point, affordable FTTH solutions would not exist. Network operators such as Daniel Island Media and Rye Telephone Company are gatekeepers of the end customer and therefore reap profits in today's market as well. Consumers, however, do not yet gain from last-mile fiber solutions. Burdened with nascent technology, high component and installation costs, and few choices for network operators, the end customer has yet to reap the benefits of this new technology.

Industry experts believe that the value landscape will begin to change in two to three years. Declining technology costs and market entry will erode the value captured by component manufacturers and solutions providers. In addition to further controlling access to end consumers, network operators will begin to raise prices as the supply and demand for high-bandwidth applications increases. At that point, end customers will begin to benefit from last-mile solutions, and innovation will lead to decreased technology costs and an increase in high-bandwidth applications.

Continuing its turbulent trend, value will change hands in four to five years. As before, component manufacturers and solutions providers will see further erosion of profits—margins will fall as customers demand cheaper equipment, competition increases, and innovation wrings costs from last-mile systems. Although robust applications will allow network operators to capture further profits, their competitive position will diminish as government intervention calls for competition in service offerings. (Similar policies allowed customers to choose telephone service providers in the past century.) End consumers, the beneficiaries of these policies, will enjoy further gains during this period.

In six years, the competitive landscape will have changed radically. Component manufacturers and solutions providers will provide low-cost, commodity-type products in a crowded and competitive space. Though network operators will continue to provide new applications, government legislation will further diminish their strength. The ultimate winner in the FTTH market will be the end consumer. As marketing guru Philip Kotler, of the Kellogg School of Management, states: "[As a market matures,] customers increasingly expect higher quality and service. They perceive fewer real product differences and show less brand loyalty. They can obtain extensive product information from the Internet and other sources, permitting them to shop more intelligently. They show greater price sensitivity in their search for value." As legislation enforces competition, equipment becomes universal, costs fall, and applications abound, the end consumer will capture the most value and emerge the triumphant winner in the last-mile fiber-optic market.

CONCLUSION

Looking Forward

Fiber optics and optical networking will experience strong growth and innovation for years to come. As Figure 2.19 shows, the need for bandwidth to transmit voice, Internet, and data is growing exponentially. This demand will drive robust growth in all elements of the optical networking market.

It is difficult, however, to predict market leaders because this sector is still segmented and the introduction of new technologies so varied and rapid. Some of today's optical giants such as Cisco and Nortel will continue to capture value in the near term, but that value capture will shrink as the network evolves and will shift to different areas such as consumers and the government. Nevertheless, we can predict the following trends in the optical industry.

Figure 2.19
Growth in Need for Increased Bandwidth

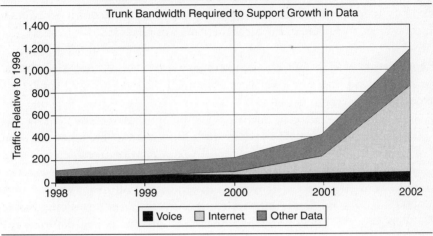

Source: RHK, 1999.

Optical-Hardware Development and Upgrades

We are at the vacuum-tube stage of optical components.

—Naser Partovi

The development and improvement of optical hardware will continue to progress at speeds similar to those predicted by Moore's law for processor speeds. We can expect the big players in the space (e.g., Cisco and Nortel), to continue to dominate. Current growth has already created a microboom in the component-manufacturing segment, as these companies strive to supply industry giants.

Consolidation

It is no secret that many start-ups have developed technologies and positioned themselves simply to be bought out by the large players in the industry.

—Morris Edwards

Even with the recent fall of technology stocks and the loss in value of equity capital, acquisition and consolidation will continue to characterize the optical-networking industry. Today's large companies, with ample cash on hand and still valuable stock, will be able to acquire those companies that offer the most promising technologies. Continued consolidation will be of great benefit to the market as a whole, as service providers will face a plethora of large component manufacturers that will meet all their hardware needs. Current market giants will actively pursue the acquisition of new technologies to widen and protect their market positions.

Migration to Fiber.   Telephone, television, and other technologies are migrating toward the optical network. Although the network will have some barriers to overcome because of consumer inertia, existing telephone and cable services will have to adapt or risk being rendered obsolete by all-optical service providers. Harry Carr, of Tellium, notes: "Switches will need both mirrors and electronics. In a couple years only optical switches will be able to keep up (in the core network), but light waves will still have to be decoded into electrons for delivery to the customers of the network."

In the access market, fiber-optic connectivity faces a growing threat from high-speed, fixed wireless connections, particularly in dense metro areas. Fixed wireless is quickly evolving to offer users more flexibility and portability, making it a viable extension to the optical network. These companies are working on the same coverage and reliability problems that continue to plague users of cell phones.

Move to Open-Source Standards.   Because standard protocols are lacking, only hardware and software from the same company can be used together. Open-source, multivendor standards will reduce infrastructure-deployment costs, device costs, installation costs, and the risks associated with choosing a single vendor or proprietary solution. Even though moving the network to an open architecture with one protocol may weaken many firms' competitive advantage, it will greatly simplify the network's operation and lower the hardware expense as both become commodity items. The current optical network comprises layer upon layer of legacy hardware and operating protocols. Unless that situation is corrected, these legacy elements will inhibit the growth and intelligence of the all-optical network. Open-source standards would allow devices of any component manufacturer to be used with those of any other manufacturer.

Consumer Access

> Currently, optical networking can be characterized by service providers touting their extensive optical backbones with customers still waiting for delivery of high-speed services.
>
> —Carolyn Raab, Vice President of Marketing,
> Quake Technologies, Inc.

An increase in the development of services to accommodate user needs will accompany an explosion in the adoption of FTTH and fixed-wireless broadband. FTTH has been the last segment of the optical industry to witness expansive exploitation. Even though fiber may not be the only answer, increased data transmission at an affordable price promises tremendous advances in service development. The number of consumers with broadband access is very small compared with the total number of network users. Service providers are still trying to overcome consumer inertia and the poor reviews of service and installation that have plagued the rollouts of cable and DSL. However, once the number of users reaches critical mass, creative research and development will take over, and solutions providers will develop new technologies to meet the varying demands of the network users. Some of these advances are already under development (e.g., three-dimensional interactive gaming), whereas others still exist only in the minds of entrepreneurs.

FTTH faces a significant threat from high-speed wireless connections. The threat is real and credible, and if the technology progresses fast enough, it could overtake the implementation of FTTH. Wireless providers have developed the technology to attain a 2Mbps connection. With less required hardware, mobile connections, and no rights-of-way concerns, wireless providers form a possible threat. However, wireless quality of service is far less attractive than that of current optical landlines. Although wireless is not suitable for all areas (e.g., rural areas), it can compete effectively in areas of high population density.

Role of Government. The proposed Internet sales tax has received tremendous public attention in recent years. The issue, however, is relatively minor compared with the potential taxation and regulation of optical networking. The government is already regulating the fees that service providers can charge for data transmission. Sources of government revenue will migrate from traditional telephone and cable-transmission activities to data transmission on the optical network. This will siphon value from network builders, service providers, and network users.

Intelligent Optical Network. Intelligent networking is a compelling area of short-term value creation. The acceptance and implementation of network intelligence will determine its long-term benefits, enable the nearly instant provisioning of new bandwidth, reduce wait time, and eliminate labor costs inherent in today's Internet connections. Intelligence will also provide better reliability, less need for redundancy, and an increased ability to garner IP-based revenue. It not only will help eliminate data bottlenecks but also will reduce total hardware demand and increase the speed and overall carrying capacity of the network.

The Final Word

Bandwidth is becoming a commodity that users can easily trade. This trend will continue throughout the long-haul, metro, and FTTH markets and will shift value from the builders of the network to end consumers, applications service providers, and software developers. In the end, consumers and businesses at the edge of the optical network will capture the most value.

As depicted in Figure 2.20, the value growth of optical networking is not unlimited: Increasing bandwidth ubiquity will cause a loss of value. A similar phenomenon occurred with legacy data systems and in the long-haul market. As base technologies are adopted, the network backbone becomes less valuable. Over time, the metro and last-mile segments will absorb all

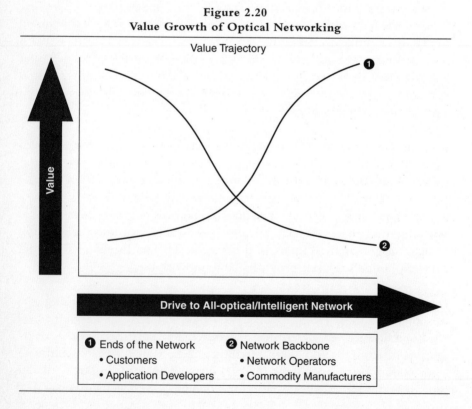

Figure 2.20
Value Growth of Optical Networking

optical solutions. Innovators capable of channeling the vagaries of the dynamic fiber-optic landscape will reap extraordinary returns.

References

"All-optical Telecom Network Faces Slowing Economy, Excess Capacity." *Wall Street Journal* (February 23, 2001).

Alpert, Bill. "Seeing the Light." *Barron's* (December 4, 2000).

Al-Salameh, Daniel Y. *Unleashing the Light™ The Brave New World of Optical Networking.* Lucent Technologies Optical Networking Group.

Bass, Evan. "Ciena's View from the Top: Q&A with CEO Patrick Nettles" (January 2, 2001).

_____. "DWDM Will Keep Fiber Flying High." *Fiber Optics News.*

Bough, Keith, et al. "Let There Be Light! The Optical Networking Revolution." In Sawhney, Mohan. *TechVenture.* New York: Wiley, 2001.

Brooks, Todd. "It's Time to Man the Optical Network." *Network World* (November 27, 2000).

Crow, Sharon. "Bandwidth Trading—Leveraging the Network." Williams Communication (February 13, 2001).

Dexhemier, John. "Wall Street Forecast: A Thousand Points of Light" (December 26, 2000).

Edwards, Morris. "Service Providers Seek Holy Grail of All-optical Network." *Communications News* (November 2000).

Fuller, Brian. "Crossing the PONs: Vendors Push Fiber for the Last Mile" (2001).

Geiling, Gregory. "Backbone! Equipment!" *JP Morgan* (September 21, 2000).

"IP over Photons to Come Sooner Rather than Later" (January 23, 2001).

Janzen, Howard. "Bright Broadband Future." *Williams Communication* (February 13, 2001).

Langner, Mark. "Beyond the Internet." *JP Morgan* (July 23, 1999).

LaserComm Inc. "Getting Closer to the 'All-optical' Goal" (December 19, 2000).

Lehman Brothers. *JDS Uniphase Analyst Report* (September 26, 2000).

Lehman Brothers. *Optical Component Forecast* (Fall 2000).

Lindstrom, Annie. "Can You Say FTTN?" (2001).

Niemela, Jennifer. "Optical Solutions Stakes Out Fiber to the Home Early" (2001).

Partovi, Naser. "Top Developments to Expect in Optical Networking" (January 11, 2001).

Peng, Peter, and Steve Hersey. *Optical NetworkDesign Considerations: Unidiretional versus Bidirectional Optical Transmission.* Lucent Technologies Optical Networking Group (November 1999).

Ponder, Daryl. "Spread of PONs Will Drive Fiber to the Home" (2000). http://www.opticalsolutions.com/Articles/Fiber percent20Optics percent20Online percent20News percent20fiber percent20opticpercent20industry percent20professionals.htm.

Proakis, John G., and Masoud Salehi. *Communication Systems Engineering.* Prentice Hall, 1994.

Raab, Carolyn. "High-Speed Optical Networking for the Masses" (January 26, 2001).

Rabin, William. "The Secret Sauce of Convergence." *JP Morgan* (December 14, 1999).

Reidy, Anna. "North American Optical Transport Market Forecast." *RHK* (November 2000).

Salomon Smith Barney. *Optical Networking Systems* (October 2, 2000).

Schmelling, Sarah. "Fiber Optics: Not Quite to the Door Yet" (2000).

Silver, Gerald and Myrna. *Data Communications for Business.* 3d ed. 1994.

Sistanizadeh, Kamran, and Sam Halabi. "Breaking the Bandwidth Bottleneck with Ethernet." *Telecommunications* (January 2001).

Solomon, Deborah. "Optics Companies Cash in on the Speed of Light." *USA Today* (June 6, 2000).

Southworth, Natalie. "Futureway Lays Down Last Mile" (2000).

Sukow, Randy. "Fiber to the Home Makes a Test in America's Heartland" (2001).

"Supplying Freshwater to Roman Cities."

Toupin, Laurie. "A New Kind of Spread Spectrum Technology for the Metro Market" (December 20, 2000).

Willhoit, Charles. "Communication Components." *JP Morgan* (December 1, 2000).

Plumbing and Mechanical Magazine, July 1989. Excerpt on the Plumber.com Web site.

CHAPTER 3

THE WIRELESS VALUE CHAIN AND INFRASTRUCTURE

In the 1990s, both businesses and consumers increased their use of wireless devices dramatically to connect with people anytime and anywhere. Productivity enhancements for workers created tremendous value, and consumers gained another social link with family and friends. But how do we define *wireless*? (The smoke signals used in primitive societies were also effective wireless devices!) Modern wireless technologies refer to radio frequency (RF), infrared (IR) beaming, and wireless optical. The chapters in this book dealing with wireless focus mainly on the cellular communications industry, which uses RF-based technology and transmits voice and data over carrier-operated, wide-area networks. Businesses associated with this industry constitute the *wireless value chain*. There is also some coverage of business and technology considerations for short range RF-based technologies such as Bluetooth and the 802.11 standard for wireless local-area networks. Space limitations allow only a limited discussion of non-RF technologies such as IR and wireless optical, as well as RF-based technologies, such as fixed wireless broadband and satellite.

This chapter first describes the wireless value chain that has developed to support the needs of customers and discusses the interactions among the players. The chain includes component makers, manufacturers of infrastructure and devices, wireless carriers, enabling software, service providers, and content providers. The discussion identifies the parts of the chain that are developing commodities and where the opportunities are for creating value now and in the future. Then we consider the expected market growth for wireless technologies around the world. Players in the chain are counting on projected advancements in the wireless infrastructure to enable new kinds of applications that will drive additional revenue growth. New technologies include 3G (third generation), location-based services, and

Bluetooth. Finally, we explore the outlook for these technologies and consider whether they are likely to add value to the chain.

The Wireless Value Chain

The increased use of wireless devices by both workers and consumers over the past decade has created a value chain in the wireless industry, as illustrated by Figure 3.1. Beginning with equipment and moving through networks, software, and services, the path through the value chain ends with the target-market segments.

Elements of the Wireless Value Chain

Equipment—Components.　The value proposition of components consists of enhancing the technological capability of devices. Critical to the future

Figure 3.1
The Value Chain in the Wireless Industry

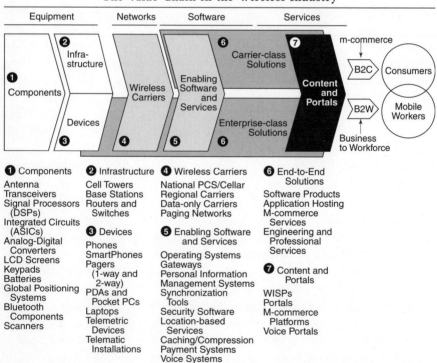

Source: Coster, 2000.

of wireless is the location functionality, which can be achieved through a global positioning system (GPS) or network-triangulation methods. Component manufacturers are responsible for the parts and subassemblies that maintain the mobility and utility of wireless devices. Also noteworthy in this category are battery suppliers, who have improved battery life, size, and weight in response to exacting demands from the market. This part of the value chain will receive a great deal of emphasis as device forms become more and more critical to the adoption rates of customers.

Equipment—Wireless Infrastructure. The value proposition of infrastructure is that it provides the points of connection that enable a backbone or network to exist. Infrastructure will continue to grow at an enormous rate to meet demand (Figure 3.2). It will face threats from competition and lack of service differentiation, causing, in turn, consternation for the equipment providers.

Equipment—Devices. Device manufacturers are the customer's key to the wireless network and, consequently, the first step in the chain for the wireless user. Wireless devices will capture more value as infrastructure becomes uniform, ubiquitous, and commodified. Device features, along with

Figure 3.2
Cell Sites in Commercial Use in the United States

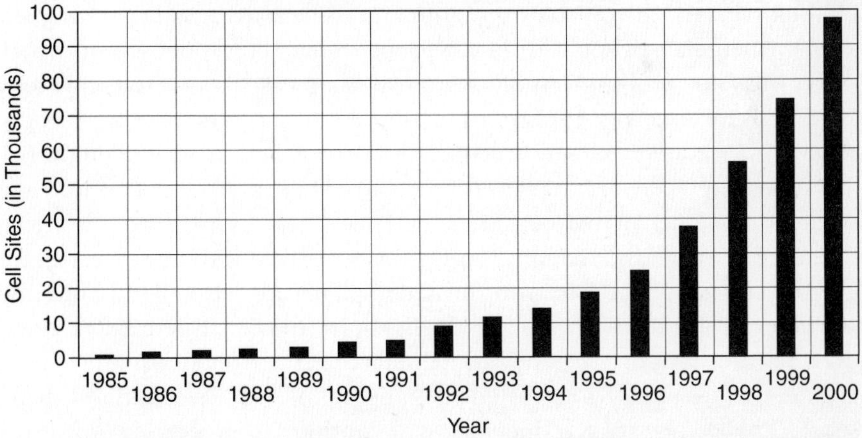

1985 = 500	1989 = 3,577	1993 = 11,665	1997 = 38,650
1986 = 1,195	1990 = 4,768	1994 = 14,746	1998 = 57,674
1987 = 1,732	1991 = 6,589	1995 = 19,848	1999 = 74,167
1988 = 2,789	1992 = 8,000	1996 = 24,602	2000 = 96,733

Source: CTIA. Reported cell cites are up 29.1 percent since June 1999.

applications, will then become the largest determinant of the consumer's connectivity and quality of wireless experience.

An analysis of the wireless application market shows that device manufacturers face a major challenge in designing devices that can provide information while integrating aesthetics, inconspicuous portability, and functionality. Some convergence in devices is inevitable, although primary consumer needs and usage patterns will prevent an all-in-one device that dominates the market with existing technology. In fact, Gartner expects more than a hundred different models of data-enabled phones by 2003. An example of this is the Research in Motion Blackberry, which has held its own against such devices as the PDA and the cell phone.

Networks—Wireless Carriers.   Wireless carriers add value by managing connectivity and service and by coordinating the billing for infrastructure. Several challenges lie ahead for carriers. One will be the transition from 2G and 2.5G technologies to a universal 3G platform. Another will be to create enough value to pay for the costly licenses that have cast doubt on the imminent rollout of 3G. The last major challenge will be to retain value in the value chain as infrastructure becomes commodified.

Software—Enabling Software and Services.   Software and services add value by expanding application solutions to business and consumer needs including security that enables m-commerce. The market is witnessing the strong emergence of application service providers such as SensCom, which offers the value propositions of lower ownership costs, access to technology specialists for enterprise solutions, and freedom to focus on core competencies. These are particularly attractive to the financial-services industry.

Numerous challenges remain for the software and services area in terms of creating value for the customer. In Japan, NTT DoCoMo's I-Mode, discussed in detail in Chapter 2, offers menu-driven browsers that can locate applications available from providers. Typically, Japanese phones do not come preloaded with wireless applications. In the United States, however, negotiations between device manufacturers and application providers are intense, as application providers compete for a share of limited menu space. This competitive framework will continue to evolve as voice is integrated into devices.

Software and Services—Carrier and Enterprise-Class Solutions.   The value proposition here lies in providing solutions through storage and/or application of information for consumers and businesses.

Software and Services—Content and Portals.   The value in content and portals lies in the one-stop-shopping convenience for consumers and the potential to attract them. The business model poses the biggest challenge in this area. Fee-based business models for content/portals have had little attraction, often leaving only the sketchy advertising-revenue model. Initially, service providers will be the best customer base for content/portal providers, leveraging existing customer bases and captive channels.

Players in the Wireless Value Chain

Some of the key publicly listed players along the various segments of the wireless value chain are shown in Figure 3.3. Historically, the largest companies in the cellular industry have been the carriers and the manufacturers of devices and infrastructure. Many of the carriers were offspring of the Baby Bells, such as Verizon and SBC, whereas manufacturers such as Nokia,

Figure 3.3
Key Publicly Traded Market Players across the Value Chain

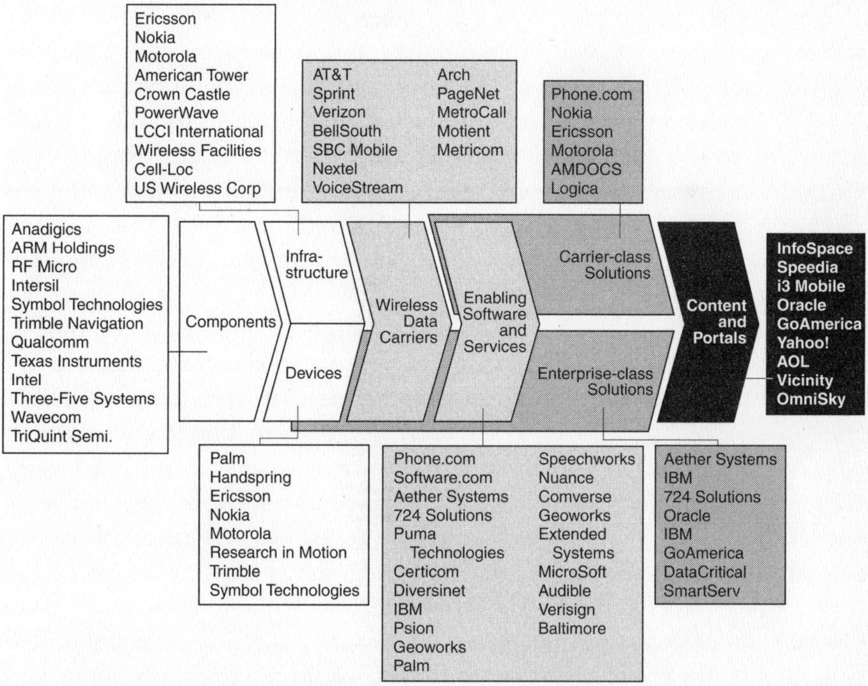

Source: Coster, 2000.

Motorola, and Ericsson rode the growth in the 1990s to become companies with revenues in the tens of billions. As the industry has moved beyond voice and continued to grow rapidly, there have been many new entrants.

The idea of the wireless Internet attracted many entrants, especially in the late 1990s. The maker of the popular Palm Pilot, 3COM, introduced the Palm VII in May 1999 to enable wireless delivery of the Internet. As part of a strategy to make the Palm operating system the system of choice for smart wireless devices, licensing agreements were made with Sony (this part of Sony's business was later purchased by Kyocera), Nokia, and Motorola. For the new entrants, partnerships with bigger players in the chain were a necessity for playing in the game. Those partnerships have not always worked, however, and as Palm's recent struggles in the wireless arena indicate, the path to profitability is fraught with pitfalls.

The Value in the Value Chain

Value is created in the value chain by facilitating access, providing content, providing infrastructure, and facilitating the exchange of content and transactions. For the wired Internet, strong consumer brands that were created in the content and portals space developed an impressive customer following. These included companies like Yahoo, Amazon, and e-Bay. In addition, some Internet service providers, most notably America Online (AOL), also developed solid relationships with their customers by providing access to the Internet. Meanwhile, the carriers—which owned the wires that transported data back and forth from the Internet to both home and businesses—were relegated to being a "dumb pipe." They were in the business of supplying a commodity and were left licking their wounds from missed opportunity.

This time around, carriers are trying to avoid becoming a dumb pipe in the wireless era, and hope to hold the critical intermediary position between all the players in the value chain and the customer. This is the now famous issue of "Who owns the customer?" discussed in *Red Herring* in April 2000. The article noted that European wireless operators balked when Nokia tried to promote wireless-application-protocol (WAP) services on its phones and added a link on phone screens to Nokia Services. Although it was an attempt to develop a wireless portal and funnel customers to the services of Nokia's partners, it was also a case of classic channel conflict. Carriers did not want those services competing with their own and hinted that they might reduce handset orders. In addition, operators wanted to control the start screen on any WAP phone they sold and create a "walled-garden approach" to accessing the Web. This strategy was reminiscent of both AOL's and CompuServe's approach in 1994, when they actually made it difficult for their users to get to the Internet.

Wireless service providers obviously want to use the walled-garden approach for as long as possible. They will do this by negotiating an agreement in their contracts (for buying devices from companies such as Nokia, Motorola, and Ericsson) that the manufacturers must include a service-provider-defined and convenient way of accessing the service provider's portal. Service providers can opt not to buy a company's phones unless it meets their demands. At least in the short- to mid-term, they should be able to do this. In the long term, they may lose some control, but they will continue to make it difficult to use services unless they have been set up by the carrier. This will mitigate forces acting to commodify the wireless service providers, and they will differentiate according to desired customer segments and services offered. The implication for others in the chain is that everyone is subject to the service providers' desires for the time being. All players in the value chain will need to carefully consider partnerships with the service providers. Keeping the service providers' motivations in mind will be a key component of executing any strategy.

The present power of the carriers does not mean, however, that they will monopolize value and that there won't be opportunities for others in the value chain. Thus far, adoption of wireless applications has been slow for reasons besides their potential value. First, the value chain in the wireless industry is tightly linked, which creates coordination costs to implement applications. Second, unlike the wired version of the Internet, the ongoing struggle between competing wireless standards, as well as languages for writing applications, makes it difficult to write applications once and make them available anywhere. Last, the lack of clear winners on several levels has encouraged the players in the chain to migrate into other parts of the chain in an attempt to capture value. As coordination costs decrease, the standards become clearer, and the industry shakes out, the pace of wireless application development and the opportunities will increase dramatically. The value of applications will then be the primary driver of the market because it will be customer-driven rather than technology-driven. For those who can identify and develop compelling applications, this will be an opportunity to capture value.

OVERVIEW OF THE MARKET AND GROWTH

The number of consumers and mobile workers using wireless phones for voice and data purposes is likely to continue growing over the next few years. Companies in the value chain that are looking to take a higher level view of the opportunity should consider two different breakdowns: one by geographic region, and one by specific cellular technology.

Market Growth by Geographic Region

According to a report in *Ovum* in January 2001, the global cellular connections are expected to grow from almost 727 million (at the beginning of 2001) to 1,266 million in 2003 and to more than 1,764 million by the beginning of 2005. Growth is also projected to increase in all regions of the world although the rates of growth and adoption are higher in emerging markets. Overall market growth between the beginning of 2001 and 2005 is estimated to be 143 percent (Table 3.1).

Western Europe is one of the most mature and advanced wireless markets in the world, and it is no surprise that it is currently the largest, at 242 million subscribers (34 percent of the market). It will retain that position in 2005 with an estimated 401 million subscribers (23 percent of the market). However, other markets are experiencing higher levels of growth, including Central Asia, which is benefiting from rapid subscriber growth in the People's Republic of China, the largest country in the world, with a population of more than 1.2 billion people. It is projected that the number of subscribers will increase from roughly 94 million in 2001 (13 percent of the market) to 355 million at the beginning of 2005 (20 percent of the market). Consequently, the Central Asia market will grow from the

Table 3.1
Expected Market Growth by Region

	Connections (Millions)		Market Share (%)		Growth (%)
	2001	*2005*	*2001*	*2005*	
Western Europe	242	401	33	23	66
Asia–Pacific	139	254	19	14	83
North America	118	258	16	15	119
Central Asia	94	355	13	20	278
South and Central America	70	234	10	13	234
Middle East and Africa	37	156	5	9	322
Eastern Europe	27	106	4	6	293
Total	727	1,764			143

Source: Scott and Respini, 2001.

fourth largest market in 2001 to the second largest in 2005—overtaking both the North American and Asia-Pacific (including Japanese) markets in number of connections.

Thus, there will be opportunities worldwide, but the developing areas will see the greatest growth. The wireless industry will have an even stronger international feel in the future, as wireless devices spread around the globe. Although players from western Europe, Japan, and North America currently dominate the value chain, as time goes on, these players likely will vacate areas of the chain where it is harder to capture value or where competitive advantage may lie in countries with cheaper labor. Also, in countries where markets are not completely free, the wireless carrier is either owned by, or has strong ties to, the government. In such cases, national wireless carriers will extract most of the value from the chain. In huge markets like China, government has a strong interest in developing the country's technological capabilities and foreign companies are eager to participate in the market in any way they can, even if it means losing money in the short term.

Market Growth by Technology

A variety of cellular air-interface technologies have been deployed around the world. This is painfully obvious in the United States, where there has been no standardization and the market has become fragmented. Much like businesses in previous standards battles, such as Beta versus VHS or PC versus Macintosh, companies providing hardware have had to either choose a single standard to support or divide resources to support more than one. In addition, service providers have been less able to hedge bets and have had to commit to specific technology-upgrade paths because of the high costs of installing and maintaining infrastructure. They also must deal with having limited RF bandwidth for customer service.

Especially in the United States, many problems that have emerged with disparate technologies are linked not only to the telecom companies, but also to the federal government. When digital wireless technology was first becoming a reality, the Federal Communications Commission (FCC) sold licenses to companies in many markets instead of issuing a few licenses for nationwide service as was done in Europe and Japan. The result was that U.S. companies chose different technologies in loading as much traffic as possible onto their networks. Whereas Europe is united behind the single global system for mobile communications (GSM) standard, the United States has more than three competing standards—the two main ones besides

GSM being code-division multiple access (CDMA) and time-division multiple access (TDMA).

Most experts agree that GSM will build on its lead in subscribers worldwide. Other second-generation technologies, such as CDMA, will also grow, but not as quickly. CDMA deployment has been significant in the U.S. and Korean markets, but penetration into other markets has been limited. As a historical note, in late 1996, CDMA was already late to market by at least two years because of technical problems. Although the technology promised more efficient use of the radio spectrum than competing digital technologies such as GSM (giving carriers more cellular capacity), U.S. companies had to decide whether they would go to market with a more mature technology or continue waiting for the problems to be worked out. Fragmentation arose partially for this reason, and CDMA has never caught up to GSM.

Accenture projects that the GSM market will grow to more than 1 billion subscribers worldwide in 2005. Figure 3.4 illustrates its projection, which shows GSM continuing to widen its lead in terms of subscribers. This momentum affects partnership and development considerations for all players in the wireless value chain. Fragmentation, however, makes

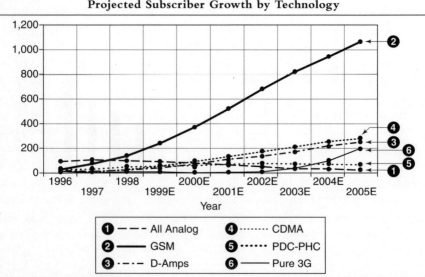

Figure 3.4
Projected Subscriber Growth by Technology

Source: Accenture, 2001.

decisions much more difficult for the firms focusing on the U.S. market (Figure 3.5).

The Wireless-Carrier Perspective on Revenue Trends

The revenues of wireless carriers in the United States have been growing impressively. The Cellular Telephone Industry Association (CTIA) estimates that the industry had revenues of over $52 billion in 2000, an increase of 31 percent over 1999.

Though growth has been impressive, service providers are concerned about declining average-month revenues per user (ARPU). A large portion of revenues is from wireless voice services, and they are becoming more of a commodity. As a result, service providers are looking for ways to bolster sagging ARPU. According to the CTIA, carriers saw a steady decline in ARPU during the 1990s, from $80.90 per month in 1990 to a low of $39.43 in 1998 (Figure 3.6). ARPU did increase to $45.27 in 2000, as the service providers enticed consumers to use their phones more through higher priced monthly rate plans offering bundled minutes. On a per-minute basis, these rates approached or equaled the price of landline calls.

Figure 3.5
Annual Service Revenues for the U.S. Market

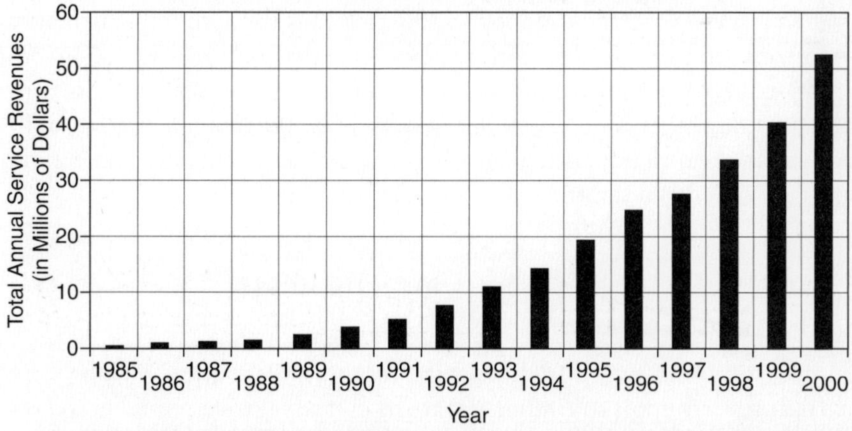

1985 = $ 482,428	1989 = $3,340,595	1993 = $10,892,175	1997 = $27,485,633
1986 = $ 823,052	1990 = $4,548,820	1994 = $14,229,922	1998 = $33,133,175
1987 = $1,151,519	1991 = $5,708,522	1995 = $19,081,239	1999 = $40,018,489
1988 = $1,959,548	1992 = $7,822,726	1996 = $23,634,971	2000 = $52,466,020

Figure 3.6
Average Revenue per User in the U.S. Market

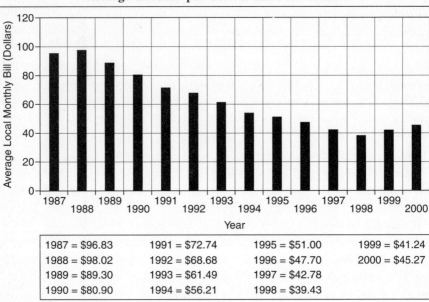

1987 = $96.83	1991 = $72.74	1995 = $51.00	1999 = $41.24
1988 = $98.02	1992 = $68.68	1996 = $47.70	2000 = $45.27
1989 = $89.30	1993 = $61.49	1997 = $42.78	
1990 = $80.90	1994 = $56.21	1998 = $39.43	

Wireless carriers are also trying to figure out how to boost the money that consumer and mobile workers will be willing to pay for wireless devices and services. One way they are doing this is through implementation and promotion of new enabling technologies that will provide additional functionality and improve the quality of service. Some of those efforts include the development of 3G wireless networks, the implementation of location-based services, and the launch of a short-range wireless connectivity standard called Bluetooth.

ENABLING NEW VALUE IN THE VALUE CHAIN

In today's business world, "value is the mother of invention," as the wireless industry attempts to find new ways to create valuable products and services that customers will pay for. New technological enablers for enhancing wireless capabilities are constantly brought into the value chain and tested against market forces. Although these enablers are not applications in themselves, they can help create new applications that ultimately add value for the customer.

Third-Generation Wireless

Wireless Generations.   The promise of 3G wireless is high-speed wireless networks capable of handling even the most bandwidth-intensive applications, such as streaming video. However technically feasible 3G may be, the question most people are asking is whether the business case is strong enough to justify the high cost of capital investment to make it happen. After a brief overview of the evolution of wireless, we discuss some of the threats to 3G networks, some potential killer applications, and the outlook for 3G technology.

1G: Analog communication.   The first cellular phones (or 1G, for "first generation") were basically fancy two-way radios, upgraded versions similar to what one might find in a taxicab or police car. They are known as analog phones and were popular in the late 1980s. Even today, cellular operators continue to provide service for 30 million users of analog phones in the United States.

Although there are several analog phone standards worldwide, the phones in North America were governed by the advanced mobile-phone system, which allowed users to share frequencies through a technique called frequency-division multiple access (FDMA). By dividing the cellular spectrum into several channels, this technology increased the number of users able to communicate at once. However, mobile-telephone companies wanted to improve their capacity even more and decided to transfer to digital systems, thus ushering in the second generation of wireless communication.

2G: Today's wireless.   Second-generation networks are largely the digital networks familiar to consumers today. They support data rates of 19.2 kilobits per second (kbps), much slower than the 64 kbps of wires. A digital phone handles voice traffic in much the same way that a compact disc player handles music: A caller's voice is converted into ones and zeros and travels through the network until it reaches another phone, where it is converted back into sound. Even though some argue that analog phones provided better sound quality than today's digital phones, digital service providers are able to compress and rearrange digital signals, allowing them to add more users, reduce their costs, and increase their billable hours.

Still, there are differences in the 2G technologies. Whereas TDMA and GSM are improvements on the old analog technique of FDMA, which slices each channel of the wireless spectrum into time slices shared by several phones, CDMA effectively broadcasts radio signals over several frequencies simultaneously. Although CDMA has some advantages over TDMA in sound consistency, it requires more complex equipment both at the cellular tower and in the handset. The CDMA signal is already packet switched (optimal for data), so the future transition to faster transmission speeds and "always-on" data will be similar to a software upgrade. CDMA carriers have a distinct advantage in this respect; in fact, later versions, such as CDMA-2000, should be able to handle up to 2 megabits per second (Mbps) of data if they have enough spectrum. This means that CDMA carriers will have the easiest transition to the next iteration of wireless technology, a fact that is not lost on the European carriers that are committed to GSM technologies.

2.5G: The bridging technology.   The term 2.5G refers to the current intermediate path from 2G to 3G; it is the bridge between 2G and the up-to-2-Mbps data rate that is often predicted for 3G technology. In Europe and for GSM networks, 2.5G will take the form of general packet-radio service (GPRS). In current wireless networks, most data that is transmitted requires a circuit-switched connection; a user must log in, receive information, and log out. Although circuit-switched connections have worked suitably for voice communications (a customer presses "send" to initiate the connection and "end" to complete it), they are inefficient for transferring data. With GPRS, packets of data can be sent over the wireless network, allowing mobile handsets to access always-on data at up to 28 kbps now, eventually moving to 56 kbps (the current speed of a modem) and then to 100 kbps. Although the GPRS handset is always connected to the network, it uses the network only when a packet of information is being sent. The true beauty of GPRS for wireless companies is that it provides a tremendous upgrade over 2G in the performance delivered to customers without the immense expense and new infrastructure that the transition to 3G will require. Essentially, GPRS is an update of an existing GSM network rather than an upgrade to an entirely new network.

Though the advantages of GPRS are readily apparent for the transfer of data over wireless networks, the packet-switching technology raises new questions for service providers as they reevaluate business models and revenue streams. Whereas current cell-phone users are charged per minute based on the connection time to the network, how should providers charge customers whose phones are always connected, thereby tying up the network but only periodically receiving information? Should they be charged per kilobit of information? Perhaps they should not be charged for every minute of connection time but for every minute of activity? Some clues on how to approach this issue can be gained by looking at the successful I-Mode service in Japan.

3G: The future of wireless.   The term *3G* refers to the International Telecommunications Union (ITU) specification for the third generation of mobile communications technology. It promises increased bandwidth and represents the new radio networks required to carry this ever faster, packet-switched data traffic. The idea of a third generation of mobile services first surfaced in 1997 with two chief aims: (1) to eliminate existing multiple standards in favor of a unified worldwide standard and (2) to provide data rates of up to 384 kbps over a packet-based system allowing for real-time, all-time access to a network. According to Ozgur Aytar of the Strategis Group, in Washington, DC, the former goal will not come to fruition, but the latter will. She argues that although a single global standard would speed up the development and implementation of new technologies, there are too many regulatory, political, and financial issues for that to occur. Both Aytar and Claire Preston, of the Australian Competition and Consumer Commission, believe that 3G wireless will eventually achieve the promised data rates and information-transfer speeds.

The basis for 3G networks will be the universal mobile-telecommunications system (UMTS); this is ITU's vision for a global family of interconnected 3G systems and is the standard to which carriers will eventually migrate their networks. Developers of the three competing networks, CDMA-2000, WCDMA, and TCDMA, have agreed to a standard that will permit connectivity among them. The UMTS is a 3G mobile technology that will deliver broadband information at speeds up to 2 Mbps. Besides voice and data, UMTS will deliver audio and video to wireless devices anywhere in the world through fixed, wireless, and satellite systems.

It is commonly assumed that Asia, and Japan in particular, have the most to gain from 3G technology. This is partly because of the penetration that wireless communications currently enjoy in Asia, partly because of the successful introduction of I-Mode in Japan (the first true 2.5G service on the market), and partly because of the strength of cellular networks in the region. Because of the high wireless penetration and low Internet penetration in Japan, consumers use their wireless handsets for much more than voice communications. During their long commutes by train, many Japanese use their handsets to send and receive e-mail or read the news. In its first year of operation, I-Mode already had 4.25 million subscribers. In that same period, largely because of I-Mode's success, NTT DoCoMo's market capitalization rose from $76 billion to $312 billion. This growth gives wireless operators everywhere hope for the future direction of 2.5G and 3G wireless.

3G Data Rates.   Sprint anticipates having a fully upgraded network capable of high-mobility data speeds of 144 kbps per second (compared with today's rate of 19.2 kbps) by early 2004. This is consistent with the following minimum requirements for data speeds that the ITU has established:

- *High mobility:* 144 kbps for rural outdoor mobile use. This data rate is for environments where the 3G user is traveling more than 120 kilometers per hour in outdoor environments.
- *Full mobility:* 384 kbps for pedestrian users traveling under 120 kilometers per hour in urban outdoor environments.
- *Limited mobility:* at least 2 Mbps with low mobility in stationary indoor and short-range outdoor environments.

Figure 3.7 shows how speed affects the download time for various files and applications. If 3G data rates are able to reach 2 Mbps, applications will be able to use richer content than just text. Still, application writers will need to consider whether it makes sense to include video just because they can. This question is addressed later in this chapter, when we discuss the future of wireless applications.

Figure 3.7
Download Times for Various Applications

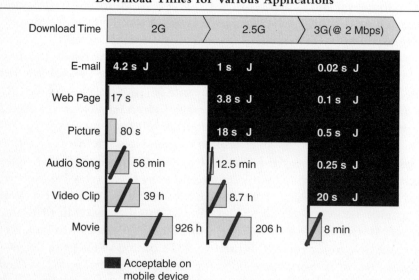

Download Time	2G	2.5G	3G(@ 2 Mbps)
E-mail	4.2 s J	1 s J	0.02 s J
Web Page	17 s	3.8 s J	0.1 s J
Picture	80 s	18 s J	0.5 s J
Audio Song	56 min	12.5 min	0.25 s J
Video Clip	39 h	8.7 h	20 s J
Movie	926 h	206 h	8 min

■ Acceptable on mobile device

Technological Threats to 3G.   Carriers are spending billions of dollars on 3G licenses, although they have not even begun to build out their networks. In the United States and Europe, it will be years before they can build these networks and deliver 3G. During that time, technologies could emerge to make 3G obsolete. The most obvious threats are wireless local area networks (WLANs) and data compression on 2.5G networks.

WLANs are becoming more common around the world. They are cheaper to install, more efficient for the area they cover, and can deliver speeds close to those of 3G. Office buildings, malls, corporate campuses, schools, and even homes are now candidates for such wireless networks. If an individual spends most of the day at work and free time at home, and both locations have high-speed wireless networks, what is the need for 3G? For college students who rarely travel outside the range of their local networks, what are the benefits of 3G? Additional similar scenarios are easy to imagine and, when combined, decrease the size of the potential population that might demand 3G. When 3G is finally ready, why would users of WLANs switch?

Just as improved modem speeds limited the attractiveness of ISDN for connecting to the Internet, data compression on 2.5G technology could affect 3G. If data can be compressed so that larger packets can travel efficiently over 2.5G networks, most of the population will be satisfied with that. Many smart companies are working on the data-compression problem right now. If they develop 2.5G compression technology before the carriers can deliver 3G, many of the carriers may go out of business because they will not be able to recoup their up-front investments in spectrum licenses and infrastructure upgrades.

In Europe, Columbitech makes a product called "3G Killer." It offers high-speed wireless service at a low cost using existing technology. That technology and others like it won't eradicate 3G, but if they catch on, they could become a significant niche service with the advantages of simplicity, far lower costs, and reliance on existing technology.

Financing Threats to 3G.   In addition to the *technological* threats that 3G networks face, there are substantial *financial* threats. Global networks requiring broadband-spectrum-license purchases, massive infrastructure upgrades, and software development and installation will necessitate tremendous investments from would-be industry players. Firms are committing billions of dollars in licensing fees alone, along with billions more in product development and testing; and marketing expenses are just around the corner. Moreover, there is no guarantee that the owner of the network will win the ultimate prize in the wireless-communication game: control over the customer and its sources of revenue. However, 3G is a technology that could revolutionize voice and data communications, and many feel that getting a seat at the table and gaining a first-mover advantage is crucial to long-term success. It's a big bet, but one many companies have already made.

The promise of a broadband wireless future has enticed telecom companies to spend huge sums on 3G-spectrum licenses. The money spent on the licenses and the additional costs to build on 3G networks, which may end up totaling close to $250 billion, could represent the largest investment spent in the shortest time by any sector in history. According to data provided by mobile-phone manufacturer Ericsson, a total of $96.6 billion was spent for 43 spectrum licenses in eight European countries and New Zealand, for an average price of $2.2 billion per license. The lion's share of that spending was in Germany and the United Kingdom, where $81.2 billion was committed for 11 licenses. That translates into an average price of $7.4 billion per license. In total, an average of $574.27 was spent for every person in those two nations. For the same money British Telecom spent on licenses, it could have put fiber into every home in the United Kingdom. In any language, those prices suggest extremely bullish expectations about the potential impact of 3G.

These huge investments will have significant financial implications for carriers and equipment manufactures. British Telecom, at the end of 1998, had debts of $1.5 billion. Those debt levels have now risen to $30 billion, sending BT's debt-to-equity ratio to a perilous 190 percent. The investment community is showing signs of a decreasing tolerance for telecom debt, and most U.S. and European carriers have seen their investment grade ratings fall to just slightly better than junk bonds.

The cost of building out an effective 3G network may lead many carriers to opt to share the infrastructure of their networks rather than build their own aerials and base stations. In the United Kingdom, where five operators committed a total of $35.4 billion for UMTS licenses, informal discussions regarding sharing of infrastructure to save costs have already taken place. Vodafone, BT Wireless, Orange, One 2 One, and Hutchison 3G are said to have begun talks to share the estimated £22.5 billion cost of rolling out new networks throughout the country. According to a BT Wireless spokesperson, there is a convergence of commercial and other interests to reduce the amount and cost of infrastructure wherever possible. Additionally, because 3G uses a higher frequency than GSM to transmit and receive information, each 3G base station has a much shorter range. As a result, 3G networks will require 4 to 16 times as many base stations to get the same coverage as GSM. Therefore, large geographic regions in the United States that lack standard technology platforms must overcome significant hurdles to deploy 3G. It is unlikely that all the existing carriers and manufacturers will survive the transition. Carriers must find compelling consumer and business applications that will enable them to recoup the massive investment.

Vendor financing is another means to mitigate the risks associated with the high cost of implementing 3G networks, and the possible shakeout of wireless providers has investors in the telecom-equipment industry justifiably worried. Wireless carriers are increasingly turning to equipment and handset suppliers for capital to build out their networks. Equipment makers have traditionally funded the purchases of their gear and will be forced to continue to fund the buildout of wireless networks if they are to meet their stretch revenue and profit goals. The levels of exposure of the global equipment industry are troubling, and 3G will only exacerbate them. The five leading equipment makers in North America have $4.8 billion (equivalent to nearly two thirds of their combined profits of $7.1 billion) of vendor financing on their books. Ericsson, Nokia, and Motorola will also be instrumental in financing the development of 3G. Nokia has invested as much as $2.5 billion into 3G development projects and is dependent on the success of carrier networks to recoup those costs. These figures increased substantially on April 2, 2001, as a British mobile subsidiary of Hutchison Whampoa secured approximately $1.1 billion in financing from three equipment vendors—Nokia, NEC, and Siemens. Then, on April 3, Nokia, Ericsson, and Alcatel trumped that figure with an even bigger pledge of $2 billion for Orange, the mobile unit of France Telecom. Equipment makers, however, are taking a step fraught with danger, joining the operators on the slippery slope of financing still unproven services, and analysts are beginning to worry. According to an analyst with Bear Stearns in Boston, to have equipment manufacturers acting as bankers indicates a serious risk because that is not their business—it means the rest of the financial markets consider undertaking this financing to be too risky.

Accordingly, lofty valuations appear to be a thing of the past. Investor uncertainty and lingering questions about the value of 3G networks relative to the prices that have been paid—and the viability of 3G in general—are beginning to move through the spectrum-valuation market. In Australia, where the government just completed its 3G-spectrum auctions, total proceeds were approximately $585 million for 48 spectrum lots. Original expectations had called for 58 spectrum lots offered for an aggregate price of approximately $1.3 billion, or $22.4 million per lot. This cut of more than 50 percent yielded an average spectrum price of only $12.2 million per license. Even more dramatically, on April 12, 2001, after only three companies registered for Singapore's auction of four 3G licenses, the government decided to cancel the auction. It then allowed the three bidders to purchase the licenses for $55.2 million, a bargain price, especially when compared with the auctions that took place in Europe in 2000. Still, the fear of missing out on the next "big thing" will drive equipment makers and carriers to continue to invest in the development of 3G networks, applications, and devices. The potential digital convergence represented by broadband wireless will bring additional players such as Palm, Handspring, Microsoft, and Sony into the competitive landscape as well. Some analysts predict that the fierce competition will result in a massive wave of consolidation that will leave only a few dominant wireless carriers in Europe and the United States. The combination of carrier bankruptcies and a glut of equipment on the secondary market could have dire consequences for equipment makers. Governments are beginning to realize that the price tag of 3G-spectrum auctions and the projected time lines for 3G services may bankrupt their domestic wireless providers. Regulators will have to relax the implementation deadlines for 3G and need to consider offering rebates or some other equitable form of relief for the winner's spectrum costs.

Additional financial challenges to the carriers will be developing and communicating to customers the benefits of applications that differentiate 3G services from existing general packet-radio services and building enough switching costs into the system to reduce customer churn. Because of the differences in existing network technologies, population density, home-based Internet penetration, and the relative strengths of carriers and equipment manufacturers, 3G applications will evolve very differently in Japan, Europe, and the United States. The tremendous success of Japan's I-Mode and other wireless interactive services has demonstrated the potential of packet-data services. What remains unclear is how the owners of 3G spectrum will differentiate their services from those available on precursor networks.

Possible Killer Applications for 3G.   Customers will switch to, and pay for, 3G only when they have a good reason to do so. The failures of past technologies and the painfully low usage rates of WAP demonstrate that "just because they can" is not a strong market position. Applications for 3G must provide a significantly better customer experience than the existing alternatives. It is likely that 3G, its predecessor systems, and future systems will all exist and compete simultaneously over the next 10 to 15 years. The key to success for 3G carriers will be developing applications that interoperate with legacy systems and demonstrate 3G's superior performance. Ozgur Aytar, of the Strategis Group, commented on the uncertain demand for 3G:

> Demand has not materialized yet, however operators have not been aggressively pursuing it either. You could define this era as "the cold war," when every player is just watching the other and not really offering services tailored to their customers' needs. New services and applications will be rolled out as data speeds increase with the implementation of 2.5 and 3G infrastructure. Billing will get diversified. However, the existing 2G and 2.5G networks are unlikely to disappear with the introduction of 3G networks. 3G will evolve even when "beyond 3G" technologies are in the picture ten to fifteen years from now. If you think about the U.S., there are still thirty million analog users that operators will need to maintain.

Regardless of the technology or geographic region, the enduring killer application for wireless communications will be voice. Simply put, people purchase wireless phones so they can make phone calls. On the surface, voice does not seem to favor 3G over existing technologies. For some carriers, however, the greater data rates of 3G can increase voice capacity and make voice services more cost-effective even if no demand for data services materializes.

Finding applications beyond voice is difficult because of the constraints of wireless devices and the differences in how consumers in the United States, Europe, and Asia use handheld devices. American consumers use their cell phones primarily for voice communication, and a niche market uses e-mail and Web browsing. In Europe, consumers have fewer computers and rely more heavily on their handhelds for e-mail, m-commerce, banking, and instant messaging. In Asia, where 3G is the closest to being implemented, consumers are accustomed to higher speeds and use applications that demand those speeds (driving directions, weather, short video clips, etc.).

Still, all three regions will implement some applications, such as gaming and messaging, which build on the success of previous Internet applications. Gambling on the Internet is part of an adult-entertainment industry estimated to be $6 billion per year. Wireless gaming sites are already appearing and are moving quickly to use the increased data speed of 3G.

Following on the phenomenal success of peer-to-peer applications like instant messaging (IM) on the Internet and short-message service (SMS), multimedia messaging service (MMS) is the most promising application for 3G. Nokia's research data indicate that heavy SMS users would be interested in audio, photo, or video messaging services as well. The majority of current SMS users are early adopters and innovators who are between the ages of 15 and 35 and live in urban areas. These SMS users are part of the attractive demographic of some 426 million "Generation Y" 18-to-24-year-olds who will outspend older adults on wireless services by 2003. As shown in Figure 3.8, as data speeds increase, the versatility of content and user benefits that carriers can provide to the millions of SMS and IM users also increase. In our mobile society, MMS could instantly send video postcards, greeting cards, music, or a clip of a baby's first steps to a distant grandparent. The 3G rollout, however, will not eliminate the previous generations of wireless technology, and the functionality of MMS will be somewhat limited by the need of 3G customers to communicate with 2G and 2.5G users. To prevent 3G from being nothing more than an overhyped bigger pipe, carriers will have to strike the delicate balance of providing a superior experience to innovators and early adopters while supporting an installed base of customers using legacy systems.

Outlook for 3G. Just as the PC industry faced incredible competitive pressure to continually churn out faster and faster computers, the wireless

Figure 3.8
Multimedia Messaging Migration Path

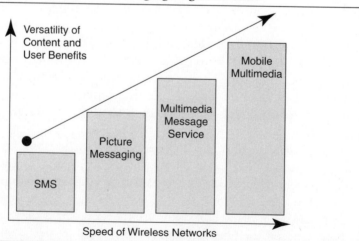

Source: Nokia, "Mobile Network Evolution to Multimedia Messaging."

industry faces pressure to build infrastructure that allows faster and faster download speeds. After all, faster is better, right? Even though faster *is* clearly better in absolute terms (who doesn't want downloading to be faster?), 3G technology faces many challenges:

- A limited range of 3G unique applications.
- Substitution of currently available technologies, such as WLAN and 2.5G compression.
- Price sensitivity.
- Standard-setting difficulty and interoperability issues.
- Unrealistic expectations of speed capabilities in a mobile environment, especially compared with landline connection speeds.
- The inability of networks and carriers to raise the capital necessary to get the projects off the ground.

Although in fall 2001, NTT DoCoMo began its 3G service in Japan, profits are not expected for the first four years. Since 3G necessarily will be the domain of very large carriers with deep pockets, its future lies in their ability to aggregate unique services, such as multimedia messaging, that use the increased speed to create value for end customers.

WILL LOCATION-BASED SERVICES BE THE NEXT GOLDEN-HAIRED CHILD?

The immediate potential of location-based services (LBS) is more obvious than that of 3G technologies, since it is not just an incremental increase in speed but also a completely new functionality. In addition, the FCC is mandating LBS in the United States for locating distress calls, so the implementation of location technologies is much more imminent.

Location-based technology, one of the fastest growing areas of the wireless-communication industry, is an integral part of the future value proposition of mobile communication. The market is already estimated at nearly $600 million and is forecast to approach $5 billion within three years.

Some of the world's largest wireless carriers, such as Verizon Wireless, Vodafone of Great Britain, and NTT DoCoMo of Japan, are promoting this technology along with dozens of other smaller companies in the United States and Europe. SignalSoft Corporation, based in Boulder, Colorado, develops software that enables tourists or business travelers to use their wireless phones to obtain location information for the closest restaurants or hotels in a given city. Cell-Loc Inc., in Canada, is already testing a wireless service in Calgary and in Austin, Texas, that delivers detailed driving directions after pinpointing the user. Some companies are even more ambitious. Webraska, a French company, received $50 million in financing from the United States and Europe to map every urban area in the world and then allow the maps to be retrieved in real time on wireless devices. TimesThree provides location content to Internet portals to make their services location sensitive, using Cell-Loc technology to implement fleet and traffic monitoring, child and pet tracking, and location-sensitive billing.

Proponents of the technology point out that LBS will enrich the mobile experience and provide consumers with cost-effective solutions that have previously been unavailable. Because location is a key element in delivering a personalized experience to each customer, LBS will be a strong factor in determining which and what type of services and goods the consumer desires most and therefore is likely to purchase and use. It will also enrich the applications of the wireless network. For example, a device that constantly updates the directions to a destination on the basis of the user's current location is much more desirable than a static map. Further, it will help people control and initiate their social relationships more easily. Users can quickly identify and locate family, friends, and colleagues using geographic buddy lists and tracking functions.

But the howl of privacy advocates continues to ring in the ears of many technology developers. Regarded by many as the crux of LBS, the detail of the technology naturally invites discussion on privacy and security. Because the LBS technology is pervasive, the successful resolution of the significant privacy concerns is paramount to many of the proposed business models.

Location-Industry Overview.   The wireless-location industry is a subset of the larger wireless-communication industry. We focus on the technology provider, the application developers, the service providers, and the consumers. This industry, however, affects many other groups. For example, the desire for richer location-based applications, such as interactive maps and driving directions, may strongly encourage device manufacturers to develop wireless devices with larger screens.

The location-based wireless industry in the United States differs from other proposed wireless services, such as video conferencing or downloading MP3s, because the FCC has mandated the ability to locate a wireless device. This implies that the wireless-location infrastructure will be built—and will be built soon. In effect, the infrastructure is a sunk cost; the industry still has to decide which form or forms of location technology and location-based services will be used.

Role of the U.S. Government.   The government provided the initial impetus for the wireless-location industry when, in 1996, the FCC announced that within five years wireless-communication providers would have to provide enhanced 911 (E911) services. The most significant aspect of the E911 service would be the ability of emergency call centers to geographically locate the origin of wireless calls. The directive involves two phases: Phase 1 requires that wireless carriers be able to provide emergency dispatchers with a 911 caller's telephone number as well as that caller's cell location; Phase 2 requires that carriers identify the location of a 911 caller in network-based solutions within 100 meters for 67 percent of calls and 300 meters for 95 percent of calls; in device-based solutions, within 50 meters for 67 percent of calls and 150 meters for 95 percent of calls.

By the end of 2001, at least 25 percent of new handsets activated had to be E911-capable. By the end of 2002, 100 percent of the new handsets activated must be E911-capable. By the end of 2005, E911-capable handsets have to reach 95 percent penetration. E911 services are free for the end user, though the wireless industry will have to pay for the necessary infrastructure. Europe and the rest of the world have yet to mandate location requirements for emergency services.

No wireless carriers were ready to deliver E911 service by the October 2001 deadline, although Sprint PCS announced that it would be the first to market with a GPS-enabled Samsung phone using Qualcomm's Snap-Track chipset technology. Undoubtedly, the technology will be employed but not as rapidly as mandated by the FCC.

Components of the Wireless-Location Industry.   Figure 3.9 shows the value chain for the entire wireless-location industry. Three segments of the industry are the focus of analysis: location technology (LT), location applications, and location-based services (LBS). These segments require attention because they are newly created by the promise of LT.

Location technology provides the x, y, and perhaps z of a wireless device. Location-based applications manage the geographic information and deliver the customer requests to the appropriate service provider; location-based services use the geographic information to provide geographically sensitive information and services. The applications and services are not sensitive to the type of LT—they merely rely on reasonably accurate geographic coordinates. Figure 3.10 illustrates how the three components interact.

Figure 3.9
Location-Based Services Value Chain

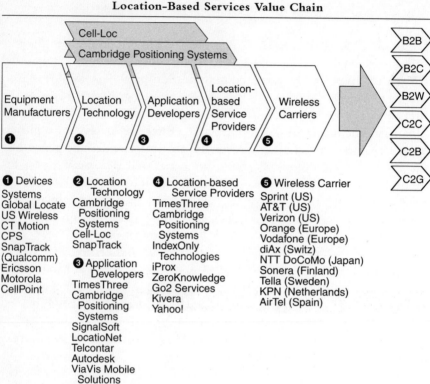

Location technology. There are two dimensions in describing the types of LT: the method of locating (GPS or network) and the method for processing the location information (the network or the device itself), as summarized in Table 3.2. It is important to understand these differences because they have implications for how LBS will be delivered.

There are two basic methods for determining the location of a wireless-communication device: triangulation through GPS or triangulation through a network. Hybrids using both technologies have also been proposed.

GPS. The global positioning system was the first global technology that allowed users to accurately determine their locations. It relies on 24 orbiting satellites, maintained by the U.S. Department of Defense, that

Figure 3.10
Components of the Wireless-Location Industry

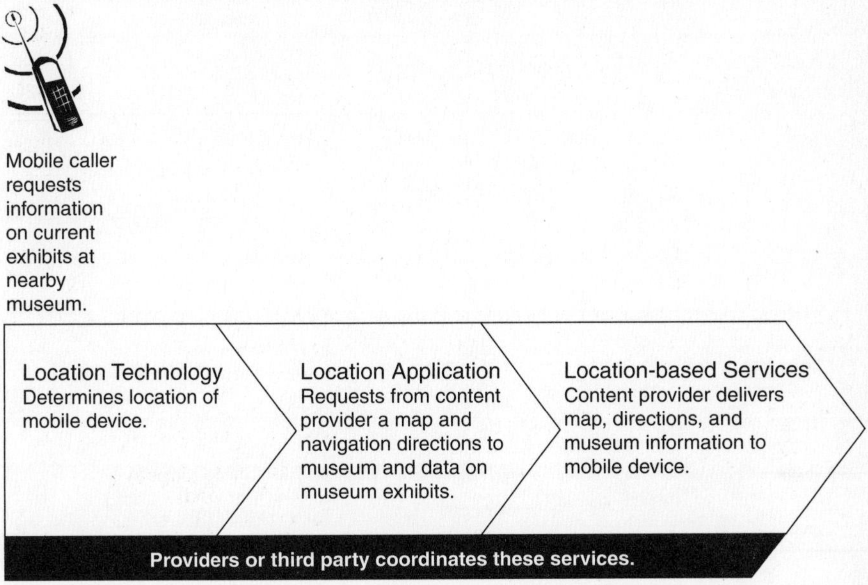

Mobile caller
requests
information
on current
exhibits at
nearby
museum.

Location Technology	Location Application	Location-based Services
Determines location of mobile device.	Requests from content provider a map and navigation directions to museum and data on museum exhibits.	Content provider delivers map, directions, and museum information to mobile device.

Providers or third party coordinates these services.

provide civilian and military users precise worldwide navigation and timing data. For users, the technology is passive. Specially designed GPS chipsets record data from three or more satellites and determine the location of the device. A GPS-based solution has several implications. Because the devices require special chipsets, legacy cell phones are not locatable. In addition, the GPS chipset creates additional power demands that shorten battery life. Network requirements are minimal—the network needs only to be able to download the GPS-derived location of the device.

To be an effective technology for LBS, GPS must overcome several shortcomings. Current GPS receivers require line of sight to the satellites. Buildings and automobiles, urban canyons, and densely vegetated areas can severely diminish GPS functionality. SnapTrack, a subsidiary of Qualcomm, has developed an enhanced GPS that is unaffected by these barriers. However, this solution requires additional network support to further process the GPS signal. Because the GPS chip is located in each phone, the user has direct control in determining if and when to use GPS.

Table 3.2
Types of Location Technology

Location Processed in	Method of Location	
	Network	GPS
Device	• Device uses OTD of network signals to determine location. • Requires special chipset in each device. • Does not work with legacy devices. • Fewer infrastructure requirements.	• Device uses GPS signal to determine location. • Needs to overcome traditional LOS limitations of GPS. • Requires special GPS chipset in each device. • Does not work with legacy devices. • Fewer infrastructure requirements.
Network	• Network determines location of device by measuring TOA of device signal. • Technology works with legacy devices. • Substantial infrastructure investment.	• Not possible—GPS needs to be recorded in device.

OTD = Observed time delay; LOS = Line of sight; TOA = Time of arrival.

Network triangulation. Network triangulation uses the signals between the device and the antenna to triangulate the device's location. Several wireless signal characteristics have been proposed for triangulation, including the angle of the incoming signal and its amplitude. The preferred method, however, is to determine the distance of a wireless device by judging the time it takes for the signal to travel between the device and the known location of the antenna, which can be achieved either in the network or by the device itself.

Even though all these technologies determine the location of the device, there are differences in where the actual computations are made. This is important, because if the network determines the location, all the end users will share the fixed infrastructure cost. If the computations are made at each device, end users pay a higher variable cost when purchasing LBS-capable devices, thus affecting their cost and pricing.

Device-dependent location. The technology whereby the device determines its position is known as enhanced observed time difference

(E-OTD). The device determines the time and therefore the distance between it and the network antenna. Because the technique requires more processing power and memory on wireless devices than is currently standard, legacy devices will not function in this environment. Compared with network-dependent location determination, device-dependent location requires less infrastructure investment but will shift the cost to the device.

Network-dependent location. The time of arrival (TOA) method depends on the network to determine the distance between the device and the network antenna. This method relies only on upgrades in the network to determine the location of devices. It works seamlessly with legacy devices. Network-dependent location determination requires a larger network investment but little or no additional device cost.

In rural areas, the small number of antennas and customers pose a potential problem for a network-based method. The low antenna density may make it more difficult to triangulate with the network. Because the high-fixed-cost network infrastructure is spread over fewer potential customers, a network model may not be cost-effective.

Multiple standards. None of these techniques are mutually exclusive. A phone with GPS capabilities could be located using GPS or TOA technology, and the network infrastructure is capable of handling multiple technologies. In fact, multiple standards could be the wisest choice. Network-based solutions are most cost-effective in high-density environments, whereas GPS devices may be the most appropriate option in rural areas. Different devices may be sold to different customer segments.

In the United States, different carriers are currently supporting different standards. Verizon and Western Wireless have chosen to develop a network-based solution, whereas Sprint PCS, Alltel, and Nextel are leaning toward a GPS-based system.

The promise of the wireless-location industry requires a solid infrastructure that will provide accurate geographic coordinates of wireless devices, and it needs to be developed and deployed wherever LBS will be delivered. It is difficult to say who will develop it and which companies and technologies will triumph because neither the technology nor the standards have been determined. In North America, only beta-networks have been deployed so far. However, the companies that are competing in this space have very different business models, which can be separated into carrier and third-party strategies (Figure 3.11).

Figure 3.11

Models for Location–Technology Infrastructure

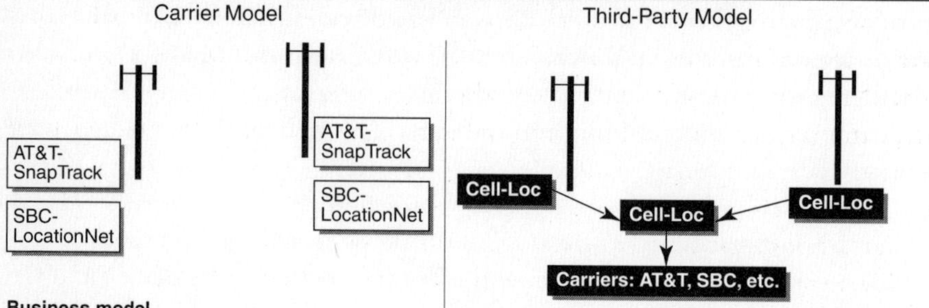

Carrier Model	Third-Party Model
Business model • Each carrier licenses and deploys LT at each cell tower • Determine x, y for their devices only	• Single LT provider, deploys technology at each tower • Determines x, y for any device across multiple carriers • Provides x, y to carriers for their end users
Infrastructure cost • High because of redundacy	• Low because only single infrastructure developed by third party
LBS • Carriers know device x, y and therefore can direct LBS "experience"	• Third party controls x, y. Carriers lose exclusive control of their customers?

Carrier model. This is the most common business model and is employed by companies such as Cambridge Positioning Systems and Snap-Track. Location technology is licensed to either the carriers or the device manufacturers. The carriers are responsible for deploying the necessary networks. The Swiss wireless carrier diAx, which operates the first commercially available LBS-enabled wireless network in the world, has installed the necessary technology to track its customers on the basis of the cell that is handling the call. The geographic information generated is used solely on the provider's network.

Third-party model. In this model, a third party installs the LT within the network with or without coordinating with the carriers. The third party provides geographic information for wireless devices across a variety of providers and technologies. Cell-Loc, which employs this model, is currently deploying LT in Austin, Texas. Cell-Loc's network is able to determine the location of any analog wireless phone call regardless of the carrier. By the end of 2001, Cell-Loc used a similar model to determine the location of any CDMA device in Austin. The LT service can be provided to the carrier or operated independently.

The service is possible because the carriers do not control the network infrastructure in the United States. Third parties, such as SpectraSite Holdings, operate antennas that allow access to LT providers. In contrast, this arrangement is not common in Canada. This business model allows LT providers to install one LT network that could operate across multiple carriers, and the carriers could license the data. The advantage for the carriers is that they will not have to develop redundant LT networks. This technology model, however, also has implications for LBS. If the customer's device carrier is not determining and handling the geographic data , the carrier has less leverage to capture value from any LBS.

Cost structures.   The different LT methods have different fixed- and marginal-cost structures. A network-based solution requires large fixed-cost expenditures, but it has very low marginal costs because it does not require device chipsets. A device-based solution requires a smaller fixed-cost investment but has higher marginal costs because chipsets are necessary in every device. Determining which of these two methods is the most cost-effective is difficult because of the rapidly changing technology.

Which LT standard prevails has implications for how quickly the technology will be adopted (Figure 3.12). High fixed costs and the necessity of retrofitting the network mean that network-based LT will probably be installed more slowly than a device-based LT system. However, because of the marginal price structure, the penetration of a network-based system will be greater because the devices should be less expensive. On the other hand, the extra cost of a location-device chipset will decrease the penetration of the device-dependent technology. Carriers and device manufacturers will have to weigh the costs and benefits of each of these technologies.

Figure 3.12
Implications of Cost Structures for Location-Technology Infrastructure

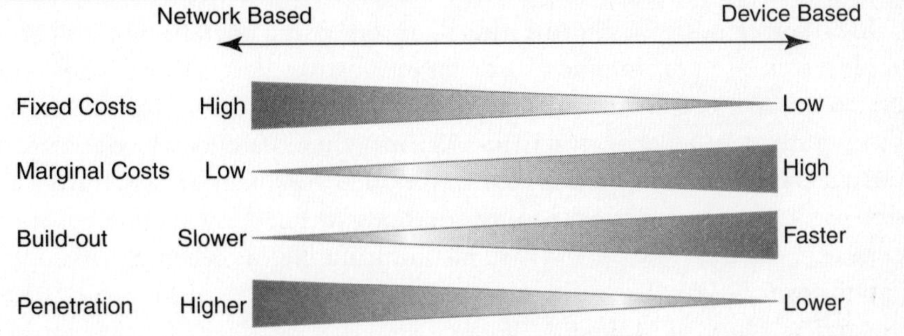

	Network Based		Device Based
Fixed Costs	High		Low
Marginal Costs	Low		High
Build-out	Slower		Faster
Penetration	Higher		Lower

Although it is difficult to predict how the LT infrastructure will develop, it is possible to outline the primary issues surrounding deployment:

- How will LT be deployed—through a high-fixed-cost, network technology or through a high-marginal-cost, device-based technology?
- Will standards be based on which standard is most cost-effective for a particular market—GPS in rural, TOA in urban?
- Will carriers develop their own redundant LT networks, or will a third party develop them?
- If a third party develops the network, will carriers lose leverage in shaping the LBS experience?

Privacy and Security Concerns.   Location-based services do have potential downsides. Ironically, the same FCC mandate that is intended to increase public safety also causes its own privacy and security concerns. Although there is great demand for LBS and interested consumers are primarily seeking safety and security, there is also an inherent paranoia and fear of misuse of the location information. In emergency situations, privacy is not an issue; however, consumers are extremely worried about the privacy and security implications in nonemergency situations. They are most concerned about (1) "Big Brother" and of being tracked without knowing it, and (2) "banner-ad invasion."

Before we jump to the conclusion that it is a great boon to be able to locate someone anytime the person is using wireless technology, we have to thoroughly address and adequately resolve the mounting security and privacy issues. Additionally, for LBS and m-commerce to succeed, mobile operators will have to persuade potential customers that such services will add significant value to their lives. If the privacy and security issues are not properly addressed, fear of Big Brother and the constant banner ad will prevail: Consumers will consider LBS to be a benefit only in emergency situations.

Business models.   Because this is an emerging market, the following applications are not intended to be an exhaustive, detailed list of all possible location-based services. Rather, we group current and potential services with similar characteristics. Within these categories, we describe characteristics and assess the business models for likely profitability. The details of the specific positioning methods or enabling technologies discussed in the previous section are not limiting factors when discussing the applications.

Applications enhanced by LT fall into the following categories:

- Emergency services.
- Push advertising.
- Pull advertising and directory services.
- Navigation.
- Tracking.
- Location-based billing.
- Social/entertainment.

Potential uses within these categories have been classified into transaction types (consumer to consumer, consumer to business, etc.) as Figure 3.13 shows.

The following framework has been used to analyze the profit potential of these applications. The profitability of an application can be disaggregated into three profit drivers:

1. Strength of the value proposition.
2. Market size.
3. Incremental profit from location.

Figure 3.13
Applications of Location Technology

C2C	C2B	C2G
• Find-a-friend • Track family, friends, pets • Track the elderly or mentally challenged • L-tokens • Find a date	• Directory services • Leisure and entertainment information • Pull advertising • Maps/navigation services • Traffic information • Comparison shopping	• E-911
B2C	**B2B**	**B2W**
• Wireless advertising/ coupons • M-commerce • Location-sensitive billing • Airline monitoring	• Delivery-service tracking • Network monitoring	• Fleet tracking • Employee tracking • Asset tracking

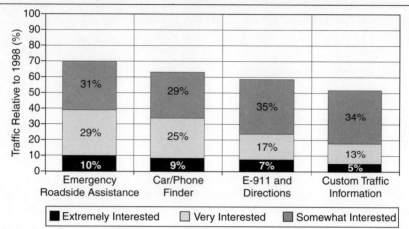

Figure 3.14
Survey of Customer Interest in Location Services

Source: Strategis Group Inc., 2000.

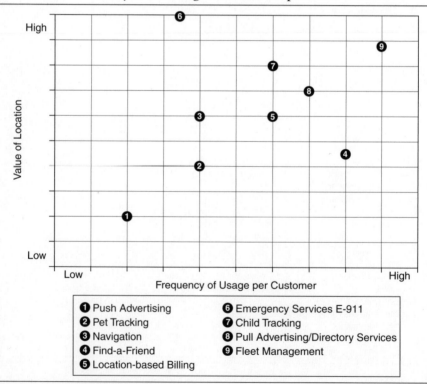

Figure 3.15
Analysis of Strength of Value Proposition

❶ Push Advertising
❷ Pet Tracking
❸ Navigation
❹ Find-a-Friend
❺ Location-based Billing
❻ Emergency Services E-911
❼ Child Tracking
❽ Pull Advertising/Directory Services
❾ Fleet Management

The first two measures give an indication of demand, and the third measure indicates profit per customer derived from the service's location element.

A customer survey (Strategis Group, 2000) was used to derive the strength of the value proposition for each application (Figure 3.14). Figure 3.15 then disaggregates the strength of value proposition into the value of location (how critical the location is to the service being offered) and the frequency of usage per customer. For example, a service that is seldom used—although location is important—is likely to be of lower value to the customer than a service that is used frequently.

Figure 3.16 analyzes the market size for each of the uses by considering the age and income brackets that form the target market. The likely penetration

Figure 3.16
Analysis of Market Size

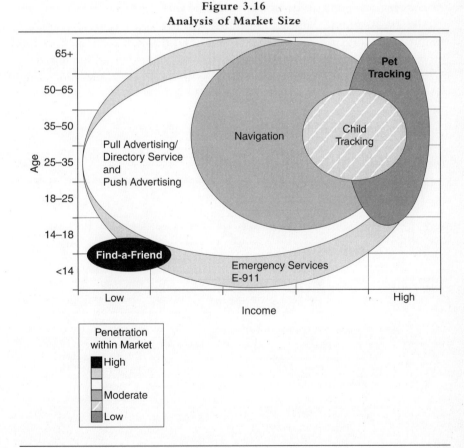

is also considered. For example, a "find-a-friend" service may be targeted at just a teenage segment but may achieve high penetration.

The three profit drivers are then integrated in Figures 3.17 and 3.18. Figure 3.17 interprets the analysis presented in Figures 3.14 to 3.16 and combines the profit drivers into a single measure of likely profitability. Figure 3.18 illustrates the findings graphically.

Emergency services. Nearly a third of the 150 million 911 calls made last year in the United States came from cell phones, according to the National Emergency Number Association. Location-based emergency services aim to improve the response to such calls and will be available for the general public without subscription. The services will consist of location-determining use of existing emergency numbers, such as 911.

Although because of privacy concerns many location-based applications are available on an opt-in basis, it is predicted that the E911 service will be mandatory. As Figure 3.14 demonstrates, it is perceived as highly valuable for quicker emergency response times achieved through accurate location information. The frequency of usage is low, however, resulting in a medium-to-high value proposition. E911 will not be a revenue-generating service (as indicated in Figure 3.18), but its extensions may provide revenue

Figure 3.17
Analysis of Applications of Location-Based Services

	B2C	C2B	B2W,C2C,B2B	C2G	B2C	C2C
	Push Advertising	Pull Advertising/ Directory Services and Navigation	Tracking	Emergency Services	Billing	Social/ Entertainment
Business Model	• Retailers pay charge per advertising impression	• Yellow Pages-type business model + increased wireless traffic	• Monthly fee per-location request	• Nonprofit but possible commercial emergency applications	• Enables location-based differential pricing	• Per-usage fee or increased wireless traffic
Strength of Value Proposition	• LOW • Intrusive, low response rates	• MEDIUM • Makes existing service more useful	• HIGH • Provides low-cost solution to new customers	• HIGH • Faster response to emergencies	• MEDIUM • Enables customers to have one phone for all calls	• HIGH • For some users, such as teenagers
Incremental Profitability from Location	• LOW • Is location really a key targeting attribute?	• MEDIUM • Location adds benefits but not essential	• HIGH • Tracking location is key to service	• FREE SERVICE • Could extend to commercial breakdown services	• MEDIUM/LOW • May be able to take usage from fixed network	• HIGH • Location essential • Small charges but frequent usage
Market Size	• MEDIUM • Users can choose to opt out	• HIGH • All cell-phone customers	• MEDIUM • Trucking, taxis, delivery services, and so on	• HIGH	• HIGH • All cell-phone customers	• MEDIUM • Appeals to some segments
PROFIT POTENTIAL ⇨						

Figure 3.18
Analysis of Market Attractiveness

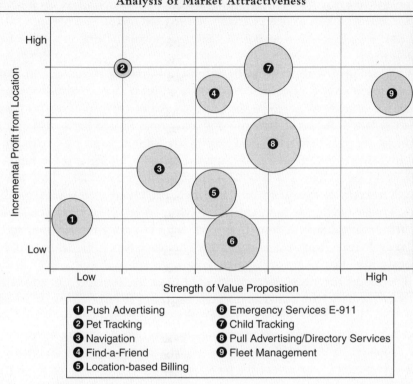

Circle size = Target market size

opportunities. For example, the same system may be made available to commercial breakdown services. A further extension could include emergency-alert services that warn customers about local dangers such as cyclones, volcanic eruptions, tsunamis, and earthquakes.

An additional commercial benefit of the government mandate is that it provides the impetus for developing technology that enables many other value-added, location-based services. The industry, however, argues that the specific technology choices should be driven by commercial applications and not dictated by the authorities.

Push advertising. Knowledge of a person's location adds a further dimension to the customer information already possessed by marketing firms. The owners of that location information have an unprecedented ability to target customers with personalized offers. For example, a customer driving along a thruway at 7 P.M. could be sent a discount coupon, via his mobile phone, enticing him into a roadside fast-food restaurant, or a person walking past a clothing store could be sent a personalized discount offer for a jacket.

One problem with location-based push advertising is that a firm may unnecessarily give a discount coupon to a customer who is already in the store and intends to purchase the product. A potential solution is to use location-based marketing to cross-sell additional related products (e.g., a financial-services firm could send loan advertisements to people in car dealerships). Smarter firms could also use the location information to predict customers' behavior, such as what regular journeys they make, how often they travel outside their state, or where they spend their evenings and weekends. Understanding an individual's behavior would be a complex task, but the firm that achieves it would have powerful targeting information at its disposal. Privacy concerns about this particular business model have been strongly raised on many occasions.

The model for push advertising would most likely involve an advertising intermediary that would aggregate advertisements from many firms on behalf of the wireless carrier. The firm wanting to advertise would be charged a per impression advertising fee, which the advertising intermediary and the carrier would share. The model's success depends on a strong value proposition, the size of the target market, and the incremental profit from location targeting. This model appears to fail on all three counts.

The value proposition for consumers is questionable. Advertising must be highly relevant for the consumer to pay attention, and it must have an

---

Spotcast is an application developer that has produced software that allows advertisers to target their intended audience by cell phone. The model involves offering subscribers one minute of free call time in exchange for listening to a 10-second audio advertisement. The user is then offered further information on the advertisement and is able to contact the advertiser. Spotcast believes location targets the right ads to the right people and that the worldwide mobile-advertising revenue will be worth $3 billion by 2003.

In evaluating this business model, we must consider the effect of a self-selected audience. Can people who will accept advertising in return for free airtime be characterized in some way, and does that segment match the advertisers' target markets?

CT Motion has produced an M-Coupon application that targets consumers with location-based promotional offers (M-Coupons). Consumers will be able to view a map of their current location, as well as detailed directions to the retailer who issued the coupon on the screen of their WAP phones. The product consists of CT Motion's M-Coupon application, City Beat, enhanced by Webraska's Personal Navigation software, which provides mapping and routing functionality.

immediate impact, producing a direct response. Well-targeted direct-response advertising has a history of single-digit-percentage response rates (e.g., direct mail), and Internet banner ads, which could be seen as analogous, suffer from low click-through rates. The low cost of transmitting advertising could make the model viable, but such intrusive advertising is likely to turn customers off. This in turn diminishes the target market, as more consumers opt out of receiving cell-phone advertising (a right they have because of privacy issues). Finally, although location does add a new level of targeting ability, it is not clear that knowing someone's location will dramatically improve response rates. We do not know what proportion of people would be distracted from their original purpose by a discount at a store they were walking past. Several companies will compete in the push-advertising arena.

Pull advertising and directory services. Most of the location-based applications currently in service are directory search engines that give customers the requested service that is closest to their location. The location element brings two main benefits to the overall value proposition that competing non-location-based search engines lack: (1) Users do not need to enter, or even know, their current locations and (2) the users receive directions to their chosen services from their current locations. These benefits are significant because users more commonly need directory services when they are outside their home location, making the location-based elements especially valuable.

The business model becomes more powerful when the cell phone also drives the transaction. A phase-one service could inform a customer where the nearest movie theater is located, whereas a phase-two directory service could convert the action into a transaction by listing the films and allowing the customer to purchase tickets over the wireless Internet. Implementing

Go2 Services launched its first location-based directory service over the wireless Web in December 1999. It has created hundreds of service- and brand-specific Web sites, such as go2Hotels or go2howardjohnson, and has signed up several well-known brands, including Coca-Cola, Ramada, Jiffy Lube, Cinnabon, and Jamba Juice. It intends to enhance its consumer value proposition through discount coupons and the provision of directions/navigation to the required service. The business model involves charging the brick-and-mortar retailers on a per location basis in a Yellow Pages manner. It plans to drive minutes for carriers and traffic, and e-commerce for retailers, and to provide a valuable service to consumers, saving them time and money.

such a service requires location technology (e.g., x, y coordinates provided by Cell-Loc) combined with mapping systems (geographic information system, or GIS, databases provided by companies like Webraska) and directory services with relationships to retailers (such as those provided by Go2 Services). Geographic mapping data is converted from complex algorithms into user-friendly driving distances and directions (e.g., those provided by AirFlash, which was recently merged with Webraska). Several companies are already offering these services. Go2 Services has teamed up with several partners to offer schemes organized by brands and service type, such as Go2Ramada for locating the nearest Ramada hotel and Go2Coffee for coffee shops.

Revenue is generated in two ways. The directory provider charges featured retailers, using a Yellow Pages model. The carrier probably gives the service away to users, relying on increased data traffic to generate revenue. Directory services can be thought of as a form of pull advertising. The location element adds significant weight to the value proposition, and the target market is all cell-phone users. As with traditional directory services, this service is easily replicable. Although it may be profitable in the

Cell-Loc's network will determine the location of the mobile-phone user. The directory service will then use Nortel's Voice Navigation System to provide directions to the location of the desired service, such as the nearest ATM.

Hutchison Telecommunications, SignalSoft, and *Siemens Mobile* have partnered to develop location-based WAP technology. Their technology was demonstrated in December 2000 in Hong Kong, an area with a high penetration of WAP-enabled devices and a high density of cell sectors. SignalSoft's Location Manager converts the cell ID, imported from the Hutchison GSM network, into latitude and longitude. The application server from Siemens takes this input and performs closest-search algorithms on the requested service.

short term, the ease of imitation will convert the service into an undifferentiated commodity.

Navigation. By combining the knowledge of current location, desired location, and map or guidance data, navigation for the lost traveler is possible. The system would automatically determine the current location, and either plain text or a voice-activated system would enter the desired location. The route would be determined in conjunction with the base-map data and, possibly, route-optimization software. Output may come in the form of a symbol-based map on a screen (PDA or enlarged mobile-handset screens highly preferred), plain text, or verbally.

The revenue model may be either a monthly access fee or a pay-per-direction basis. Monthly fees may be more applicable to the rental-car businesses and government agencies as value added to their existing businesses, while a pay-per-direction model would aim to capture the maximum value from the lost traveler.

Many inexpensive alternatives are apparent, including paper-based maps and other traditional navigation methods, although the automatic location information would regularly prove especially valuable to the time-conscious consumer. Ease of use for the consumer is paramount to introducing such a service and would be enhanced by the previously mentioned visual displays available with the currently larger PDA screen.

Privacy issues are not immediately apparent if the system is discontinuous (i.e., navigation is available on demand but generally not in the form of continuous tracking).

The target market for a navigation service spans all mid- to high-income drivers, although drivers who frequently drive to new destinations will benefit most from this service. Companies with fleets of vehicles (e.g.,

> *NTT DoCoMo* has had encouraging results selling the first mass-market GPS-based mobile personal-navigation service, called DokoNavi. Snap-Track Inc. (a Qualcomm division) developed the product. Its success is encouraging for the future of mobile-based navigation services. When evaluating this success, however, it is important to realize that Japan's cities are notoriously difficult to navigate. Selling a navigation system in other countries may prove more difficult.

taxi firms, haulage firms, sales representatives) will find the service valuable. However, screen limitations and usability for single drivers are likely to limit its utility.

Tracking. Wireless LT provides a cost-effective solution for tracking valuable assets. There are both business applications (e.g., tracking a firm's fleet of taxis or trucking vehicles) and consumer applications (e.g., tracking children or pets). Wireless tracking could also detect traffic congestion.

Fleet management. Fleet-management services provide for the tracking of location and status of mobile assets. Location and status information is received via the existing wireless infrastructure and compiled in a central location to be matched to a GIS database. Authorized parties can then use the information centrally and also for remote access. The service can be used by both a supervisory group and managed entities. The supervisory group may use the location and status information to optimize services, while the managed entity may access the services for information on system demands and other managed entities. Mobile-station devices (mobile phones or personal digital assistants—PDAs) would facilitate the transfer of the positioning information and would also serve as communication devices to access transfer status and use information.

This model has immediate benefits for traditional fleet management such as road-based transportation systems. Applications may also extend to stolen-vehicle location and employee use in the taxi and package-delivery industries. Zone-based applications may also be used for billing purposes and include concepts such as car insurance billing depending on zone usage. Activation of fleet-management services would most likely be conducted via a monthly fee per mobile asset plus a license fee for management software. Access to the location and status information, depending on authorization, could be provided within the system using Web-enabled devices and also for supervisory services via traditional systems. The value offered by the service is in the optimization of transportation activities. Even small improvements in efficient route selection and carrying use can result in significant bottom-line gains. Traditional alternatives generally offer circumspect prose, often based on inaccurate data and/or limited big-picture perspectives. In comparison, this real-time decision-making ability can capture value immediately through improved efficiencies and information services.

The target user group is likely to be limited but extends beyond trucking companies. Although users within this model can access the information system, it is also proposed that a customer could access the location information to better time interface activities. This may be a manufacturer waiting for a delivery but would also be applicable to a customer waiting for a taxicab or a courier service waiting for the pickup service.

Privacy issues are limited, as the service/information would be supplied only to companies tracking their own mobile assets and their respective customers. The accuracy of the location information is not critical, since it is expected that ±125m would be acceptable. Response time is similarly not critical, as information at five-second intervals is more than adequate given the speed of the assets and decisions made. To offer continuous tracking, however, service would be constant, and it therefore needs to be considered in future infrastructure planning.

Wireless-location information makes this service possible as a cost-effective solution. Potential customers perceive it as highly valuable, as Figure 3.14 shows, because of the value associated with the tracked asset. Combined with an expected high frequency of use, fleet management results in a strong value proposition (Figure 3.15). The market size, however, is limited to corporations that need to track valuable assets. This analysis is summarized in Figure 3.17. Of those analyzed, Figure 3.18 shows fleet management to be the most attractive market segment.

Ericsson has high expectations for fleet management as a revenue generator. It has estimated that the trucking sector in Sweden alone is worth $18 million in revenue per year based on the following figures:

Number of trucks = 35,000
Number of position requests per week = $100
Charge per request = $0.10

Child or pet tracking.   Anxious parents would greatly value the peace of mind provided by a system that could track the whereabouts of their children. Similarly, pet lovers might also appreciate a system to locate their animals.

A revenue model could be based on a monthly access fee or a pay-per-find basis. The strength of the value proposition is high because of the pricelessness of peace of mind and the lack of any suitable alternative system.

Accuracy of ±25m is desired, and the target market would be fairly large, given the number of children and pets. Mobile handsets are not necessarily required, as chip technology is proposed for clothing, watches, collars, and embedding under the skin of animals. Significant privacy concerns are apparent because access to the location of a child might be available to external parties who corrupt the system.

As with fleet management, potential customers perceive child or pet tracking as highly valuable because of the value associated with the tracked asset. However, both the frequency of use and the value of the location will be reduced for child tracking and markedly reduced for pet tracking. Combining these with medium-size potential markets and questionable market penetrations results in medium- and low-value propositions result (Figure 3.16).

Traffic monitoring.   Traffic congestion can be detected by wireless LT. By finding many mobile devices clustered in a row, a system can predict traffic congestion. In fact, the Dutch government has proven the effectiveness of a system that uses the location of mobile devices to detect traffic congestion. When the system detects 100 to 200 devices bunched closely together, it is likely to have found a traffic jam. The success of the system relies on a sufficient penetration of location-enabled wireless devices among vehicle drivers. Traffic monitoring using cellular devices would be significantly cheaper than installing and maintaining fixed monitoring systems along roads and would allow monitoring a broader network of roads.

A monthly access fee might be appropriate for the supply of such information, or this service might form part of a suite of location-based services provided by a carrier to drive wireless Internet traffic. The information might also form part of a navigation service that would reroute the customer's travel path to avoid congestion. This system would be most valuable to consumers with tight time schedules. Taxicabs might also benefit from such a service. Note that avoidance of congestion must be the net result as opposed to simple identification of congestion, and that depends on external factors such as adequate alternative infrastructure and access to it.

Both the accuracy of location, say ±10m, and response time are important to determine speed within acceptable tolerances. Privacy issues also have a negative impact on this proposition, as there would need to be limitations on collection of user identification. Figure 3.14 indicates, however, that of the potential LBS applications, traffic monitoring is likely to be valued slightly less than others.

Location-based billing makes it possible for a carrier to charge different rates depending on the customer's location. The rates may apply to a part or the full length of a call and may also be time dependent. Location-based billing allows the cellular provider to compete with fixed-network phone services while maintaining a premium price for truly mobile calls. The carrier can reduce rates to compete with the fixed networks when the customer is at home or in another specific location.

Customers should be notified of billing rates or zones and when those change. The service is likely to be incorporated into carriers' existing business models and will require customers to nominate such zones at registration. No service fee or monthly charge is required, as this service helps the carrier maximize profit with each customer. Accuracy depends on the size of the billing zone, but ±25m appears acceptable. Location information is required only during call periods; therefore, usage is not constant, and privacy issues will limit information transfer between the carrier and the user.

This value proposition appears to have medium strength, and the target audience is large, since the customer would be every mobile-phone user. Carriers also need to make up for the expenditures to acquire 3G licenses and simultaneously find new revenue sources now that mobile phone calls are declining.

Social uses/entertainment. Many user-experience applications are possible with location information. Such applications include Find-a-Friend and L-Tokens and may lead to similar models such as "find-a-date" or location-based gaming.

Wherify Wireless Location Services will soon be selling a $300 device that is the size of a wristwatch. It is targeted at parents and caretakers who want to track children or the elderly. The tracking-service cost is estimated to be $25 per month. The company realized it has to be careful not to use scare tactics in the marketing of its product. The technology is GPS based.

Yahoo Find-a-Friend. CellPoint, a Swedish developer, in cooperation with Yahoo!, is offering location-based service to carriers. It is aimed at users who want to keep tabs on friends and is popular with teenagers.

This value proposition appears to be high; for now, however, it is a limited but growing user group. The Find-a-Friend model is currently proving successful among Japanese teenagers. Significant privacy issues abound concerning access by external parties to personal location details, and any system will require secure acceptance of authorized parties to an individual's location information.

Any business model in this category will be an added benefit offered by carriers and will simply stimulate additional airtime or wireless Internet usage. Premium charging may be appropriate. Over time, however, the service would be provided at regular calling rates. Accuracy needs to be at least ±25m.

Figure 3.17 summarizes the analysis of the business models for potentially successful services. For each LBS horizontal-application type, the figure disaggregates the likelihood of success into the strength of the value proposition, the incremental profit from knowing location, and the target-market size to predict the potential profit. Predictions give tracking services, such as fleet management, the largest potential profit margin because of the large potential market size and the strength of the value proposition. Location-based directory services are likely to have the next highest potential. Social/entertainment services and child-tracking services could be profitable applications in specific customer segments. Despite the industry excitement surrounding push advertising, this market probably has low potential because of the low response rate of analogous channels and the ability of customers to refuse the service.

Outlook for Location-Based Services. We propose a framework to evaluate how LBS offerings will develop based on the technology required to

AirFlash (U.S.) is working with Orange Telecom in Europe to offer location-specific instant messaging. The messages can be sent to friends within a certain area or at a specific location.

Times Three has developed an L–tokens application, whereby, for example, a person can send location tokens (L–tokens) to friends with details of the location of a party. Guests can then use the L–token to find their way to the party.

deliver LBS as well as customers' willingness to accept the technology (Figure 3.19). It is apparent that the services will evolve in three stages—informational, tracking, and interactive.

Informational stage.   The first set of LBS services will be extensions of current wireless offerings but will include the added feature of location. These services will be initiated by customers as they request (B2C: directory services) or deliver information (B2G: E-911). Directory services will be available either through browsers or voice-based delivery. The information requested can range from the nearest car-repair shop to the local ski conditions. This type of LBS will develop first because customers are used to interacting in this kind of relationship and the databases and technology

Figure 3.19
Evolution of Location–Based Services

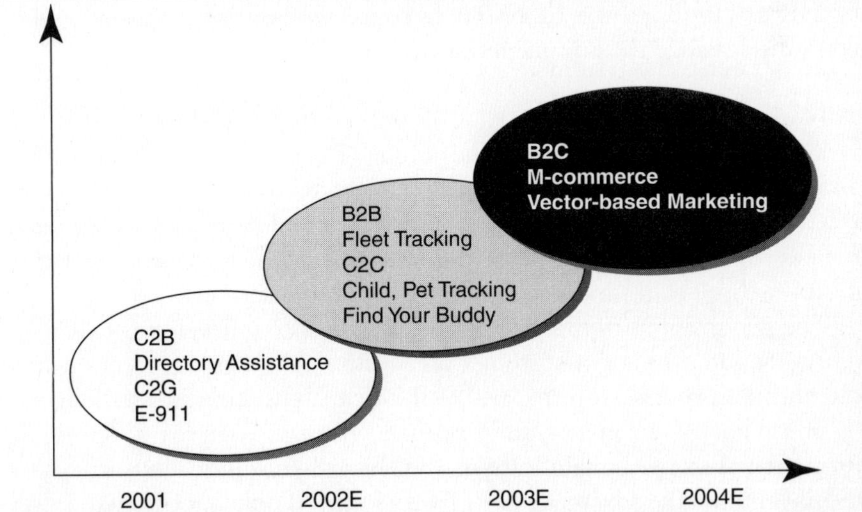

Adapted from JPMorgan, 2000.

are readily available. In addition, the technology is seamless for the consumer and will provide richer, more relevant data and services. These services do not require customers to change their habits.

Tracking stage. The next LBS that will become attractive to consumers and businesses is tracking. The ability to determine the location of one's children, friends, employees, and assets will be compelling for consumers and businesses. The technology to determine the location will be readily available through LT. For several reasons, however, these services may evolve more slowly. The display of tracking information on current devices is not optimal. On most, it is not possible to plot a real-time, dynamic map locating the target. Until devices have better screens and bandwidth, most tracking will be directed through Web browsers, which may slow the development of tracking applications.

Tracking technology will most likely be accepted by businesses more quickly (B2B). Businesses are accustomed to managing their employees and assets, and the ability to monitor their location and to communicate will be a valuable tool. Privacy will not be as large an issue in B2B location-based services because the privacy issues in the business realm are better understood.

Tracking in the C2C area will be slower to develop. Consumers will have to learn how to use the technology. How easy is it to make an alarm sound when a child leaves school during school hours? Additionally, tracking raises privacy issues. Do users really want their whereabouts known to friends or family all the time? These concerns, however, will fade when consumers realize the advantages of tracking.

Interactive stage. Interactive LBS will be the slowest to develop. Services include m-commerce and the ability of marketers to deliver personalized advertisements and promotions. Interactive services will be both B2C (an airline pulling up a flight reservation and customer profile when the passenger enters the airport) and C2B (a customer accessing real-time location-based flight information and purchasing a ticket).

The reason interactive LBS will be the slowest to develop is that it requires the interlinking of customer preferences and customer location with the business processes. In the case of the airline checking in a passenger as he or she enters the airport, the customer will have to agree to release information about personal location, and the airline will have to install the technology to take advantage of it. Every business that wants to participate in m-commerce will have to accommodate the technology in its business process. That will take time.

The Largest Share of the Value Chain. In reference to Figure 3.9, we have predicted who will be the likely winners in the location-based industry.

Equipment manufacturers and location-technology providers. Technology manufacturers do not have a great deal of room for differentiating their LT. The component manufacturer who develops the most accurate, least expensive LT will achieve a short-term advantage. It is relatively easy to imitate LT, as evidenced by multiple viable technologies already in the market. Long-term differentiation and above-average profitability are unlikely. The cellular-device manufacturers may promote location services to drive sales of Internet-enabled phones. The manufacturer that provides the best user experience, a function of screen and operating system, will have a short-term advantage.

Application developers. Software applications such as directory services or mapping tools that are easily reproducible are unlikely to sustain a competitive advantage. But the companies that develop complex, unique software, such as routing algorithms (e.g., Webraska) or integrated m-commerce/location platforms, will be able to maintain higher profit margins.

Location-based service providers. Currently, the wireless carrier acts as the wireless Internet portal and will manage location-service delivery as a natural extension. Thus, Sprint could determine the x,y coordinates of the device and act as a gateway between the consumer and the location-sensitive content providers. It is unlikely that the wireless carrier will maintain a competitive advantage because content providers will want nonexclusive agreements with all carriers. Perhaps Internet service providers or portals, such as AOL and Yahoo!, are better positioned to manage location-based services. To date, location-content providers do not appear to have offered any unique services (e.g., Go2 Services). The imitable nature of their services results in a low share of the value chain.

Wireless carriers. In the short term, wireless-location services will be a competitive advantage for the first carriers that introduce them as a differentiator, but that advantage will diminish as all carriers offer location services. The question is whether one carrier can provide markedly superior services.

Value Migration. What is the long-term future of LBS? If it is a "killer app," who will benefit from it—the infrastructure providers, the LBS providers, the carriers, or the customers? None of the location-based services appears to be unique; all are imitable, and versions can be copied by any of the carriers. Information and monitoring of LBS will definitely be available across all carriers.

Figure 3.20 proposes a framework for the evolution of the competitive landscape of LBS. It illustrates how the carriers will introduce different LBS services and how that will affect the value of LBS. Because different carriers will not introduce it at the same time, LBS will differentiate carriers at this early stage. That is how diAx, of Switzerland, successfully used location-sensitive information services to differentiate its mobile service from the incumbent service.

An optimization phase follows the differentiation phase. Local competitors soon match the initiator of the LBS in the local market, as happened in Switzerland, where Orange has signed with SignalSoft to deliver services similar to those of diAx. Competition in the LBS market focuses on delivering superior LBS products, so carriers will compete in signing the widest array of LBS. However, particularly because LBS is imitable, in the long run it will become a commodity service, and the carriers will offer

Figure 3.20
Value Migration

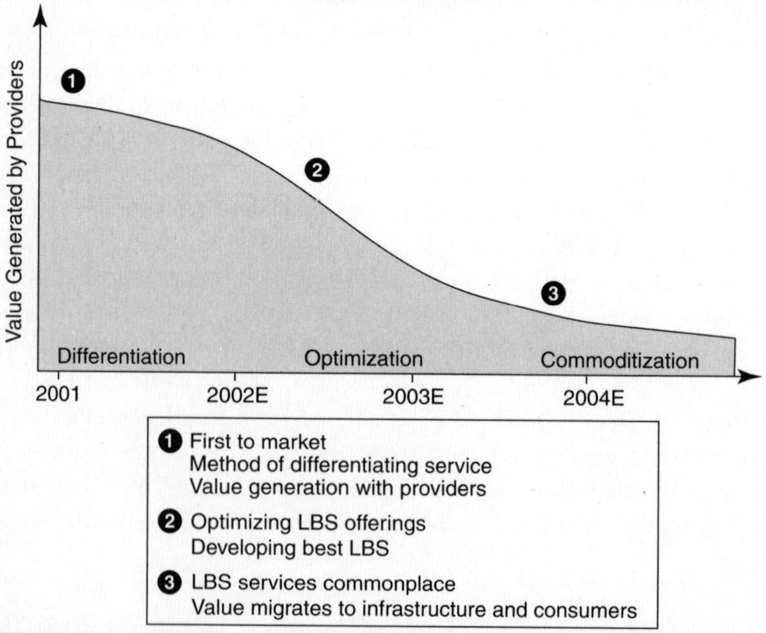

- **1** First to market
  Method of differentiating service
  Value generation with providers
- **2** Optimizing LBS offerings
  Developing best LBS
- **3** LBS services commonplace
  Value migrates to infrastructure and consumers

similar services. The winners could be best-in-class application providers that can charge a toll for every use or technology providers whose solutions become widespread de facto standards.

Next, we examine an enabling technology called Bluetooth. It is different from 3G and LT in that it does not involve wireless-carrier networks at all. In fact, it has no revenue-generating potential for the wireless carriers, and some of the biggest drivers of the technology are mobile-phone makers who want to make short-range data transfer between phones and other devices easier. Although there are several applications, they want, most of all, to make their devices the center of the customer's universe by creating a dependency level that outstrips that of the PCs. To be fair, it must be said that the technology has the potential to provide many benefits to end customers (including PC users). However, Bluetooth has been slow to arrive, so the question is whether this technology can gain momentum and become a lasting enabling technology that lends value to wireless devices for end customers.

BLUETOOTH: UNLEASHING THE BITE

Bluetooth is an innovative short-range wireless technology and standard that can network everything from PCs to mobile phones to accessories. In its simplest rendition, Bluetooth offers freedom from the tangle of cables and wires that connect all those elements in today's computer environment. At its height, Bluetooth promises to deliver new device-to-device communications, eventually creating seamless, wireless Personal Area Networks (PANs) in which devices automatically detect, communicate, and synchronize with one another.

Bluetooth, however, is still a network-externality story, and the main question is whether it will deliver on its promised benefits, and if so, when. First, we examine the role of Bluetooth in relation to alternative wireless technologies and discuss which will take control in the marketplace. Second, we outline the current state of the technology and the obstacles that lie ahead as Bluetooth moves toward sustainability. Finally, we inventory the products we are most likely to see in the next two years and the estimated times of Bluetooth product rollouts.

Promise of Bluetooth

To the novice, Bluetooth is no more than a radio that transmits information from one place to another. But this little radio, because of its size, range, speed, and portability, may prove to be one of the most versatile inventions of the past 10 years. Bluetooth is a miniature radio that can be installed in virtually every computing device or home/office appliance. More importantly, it allows all these devices to automatically communicate with each other in a seamless personal network.

We can imagine the functionality of the Bluetooth-enabled home environment. As the homeowner walks in the door with a Bluetooth-enabled PDA, it checks for messages on the answering machine. Next, it automatically detects changes in a calendaring system, adding relevant dates and appointments. Then it checks for the latest e-mail and sends the VCR instructions to record a favorite TV show—all before the user can get a quick bite to eat from the fridge. And, instead of sitting down at a computer to finish up a few notes on a report, the user may spend some time on a treadmill or stationary bike, dictating notes via a Bluetooth-enabled wireless headset.

Likewise, for an employee in the Bluetooth-enabled office environment, an array (or disarray) of cables would disappear from the landscape (Figure 3.21). Dangling wires would no longer connect keyboards or mice. Laptops could connect to network environments, printers, scanners, and fax machines anywhere without carrying or using any cables. Moreover, wireless headsets would double as phones and personal intercom devices replacing all cord-attached handsets.

Figure 3.21
Envisioned Freedom and Productivity

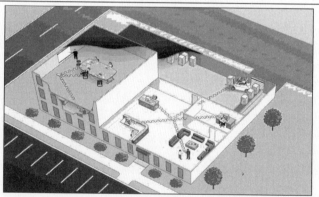

"I want the ability to access information instantly
anywhere, anytime, as if I'm at my desk."

Source: Toshiba, 2001.

Those examples illustrate the real "bite" that Bluetooth could unleash. The advantages are twofold—freedom and productivity. First, users would enjoy release from the tangled cables and wires that hinder mobility and functionality. Although Bluetooth's current range is only 10 meters, future development could extend that distance and allow users to move from office to conference room and later to production floor while never losing contact with a seamless PAN that would travel anywhere. Second, through Bluetooth-inspired applications, users everywhere would experience a heightened sense of productivity not only at work, but also at home, where time management is increasingly important.

But is Bluetooth actually all bark and no bite? To answer this question, it is important to discuss Bluetooth in light of its alternative technologies, such as IEEE (Institute of Electrical and Electronic Engineers) 802.11b. Indeed, IEEE 802.11b has enjoyed a faster adoption rate in the wireless local-area network (WLAN) arena, but its higher power consumption still makes it inefficient for smaller computing environments.

Moreover, Bluetooth faces its own implementation challenges and impediments before it can become a reality. Standardization, interoperability, and security remain concerns. Whether these become crippling obstacles or burgeoning opportunities is a topic of discussion as the technology moves forward. This chapter looks at how well the industry is overcoming the barriers—whether perceived or real—and which ones might keep the technology grounded.

Finally, Bluetooth applications have been highly anticipated, but where are they? The following discussion also highlights and reviews Bluetooth applications and the current road map for product delivery. Indeed, Hewlett-Packard, Intel, Motorola, Ericsson, Toshiba, and Nokia have all announced new Bluetooth-enabled products for sale. However, in light of Microsoft's April 2001 announcement that it would withdraw support for a seamless Bluetooth platform on the release of its newest operating system, the lingering question is . . . Is Bluetooth too late?

Alternative Technologies: Substitutes or Complements?

Defining the relationship between the technologies surrounding Bluetooth involves examining each technology in the broader context of the overall wireless landscape. Much has been said and written about the competitive dynamics among wireless networking technologies. Will IEEE 802.11b destroy HomeRF in the marketplace? Will Bluetooth replace IR as the primary means of short-range data exchange? Some analysts have even postulated that Bluetooth and IEEE 802.11b are in a competitive battle to the death, ignoring basic functional differences between the two technologies. Much of the confusion surrounding the wireless–technology landscape occurs because multiple dimensions must be considered to understand the trade-offs in using one technology versus another. Therefore, to judge the future potential of Bluetooth, it is critical to first analyze the wireless networking landscape in depth and develop a sharper outlook on how these technologies will interact in the marketplace.

Relationship between 3G and Local–Area Networks. On the most basic level, wireless technology involves the exchange of information using the radio-frequency spectrum. The most natural dimensions to use in a first-cut analysis of the landscape are speed and range. If the objective is information exchange, the key dimensions to measure are how quickly data transfer occurs (Mbps) and over what range (distance) each wireless technology communicates.

Using speed and coverage as the only analysis tool, the objective of the wireless game is reduced to obtaining the highest bandwidth with the greatest range. The greatest hype surrounds the rollout of the next generation

Figure 3.22
The Wireless-Data Landscape

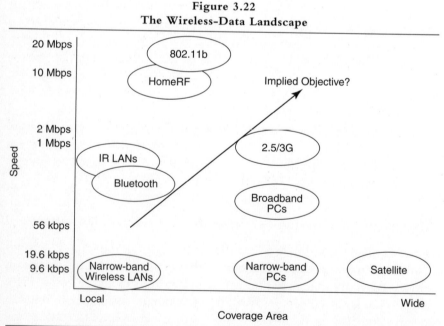

Source: Arthur Andersen, 2001.

of mobile telephony, known as 3G. The apparent promise of 3G is its ability to deliver relatively high-speed wireless communication (several hundred kbps) over a wide coverage area. Because of such broad capabilities, it is tempting to conceptualize 3G networks as a one-size-fits-all solution to communications (Figure 3.22).

That perspective on 3G is one reason for the exorbitant prices paid for spectrum in the 3G auctions across Europe in 2000 (more than $300 billion). Bidders justified their purchases with business models that promised seamless broadband access to the Internet anywhere, anytime. Their business cases were based on two assumptions: first, that there will be widespread adoption of 3G technology resulting in a large user base and, second, that there will be ‑ new opportunities for value creation through the convenient connection of individuals to information anytime, anyplace, whether the individual is stationary or on the move (Figure 3.23). According to Arthur Andersen,

Figure 3.23
The Effect of WLAN on 3G

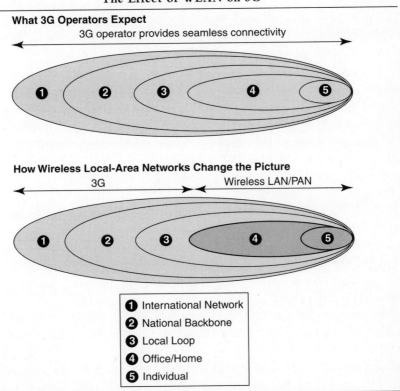

Source: Arthur Andersen, 2001.

however, local- and personal-area-network technologies such as Bluetooth, IEEE 802.11b, and HomeRF will likely siphon off some value from these assumptions in the local interactions because of cost, bandwidth, and access-device considerations—a concern mentioned earlier in this chapter.

In local contexts such as airports, shopping arcades, and other major centers where people browse for information, a business model involving a one-time Bluetooth server costing approximately $3,000 has the potential to provide significant savings over ongoing 3G airtime costs by effectively creating a low-cost, fixed-network infrastructure for all types of data transmission. As a result, it is constructive to revise the 3G providers' view of the future wireless value chain to include the vision of complementary WLAN and PAN technologies.

The complementary relationship between WLAN technologies and 3G is best illustrated using a concrete example. In Finland, customers carry out vending-machine m-commerce by placing a mobile call to a number listed on the machine and keying in an identification number for the product purchased. This is the use of wide-area-network bandwidth for a local transaction. In more advanced 3G applications, each device involved in the transaction will require expensive transceivers, and base stations will need sufficient capacity to carry an ever-increasing load of traffic.

In the real world, cost considerations are a major factor driving technology-adoption trends. If costs increase with faster and wider coverage, as analysts predict in the case of 3G, then the business case for a range of complementary local wireless technologies gains significant strength. Adding new dimensions such as cost to the analysis of the wireless landscape makes the need evident for WLAN technologies that function as complements to wide-area-networking technologies such as 3G.

WLAN Technologies. The next task is to differentiate the technologies within the WLAN field. The first step is to return to the speed-versus-coverage analysis to see that there are two groups of technologies: One fills the PAN space (10 meters) at relatively modest speeds of approximately 1 Mbps; the other fills the LAN space (50 to 100 meters) at faster speeds of 10 to 11 Mbps (Figure 3.24).

Bluetooth and infrared fall into the first group, whereas IEEE 802.11b, called Wi-Fi; HiperLAN2; and HomeRF fall into the second. Once again, this framework encourages jumping to the conclusion that IEEE 802.11b, HiperLAN2, and HomeRF will naturally win the battle to cover the entire WLAN space because they provide faster and wider network access. Yet, when additional layers, such as the type of access device, are added to

Figure 3.24
Local Wireless Technologies

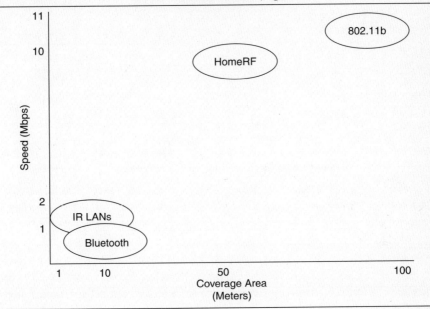

the analysis, it becomes obvious that there is a role for both types of technology, and the winners in each category become apparent (Table 3.3).

Access Device. Comparing wireless technologies according to the type of access device highlights a critical battle being waged between hardware manufacturers in the computer and telecommunications industries to produce the device of choice. Until recently, PC manufacturers maintained secure control over the access point to the Internet. However, with the advent of more advanced wireless telecommunications networks built with the express purpose of handling data, the PC industry's stranglehold on the Internet access point is rapidly loosening. The notion of anytime, anywhere connectivity plays directly into the hands of the manufacturers of small mobile devices such as PDAs and wireless handsets.

In the short term, neither side is going to win the battle. There is an inherent trade-off between screen size and portability. More likely, there will be a proliferation in the number and types of computing and telecommunications devices, which alone can provide a short-term market opportunity for Bluetooth. Already work spaces are clogged with an ever-increasing

Table 3.3
Comparison of LAN Technologies

	IEEE 802.11b	HomeRF	Bluetooth	Infrared
Speed	11 Mbps	1, 2, 10 Mbps	30–400 Kbps	1–4 Mbps
Range	100 meters	50 meters	10 meters	1 meter
Power Usage	100 mW	100 mW	1 mW	100 mW
Cost of Device	$150	$150	$5	$5
Use	Office or campus LAN	Home office, house, and yard	Personal–area network	Direct 1–1 transfers
Type of Terminals	Laptop and desktop	Laptop and desktop	Anything electronic	Built into laptop, cell phone, and PDAs

tangle of wires. Bluetooth is designed to seamlessly connect the rapidly expanding universe of devices into wireless personal area networks. More interesting, however, is the notion that the different types of devices have very different benefits and limitations that will dictate the use of specific wireless technologies.

First, small mobile devices such as PDAs and wireless handsets have severe power constraints. Without a grounded power connection, these devices rely on a limited supply of battery power. Bluetooth has a hundredfold advantage over IR, 802.11b, and HomeRF in regard to power consumption (1 megawatt versus 100 megawatts). The power limitations of small battery-powered devices will naturally drive them toward Bluetooth for wireless connectivity. This factor has large implications in defining Bluetooth's niche market. Bluetooth will likely capture the market for devices such as PDAs and wireless handsets primarily because of this issue. In addition, Bluetooth's hold on the small-device market will ensure its inclusion in the laptop and PC market because of the need to synchronize and exchange information between devices.

Second is the cost issue. An 802.11b WLAN involves the purchase of $150 to $200 adapter cards for every device using the network. Such a cost element is much more palatable for a $1,500 to $4,000 laptop computer that will be used for high-speed, wireless Web surfing than it is for smaller, less expensive devices. The cost of the adapter doubles or triples the cost of a mobile-phone handset that will most likely be used only for accessing limited amounts of highly selective data (because of the small screen). Therefore, the estimated $5 cost target of an embedded Bluetooth radio makes Bluetooth the wireless technology of choice for small devices.

An examination of the trade-off of cost versus functionality illustrates a major difference between a WLAN and Bluetooth. Granted, WLAN technologies provide higher-speed access over wider areas; however, the 15-fold cost increase of this higher performance is not justified for devices that are unlikely to be used for surfing the Web in the short term. Furthermore, by achieving the lower cost base, Bluetooth can be installed in a great range of devices, from refrigerators to VCRs, thereby opening the door to a vast number of potential applications. In sum, there is a role for both the more expensive, faster WLAN technologies and the cheaper, slower PAN technologies.

Solutions using the IEEE 802.11b standard are already being deployed on a widespread basis. Large corporations, universities, and school districts are building 802.11b networks as an alternative to running cables through office buildings, dormitories, and classrooms. Hotels, conference centers, and airports are also beginning to build out 802.11b networks, enabling people to use PC cards for WLAN access.

The rollout of the 802.11b networking standards is supported by more than 70 companies, including Apple Computer, 3Com, Cisco Systems, Dell Computer, and Sony. Even though the heavy hitters (Intel, Motorola, and Hewlett-Packard) also backed the competing standard, HomeRF, it was originally marketed to the home-office customer and has failed to gain a strong foothold in the market. As a result of the rapid adoption rate of 802.11b in the corporate market, HomeRF is facing an increasingly uphill battle because end users are reluctant to have two separate wireless networking cards—802.11b for work and HomeRF for home. In fact, Intel decided to back the 802.11b standards and drop its support of the HomeRF standard.

Solutions based on IEEE 802.11b seem likely to gain a dominant share of this market over the next two years before new 5 GHz systems based on IEEE 802.11a and/or HiperLAN2 replace them. Although the initial rollout will take place in Europe, HiperLAN2 backers think North America may be ripe for the picking as well. HiperLAN2 hopes to become a WLAN success story with its high data rates and ability to combine data with voice and video, using the spectrum in the 5 GHz band. A joint project of the telecom equipment giants Nokia and Ericsson, the technology is almost assured a future in Europe.

Nevertheless, the power consumption and cost weaknesses of the WLAN technologies create a powerful niche market for a PAN technology such as Bluetooth. It will not replace WLAN equipment, since its maximum throughput is less than 1 Mbps. Yet it will become a low-cost, low-power consumption technology to eliminate wires and cables and to create wireless PANs that will spawn an entirely new generation of applications. Bluetooth will overtake IR because of IR's limitation in range (one meter) and the requirement of a clear, line-of-sight view from one device to another. In the near term, IR will not disappear because it has a large installed base in the marketplace and strength for person-to-person applications. But in the long term, the limitations associated with IR give the advantage to Bluetooth (Figure 3.25).

Over the next two years, the market will witness the mass deployment of both Bluetooth and IEEE 802.11b technologies. The design characteristics of the two will allow the segmented targeting of different applications to similar but different market spaces. Both types are striving toward the standard networking goals of achieving interoperability and security, but they have distinctly different design goals. Bluetooth is designed for short-range, low-cost communication, whereas IEEE 802.11b is for high-speed network access between computers. The limited overlap between these two technologies will enable both standards to carve out unique market positions.

Figure 3.25
Complementary Technologies

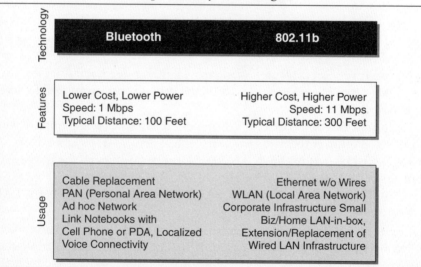

Impediments: Obstacles or Opportunities?

Considering the market potential, some are wondering what has delayed the deployment of Bluetooth-enabled devices. Perhaps the media is partly to blame for overhyping products and creating unrealistic expectations for the proliferation and performance of upcoming Bluetooth technologies. But media hype aside, Bluetooth faces real obstacles as it enters the wireless space. For the consortium of core Bluetooth developers, standardization remains the primary difficulty, followed by technological hurdles dealing with specifications, quality control, and security of data. Finally, the lack of applications in today's market threatens consumer confidence in Bluetooth as a viable wireless technology. Weak consumer confidence will only serve to slow the pace of Bluetooth adoption. However, it is this very dissatisfaction that drives the dedication and renewed focus of Bluetooth developers. Rather than pitching Bluetooth as a technology that does all things for all people, developers are once again focusing on need-to-have applications that target niche markets. The end result will be the successful introduction of key Bluetooth applications throughout 2002 and the full proliferation of Bluetooth products and applications through 2004 and beyond.

Standardization.   Interoperability and standardization are at the forefront of Bluetooth development. Since the creation of the special-interest group (SIG), developers have constantly worked to create a single standard through which all Bluetooth-enabled devices would communicate. The original specification for Bluetooth, BT v1.0b, introduced in July 1999, was described as ambiguous, and tests of products following that specification exhibited interoperability problems. In November 2000, the SIG released an updated set of standards called BT v1.1 to replace the confusing BT v1.0b; it includes clarifications and corrections that ensure improved interoperability. The updates are software based and easy to adopt, which means the new specification should not cause significant delays for semiconductor companies.

Although the Bluetooth specification attempts to set clear rules for building products, the qualification process, under the authority of the SIG, guarantees that all Bluetooth devices can communicate with each other. Merrill Lynch reports that Bluetooth will have several testing centers located around the world responsible for rejecting or approving Bluetooth-enabled products. In the race to market, however, many companies are seeking third-party testing, while others are doing self-tests and sending their results to the Bluetooth Qualification Body, which must approve products that want Bluetooth backing. Furthermore, many of the qualified products were built using the BT v1.0b specification, which is being phased out because of errors and possible interoperability problems.

Interoperability.   Bluetooth devices operate on the Industrial, Scientific, and Medical (ISM) applications band that is available free to most parts of the world. The 2.4 GHz frequency is a noisy, crowded band that is shared by almost every appliance, including microwave ovens, wireless speakers, and garage-door openers. Because Bluetooth uses low transmission power, it is susceptible to interference from that noisy environment. However, because Bluetooth technology is a fast frequency hopper at 1,600 times a second, it is shielded from losing connectivity. IEEE 802.11 also works on the 2.4 GHz band but might eventually move to the 5.2 GHz band, where data rates are much faster and can support heavier multimedia applications. Frequency problems are expected to continue as the number of Bluetooth devices grows to the billions, and even the SIG admits there is a chance of performance degradation in the crowded space.

Cost.   Perhaps the greatest impediments to Bluetooth adoption are the cost and size of radio chips. The hardware to integrate Bluetooth into devices is expensive, and to persuade equipment manufacturers to include the technology, the production cost must be low. Industry experts point to the success of IR interfaces introduced to mobile phones and PCs with a target cost of $5. Today over 90 percent of portable PCs have built-in IR interfaces. The challenge for Bluetooth, a technology that is more complex than IR and therefore more expensive, is to come up with a low-cost, unobtrusive chip.

As with most technology innovations, upgrades are fast on the way. Today unit prices range between $20 and $30, and the competition among chipmakers is fierce. At the forefront of the excitement is Cambridge Silicon Radio (CSR), a start-up based in the United Kingdom that is ahead of the pack with cheaper Bluetooth-enabled chips. CSR, and Texas Instruments, along with several more companies (Infineon and Alcatel), are saying they will be competing in the $5 price range. Expectations are high that chips will fall below $5 by 2003.

Security.   As companies rush to launch new products in the wireless market, attention to security also gains greater importance. According to the Gartner Group, computer scientists from the University of California, Berkeley, announced in February 2001 that they had discovered a flaw in the IEEE 802.11b wired-equivalent privacy (WEP) protocol that allows hackers to intercept the transmission of data, read it, and modify it unnoticed.

A failure of IEEE 802.11b security occurred in January at an exclusive annual meeting attended by the leaders of business and government in Davos, Switzerland. The entire town was equipped with 802.11b access points, and every delegate received a PDA fitted with a transceiver card. Representatives could walk around while sending and receiving data at broadband speeds. But despite a large police force, meeting participants were not entirely protected. A group of hackers managed to break into the Davos network, pilfering personal information including Jeff Bezo's cellphone number, Yasser Arafat's network passwords, and Bill Gates's e-mail address.

This is in contrast to the Bluetooth security specification that supports authentication (one-directional or mutual) and encryption. Authentication prevents unauthorized parties from accessing data, while encryption prevents outsiders from reading data. Authentication, encryption, frequency hopping, and a small frequency range give Bluetooth a strong defense against security breakdowns.

Although Bluetooth ad hoc networking makes it more secure, Bluetooth security still has flaws, and they do not always point to the technology. Even though vendors rigorously integrate security technology—protocol stacks, encryption, and shared keys—users fail to use the security features properly. According to Nigel Ballard, the vice president of products strategies at Portland-based Cerulic, Inc., "People don't even take the time to change their passwords from their defaults 'public' or '101.'" The passwords are intended to protect individuals and their data in the same way that a login password secures access to data on a PC. To achieve that goal, the public must be educated in the proper and effective use of these security features.

Network Externalities. The Bluetooth rollout also relies on the extensive proliferation of Bluetooth-enabled products, but repeated delays have impeded the network's growth. Certainly Microsoft's decision to pull Bluetooth from its Windows XP launch, while including support for Wi-Fi, delivered a serious blow to Bluetooth's credibility and growth. Beginning in September 2001, laptops were slated to be Bluetooth-enabled with 13 user profiles, while PDAs and cell phones might have only 3 or 4 profiles. Profiles are applications that allow devices to communicate and exchange data. For example, one profile is called the headset profile, and only devices with the headset profile can exchange data with one another. Audio profiles are in the works. Bluetooth-enabled devices will not be able to exchange information with all devices unless they contain a full set of profiles.

Despite the delays, Bluetooth is still projected to be a $5 billion market within the next five years, and as chip prices continue to fall, applications will follow. The next step is to examine the second generation of Bluetooth-focused companies vying to own the application space.

Applications

Bluetooth technology was initially developed to replace cables and connect devices with a short-range radio link. It has evolved into a more promising technology that will enable easy synchronization, quick ad hoc networking, and great mobility through wireless connections. The Bluetooth application road map (Figure 3.26) outlines the development trends and relationships between segments of Bluetooth functions and applications.

The most immediate and short-term benefits of Bluetooth technology are cable replacement, synchronization, and ad hoc connectivity. These will be enabled through Bluetooth chipsets added to existing products such as laptop computers and mobile phones. Other than handsets, PCs, and laptops,

Figure 3.26
Bluetooth Application Road Map

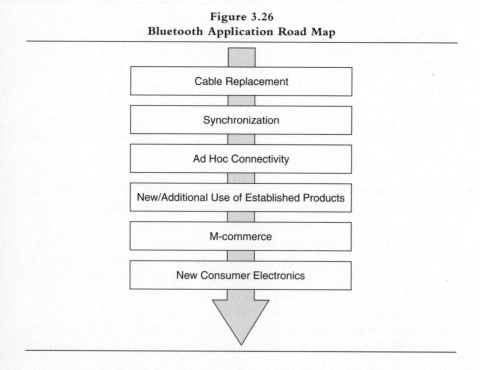

a whole host of products will be driving the adoption of Bluetooth technology. These products, either in new models or in existing models with improved features, include digital cameras, digital TV set-top boxes, modems, printers, and industrial appliances. The Bluetooth penetration rate for digital still cameras, which was 2 percent in 2001, is expected to reach 60 percent in 2006. Moreover, the same rate for digital TV is expected to hit 65 percent in 2006.

The emergence and adoption of Bluetooth technology would also facilitate m-commerce. Like digital wallets, Bluetooth-enabled phones or other mobile devices would offer the means to pay for transactions without repeatedly entering credit card numbers or risking the storage of such numbers on the wireless device. As consumers become more comfortable with quick, easy, and secure communications and transactions over wireless devices, m-commerce revenues will increase. Companies will compete for revenues from data access, m-commerce, and advertising. According to analysts' pricing estimates, this could translate to $18.5 billion of data-access revenues, $2.4 billion of m-commerce, and $1.2 billion of advertising revenues by 2005.

Major Bluetooth Applications.   Cable replacement. Bluetooth enables users to connect a wide range of computing and telecommunications devices easily and simply without buying, carrying, or connecting cables. Thus, it eliminates the need to purchase additional or proprietary cabling to connect individual devices. Because Bluetooth can be used for a variety of purposes, it can potentially replace multiple cable connections via a single radio link.

Automated synchronization.   The proliferation of different devices makes data synchronization and aggregation services extremely complex yet very important. There are three types of synchronization: Point-to-point synchronization involves data exchanges between two devices; multipoint synchronization involves data updating of connected devices through a central data repository; and multidevice synchronization involves data exchanges between multiple devices via a central data repository. With Bluetooth enabling connectivity between any two devices, users could automatically synchronize information among any computing devices (e.g., contact and calendar information among desktop, notebook, and palmtop computers).

Ad hoc connectivity.   When two Bluetooth devices come close together, they automatically detect each other and establish a network connection, delivering opportunities for rapid ad hoc connections and possibly automatic, unconscious connections between devices. This creates a new form of networking—unmanaged, dynamic networks of devices that spontaneously and unpredictably join and leave the network.

Wireless personal-area networks (WPAN). Ad hoc connectivity can be extended to more than two devices within a user's personal operating space. This multipoint connectivity among wireless devices creates a network called a wireless personal-area network.

Major Bluetooth Market Segments

The unique components that make up a Bluetooth communication network create a huge potential for applications in at least four key market segments: home networking, interactive office, mobile e-business, and automotive and industry applications.

Home Networking. Bluetooth would allow almost all electric and electronic appliances in the home (entertainment systems, refrigerators, washers, dryers, security systems, and control systems) and mobile electronic devices (such as smart phones, PDAs, and notebook and desktop computers) to interact and communicate wirelessly.

Three-in-one phone. At home, a phone would function as a portable phone. For a user on the move, it would function as a mobile phone. And when the phone came within range of another mobile phone with built-in Bluetooth wireless technology, it would function as a walkie-talkie. Benefits would include user-based optimal pricing (fixed charge when functioning as a portable phone, mobile charge as a mobile phone, and no charge as a walkie-talkie), with "one telephone, one number" regardless of location.

Universal remote. As more and more home appliances become equipped with Bluetooth technology, it is likely that any personal Bluetooth device, such as a PDA or smart phone, will be able to query and control other devices. Thus, a user could arm the security system, change channels on the television, or receive an alert from the dryer to take out the dry clothes.

Interactive Office. A Bluetooth network in the office would enable users to connect to the network from virtually any location. Furthermore, each Bluetooth device could be connected to 200 other devices, making the connection between every other device possible. Since it supports both point-to-point and point-to-multipoint, the maximum number of simultaneously linked devices would be virtually unlimited.

Ultimate LAN. Bluetooth technology connects all office peripherals wirelessly. Users can connect notebooks to printers, scanners, and faxes. Even the mouse and the keyboard need not be connected to the computer.

Interactive conferences. In meetings and conferences, documents could be transferred instantly among participants. Notes from Bluetooth-enabled whiteboards could be sent directly to participants' computers or palmtops. Electronic business cards could be exchanged automatically.

Mobile E-Business. Bluetooth is well suited for mobile e-business since it could be used to complete transactions locally between two communicating peer-to-peer devices. Its built in security mechanisms enable secure transactions.

Walk-up kiosks. Walk-up kiosks could provide local information in many venues, such as shopping malls (maps, coupons, special offers), airports (maps, flights, parking), team or exhibitor data, and contest entries. Bluetooth-capable kiosks could allow multiple users to access the kiosks simultaneously. They also enable mobility, in that the information could be transferred to a personal device and thus be available even when the user was not near a kiosk.

Ultimate "queue killer." Peer-to-peer transactions would enable local e-commerce transactions without the user's having to stand in line for access to a resource (machine or person). Consumers could make purchases, get discount authorizations, and complete other transactions at the point of presence.

Automotive and Industry Applications. Industry observers have raised their expectations of the penetration rate of Bluetooth in cars and industrial applications. They have seen scenarios where five Bluetooth radios are installed in one car. The majority of these applications would be application-specific (designed to perform only one function and to interact with only one other Bluetooth module). At a 2 percent growth rate, the Bluetooth penetration rate for cars is projected to increase from 5 percent in 2002 to 60 percent in 2006, meaning a total of 34 million Bluetooth chipsets installed. By 2006, there will be more than 57 million Bluetooth chipsets in industrial applications.

Company Profiles and Product Rollout. Bluetooth technology has moved quickly in terms of standards adoption, early release of chips, and a few demo products. Progress was fueled mainly by the formation of Bluetooth SIG, led by the Promoter Group of Bluetooth SIG, comprising Ericsson, Nokia, IBM, Toshiba, Intel, 3Com, Motorola, Lucent Technologies, and Microsoft. Bluetooth SIG has more than 1,600 members and is one of the fastest-growing SIGs. This is the first big effort by all the major companies of the world to come out with a global standard for wireless connectivity in a homelike environment since first- and second-generation cellular communication.

Nonetheless, Bluetooth is in the early stages of development from the point of view of end-user applications. Many of the first Bluetooth products are add-on devices for existing laptop and personal computers, and the high cost of those devices has hampered adoption. Key chipmakers that have started full production of the add-ons are Broadcom, Lucent Technologies, and Motorola along with start-ups like Cambridge Silicon Radio and Silicon Wave. Aside from the high cost, the size of the current generation of chips is also a problem. Companies such as Palm that have pledged to adopt the technology are counting on the reduction in cost and size of the chips.

Bluetooth has seen little progress in reaching the mass market. Microsoft blamed a lack of Bluetooth-enabled hardware for its decision to omit Bluetooth from its 2001 version of Windows XP. Nevertheless, supporters note that other standards, such as Ethernet, as well as many of the cell-phone protocols, took much longer to develop. Some of Bluetooth's promise is already visible. In March 2002, manufacturers such as Hewlett-Packard, Ericsson, and Psion were showing off Bluetooth devices. Hewlett-Packard unwrapped the DeskJet 995C, the first integrated Bluetooth printer.

Aside from products, industry applications have also shown progress. Registry Magic launched the world's first consumer payment network in January 2001, which leverages Registry Magic's patented biometric access-security system (BASS) authentication and authorization services and Bluetooth technology to enable a customer's cell phone to be a one-stop device for everyday consumer transactions such as making purchases, interpersonal communication, and identity validation.

In the current phase of Bluetooth technology, the first release of specifications has been developed and adopted by the core members. Chipsets have been developed by several vendors and released to systems integrators. Major vendors have also released software development kits. Figure 3.27 is a road map for rollout. Developers' conferences have been held in Europe

Figure 3.27
Product and Application Rollout

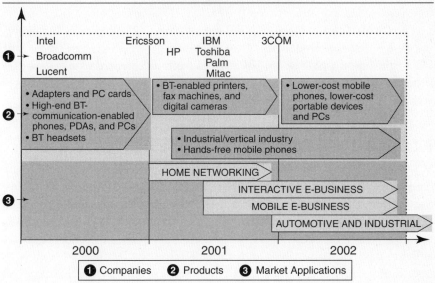

and North America, and now the second level of developers, such as 3Com and Extended Systems, have got into the act to create systems-development tools that business-application programmers can use. The highlighted product profiles give a closer look at existing and upcoming Bluetooth applications and their underlying technologies, as well as the values they create in wireless communication.

The majority of market forecasting for Bluetooth applications remains in mobile phones, headsets, PDAs, and PCs, accounting for over 80 percent of units by 2006. Even though it is still too early to tell how quickly, and by how much, price competition will erode profits, many industry watchers still prefer to err on the side of optimism. Numerous applications such as toys, consumer appliances, and electronics could emerge after a robust launch and widespread consumer adoption of the Bluetooth technology.

Product Profile Integrated PC Cards: Xircom's RealPort Families

Xircom's wireless-product families include a CreditCard Bluetooth adapter, a RealPort Bluetooth adapter designed for notebook computers, and a

SpringPort Bluetooth module that fits into the Springboard slot on Handspring Visor devices. The RealPort integrated PC card family has all the features needed to connect to information in the office or on the road.

The form-factor evolution diagram in Figure 3.28 illustrates the evolving design and functionalities of several generations of Xircom's RealPort PC adapter products. Xircom has evolved from its patented external-pocket Ethernet adapter to a smaller, less cumbersome, internal PC card adapter with custom cables to today's single integrated wireless PC card.

FUTURE OUTLOOK FOR BLUETOOTH

Without question, Bluetooth has the potential for revolutionizing the computing landscape. It provides a world free from the tangle of cables, thus releasing computer users from the confines of a workstation or wired network environment. And that's just the beginning. This technology can free scanners, printers, visual-projection equipment, and other peripheral devices from cables and immediately provide the end user with new mobility, functionality, and heightened productivity. Though not initially a standard as defined by the IEEE, the IEEE now has a formalized development in process for Bluetooth known as 802.15.1 and is exploring its enhancement with a high-data-rate standard, 802.15.3. A

Figure 3.28
PC Card—Form-Factor Evolution (1998 to Present)

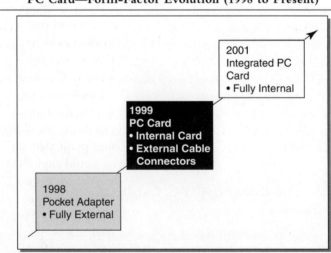

high-power/high-speed version of Bluetooth might someday be seen as a viable WLAN service.

Bluetooth can go far beyond cable replacement and proposes to offer something more—a complete personal-area networking solution, whereby computers, mobile phones, laptops, and PDAs will use intelligent software to detect, communicate, and transfer relevant information on a continuous, automatic, and unencumbered basis. With the right security clearance, these devices could automatically transfer and synchronize e-mail, files, news, credit card information, and other electronic information, enhancing not only user mobility, but also user productivity.

But are Bluetooth's plucky claims too late? The computing industry has speculated about, hyped, and promoted Bluetooth since 1998. What has appeared since is the Bluetooth SIG, a consortium with 11 promoting companies and more than 1,600 developing companies that are supposedly working together to develop a Bluetooth standard so that all Bluetooth-enabled products will function seamlessly. Products have been slow to come to market, and the few that have arrived are stymied by the same standardization and interoperability problems that the SIG was supposed to fix.

It appears today that dominant companies such as Microsoft are saying enough is enough. Microsoft's omission of support for Bluetooth in its operating system added relevance to the question whether Bluetooth would survive before it really got started. So Bluetooth is entering a crucial stage as it struggles to gain traction. Will it succeed in light of Microsoft's original criticism of the technology? Intel has countered with claims that Bluetooth "was never a race"—that instead, Bluetooth is about creating a standard and delivering a platform in which all users will find satisfaction.

In fact, HP has introduced new Bluetooth-enabled printers, computers, and PDAs into the market. Bluetooth remains a network-externality story—a chicken or egg game—where the benefits will only begin to become apparent as a function of manufacturers' willingness to introduce new products and make Bluetooth a persistent element in the industry.

Thus far, Bluetooth has stumbled in creating its market, and 2002–2003 will be very telling as to whether it is a sleeping giant that will arise or will become just another good idea that no one could capitalize on. The most likely scenario is somewhere in the middle. Although the ubiquity of Bluetooth may not reach previously promised levels, especially in the short term, it will likely find its niche in the market with its many potential applications. Since no revenue-generating potential is possible for wireless service providers, there is no incentive for these powerful drivers of the future vision of the mobile-phone industry to support the technology. Still, we optimistically await the future.

CONCLUSION

This chapter gave an overview of the wireless industry and the value chain that delivers products and services to end customers. There are many players in the chain, but wireless carriers have had the luxury of being the intermediary between the end customers and all the other players. This allows the carriers to capture value. However, as competition has increased and revenues for wireless voice communications have declined, wireless carriers have become interested in providing customers with value-added data services that can halt the trend of declining revenues. All the members of the value chain are looking for ways to add value to the chain. This has spurred efforts to develop new enabling technologies such as 3G, LT, and Bluetooth that can enrich the wireless experience for end customers. Although progress surrounding these technologies has fallen short of the initial hype, it is too soon to pass final judgment on their impact.

References

Abbey, Allen. "MessageVine Makes Wireless Messaging Its Top Priority." *InternetNews* (February 2001).

Anderson, Christoffer. "Mobile Positioning—Where You Want to Be!" (2000).

Angell, Chris. "Bluetooth as a 3G Enabler." *Intercai Mondiale* (2001).

Arthur Andersen. "Fast Forward: Bluetooth—Treading on 3G Territory?" (2001).

Baker, Stephen. "A Killer App for the Wireless Web?" *Business Week* (January 15, 2001).

Bernstein, Jeffrey, Shinichi Yokohama, and George Riedel. "Asia Revalued." *McKinsey Quarterly* (2000).

Bourrie, Sally Ruth. "Location-based Services and Privacy: A Brave New World of Services—or Intrusions?" *Inside Mobile Data* (2000).

"Briefly . . . ," *Wall Street Journal* (April 12, 2001).

Briody, Dan. "Smart Phones Are Dumb." *Red Herring* (March 6, 2001).

Calvert, Michael. *Management Update: A Hot Market Will Force the Outsourcing of Testing Mobile Applications.* Gartner Group (2000).

Charney, Ben. "For Cell Phone Makers, Gen Y = Gen $." *CNET News.com* (March 20, 2001).

_____. "Gambling Fever Spreads to Cell Phones." *CNET News.com* (March 22, 2001).

_____. "IBM and Webraska Push Location Services." *ZDNet News U.S.* (February 2001).

Cornell Data Networking: Wired versus Wireless. Cornell University Office of Information Technologies (2001).

Coster, Paul. "Out of Thin Air." *JP Morgan Securities* (September 29, 2000).

Cukier, Kenneth Neil. "Who Owns the Customer?" *Red Herring* (April 2000).

Deelman, Wouter. "On the Right Track—A Discussion of Location-based Services." *Logica Views Archive* (2001).

Dornan, Andy. "Wireless Ethernet: Neither Bitten nor Blue." *Network Magazine* (April 2001).

"FCC Adopts Rules to Implement Enhanced 911 for Wireless." *CC Docket FCC* (June 1996).

Foley, Theresa. "U.S. Wireless Carriers Send 3G into a Spin." *Communications Week International* (April 2, 2001).

Gold, Steve. "Location-based WAP Technology Tested in Asia." *Newsbytes* (December 2000).

Goldman Sachs. *Mobile Internet Primer, Technology: Mobile Internet.* (2000).

Hamblen, Matt. "Location Information Could Invade Privacy of Wireless Users, Analysts Warn." *Computerworld* (September 2000).

_____. "Why Wireless Needs a Hard Look—It Can Be a Prime Business Driver or Simply a Money Pit." *Computerworld* (March 2001).

Kapner, Suzanne. "Wireless Companies Ask Suppliers to Share Costs." *New York Times,* online ed. (April 4, 2001).

Kwan, Joshua. "New Wireless Technology Tracks Location." *Mercury News* (October 2000).

Latour, Almar. "Swedish Entrepreneur Sees Shortcut to Wireless Services." *Wall Street Journal* (March 23, 2001).

Li, David. "This Could Be Watching You." *New York Post* (January 2001).

LM Ericsson Telephone Co. "3G Spectrum Auctions." (February 20, 2001).

Logica Mobile Networks. "3G: Is the Message Clear?—The Future of Messaging." (2000).

Mathieson, Clive. "Holders of 3G Licenses May Share to Cut Costs." *Times of London,* online ed. (March 3, 2001).

McDonald, Iain, and Graham Morgan. "Modest Bids Mark Australia's 3G Auction." *Wall Street Journal* (March 23, 2001).

Merrill Lynch. "Bluetooth and 802.11b—The Right Tools for the Job." *Merrill Lynch Comment* (December 4, 2000).

_____. "Bluetooth Update—It Will Not Be a Bluetooth Christmas." (November 14, 2000).

_____. "Bluetooth Update—We Are Getting Closer." *Merrill Lynch Update* (February 8, 2001).

Mobile Lifestreams. "Data on 3G: An Introduction to the Third Generation." (2001).

Nokia Networks. *Early Demand for Nokia Multimedia Message Service: A Market Study of MMS* (1999).

"Only Fakirs Need Apply: The Tide Turns against 3G." *Economist* (February 3, 2001).

Pescatore, John. *A Lesson in Managing Security Risk of New Technologies.* Gartner Group (2001).

Romero, Simon. "Locating Devices Gain in Popularity but Raise Privacy Concerns." *New York Times* (March 2001).

Rosenbush, Steve, et al. "Bad Loans Rattle Telecom Vendors: When Upstart Carriers Default, Their Suppliers Take a Hit." *Business Week* (February 19, 2001).

Scott, Nicky, and Ines Respini. "Global Mobile Markets 2001–2005." *Ovum* (January 2001).

Sepenzis, Thomas, Dale Pfau, and Earl Lum. *Unstrung: The Birth of the Wireless Internet.* CIBC World Markets Equity Research (2000).

Smith, Brad. "Another Standard in the Wind." *Wireless Week* (July 6, 2001).

"Sprint, Cingular to Launch 3G Service." *Bloomberg News* (March 20, 2001).

Strategis Group. *Location-based Wireless Services: Consumer Survey 2000* (2000).

"Teething Trouble." *Economist* (December 2, 2001).

"A $250 Billion Gamble: The Telcom Sector Has Overreached Itself." *Economist* (January 27, 2001).

"Two Stumbling Steps to 3G." *The Economist* (December 7, 2000).

Wohlert, Randolph. *Location Based Services—Service Requirements Document.* GSM North America (2001).

Wong, Wylie. "Home Wireless War Rages over Standards." *CNET News.com* (November 28, 2000).

SECTION II

BUSINESS MODELS AND MARKETS

CHAPTER 4

INTERACTIVE TELEVISION

Television has remained relatively unaltered over the past several decades. The methods of broadcasting, the business models, and the roles of the broadcasters and advertisers have been stable and even resistant to change. Interactive television, however, promises to dramatically transform the industry (see Figure 4.1).

In this chapter, we identify the key changes that need to take place in the industry, suggest how interactive television promises to change the players' roles and interactions, and examine the likely evolution of technology and offerings.

HISTORY OF INTERACTIVE TELEVISION

Since its inception, television has been a one-way broadcast medium. Television's search for interactivity with its audience, termed *interactive television* (iTV), has spanned several decades. By examining the history of iTV, we can gain an appreciation for all that has been learned in earlier trials, as well as understand some of the issues facing the iTV initiatives today and tomorrow.

The first truly interactive television program, *Winky Dink and You,* aired from 1953 to 1957. The interactive element of the children's show relied on special plastic sheets that children could attach to the television screen and draw on with crayons. At various times during the show, the children would be asked to draw items on the plastic screen, and the cartoon characters would react to the drawings. CBS eventually canceled the series because of parents' complaints that children were not using the sheets, but instead were drawing directly on the television screen.

In 1979, the English government offered Teletext, which allowed BBC viewers to trade text messages via the telephone. Teletext used the black vertical blanking interval (VBI) between lines of video to transmit data,

Figure 4.1
Continuum of Assumptions

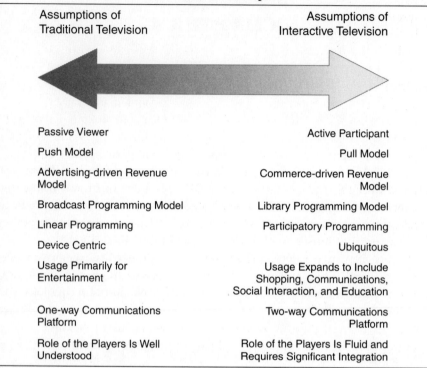

Assumptions of Traditional Television	Assumptions of Interactive Television
Passive Viewer	Active Participant
Push Model	Pull Model
Advertising-driven Revenue Model	Commerce-driven Revenue Model
Broadcast Programming Model	Library Programming Model
Linear Programming	Participatory Programming
Device Centric	Ubiquitous
Usage Primarily for Entertainment	Usage Expands to Include Shopping, Communications, Social Interaction, and Education
One-way Communications Platform	Two-way Communications Platform
Role of the Players Is Well Understood	Role of the Players Is Fluid and Requires Significant Integration

which was displayed on the screen as a page of text. The United Kingdom's Teletext model was adopted by more than a dozen countries. An attempt at U.S. adoption was unsuccessful largely because the FCC chose not to set U.S. Teletext standards. Without such standards, television manufacturers were unwilling to build Teletext functionality into television sets, and having consumers purchase separate hardware to provide the functionality was prohibitively expensive.

The first major iTV service in the United States was Warner Communications' Qube, which began in Columbus, Ohio, in 1977. Qube offered 30 channels of television divided equally between broadcast, pay-per-view, and original interactive channels. The viewer accessed Qube programming with a proprietary remote control that was connected by wire to the set-top box and was used to select channels, order pay-per-view movies, and respond to interactive programming. The interactive programming buttons could be assigned different meanings for different shows such as to poll the audience, respond to questions on live talk shows, answer questions on a quiz show, play interactive games, or purchase goods and services. Although Qube's innovative programming was popular, it was not a sustainable business model because of the high costs of its set-top boxes and other equipment.

In 1994, Time Warner tested the Full Service Network (FSN)—the world's most sophisticated and expensive interactive television service—in Orlando, Florida. FSN offered interactive shopping, games, sports, news, and an electronic program guide, as well as movies on demand. FSN was incredibly complex. File servers stored movies and other content in digital form, and ATM switches transferred the data to a set-top box at a speed of 30 pictures per second. The box itself had five times the computing power of a top-of-the-line PC. Although FSN had tremendous potential, three problems led to its demise. First, Time Warner attempted to do too much too fast and discovered that the complexity of integrating all the services was overwhelming. Second, the high overhead and infrastructure expenses surpassed the market opportunity. Third, the service predated customer demand.

Despite the apparent failure of previous iTV initiatives, they offer several important lessons. First, audiences should not be expected to change their media habits overnight. Television viewing has long been a passive entertainment, and producers of iTV content should be sensitive to this pattern. Second, the integration of iTV services is tremendously complex and requires coordination among several parties including content providers, advertisers, and cable/satellite companies. The costs and difficulty of such an undertaking must not be underestimated. Third, the costs of developing iTV cannot be greater than the value created for consumers. Providers must control the costs passed on to consumers directly through subscription fees. Fourth, producers must learn to be creative with the new medium. To win over the consumer and promote adoption, iTV must provide a compelling value proposition, as well as a killer application. Finally, the full adoption of iTV requires establishing standards because the lack of such standards will discourage the platform-specific investments that are key to providing the most promising services.

Despite the highly publicized iTV failures, companies such as AOL Time Warner, Microsoft, and OpenTV think they will finally make iTV a reality because the Internet experience has given viewers expectations for interactivity. In addition, it is now cheaper and more efficient to deploy iTV, as the existing digital infrastructure greatly reduces technology and hardware costs. For example, adding interactivity through a set-top box costs only 10 percent of what it did just six years ago. These two factors will be the key enablers for the success of iTV in the early twenty-first century.

EVOLUTION OF INTERACTIVE TELEVISION

Before discussing the evolution of iTV, we must define it. For our purposes, iTV refers to the convergence of computing, communications, and entertainment on a television (see Figure 4.2).

Interactive television can offer many services including e-mail, games, shopping, video on demand, access to local community information, and electronic programming guides. The interactivity of iTV can be further defined as simulated, delayed, or real time. In simulated interactivity, interactive functions are performed at consumers' homes without a return path. An example is an electronic program guide (EPG). Delayed interactivity relies on telephone lines to provide upstream paths from set-top boxes. Examples of services are online banking and e-mail. Finally, in real-time interactivity, a high-speed two-way connection between the television and the cable operators and programmers allows for greater manipulation of content. Multiplayer games and interactive programming are examples of real-time interactivities.

Figure 4.2
Convergence of Computing, Communication, and Entertainment in iTV

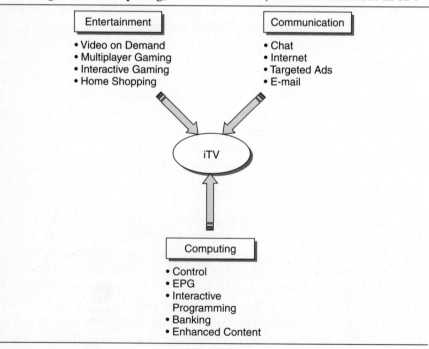

Three models for iTV have emerged. These models and others will determine the shape of iTV in the early twenty-first century.

Personal Video Recorder (PVR) Model

The PVR model (Figure 4.3) is based on the theory that people do not want interactive television; what they want is more control over what they watch. Equipment and services would allow viewers to digitally record video content; to pause, rewind, and impose slow motion on live television; record favorite shows; skip commercials; and easily find programs via an EPG.

Multiple Service Operators (MSO) Model

In the MSO model (Figure 4.4), two-way communications, and the ability to manipulate the information on a viewer's television screen, would be delivered to digital set-top boxes via a cable or satellite provider. This model creates the possibility of customized, targeted programming and advertising determined by viewers' individual preferences. It allows viewers to shop online, conduct online banking, receive targeted advertisements, watch video on demand, play interactive games, and send e-mails to other viewers. In addition to PVR functionality, it gives customers a taste of real interactivity but in a closed space ("walled garden").

Internet Model

In the Internet model (Figure 4.5), content can be delivered via the Internet. This model includes the PVR and MSO model capabilities, as well as

Figure 4.3
PVR Model (TiVo Web Site)

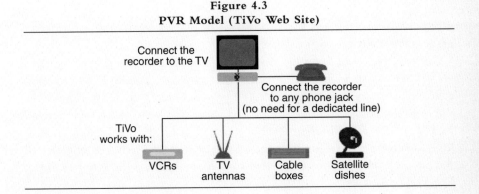

Figure 4.4
MSO Model (WINK Web Site)

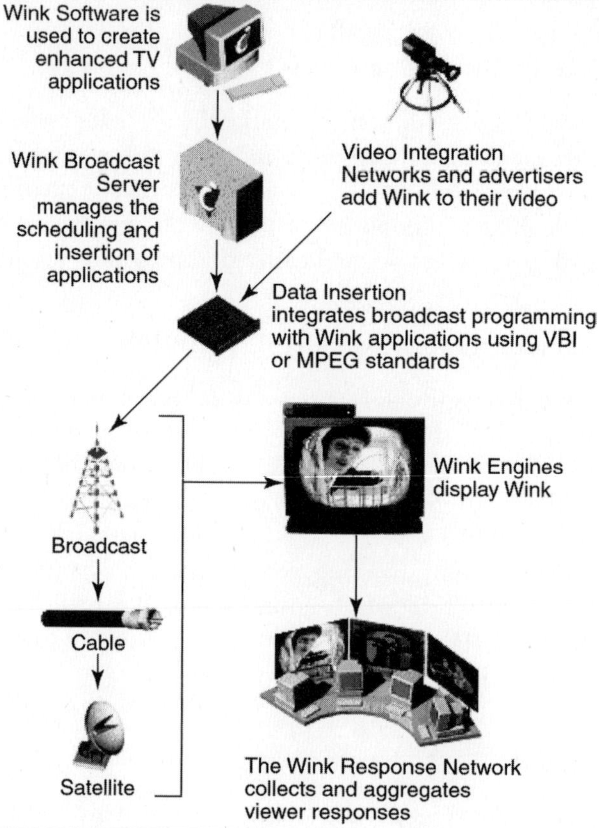

Wink Software is used to create enhanced TV applications

Wink Broadcast Server manages the scheduling and insertion of applications

Video Integration Networks and advertisers add Wink to their video

Data Insertion integrates broadcast programming with Wink applications using VBI or MPEG standards

Wink Engines display Wink

Broadcast

Cable

Satellite

The Wink Response Network collects and aggregates viewer responses

other functions, such as surfing the Web, playing real-time multiplayer games, and chatting with other viewers.

An example of the Internet Model is Yahoo! FinanceVision, with which a viewer can watch anchors read tech-stock stories, explore links to information applicable to the stories, monitor a personal portfolio, get stories for the stocks in the portfolio, trade stocks, and search the Web—all on one screen.

The models differ in their level of interactivity and functionality. Therefore, a convergence of functionality is likely as well as a movement toward the higher levels of interactivity that can be obtained via the Internet model (see Figure 4.6).

Figure 4.5
Internet Model (OpenTV Web Site)

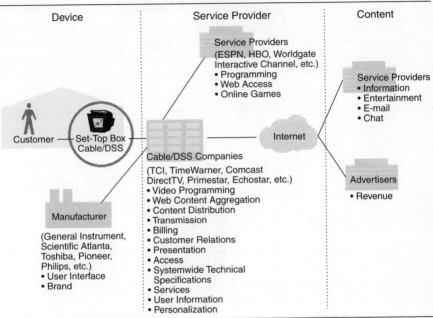

Figure 4.6
ITV Service Offerings by Model

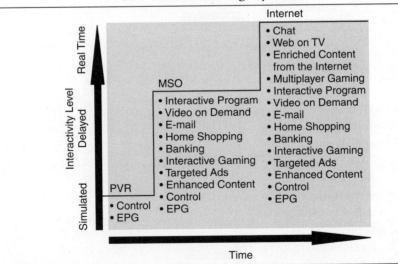

Adoption Forecasts

The adoption dynamics of iTV will likely follow an S-curve: The number of users will grow slowly during the launch, increase rapidly as positive feedback and network externalities kick in, and then taper off as the market nears saturation. At the beginning of 2001, the number of iTV users was approximately 1.7 million. However, many MSOs are currently conducting trials and digitizing their networks to allow for iTV. That number, therefore, is expected to reach 29.4 million users by 2004, 39.5 million users by 2005, and eventually approximate the number of households with television sets, which is nearly 100 percent in the United States. By early 2001, the adoption was in the launch phase: The market was growing slowly and service offerings were being developed. Prior to 2004, however, the iTV industry will face several challenges. How it addresses those challenges and adapts to the needs of users will determine the industry's fate (see Figure 4.7).

First, current iTV users, the innovators and early adopters, are willing to endure bugs and glitches and are technically competent. Nevertheless, to win over the early majority of consumers by 2004, iTV will need to provide a high level of support, compatibility, reliability, and integration. This positioning will require significant enhancements to the technology and significant investments in the support infrastructure. In addition, a killer application must be introduced to attract the early majority.

Figure 4.7
Challenges of iTV

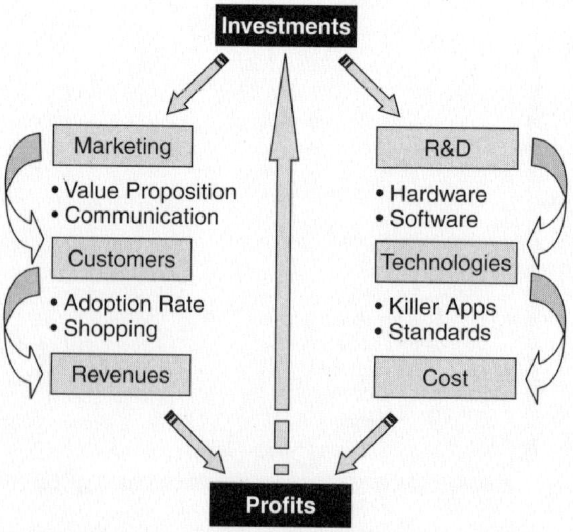

At this point, it appears as though the PVR could be such a killer application. Forrester Research estimated that 80 percent of U.S. households will have a PVR by 2009. However, the market is not developing as quickly as analysts' initial estimates. For example, they expected TiVo to have more than 300,000 subscribers by the end of 1999, but as of the first quarter of 2001, it had only 153,000 subscribers.

The primary reason for the slower-than-expected adoption of this technology is the cost of creating a mass market. Firms in the PVR industry need not only to build brand awareness but also to educate the mass market on the features and benefits of their offering. In fact, TiVo spent more than $50 million in advertising in 2000, but the ads focused on branding and failed to communicate the features and benefits of the product. TiVo claims that branding is central to its marketing strategy and subsequent ads will focus on functionality.

The slow speed of adoption must be taken in context. The rate of adoption for the PVR is greater than the acceptance rate for comparable consumer electronics products such as the VCR and DVD player. As such, many analysts still view the PVR as the killer application of iTV, as indicated by the investments of several prominent companies. For example, AOL invested $200 million in TiVo in September 2000, and work is in progress to combine its TV-based Internet service, AOLTV, with a TiVo box. Also, in 2001 Microsoft began selling its own PVR, UltimateTV, which has essentially the same functionality as a TiVo box, except that it comes with two tuners allowing users to record two programs at the same time. These are positive developments for the industry. Even though TiVo is well financed, it does not alone have the financial resources necessary to create the mass market. The industry will benefit both from the financial resources of AOL and Microsoft in educating the market on the product's unique benefits and from these firms' experience in marketing new and unproven products.

Second, the early majority of consumers will likely be technically less savvy than early adopters, so the iTV interface will need to be simple and intuitive. The task of making it so will be complicated by the users' reliance on a remote control or a keyboard to interface with iTV.

Third, the early majority will be more price sensitive than the innovators and early adopters making it unlikely that the investments in technology and the support infrastructure can be fully passed through to consumers via subscription fees, thus requiring a new revenue model.

Finally, lack of a dominant standard will cause hesitation in adoption, as well as inefficient development efforts.

THE CURRENT STATE OF INTERACTIVE TELEVISION

Interactive television is the dream of science-fiction writers, businesspeople, and engineers—but we are still not sure if anyone else wants it.

—James Stewart, Edinburgh University

Value Propositions

Incumbents. Interactive television provides incumbents in the television industry, such as MSOs, software providers, hardware providers, content providers, and advertisers with a compelling value proposition. For multiple service operators, iTV can provide a competitive advantage by making it possible to deliver the relevant, personalized information viewers want, when they want it. In addition, it allows them to earn additional revenue through a percentage of sales conducted online. For software and hardware providers, it represents an opportunity to enter and potentially shape an emerging high-growth industry. Content providers have a new medium for enhancing traditional television storytelling techniques by giving viewers engaging detail not obtainable in traditional programming. It also provides them with additional revenue opportunities such as product-placement advertising and commerce-revenue-sharing arrangements. Finally, advertisers may have an even more compelling value proposition. With interactive television, they can create richer advertisements and make it easier for consumers to purchase products online. In addition, advertisers can buy space in the interactive portion of the screen in the form of logos or graphics that can be on screen throughout a broadcast, not just in commercials. Most important, the data-collection and aggregation potential of middleware, set-top boxes, and servers could provide detailed demographic and behavioral data about viewers that would allow targeted advertising and more accurate assessment of advertising efforts. It is obvious that businesspeople and engineers "want their iTV," but whether consumers also want it is still an unanswered question (see Figure 4.8).

From the viewer's standpoint, iTV's value proposition is a richer viewing experience. Viewers will have fewer, and presumably less expansive, choices than the Web offers, but the images will be easier to manage on a TV screen with a remote control. Interactive television will by nature be more passive than the Web: It will require less effort on a viewer's part and will be better integrated with the viewing experience.

There may be differences in what viewers perceive as value added and what businesspeople and engineers view as value added. According to a

Figure 4.8
Demand for iTV Features

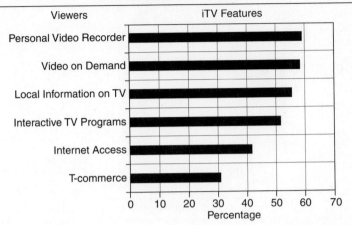

Source: eMarketer, 2000.

Jupiter survey, the most preferred features correspond to existing PVR functionality. Functions such as Web surfing, e-mail, games, or online shopping are not desired, perhaps because people think that they already have them in their console game or computers. Although *Jupiter* considers video on demand (VOD) to be "not economically viable in near-term" for its high cost of implementation, users ranked VOD as the second-most-desired feature in the last Forrester survey. Even if interactivity would attract innovators and early adopters, the iTV market will grow only if companies prove its benefits to the mass market. Therefore, companies will have to create the need for interactivity in the consumer's mind.

Revenue Models

According to *Jupiter,* iTV will generate $9.9 billion in *new* revenues in 2004. As cable and satellite companies compete and incorporate the new interactive service in their costs, commerce, advertising, and access will split the new revenues. Subscriptions and licensing are expected to generate little new revenue because users want interactivity without incurring extra cost (see Figure 4.9).

At present, television revenues come from access, which includes pay-per-view and subscription, advertising, program licensing, and shopping. The iTV revenue model will likely be similar, with some exceptions.

Figure 4.9
ITV Revenues Split in 2004

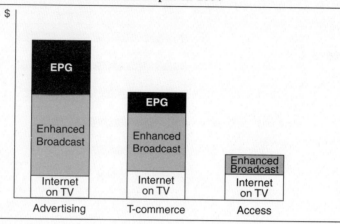

Source: Forrester.

Access (Subscriptions and Pay-per-View). Some pure-play companies, like TiVo, charge a fee for interactivity features such as EPG. *Jupiter* reports this revenue model is not sustainable. Television operators will encourage penetration of interactive services and the revenue streams they provide (i.e., commerce, advertising) by offering interactive services at no additional charge to subscribers, even if a customer does not buy additional digital channels.

Advertising. Advertising has always been the main revenue source of broadcasting and represents 54 percent of television revenues today. Compared with traditional TV advertising, interactive advertising will offer better targeting opportunities. It will also inherit Web advertising techniques such as banners.

According to *Jupiter,* the installed base of users will not reach the critical number necessary to attract mass advertising until 2003. Interactive advertising revenues are expected to increase from $60,000 in 1999 to $1.6 billion in 2003 to $4 billion in 2004.

In the future, TV advertising will come from both infomercial (which currently represents $1 billion) and direct-response advertising (now representing $20 billion). Traditional brand advertisers are very interested in iTV, and many industries like the automotive (e.g., Ford, Daimler-Chrysler), financial services (e.g., Schwab, Wells Fargo), health (e.g., Pfizer), and consumer-packaged goods (e.g., Clorox) have begun testing interactive advertising on Wink. According to Forrester, advertising revenues will come mainly from enhanced broadcast (56 percent), EPG (29 percent), and Web on TV (15 percent).

Program Licensing.   Program licensing today represents 9 percent of TV revenues. In the absence of standard iTV protocols, *Jupiter* expects that iTV programs will be specific to each platform or region and no new revenues will be created from licensing iTV programs.

Hardware.   Consumers now buy set-top boxes for local interactivity. Cable and satellite companies will start to compete and subsidize the hardware in their set-top boxes. Therefore, interactivity will be included in the infrastructure provider's costs and will not generate new revenues.

T-Commerce.   Interactive television's ubiquity and ease of use will enhance the shopping experience and increase t-commerce (or television-based e-commerce) revenues. It will also be a perfect medium for financial services. According to *TechTrends,* even among the consumers interested in banking and investing through iTV, only 6 percent are willing to pay more than $3 per month for the service. Three types of t-commerce will emerge.

Push commerce.   Push commerce will make special offers through commercials or programs. For example, when WebTV viewers in San Francisco were offered a 30 percent discount coupon for Melissa Etheridge CDs from CDNow, the interactive ad's response rate was 22 percent, compared with the typical online response rate of less than 1 percent.

Enhanced shopping channels.   Enhanced shopping channels will give consumers the opportunity to make purchases online. The channels are expected to increase impulse buying.

Virtual mall.   The virtual mall will provide a catalog of products that viewers can access, browse, and order from at any time.

Twenty percent of U.S. households made purchases from a home-shopping network in 1999. Judging by the evolution of Internet shopping, *Jupiter* estimates that iTV commerce will grow from $100,000 in 2001 to $2.2 billion in 2003 and to $5.7 billion in 2004. According to *TechTrends,* 46 percent of U.S. consumers are interested in t-commerce. In addition, *TechTrends* estimates that 80 percent of active home-shopping-network users are interested in t-commerce, and 27 percent are willing to pay a monthly fee for the service. The eventual revenue model of iTV is dependent on the model of iTV that evolves.

PVR Model. After Replay's failure, TiVo is trying to prove that a revenue model based on selling hardware and subscriptions is possible. The subscription supports services such as EPG that make recording easier.

The PVR model's subscription-based revenue model is not viable for the long term, as firms will not be able to continue to charge a fee for providing a simple service. The industry has attempted to overcome this problem by enticing consumers to pay a one-time subscription fee, but this effort has met with limited success for several reasons. First, customers are not willing to pay for a long-life service if they do not know its worth. Second, customers value the flexibility to change from one service provider to another. Third, TiVo's long-term viability, as well as the long-term viability of the embryonic PVR industry, is uncertain.

Another stream of revenues could be generated from advertising. As EPG is the portal to access the programs, advertising on EPG will reach every customer. But if customers do not like seeing advertising on a service they pay for, the PVR model may have difficulty drawing revenues from EPG advertising.

MSO Model. In the MSO model, new revenue streams are possible. First, VOD and interactive games will add pay-per-use revenues to subscription fees. Services like banking, enhanced content, and interactive programming should increase subscription fees. Since access revenue is a mix of subscription and pay-per-use fees, it is unclear which one will be the main driver of revenues. Initially, consumers will pay for the interactivity, and the proportion of pay-per-use fees will increase. Then, competition will drive players to compete on an all-included fee, and a subscription fee will become the main access revenue.

Second, advertising will become more targeted, resulting in a lower cost per target customer for advertisers and premium pricing for iTV companies. In this model, iTV advertising will be perceived as similar to TV advertising—an inconvenience to consumers yet necessary to finance these channels.

Third, the MSO model offers opportunities for higher shopping revenues. Using the same revenue streams as current shopping channels, but being easier to use and more convenient, the MSO model will increase the volume of users buying online.

Internet Model.   The Internet model has mainly the same revenue streams as the MSO model. Additional revenues would come from Internet access and cross-media promotions. For example, the Internet model will allow iTV companies to charge customers higher subscription fees for Internet broadband access, while the click-through fees from cross-media promotion will generate extra advertising revenues (see Figure 4.10).

Summary for Revenue Models.   Because the PVR revenue model is not sustainable, it will merge into the MSO model. The MSO model will evolve toward the Internet model as consumers demand more interactivity, and competition will push MSOs to compete on services rather than on price. As discussed, different players in the value chain favor each model, and their biases will likely affect the evolution of the iTV revenue model. It will evolve toward an increased proportion of t-commerce and advertising. Pay-per-use access fees will increase in the MSO model, whereas subscription fees will increase in the Internet model.

Because of delays in adoption, analysts have cut forecasts for industry revenues dramatically. *eMarketer* estimates that by 2004 iTV revenues will reach $11.4 billion, a far cry from projections made earlier by research firms.

By comparison, Forrester Research cut its iTV forecasts from $20 billion in 2004 to $15.4 billion, and the Myers Group now projects iTV revenues to reach $13.7 billion for the same period (see Table 4.1).

Figure 4.10
Revenue Streams for Different Interactive IV Models

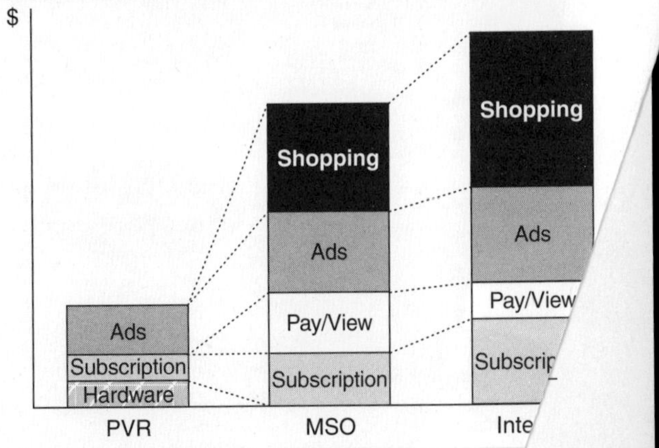

Table 4.1
Comparative Estimates

ITV Value Chain
Comparative Estimates: Total ITV Revenues, 1999–2004 (in Millions)

	1999 ($)	2000 ($)	2001 ($)	2002 ($)	2003 ($)	2004 ($)
eMarketer	665	1,636	3,001	4,672	7,406	11,432
Myers Group	665	920	1,680	4,040	7,300	13,650
Forrester Research	665	1,665	3,509	5,994	10,262	15,389

Data Source: eMarketer, 2000; www.eMarketer.com; various as noted. © 2000 eMarketer, Inc.

The iTV value chain consists of five main segments, as shown in Figure 4.11.

Infrastructure Providers (MSOs). The main role of the MSOs is to provide "pipes," or channels, to transfer data to a viewer's home. The data may be in the form of video or sound. The MSOs also bundle the programming ntent so that the viewer receives all channels through a single pipe.

players. There are three key players in this space: cable pro-
igital satellite providers, and telecommunications companies (see
12).

Figure 4.11
Current iTV Landscape

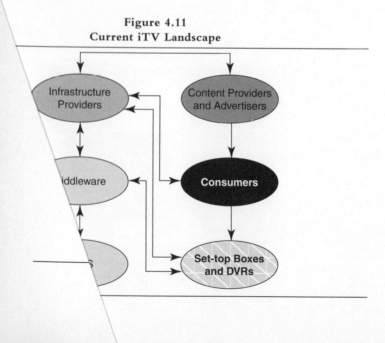

Figure 4.12
Traditional Infrastructure Layout

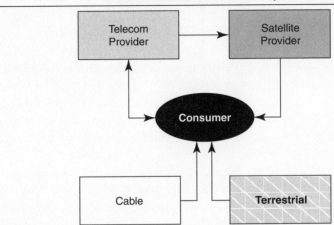

Cable providers have been the traditional carriers of television, and for over three decades they have dominated the transmission of TV to homes. With the acceptance of the Internet, cable providers needed to provide higher bandwidth to increase data-transfer rates and to provide two-way communication capabilities. As a result, they invested, and are investing, in hybrid fiber coax (HFC) and two-way optical fibers.

In the past few years, the digital broadcast-satellite (DBS) providers have been increasing rapidly. In fact, the digital broadcast-satellite industry has more than 14 million paying subscribers. DBS services grew quickly because the digital signal provided better picture quality, and satellite broadcasts could reach places where cable could not. DBS services, however, can provide only one-way interactivity and must partner with the telecom providers for two-way interactivity. The main DBS players in the United States are EchoStar and DirecTV, both of whom have made EPGs available on their set-top receivers. They have also been aggressively building alliances through strategic technology and marketing partnerships with companies such as OpenTV, Microsoft's WebTV, and TiVo.

Telecommunications companies are providing broadband technologies, such as integrated-services digital network (ISDN) connections, xDSL (where the x stands for several variants, such as A,H,S,V), T-1 and T-3 pipes, and fiber.

Sensing a threat from DBS, the cable providers invested billions in their movement from analog systems toward digital cable. This enables them to supply more channels as well as a platform for interactivity. Players like

AT&T, Insight, and Comcast are adding interactive applications such as video on demand on their digital cable network. These actions have led to strategic alliances between the cable companies, studios, and solution providers, such as DIVA, SeaChange, nCUBE, and Intertainer.

A major factor shaping the landscape of the iTV industry is the AOL Time Warner merger. It brings programmers and broadcasters together and gives them incentives to develop interactive content that will be carried over AOLTV's service network. Thus, the AOLTV platform is fueling the rapid growth of the industry by developing new interactive programming and by expanding the reach of interactive offerings. AOLTV allows consumers to access popular AOL tools such as e-mail, instant messaging, and chat while watching regular television programming. AOL has also heavily invested in General Motors' Hughes Electronics, which owns DirecTV, and has struck partnerships with iTV middleware providers such as Liberate and TiVo for the AOLTV platform. AOL and TiVo have announced a three-year strategic agreement in which TiVo will become an AOLTV programming partner, offering AOLTV subscribers access to features of TiVo's Personal TV Service. Under the agreement AOL and TiVo will work together to develop a dual-purpose AOLTV-branded set-top box, and TiVo will become the exclusive provider of personal TV features on these boxes.

Key issues.   Five major issues converge on the infrastructure arena:

1. *Migration to digital.* Whereas satellite companies already broadcast digital signals, cable companies will need to migrate from analog to digital platforms to offer interactive services. This will require an investment of billions of dollars and will take time to complete.
2. *Pressure on profits.* Since many players are competing for market share in the backbone infrastructure, the intense rivalry will fuel the need to keep costs down and simultaneously ensure better service. As infrastructure companies try to attract customers to spread their fixed costs, they will enter into a battle to add more and more features to their services or compete on price. Added features and lower prices will accelerate growth but will also drive the infrastructure providers' profit down, perhaps limiting the investments they are willing to make.
3. *Customer-service skills.* The infrastructure providers currently charge the consumer for providing the basic service of data transfer. However, as interactivity and commerce via iTV grow, the MSOs will have to invest in billing systems and customer-service capabilities. They will have to provide support to their customers and continuously upgrade services to compete effectively.

4. *Control of the consumer interface.* As t-commerce grows, MSOs will compete with other segments of the value chain to control the consumer interface. This rivalry will be costly for all parties involved.

5. *Strategic partnerships and mergers.* As the need to provide greater interactive content increases, MSOs will have to form strategic alliances with content providers and software providers, who will ensure that the consumer receives seamless interactive content.

Software Providers. *Middleware* is a general term for any programming that serves to mediate, or "glue together," two separate and usually already-existing programs. Middleware in iTV manages the video display and other basic television functions; serves applications such as the EPG; accesses the Internet, e-mail, and interactive graphic walled-garden environments; provides video on demand, and enables services such as multicamera digital-video switching.

Key players. This industry is in its embryonic state: It is highly fragmented, and there are many competing technologies. Our discussion is limited to a few prominent middleware platforms such as Liberate, OpenTV, and Microsoft TV.

Liberate has a modular platform based on open Internet and international broadcast standards. To proliferate its platform, Liberate established programs to educate content and software developers. It also made strategic mergers with MoreCom (a complex, IP-over-cable middleware platform) and SourceMedia (middleware for thin set-top boxes—those with a small hardware footprint such as DCT-1200s and 2000s) and with iTV portals such as MetaTV to extend capabilities.

OpenTV has been successful in installing its proprietary middleware platform on DBS networks in Europe, Latin America, and now with Dish-Network in the United States. OpenTV merged with Spyglass (developer of small-footprint, IP-based middleware) to offer access to the Internet and to appliances such as set-top boxes and televisions.

On the other hand, Microsoft has developed a complete end-to-end iTV back-end architecture platform called Microsoft TV (MSTV), which incorporates Windows CE and WebTV software. WebTV introduced a stand-alone set-top box with an information and Internet service in 1996. It quickly grabbed media and consumers' attention with low prices and ease of access. WebTV (purchased by Microsoft in 1997 for $400 million) has a subscriber base of more than one million. It obtained space on several MSOs' set tops in Europe and Japan, as well as on DishNetwork. MSTV offers services such as watching TV with the image of another channel reduced on screen (called "picture in picture," or PIP), a walled garden, Javascript support, banking and bill-payment services, surveillance software, an EPG, and Web-page-building tools. WebTV's set-top products include Classic, Plus, and WebTV for Windows 98—the last two featuring two-way VBI broadcasting. To ensure deployment with a prominent cable operator, Microsoft paid AT&T $5 billion and has invested in networks around the world. In September 2000, however, Microsoft announced it was unable to deliver MSTV to AT&T or to UPC in full, causing both companies to sign with Liberate. Thus, it is not clear whether cable operators will truly buy into this Windows-based, resource-intensive system.

Data-Enhancement Broadcasting Services.   Data enhancements appear as graphic and information elements on the overlaying screen. They may be opaquely colored and cover the broadcast in part or may be transparent or semitransparent. Elements such as icons, banners, labels, menus, interface structures, open text fields in which the viewer can insert his or her e-mail address, forms to fill out to buy a product, or commands to retrieve and manage video streams and graphics on a relevant Web page are most common. Enhancements can be part of the television program or may be irrelevant to the current programming, such as news, stocks, scores, weather, and so on.

Key players.   This space is also in its embryonic state and has many competitors. We focus on prominent players such as Gemstar's TV Guide, Wink Communications, TiVo, WorldGate, RespondTV, and Mixed Signals.

The most commonly used example of enhancement is EPG, widely available on digital cable and DBS systems. An EPG appears interactively when one calls it to view by pushing a button on the remote control or by some other method. Once it displays, the EPG allows the viewer to easily navigate or search for programming by time, theme, channel, and so on. The Gemstar TV Guide merger is leading the development of EPGs. Because EPGs are the portal application to the new television experience, many companies are trying to develop their own versions of the EPG out of Gemstar's purview. Software providers, such as MetaTV, are offering software solutions that enable the networks to create their own portals across different middleware platforms and set-top boxes. This allows network operators to scale their interactive content and programs rather than customize for each set-top-box platform. The idea of a cable-network-branded portal is very appealing to the network operators, but the resolution of EPG patent issues concerning Gemstar remain to be seen. Gemstar controls many of the patents surrounding this technology and is vigorously pursuing patent-infringement litigation.

TiVo leads the deployment of EPGs by coupling an online data-service broadcast through the phone line to a set-top box with a recordable digital-video hard-disk drive. These units influence how the average person becomes familiar with the availability of such video-based interactive services.

Another player, Replay TV, was also involved in the deployment of EPGs through PVRs. However, Replay TV's business model was very expensive because it manufactured and sold its PVRs without charging a subscription fee. In October 2000, Replay changed its business model from manufacturing and selling PVRs to licensing its technology to MSOs. In January 2001, it was acquired by SonicBlue, and in addition to licensing, the company is now trying again to sell high-end PVRs to early adopters as its ReplayTV 4000 product line.

More examples of iTV-like video programming include the data boxes, or elements that appear in the corner of the TV screen during music videos on MTV or when a game player sets up a Nintendo, PlayStation, or Sega console. Here the player navigates graphic or text elements with a keyboard or joystick to select the difficulties of the game or learn about its rules. One of the major players behind technology for enhancement software is Wink Communications. Wink's services include downloadable software to a set-top box, a proprietary and Advanced Television Enhancement Forum (ATVEF)-compliant data-enhancement broadcasting service, and a special back-end tracking and billing environment called the Wink Response Network. Wink has established many partnerships with prominent media companies such as MSNBC, the Discovery Channel, the Weather Channel, E! Entertainment Television, DirecTV, and others. It also received multimillion-dollar investments from Microsoft and Paul Allen's Vulcan Ventures. Wink tries to provide a limited, yet interactive, choice to the viewer. When the icon *i* is presented on a WebTV screen, for example, the viewer can click on it to bring up the interactive enhancement from an advertiser or content provider. In a Wink environment, it might be a simple query to ask if the viewer wants more information on a product from the advertiser or data from a content provider such as the Weather Channel.

Another competitor in this space, WorldGate, delivers a URL trigger within network broadcasts that viewers can click with the remote. Called Channel Hyperlinking, WorldGate's system is proprietary, although it has announced support for ATVEF.

Two other companies focus on iTV broadcasting-infrastructure technologies and services, RespondTV and Mixed Signals. RespondTV and

Mixed Signals pride themselves on their broadcast servers and enabling technologies, which permit them to send out full ATVEF-compliant data broadcasts wherever the VBI and, eventually, digital signal will carry them. RespondTV has had much success signing advertisers and content providers to its services (e.g., Bloomberg, HGTV, MSNBC, Domino's, Purina). Mixed Signals has a special arrangement with Sony's Columbia Tri-Star and Game Show Network to present the iTV version of various game shows.

Key issues

- *Lack of standards.* The software market of iTV is rich with new players and technologies. In fact, this link of the iTV value chain has the highest number of new players and technologies. The reason may be that the space is still evolving and is at the innovator/early adopter stage, which means that no single software provider has enough power to make its technology the software standard. So a standards battle will erupt in iTV just as it did in the high-definition-TV industry.
- *Many languages.* Three main languages are used in the software for iTV: Windows CE, Java, and HTML. It is unclear which language will emerge as the standard.
- *Alliances and partnerships.* Problems in the software space are compounded by uncertainty and by the lack of standards, killer applications, and compatible software. The situation is forcing many alliances and partnerships between software providers and players up and down the value chain.

Hardware Providers—Set-Top Box Manufacturers and PVRs. The main role of the hardware providers is to provide hardware that will enable existing television sets to interact with the Internet and to receive and decode television broadcasts. The hardware also needs to provide PC-like functions such as memory, processing, and storage of data. The hardware market consists of strong incumbents as well as new entrants. The incumbents focus on products like set-top boxes, which have been in use for some time, whereas new players are introducing new hardware platforms.

Key players. The main manufacturers of set-top boxes are Motorola (which acquired General Instruments in early 2000), Scientific Atlanta, Pace Micro, Mitsubishi, Sony, and Thomson. Their boxes contain video and audio microprocessors, memory, conditional-access technology, a cable modem, middleware to control or to enhance their capabilities, and other technologies.

For the other piece of hardware, the PVR, the market leader is TiVo, which contracts out the manufacturing of its boxes to firms such as Sony and Philips. As of December 31, 2000, TiVo's installed subscriber base was 136,000, a growth of 86 percent over the previous year. Forrester projects that sales of PVRs should increase to 53 million by 2005. Constraints on the adoption of this technology include the complication of setting up the units and their expense. Deals by TiVo, such as the one with AOLTV, may encourage the diffusion of TiVo's technology.

Key issues

- *Lack of standards.* Standards issues plague this segment of the value chain as well. Current standards increase the power of incumbents. If interoperability increases with open standards, however, power may shift from the incumbents to innovative new entrants.
- *Manufacturing capabilities.* The hardware market is expected to show rapid growth, in tune with the overall industry, although uncertainty in adoption rates will cause challenges in planning manufacturing scale.

Content Providers and Advertisers. Content determines the popularity of programs and channels—it is the main offering to the end consumer. Thus, it is essential that as iTV evolves, the content increases interactivity with audiences. Content providers and advertisers have a symbiotic relationship. Content drives audiences, and advertisers are attracted to audiences driving revenues of content.

Key players. The key content players are TV studios—Paramount TV, Universal Studios, Sony Entertainment, Columbia Tristar, CNBC, and CNN. Content providers also include firms in the film industry such as Walt Disney, DreamWorks, Fox Movies, New Line Cinema, and Paramount. The advertisers are companies that create advertising and manage the media monies of their clients. Their major clients include the automobile manufacturers, the packaged-goods manufacturers, and services. Even in these early stages, certain types of iTV programming are beginning to thrive in the commercial setting. They include EPGs, synchronized TV applications, and integrated iTV programming such as interactive news, sports, 3-D games and game shows (like MTV's *WebRiot*, Columbia-Tristar's *Jeopardy* on WebTV, and ABC's enhanced *Monday Night Football*), home shopping, court programs, weather channels, educational documentaries, and advertising.

Key issues

- *Lack of standards.* There are no standard formats for making content. Because of the inefficiencies in enhancing content for multiple platforms, there will be a need for common standards as iTV evolves, to make formats transferable across content providers.
- *Greater customization.* Those producing iTV shows and applications need to customize their offerings more and more on an interest-group level, each with a different perspective, agenda, and style of communication. This will ultimately evolve to highly personalized content, maybe even on an individual basis.
- *Need to increase production budgets.* A producer now spends between $70,000 and $3 million developing interactive content. These budgets need to increase as technology improves and audiences demand more choice and functionality.
- *New sources of revenues.* Revenues may come from the viewers through tiered subscriptions or through revenue-sharing agreements with other providers in the value chain. Additional revenues will come from interactive and/or targeted advertising. Viewers may enjoy the accessibility of products relevant to the programming.
- *Change in programming approach.* Creators of content presently follow a linear/script-driven approach. For iTV to become a reality, the programming must be more interactive; and to achieve that, content providers and advertisers will have to change the way they make content or ads. The iTV landscape is summarized in Table 4.2.

THE FUTURE OF INTERACTIVE TELEVISION

Sometimes viewers want to relax and let producers and schedulers control the flow of the narrative and the programming. Other times, viewers are looking for information, trying to learn, or sharing time with friends. In the future, ITV will reflect these multiple uses. Personal computers will not take over television, nor will interactive television take over the PC. The question is not whether the PVR model, MSO model, or Internet model will dominate—it is how these very different services and models, each with its own distinct advantages and disadvantages, will converge to increase value to the consumer.

Table 4.2
Summary of the Current iTV Landscape

	Key Payers	Key Issues
Infrastructure providers	Echostar, DirecTV, AT&T, Insight, Comcast, AOL Time Warner	• Migration to digital • Pressure on profits • Customer-service skills • Control of consumer interface
Middleware and DEBS	Liberate, OpenTV, Microsoft TV, Wink Communications, TiVo, Ultimate TV, Meta TV	• Lack of standards • Many languages • Alliances and partnerships
Set-top boxes and PVRs	Motorola, GI, Scientific Atlanta, Pace Micro, Philips, Sony	• Lack of standards • Manufacturing capabilities
Content providers and advertisers	Paramount TV, Universal Studios, Sony, CNN, Clients like Packaged Goods, Auto Manufacturers	• Lack of standards • Greater customization • Need to increase production budgets • New revenue sources • Programming approach

Consumer-Centric Approach to Functionality

The fundamental shift just described will focus on key benefits that will provide utility for viewers. These benefits include convenience and productivity, enhanced entertainment, and social interaction. To achieve these benefits, television will be transformed from a broadcast, passive, linear, entertainment experience to an on-demand, two-way communications platform. It will be broadband, participatory, and nonlinear; and it will feature infotainment and targeted-advertising (see Figure 4.13).

Convenience and Productivity. The key benefits that iTV will provide are convenience and productivity. As people continue to become more time starved, they will increasingly look for convenience and time-saving services as key sources of value. The functionality of iTV will develop with this consumer benefit in mind. The industry will accomplish this in several ways.

First, iTV will allow users to exercise more control over their viewing experience and will permit them to do so at their own leisure. Examples exist today in products such as PVRs and EPGs. The evolution of

Figure 4.13
Consumer Benefits and Value Creation

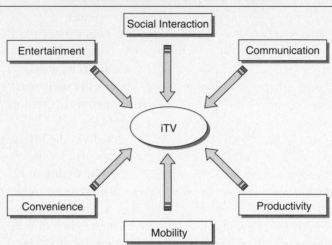

convenience offerings will likely be much more robust in the future. No longer will viewers need to program a device to record shows for later viewing, but they will be able to access distributed recordings of shows to watch at will. There will be less reliance on broadcasting, as more of a "library model" develops, whereby viewers download programs, much like they borrow books or rent videos today. This will likely evolve from a system that digitally stores content on large servers and sends it to viewers on request to a peer-to-peer system in which individuals store and serve programming that can be shared with the world.

Evolution will likely mirror the current evolution in the distribution of other types of media, such as music files, but will take place much more slowly because of the enormous storage and bandwidth requirements for audio and visual media. Privacy and intellectual-property restrictions also will hamper development.

Second, iTV will allow individuals to tailor content to their needs. This evolution is being observed on Internet services such as MyYahoo! which allows users to tailor content such as news and weather to their liking. In the world of iTV, this tailoring will be much more robust. Viewers will be able to tailor not only the type of news content that they watch (local, business, international, etc.) but also the source of the content in an à la carte manner (CNN for breaking news, ESPN for sports, Financial Times for international news, etc.). In addition, viewers will be able to specify the level of detail, the medium used (video, text, photo), and how they are notified (e.g., breaking news is automatically pushed to the viewer, whereas the viewer must pull less critical news). Intelligence built into the software will automatically suggest content of interest to the viewer.

Third, advertisers will be able to narrowly target users and deliver the right advertising to the right person. However, users will have more control over this (such as being able to choose which ads to watch) and will be able to extract value for their time via arrangements such as allowing the iTV company to use their personal data for targeted advertising in return for lower subscription fees.

Fourth, many services that are currently offered via the Internet, such as home banking and shopping, will become available via iTV. Interactive television will provide an easy-to-use and convenient way to shop at home. It will evolve from an online catalog model to a much more open model in which consumers can retrieve additional information, make product comparisons, virtually try on clothing, and purchase items at the click of a button. The goods that are advertised, placed in programming, or shown in the virtual malls will be adjusted to the individuals' tastes and preferences on the basis of demographic data, individual profiles, or past behavior. Other services also will evolve. For example, telemedicine may help to provide people in rural areas with access to specialists. It could also spare patients with chronic illnesses the inconvenience of having to repeatedly visit a clinic for testing.

Finally, iTV promises to provide a rich medium for on-demand, interactive educational services. Educators do not anticipate that iTV will take over the classroom, which provides students with important behavioral and social learning experiences, but they believe it can supplement the classroom. This is especially desirable for continuing professional education classes, where geography and logistics are a barrier, and for rural or poor communities that lack the resources to provide broad educational opportunities.

Enhanced Entertainment. Interactive television promises to provide users with richer, personalized entertainment. No longer will consumers receive only mass-broadcast static content—they will be able to interact and control the content. In the short term, the enhanced entertainment will include individualized tailoring of content; games on demand; polling; and interactive game shows, talk shows, and children's programming. In the long term, more interesting possibilities emerge.

Viewers will be able to control the content of programming and even be part of it. Examples include "be-your-own director," multithreaded programs, "thinkies," virtual reality, and smart characters. In be-your-own-director programming, the viewer would have control over camera angles, camera placement, and the action of the characters. Stories could unfold in different ways according to the viewers' decisions. Likewise, a multithreaded program would allow the audience, either in aggregate or individually, to make choices throughout the program that would result in different situations and different outcomes. This style of programming is analogous to the "choose-your-own-adventure" children's books. Finally, thinkies would allow the viewer to take the role of a character in a nonlinear program and to interact with "smart characters" with built-in behavior patterns. This type of entertainment experience would be unlike anything available today because it would not be based on a script or set of outcomes. The viewer would actually control the entertainment experience on an individual level.

The advent of virtual reality will take these experiences one step further. Similar entertainment experiences will be available, but the viewer will be able to experience the entertainment in a multidimensional, multisensory fashion. The technology will also offer viewers additional entertainment experiences such as virtual vacations.

Social Interaction.   Interactive television will evolve toward a new level of social interaction. In a first step, interaction will be between users at home and a group of users in a studio. For example, users at home could answer questions during a show and if their responses were correct, they could participate live (which presupposes that iTV users would have a camera and two-way video-network access at home). In the future, there is likely to be more social interaction between users. Audio/visual chat will allow users to discuss a program and to virtually come together in social situations. Multiplayer games will give users opportunities to play championships and interact with each other. Another type of one-to-one interaction includes videoconferencing (see Figure 4.14).

Migration to the Network Model

To imagine the evolution of iTV in the long-term future, we examined trends affecting the Internet (tailored information and convergence of data, sounds, and video), current technologies (LCD, digital light projection, synchronization and convergence of devices, improvement of remote control, image and sound quality, wireless-communications infrastructure). We then projected the evolution of those technologies in terms of consumer needs and wants.

The three distinct models of iTV described earlier will not survive into the long-term future. Each has certain benefits that consumers will value, but

Figure 4.14
Consumer Benefits and Value Creation

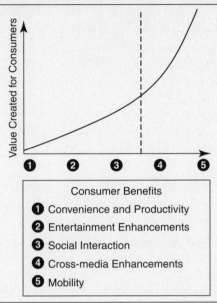

each also has certain limitations such as lack of mobility and the device-centric nature of the models. These three models will converge and evolve into what we term the "network model" of iTV. It will contain the best features of each model, such as the control functionality of the PVR model, the enhanced-entertainment and convenience aspects of the MSO model, and the communications and rich media capabilities of the Internet model. The primary differences of the network model are that intelligence and content will be distributed to the network, iTV will become increasingly mobile, and multiple technologies and media will converge in one device or be built into many different single devices. No longer will iTV be device centric, as it is today, but it will become network centric and become an increasingly inseparable part of our lives (Figure 4.15).

Cross-Media Enhancements. Cross-media enhancements refer to the convergence of media such as broadcast, video on demand, program on demand, multiplayer games, Internet and videoconferencing, and mobile communications, linked with an enhanced experience of watching television.

New technologies will improve the interaction between users and devices. The old-style remote control or keyboard will be improved to fit new functions such as games, Web surfing, participation in shows, or

Figure 4.15
Migration/Convergence to the Network Model

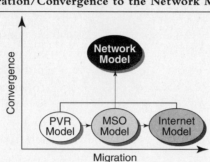

communications with people. In the long term, there will be new and more intuitive interfaces, such as voice recognition or other biometric controls. Through these new interfaces, users will benefit from enhanced functionality, simplicity, and ease of use.

Thanks to the improvement of screens and the quality of high-fidelity systems, iTV will enrich the user experience. Better imaging and sound clarity will help users to experience a more virtual and entertaining experience. Digital-image projection and LCD screens suggest what iTV will look like. The television set of today will give way to flat, pliable screens and digital projection. People will be able to project images on any support or even in the air. Interactive television will conveniently migrate to any place where an image is visible and could be an easy way to decorate a house or an office. Experiments on digital glasses, three-dimension, and holograms are the first step toward virtual television.

Some features, such as interactive games and the programming-on-demand features of the cross-media model, will need high bandwidth and storage capacity. As computers and servers move toward more processing power and storage capacity, networks will evolve toward higher bandwidths. Within 20 years, a large portion of the U.S. population will be connected to networks through fiber to the home, which will have a dramatic effect on the services and content that iTV can offer.

Mobility Enhancements. In the PDA industry, Palm accomplished a breakthrough with a device that complements, rather than substitutes for, the personal computer. In the same way, iTV will develop toward devices that complement, rather than substitute for, television. A portable iTV will not be the transposition of iTV onto a wireless device. To be viable, it will have to complement iTV and create new customer benefits.

Mobility enhancements presuppose that hardware will converge toward a lightweight and connected device that will allow consumers to use it anywhere. Miniaturization is the enabling technology of mobile iTV.

As ISP and portals give people space to store data or create their own pages, iTV will evolve toward a distributed storage device for personal video, music, and information on servers that users will be able to retrieve from anywhere. Mobility also suggests that many devices will share data, which assumes a function of automatic synchronization.

Impact on the Players' Landscape

The long-term emergence of the network model will radically affect the iTV players' landscape.

New Networks.   New networks that are not now a part of the iTV landscape will start interacting with the current iTV network as defined in Figure 4.11. The following three additions are likely:

1. A financial network consisting of billing systems, credit-card companies, and credit providers.
2. A mobile communications network consisting of an entire m-commerce value chain from devices to content providers.
3. A supply/demand chain consisting of networks of all firms participating in t-commerce. It will include their manufacturing, distribution, and logistics systems, as well as the systems of their suppliers (see Figure 4.16).

Peer-to-Peer Networking.   Another change will be that peer-to-peer (P2P) networking will develop among consumers. Thus, the networks of one consumer will interact with the networks of other consumers, and consumers will share services such as a library of programs with each other (see Figure 4.17).

Value in the Networked Landscape.   Our final predictions for the industry landscape are based primarily on a framework developed by Mohanbir Sawhney and Dave Parikh in "Where Value Lives in a Networked World," which appeared in the January 2001 issue of the *Harvard Business Review*.

Figure 4.16
Interaction of Different Networks Creating the iTV Network Model

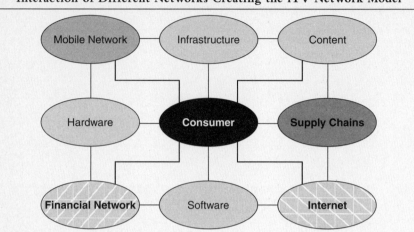

The section on the iTV value chain earlier in this chapter provides a detailed discussion of the key issues (see Table 4.3).

Network externalities through partnerships. We predict a huge increase in alliance and partnering activities across value chains to maximize the externalities of different networks. New business models that reflect complex revenue-sharing arrangements among producers, set-top box vendors, software providers, MSOs, shopping vendors, ISPs, advertisers, and billing vendors will be developed. These arrangements will require partnerships and increased interaction among the members of the value chain.

Figure 4.17
P2P Networking of Consumer Services in the iTV Network Model

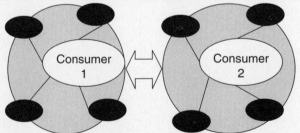

Table 4.3
Expected Industry Patterns

	Key Issues	Expected Response	Intelligence Migration	Value Migration
Infrastructure providers	• Migration to digital • Pressure on profits • Customer-service skills • Control of consumer interface • Alliances and partnerships	• Greater investment required • Economies of scale more important • Alliances with billing/finance companies • Centralization required • Network with lots of players in value chain	• Core—consolidated, centralized, scalable	• Core—value migrates to core. Those that establish the preeminent networks extract greatest value.
Software providers	• Lack of standards • Many languages • Alliances and partnerships	• Standards • Open languages used • Networks with hardware providers, content, infrastructure, and so on formed	• Distributed—more modular, decentralized, flexible, personalized	• Distributed—value migrates to periphery of network
Hardware providers	• Lack of standards • Manufacturing capabilities	• Standards • Many new devices, especially mobile and tablet devices	• Distributed—multiple devices, modular, flexible	• Distributed—value migrates to periphery of network
Content providers and advertisers	• Lack of standards • Greater customization, changed programming approach • Need to increase production budgets • New revenue sources	• Standards • Flexible, personalized programming • More flexible and decentralized to raise new revenues • Decentralized, contextualized programming	• Distributed—decentralized, user centric, personalized, contextual content, highly intelligent at front end	• Value migrates to periphery of network

Value remaining at the core.   The current subscription or access monies for infrastructure players may dry up. Set-top boxes may become free, and consumers will not have to pay subscription fees, as the revenue model will be focused on t-commerce and advertising. As the shift happens toward t-commerce, greater centralization, scaling, and increased robustness of infrastructure will be necessary. These activities will create value at the core that infrastructure providers will capture as utility or service suppliers to the rest of the value chain.

Value migrating to the periphery.   As the industry evolves and standards are established in content, software, and hardware, many new players employing common standards will emerge, and fragmentation will increase in the content, devices, and software networks. Those firms that are best able to adapt to the fluidity of the industry architecture will reap the rewards.

Challenges and Considerations

Privacy.   As iTV becomes an increasingly digital environment, privacy takes on significance. The risk is that servers, middleware, and databases will potentially be able to track viewer behavior and preferences and will share the information with third parties such as advertisers. Efforts at regulating this space have so far been unsuccessful. California State Senator Debra Bowen introduced a bill to regulate privacy standards, but it was defeated by strong pressure from ISPs, Microsoft, and AOL. However, as t-commerce becomes more significant, the pressure will intensify for either industry self-regulation or legal regulation.

Standards.   The lack of uniform technological standards could prove the biggest obstacle to widespread use of ITV in the near future. It affects the industry in many ways. Without standards, MSOs are understandably hesitant to invest millions of dollars in upgrading their plants and equipment because those costs would be sunk should an MSO choose a format that does not emerge as the standard. Also, a lack of standards causes unnecessary duplication of effort in the creation of enhanced programming and restricts the content because the costs of enhancing a program are the same whether the program is shown in five cities or fifty.

Common specifications will accelerate the creation and distribution of enhanced television programs and allow viewers to enjoy such programs cost-effectively and conveniently, no matter which transport or broadcast receiver they use. Such a specification would also allow content providers and distributors to choose from several enhanced-television business models and delivery methods.

The two primary organizations shaping iTV standards in the United States are the ATVEF and CableLabs' OpenCable project. AVTEF has defined protocols for television programming enhanced with data such as Internet content. Its goal is to allow content creators to design enhanced programming for delivery over any form of transport (analog or digital TV, cable, or satellite) to all types of broadcast receivers. The founders of AVTEF are among the most prominent companies in the broadcast and cable industry, the consumer electronics industry, and the computer and software industries. They include CableLabs; CNN; DIRECTV, Inc.; Discovery Communications, Inc. (DCI); Walt Disney Company; Intel Corporation; Microsoft Corporation/WebTV Networks, Inc.; NBC Multimedia, Inc.; Network Computer, Inc. (NCI); NDTC Technology; Public Broadcasting Service (PBS); Sony Corporation; Tribune Company; and Warner Brothers. Over 130 companies have adopted the AVTEF standards.

CableLabs is a nonprofit research and development consortium of cable-television-system operators representing North and South America. Its members, such as ALLTELL, AT&T Broadband, CableOne, and Time Warner Cable, serve more than 85 percent of cable subscribers in North and South America. CableLabs' OpenCable project is an interoperability initiative supported by more than 400 cable-television companies, software-technology companies, and hardware manufacturers. Its goal is to attain interoperable standards for digital set-top boxes and other advanced digital devices manufactured by multiple vendors. OpenCable reached its initial goal—a standard for a common hardware platform for digital cable-television set-top boxes and other digital devices deployed by North American cable operators—in mid-2000 with the availability of interoperable point-of-deployment (POD), or removable security, modules. Since then, it has been working on setting standards for middleware. In March 2001, CableLabs released for comment the OpenCable Application Platform (OCAP), or middleware, specifications. The specification has two major components: An execution engine (EE) will provide a programmable environment, and a presentation engine (PE), similar to a Web browser, will support the creation and use of the Web's standardized markup and scripting languages—HTML and ECMAScript. Although OCAP is a separate effort from the ATVEF's content specification, it calls for support and extension of ATVEF as a part of the PE requirements.

Intellectual Property.   The future of iTV is content and technology. As iTV becomes more distributed, and the supporting infrastructure for efficiently transferring content is developed, intellectual-property rights will become a critical issue. The two types of intellectual-property protection that will be important are copyrights and patents.

Copyrights protect "works of authorship" from unencumbered copying and dissemination. Interactive television content such as programming will fall under this category. Cases such as *RIAA v. MP3.com* provide insight into how network technology can dramatically affect information and digital-content businesses and disrupt every element of the value chain. Because of the difficulty of enforcing copyright in a distributed network, technologies to protect iTV content from piracy, such as digital-rights management, will become critically important.

Patents, which provide legal monopoly rights to the inventor of a useful, nonobvious machine, article of manufacture, or composition of matter, are a second significant source of intellectual-property protection. As a result of the *State Street Bank v. Signature Financial* and the *AT&T v. Excel Federated* court rulings, software and business processes embedded in software are now considered patentable. Because the industry is still adolescent, many innovations are appearing in iTV technologies (middleware, hardware, data enhancement), and new business models are likely to emerge. Therefore, the ownership of intellectual property with respect to innovations will be a critical enabler of sustainable competitive advantage. It will provide inimitability and give firms possessing the property advantages in the standards battle and in locking in consumers. An example of this phenomenon is Gemstar, which controls many of the patents relating to EPG technology and vigorously litigates for infringement.

CONCLUSION

The future of television is not a broadcast, passive, linear entertainment experience: It is an on-demand, participatory, nonlinear, infotainment, targeted-advertising, broadband, two-way communications platform. The concept of television as a device in the living room with the family seated in front of it will soon seem as archaic as the days when families huddled around a radio. Interactive television will become a more ingrained piece of our everyday lives. It will be something we can access at any time, from any place, for most every use. Not only will it provide us with entertainment, but it also will make us more productive, provide us with information and education, and encourage social interaction.

The radical changes that iTV will bring will be disruptive not only to television viewers, but also to the incumbents of the television industry. Interactive television promises to radically change the revenue models and the balance of power among infrastructure providers, hardware providers, software providers, and content providers. Infrastructure providers can retain some value in this new architecture by being a utility service for the other players in the value chain. However, a significant unbundling will occur in other areas of the value chain as firms compete in a fluid, modular, decentralized arena.

What will iTV look like in the future? The only limitations are the needs and wants of the consumer.

References

Beacham, Frank. "Movies of the Future: Storytelling with Computers." *American Cinematographer* (April 1995).

Besert, Jessee. "It's Baa-aack. How Interactive TV Is Sneaking into Your Living Room." *ZDNet* (2001).

"Blockbuster Going Broadband." *abcNEWS.com* (July 20, 2000).

Brewster, Jason. "Interactive Television: Where Does Advertising Go from Here?" *Online Daily News* (2000).

Brown-Kenyon, Paul I., Alan Miles, and John S. Rose. "Unscrambling Digital TV." *Mckinsey Quarterly* (2000).

Card, David. "ITV Platforms: Balancing Capability with Deployment." *Jupiter* (2000).

_____. "ITV Portals: Defining and Controlling the Home Screen." *Jupiter* (2000).

_____. "Television: Interactive TV Projections." *Jupiter* (2000).

Chen, Christine. "TiVo Is Smart TV" (March 19, 2001).

Elmer-Dewitt, Philip. "Ready for Prime Time? Time Warner's Full Service Network Is the Cadillac of Interactive-TV Tests." *Time* (December 26, 1994).

Freed, Ken. "Early Broadcasters Tried Interactive TV." *Media Visions Webzine* (2000).

_____. "Interactive Teletext." *Media Visions Webzine* (2000).

"Forrester Predicts Dramatic Shift in Television Business Model." *ITV Report* (July 23, 2000).

Garcia, Jon C., and Jon Wilkins. "Cable Is Too Much Better to Loose." *Mckinsey Quarterly* (2001).

Gilman, Brian. "Is ITV Ready for Prime Time?" *eMarketer* (October 16, 2000).

_____. "I Want My ITV!" *eMarketer* (June 5, 2000).

Hammer, Ben. "Interactive Wait-and-See TV." *The Standard* (April 3, 2000).

"ITV Commerce Infrastructure Challenges: Carriers Must Resist Becoming ASPs for Merchants." *Jupiter* (January 10, 2001).

Jensen, Jens F. "Mapping Interactive Television" (1996).

Jesdanun, Anick. "It's Not Your Ordinary TV." *abcNEWS.com* (January 17, 2000).

Komisar, Randy, and Ken Lineback. "The Monk and the Riddle." *HBS Press.*

Krebs, Brian. "FCC Launches Interactive Television Inquiry." *Newsbytes* (2001).

Kwatinetz, Michael. "Interactive TV Is Ready for Wide Adoption—Really." *Red Herring* (January 30, 2001).

Lake, David. "Cable Subscribers Want Their ITV." *The Standard* (January 10, 2001).

La Franco, Robert. "Teledivision." *Red Herring* (August 2000).

Levin, Stanislav. "T-commerce Land of Opportunity." *iTVreport.com* (2000).

Lewis, Nichole, and Lydia Loizides. "ITV Commerce Infrastructure Challenges." *Jupiter* (January 2001).

Moore, Geoffrey A. *Crossing the Chasm.* New York: HarperBusiness, 1999.

Murarka, Anup. "Reclaiming the Attention of Viewers Worldwide: The Promise of Interactive Television." *OpenTV* (2000).

"OpenTV Solutions for Interactive Television." *OpenTV* (2000).

Roche, Paul J. "DSL Will Win Where It Matters." *Mckinsey Quarterly* (2001).

Salkever, Alex. "What ITV Needs to Grow Up: Fewer Standards." *Business Week Online* (September 8, 2000).

Sawhney, Mohanbir, and Dave Parikh. "Where Value Lives in a Networked World." *Harvard Business Review* (January 2001).

Schonfeld, Erick. "Don't Just Sit There. Do Something." *eCompany* (November 2000).

Sean, Alexis, et al. "TiVo, Inc." Kellogg Graduate School of Management.

Shapiro, Carl, and Hal R.Varian. "Information Rules." Boston: Harvard Business School Press, 1999.

Shim, Richard. "TiVo Adds New Features to TV Recording Service." *CNET* (January 6, 2001).

Stewart, James. *Human and Social Factors of i-TV: Interactive Television at Home.* Research Center for Social Sciences. Edinburgh, Scotland: University of Edinburgh, 1998.

Stone, Amey. "Interactive TV's Really Big Picture." *Business Week Online* (September 7, 2000).

Swedlow, Tracy. "Interactive Enhanced Television: A Historical and Critical Perspective." *InteractiveTV Today.*

"Television: Online Landscape." *Jupiter* (1999).

"TiVo Sells over 80,000 Units during Fourth Quarter." *ITV Report* (January 31, 2001).

Werts, Diane. "Transforming Television." *Our Future* (2001).

CHAPTER 5

WIRELESS APPLICATIONS

Back in 2000, everyone was excited about wireless handheld devices and services. As reported in an *Upside Today* article entitled "Wireless Craze," wireless proponents used forecasts from research houses to show the world the market's potential. The Yankee Group reported that there were 469 million wireless users worldwide at the end of 1999 and predicted that the number would increase to 1.26 billion by 2005. Datacomm Research predicted that shipments of "smart" phones and handheld Internet devices would exceed 350 million units globally by 2003. International Data Corporation (IDC) predicted that U.S. wireless Internet users would increase to 61.5 million in 2003 from 7.4 million in 1999. Those predictions of hockey-stick growth seemed to promise a wireless nirvana. Still, concern about growth was evident on some people's faces (Figure 5.1).

For the most part, the uptake in wireless Internet and wireless applications has been a much less remarkable trend. In 2000, the Yankee Group reported that mobile-phone penetration in the United States had reached 38 percent, with penetration of 6 percent for new browser-enabled wireless phones. Actual use of the browsing capability, however, trailed far behind, at just 0.3 percent penetration (Table 5.1). The prediction was for the gap between the penetration and use of browser-enabled phones to continue for the next few years, as usage penetration would rise to only 7 percent by 2003 before shooting up to 20 percent by 2005.

ARGUMENT FOR APPLICATIONS

The buildup surrounding the wireless Internet has subsided considerably, and now companies are focusing on how wireless technologies really do add value. Although users may occasionally browse Web sites on a mobile device while out and about, surfing Web sites on the tiny screen of a

Figure 5.1
Concern on Alan Greenspan's Face

mobile phone or personal digital assistant (PDA) just does not provide the same user experience as viewing them on a computer monitor. As discussed in Chapter 2, other factors have contributed to the slow uptake of wireless applications including competing standards, turf wars, and high coordination costs between players in the tightly interlinked value chain. In addition,

Table 5.1
Wireless Web Access Slow to Catch On

U.S. Internet Access and Browser Usage via Cell Phone							
	1999 (%)	2000 (%)	2001 (%)	2002 (%)	2003 (%)	2004 (%)	2005 (%)
Own a wireless phone	32	38	44	50	54	59	62
Own a browser-enabled wireless phone	1	6	12	25	39	51	60
Browse the Net on a wireless phone	0.1	0.3	1	3	7	13	20

Source: Yankee Group, October 2000; Copyright © 2000, Standard Media International.

technological barriers, including security and slow data rates for 2G networks (which affect response times for applications), are being overcome as security solutions become more mature and 2.5G networks are being rolled out. Very soon, the only factors retarding the value of wireless applications will be the quality and utility of the applications themselves. When the market matures to that point, customer needs, instead of technology constraints, will drive wireless applications.

So how does wireless technology add value to applications? Wireless can bring at least two extras to the table: real-time interaction and location information. It can promise that no matter where users are, they will be able to interact with information in real time. No more being glued to a desktop computer while waiting for that urgent e-mail. Location information can be useful simply to locate the nearest Chinese restaurant or to monitor the progress of truck shipments. A portable device also can increase the personalization of interactions since it can carry user profiles anywhere (e.g., a user's preferred credit-card information). For full impact, wireless applications need to take advantage of these value-adds over desktop applications.

Differences in usage patterns have also become evident. Research suggests that PC users tend to access the Web 3 to 4 times a day for periods of 20 to 60 minutes on each occasion. For wireless devices, the model is a higher frequency of usage, such as 10 times a day, but for only 3 to 4 minutes each time. So the focus now is on streamlining interactions with wireless applications and targeting focused tasks as opposed to general surfing.

The market for wireless data applications is still relatively new. Enabling technologies such as location-based services and other personalization features will allow the fine-tuning of current applications, and innovative applications will emerge to meet the needs of consumers as well as businesses. The enterprise market offers an especially exciting opportunity, as demand for wireless business applications is increasing for several reasons:

- Incremental revenue through increasing market share and frequency of use.
- Improved productivity through greater effectiveness and efficiency, faster decision-making processes, and reduced costs.
- Greater customer loyalty through personalized content and services.

Recent reports such as one by Forrester Research have noted that as many as 40 percent of Fortune 2,500 businesses in the United States had equipped or were equipping their workforces with wireless tools and that an additional 30 percent were considering it.

The constituents of the wireless value chain are all working to drive new innovations; the high motivation of wireless carriers to stabilize declining average-month revenues per user will spur other firms in the chain to try to fulfill the carriers' desires. The demand and technology are now falling in line with the motivation by the players in the value chain to position this market for growth. And herein lies the opportunity: compelling applications will be the primary driver of that growth.

FRAMEWORK

Since a lot of hype has surrounded the convergence of wireless and the Internet, this section examines specific applications that will be driving wireless data traffic. Segmenting the market in terms of industry verticals is a systematic way to analyze the opportunities. Vertical applications are customized solutions for the needs of a particular industry. For example, specific applications in the health care industry include electronic prescriptions, which are transmitted wirelessly from a doctor's PDA to a pharmacy. This application is not relevant to other industries although the underlying technologies could be used for other purposes.

On the other hand, some applications could be used universally across industry verticals and by consumers, much like word processing or the telephone. These horizontal wireless applications include knowledge applications, communication, m-commerce, and telemetry and tracking. Knowledge applications include personal information management, as well as office tools such as document sharing. Communication includes applications for sending messages between people, such as short message service (SMS) and e-mail. Mobile commerce (m-commerce) includes any applications that aid commerce, such as those that support buying and selling or even advertisements. Finally, telemetry and tracking allows either tracking or transmittal of data from remote sources and includes applications that shipping companies use to monitor the progress of trucks toward their destinations. Figure 5.2 summarizes the vertical and horizontal application areas.

HORIZONTAL WIRELESS APPLICATIONS

Many horizontal wireless applications already exist in some shape or form. Mobility mainly enhances the accessibility and the potential integrity of data and communications through real-time interaction. Consequently, most of the exciting horizontal wireless applications are extensions of

Figure 5.2
Horizontal and Vertical Application Areas

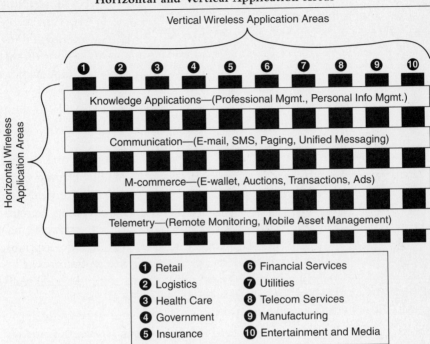

Adapted from Bear Stearns, 2000 and Gulati and Panas, 2001.

existing computing applications. However, wireless can also add context, such as location and personalization, which enables more powerful applications. As costs decrease over time, horizontal applications have the potential to become widely used consumer applications.

The following section provides a detailed discussion of the four horizontal applications: knowledge, communications, m-commerce, and telemetry and tracking.

Knowledge Applications

Businesses have used specialized wireless applications for more than a decade. Many of these wireless devices and applications are extensions of the wire-line platforms for general-purpose business applications, but they also include new uses that have been spurred by the ability to access and update information in real time. Many of the applications are professional-management or personal-information-management tools to increase the productivity and efficiency of people in the workplace, in their personal lives, or both.

The cost-savings model of business adoption is based on the idea that widespread use of wireless-enabled devices will occur when the benefit derived from employee access to instant information clearly exceeds the installation and operational costs of corporatewide wireless networks. In addition, rapid adoption of wireless models will occur where businesses obtain a competitive advantage is obtained by being able to access information in new ways and from locations that are not easily available in the wire-line world.

Value Proposition of Knowledge Applications.   The main customer need that knowledge applications meet is instantaneous and ubiquitous access to business-critical data. Enterprises will demand this productivity-enhancement value proposition, and will have large ROI (return on investment) expectations on implementation. Most enterprise customers will be agnostic to the technology that suppliers use for wireless data transmission; they will look for end-to-end solutions that meet their mobile data bandwidth, availability, and security requirements. Thus, the same enterprise applications and device will have to work seamlessly between the wireless LAN in the office, the broadband wireless system at home, and the preferred carrier's public network everywhere else. The information that the application accesses, displays, and modifies may vary in content and richness depending on the bandwidth of the network to which the device is linked, but for fast adoption, the change in functionality must be intuitive and transparent to the user.

The pull for instant information at the fingertips will be especially strong within the manufacturing and service industries, where it can provide efficiency improvements or competitive advantages. Corporate information available on personal computers (desktops and laptops) will be extended to a mobile handheld device that employees can carry with them to meetings within and outside their corporate offices. This will happen as the corporate intranet extends beyond the PCs into mobile handheld devices.

The following five applications are in the forefront of the adoption curve in the knowledge-management space:

1. Corporate database access and entry of data.
2. Intranet access and entry of information for applications such as network-hosted calendars, to-do lists, address files, and memos.

3. Access to supply chain-management applications.
4. Access to customer-relationship-management (CRM) applications.
5. Training or troubleshooting materials that can be pulled on demand by workers in the field.

Providing people with wireless data access can enhance the productivity of a mobile sales force. For example, integrating wireless functionality into CRM (customer relationship management) applications provides an additional level of salesforce automation. Also, with always-on connectivity, sales representatives can be better informed about their customers, access the information needed to complete sales, and communicate any status to the central office in real time. Such applications will be even more effective by providing real-time inventory and product-availability data to the sales personnel. These applications focus on enhancing customer satisfaction, shortening the sales process, and improving the information flow within an organization.

Westinghouse mobile satellite terminals and dome antennas provide AT&T Network Computing Services maintenance crews with seamless communication regardless of location. The technicians have access to data-communications services, mobile telephone, and fax to help troubleshoot problems. Sears has equipped its home-repair service crews with PDAs that operate on Motient's network using both terrestrial and satellite connectivity. It allows the technicians to access real-time information about pricing, schedule changes, inventory, and routing, not only improving their efficiency but also providing better customer service. The connectivity optimizes workforce utilization by prioritizing customers and fulfilling rush orders.

Challenges. Wireless knowledge applications will essentially be extensions of desktop applications. The challenges faced by widespread implementation and adoption of such extensions are related to technology, user experience, and cost. A typical system is shown in Figure 5.3. The technology already exists to extend applications into the wireless environment. For example, there are content-transformation tools that can take HTML Web pages and transform them into Wireless Markup Language (WML) cards for presentation to wireless devices. The biggest technological challenges are related to security and to speeding up the response times for applications. The 2.5G services will help with response times, but security will have to evolve through stronger encryption technologies and digital signatures.

Figure 5.3
Typical System Architecture for the Implementation
of Wireless Knowledge Applications

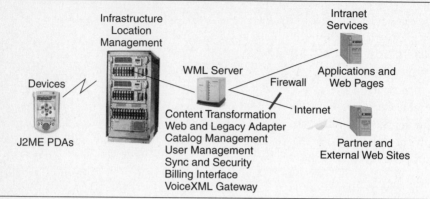

The biggest challenge from the user's standpoint is taking the experience and expectations from desktop applications and transforming them into something reasonable on a wireless device. Limited screen sizes, presentation area, and keypads will force applications developers to think of application extensions to the mobile domain as *complements*, not as *substitutes*, for the core use of an application on a desktop computer.

Cost will also be factored into the purchase of systems or services to enable wireless access to knowledge applications, and there will be competition to bring the cost of solutions down. For some applications, customers will seek solutions that use no–service–cost wireless local–area–network technology to interact with knowledge applications while in the office but that also allow seamless switching to access through 2.5G or 3G networks outside the office. At any rate, it is likely that wireless access soon will be narrowly targeted at specific knowledge applications such as CRM and field–service–support tools, which are the areas of immediate opportunity. In the long run, the challenge will be to reduce the cost until the return from everyone's having wireless access to the full range of desktop knowledge applications is similar to the return from everyone's having a computer.

Summary.   The adoption rate will initially be driven by the need for constant access to specific business applications as well as by the decreasing cost of implementation. The adoption rate should be high since corporate implementation can drive the standardization of platforms and applications.

"Smart" network architecture for enterprise information systems and in-tranets will facilitate the adoption of knowledge applications: The data and applications will reside on nodes of the corporate data network. Wireless devices will access knowledge applications on an as-needed basis after an employee login, as neither data nor applications are stored on the device it-self. This system will enhance the security of corporate data in case of loss of the wireless device, as well as reduce the processing and data-storage re-quirements of the access device. It will also allow the device to be interop-erable between employees and applications. The availability of low-cost (under $200) devices that can operate across multiple wireless transmission protocols such as 802.11, and 2.5G or 3G, will facilitate the widespread adoption of knowledge applications.

Communications

This section concentrates on communication and messaging, mainly text. Voice communications, while important, are excluded because the focus is on text-messaging applications such as SMS (short message service) and wireless access to e-mail. The popularity of messaging is evident in many ways. The GSM (Global System for Mobile Communication) Association estimated that at the end of September 2001 nearly 750 million SMS mes-sages were being sent *per day*. This service is a major contributor of rev-enue and profits to many European mobile operators. Electronic mail (e-mail) is a killer application in the wired world, and wireless access to e-mail is a highly desired mobile application, as proven by the popularity of the research-in-motion (RIM) Blackberry pager and similar devices. In addition, a survey from Jupiter Communications showed that 50 percent of those surveyed wanted e-mail on their mobile device. Market estimates hover around $10 billion, a significant figure.

Value Proposition of Communication Applications.   Text communication in the form of e-mail has existed since the 1970s, but it did not become popular until the Internet's growth spurt in the 1990s. Millions of people use e-mail, and therefore the application has proven value for a huge num-ber of consumers and enterprises.

On one level, text communication has intrinsic value. First, it allows users to process information in parallel. It is easy to decide which piece of information is important on a page of text. On the other hand, people pro-cess voice communication serially. They must listen to voice mail in the order it was recorded to find the information of interest. Second, text is easy to reference (e.g., it is generally preferable to read driving directions than to listen to them). The real value, above and beyond the intrinsic value of text communication, is that it is a networked application, and many people are attached to the network. If only two people in the world had e-mail, it would be merely a novelty. However, as more and more people get e-mail, it becomes more and more useful. The value of the application increases with the size of the network (Figure 5.4). When wireless text communication was created, millions of people were already tied to the network. Thus, it became merely an extension of the existing e-mail network but added an aspect of portability that previously did not exist.

Challenges.   Text communication is already viable, and several companies are competing in this space. Those offering solutions for wireless access to e-mail include RIM, OmniSky, and Palm.net. RIM offers a full, end-to-end

Figure 5.4
Network Extension of Text Communication

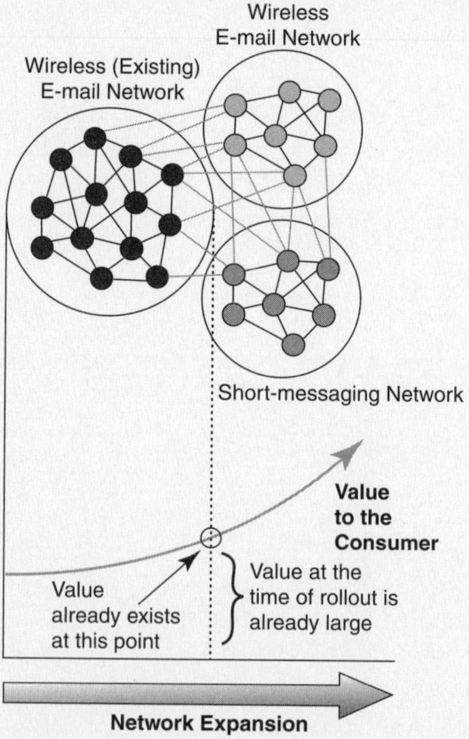

solution by providing server software, hardware (Blackberry device), and software for the Blackberry. Both Omnisky and Palm.net provide the client software that runs on either Palm or Windows CE devices. The infrastructure behind e-mail was in place, and access was extended to wireless devices.

Short-message service (SMS) has existed for several years. Its rapid adoption was facilitated by its incorporation into the global system for mobile communications (GSM) standard, which sets standards not only for air interface protocols but also for core features. Unlike today's mobile e-mail, SMS messages are transmitted in the control band of cell phones, a small amount of bandwidth that voice transmission does not use. The original intention was for telephone companies to use the control band to send messages to their mobile users.

Nonetheless, horizontal wireless applications face technological obstacles that hinder their adoption by consumers and mobile workers. Some of them are applicable not only to the marketing of communications applications but also to the adoption of wireless solutions among different horizontal and vertical markets. The main obstacle to the deployment of wireless communication or mobile-commerce tools is the lack of security for data transmissions among wireless networks. The risk of violation or distortion of critical information by others limits the demand for wireless communication tools. In the United States, multiple standards and dated circuit-switched network configurations constrain the development of a secure communications environment.

Small screens and the limited scope of input capabilities have been obstacles to handling a broad range of data patterns through wireless devices. At first glance, there seem to be two contradicting attributes in wireless communications that the industry must reconcile to optimize the value proposition: the size of the equipment and the interfacing features provided. The development of speech-to-text converters may eventually optimize both attributes.

In addition, mobile users need filtering tools to facilitate the efficient screening of messages. Because the information they may require in the field is time critical, junk mail may damage the functionality that wireless is intended to provide. Potential customers are unlikely to be interested in paying to be bothered.

When attempting to integrate horizontal communications platforms with enterprise systems—an accomplishment that may leverage the deployment of horizontal wireless communications platforms—corporations find four challenges:

1. Mobile workers handle diverse devices with different operating systems that make the integration of individuals into internal legacy systems difficult.
2. When wireless workers do not have PCs, firms may find synchronization with central data stores costly.
3. Corporations need the capability of maintaining software remotely to achieve cost efficiency.
4. Diverse personal end-enterprise communications media should be integrated or synchronized with a single mobile device/operating system (unified messaging).

Summary

Though the United States is behind in the adoption curve for text messaging, rapid growth is certain for this method of communication. Wireless carriers support SMS messaging at much lower cost than when handling voice calls and can count on SMS to generate revenues that compensate for declining revenues from voice calls. Some issues, however, pose doubts about the ability of horizontal wireless-communications applications to capture significant value. Both e-mail and messaging are basic tools with a low degree of complexity. These applications will soon be commoditized and become part of the ante to play in the game. If so, value will be captured by e-mail/messaging service providers or by those players that develop ancillary technical-support technologies to improve speed, variety, and security of transmitted information, not by the companies that develop solutions for these applications. Also, as prices for these services decrease, end customers will find text-communication services more attractive and valuable.

M-Commerce. Mobile-commerce applications facilitate monetary transactions via a mobile device. In the United States, people think of mobile commerce as traditional electronic commerce via a mobile device (e.g., using an Internet-enabled mobile phone to purchase a book from Amazon.com while waiting for the train). It is not surprising that true mobile commerce has failed to take hold here. Compared with e-commerce, the m-commerce experience is slow, lacks depth and graphical aids, has costly charges per minute, and is hampered by the difficulty in entering payment information. Generally, it is easier to call a customer-service representative and place an order over the phone. However, as operators move to 2.5G and 3G systems, m-commerce will improve because of faster downloads and response times.

Mobile payment services will probably evolve until one or two standards emerge; increased consumer acceptance will then establish them as common wireless alternatives. Early attempts at mobile payments have involved using a traditional bank credit or debit card in conjunction with a cell phone. After ordering a product by phone or over the Internet, the customer receives an SMS message with the price and completes the payment transaction by inserting the bankcard into the phone's slot and keying in a password.

Companies are also pursuing mobile-payment services that do not require smart cards. Sonera, formerly Finnish Telecom, has orchestrated a cardless "pay-by-GSM phone." Customers purchase an item by dialing a special number provided at the point of sale (e.g., a parking meter). The network operator acts as a clearinghouse and credits the customer's predetermined billing account. Bluetooth technology, which allows nearby devices to communicate via high-speed, short-distance radio waves, is also expected to play an important role in mobile payments at point-of-sale locations.

Another promising concept, still in its experimental stages, is mobile cash: A wireless network loads cash onto a mobile device, typically through a smart card. Telephone companies (e.g., NTT DoCoMo and Sonera) and credit-card companies (e.g., MasterCard and Visa) are rapidly building microbilling and electronic-wallet businesses. Two such services are PayPal and Remit.com, which enable individuals and businesses to transfer money to each other from their banking or credit-card accounts.

Value Proposition of M-Commerce Applications. The next generation of mobile commerce will be a much better value proposition for both the consumer and the seller. Bluetooth and location-based technologies will enhance the functionality of wireless devices, enabling mobile commerce to offer unique benefits over electronic commerce. Location technology will enable retailers to send time-sensitive and location-sensitive coupons to shoppers. Consumers will be able to use their phones as electronic wallets to beam money to friends or to pay for goods in stores or at vending machines. Over time, mobile devices could become a vehicle for transmitting digital money, tracking transactions, and compiling spending reports for their users (see Table 5.2).

Mobile commerce is a significant opportunity for all parties involved. On the consumer side, traditional e-commerce sites have been expanding their reach to a new channel, the mobile customer. As enabling technologies become integrated in devices and networks, the prospect of

Table 5.2
M-Commerce Applications

Enterprise	Consumer
• Point-of-sale retailing • CRM data gathering • Expense tracking (automatic expense reporting for business travelers)	• E-commerce • Point-of-sale transactions • E-wallet applications • Person-to-person payments • Expense tracking

m-commerce becomes drastically more compelling. For example, location services could make it easy to find nearby restaurants and order off the menu before arriving for pickup. Transactions could become more convenient and efficient with Bluetooth-enabled devices. In February 2001, Holiday Inn unveiled its first hotel with Bluetooth-enabled room-service menu downloads and checkout. In a vote of confidence for the technology, Bass Hotels, Inc., plans to use Bluetooth in all of its properties, which include the Crowne Plaza and Intercontinental chains as well as the Holiday Inn chain.

Mobile commerce has seen significant development in vertical business markets from finance to government. As technology advances and new applications emerge, wireless commerce can be leveraged across vertical markets to address a much larger customer base. These applications include wireless hosting, or gateway services, that convert information from a firm's legacy system into a form viewable on a mobile device.

Mobile commerce has received both positive and negative press over the past several years. The question remains not if but when will m-commerce applications really offer to the consumer the value that they proclaim.

Challenges. Mobile commerce is less an application than a network of enabling technologies that facilitate transactions. Technology can meet the challenges for m-commerce in three main areas: transaction enablers, security providers, and translation/integration services (Figure 5.5).

Transaction enablers. Transactions occurring between the customers and their carrier provider will pave the way for broad-based mobile-commerce applications. Effective billing technology is the most important missing component of any broad-based m-commerce solution. Real-time

Figure 5.5
Network of Technologies That Facilitates Transactions

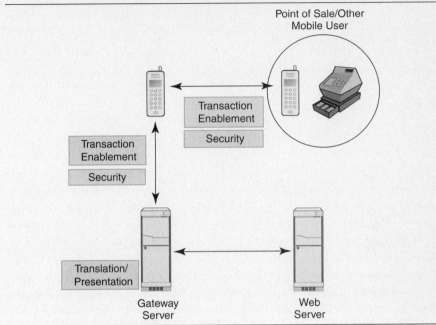

billing will most likely fill that void. This solution is already in place and is being used in prepaid wireless; it could serve as a driving force behind the imminent convergence of the wireless horizontals.

Real-time billing for m-commerce can be adapted from prepaid wireless to create a payment model in the form of an integrated prepaid wallet. Using a credit card or check, a customer would be able to fund a prepaid account through either a "wallet provider" or an operator. Once the account was established, the subscriber would be able to make calls, send and receive text messages, and purchase goods and services by phone. A customer could simply enter an ID code into the phone to request a ringing tone, a simple video game, or a song from a content provider. The content provider would then validate the code, check the account balance, deliver the service, and debit the subscriber's prepaid account.

The demand from the rapidly growing youth market and the limitations to other solutions make this real-time billing solution even more likely. If current growth rates in the youth segment continue, the revenue forecasts for mobile entertainment transactions are substantial. According to the

Yankee Group, revenue from graphics, games, audio, and video will reach $1.13 billion by 2005, up from just $41 million in 2000. The increasing popularity of prepaid phone solutions makes it likely that real-time billing technology coupled with teenagers' need to be "cool" will drive m-commerce forward.

Security providers.   Security is a necessary enabling technology for con-ducting m-commerce. As mobile commerce becomes more widely adopted, security will be a significant challenge. Unlike computers in the wired world, mobile devices have limited memory, rendering traditionally strong encryption and authentication technology impractical. Although most soft-ware developers have access to a scaled-down version of secure socket layer (SSL) for wireless devices, the wide variety of devices, each with its own security protocol, will make things more challenging. Although the wire-less application protocol (WAP) has its own security—wireless transport-layer security (WTLS)—a point of weakness occurs at the wireless gateway, where the wired world meets the wireless world. The gateway server must decrypt the information received from the wired Internet and re-encrypt that information in WTLS. Companies hosting their gateway servers be-hind firewalls get around that complication.

Wireless devices, unlike their landline counterparts, have a much higher chance of being lost or stolen. This presents an additional challenge to se-curity providers—authentication. How does a merchant know that the per-son making the purchase is actually the person who owns the device? This will become a critical issue for point-of-sale transactions (at the cash reg-ister) and is also a grave concern for enterprise customers who may put valuable company information at risk.

Translation/integration.   Though the technology for automated trans-lation of HTML pages to WML cards exists, improvements will be neces-sary to ensure an satisfactory user experience on wireless devices. As with wireless knowledge applications, creating a complementary m-commerce user experience for e-commerce applications will be necessary, since the richness of regular Internet content will not be replicable. In the short term, application developers will struggle with the trade-offs of reducing imple-mentation effort by writing generalized applications versus customizing the user experience on the basis of the access device (computer or wireless).

Summary.   The addition of incremental enabling technologies such as location-based services, Bluetooth, and ultimately broadband to communications devices will rapidly enhance their value in m-commerce. Furthermore, improvements in security will make hosted applications a useful and viable reality for businesses.

The face of mobile commerce could change for the consumer with the establishment of these services. Because location information is unique to mobile devices, it can add value to other applications. For example, retailers will be able to send out time- and location-sensitive coupons directly to users' mobile devices. These customers can then go to the store offering the promotion and receive discounted opportunities. Highway hotels will be able to send pricing and availability information to midnight drivers on the nearby thruway to help fill empty rooms.

Additionally, once broadband becomes a reality, the mobile-shopping experience could become graphically rich. Current thinking is that m-commerce will be tailored to purchases and services that people perform during downtime, such as banking or bill paying, or time-sensitive purchases, such as stock trading. The simple text-based interface of today precludes many online retailers from doing business via wireless devices. When broadband is available, m-commerce may be able to offer a user experience more like that of regular e-commerce.

Limitations in screen size, keypad size, and security make it unrealistic to expect widespread Web browsing and purchasing to occur on wireless devices in the near future, but simpler transactions will proliferate the landscape. In the important youth segment, "m-tertainment"—MP3s, ringing tones, videos, games, and other low-price items—will drive m-commerce applications. Offerings such as these are perfectly suited for the real-time billing technology that already exists. As a result, more and more services will emerge and eventually rival today's information and "infotainment" portals.

The integrated prepaid-wallet mode provides customers with a simple payment vehicle that leverages the highly effective microtransaction-payment services entailing payments of small amounts that are already available. With real-time, microtransaction billing already in place, and a youthful consumer base for m-commerce goods and services, applications that bring the merchants and the carriers together are all that is necessary. This model provides value for both consumers and carriers. For consumers, it will provide convenient, low-priced features. On the carrier side, it will generate revenue incrementally but at lower margins than the ones associated with the delivery of voice and data services. The model's attractiveness lies in supplementing revenues from existing services by increasing a prepaid customer's lifetime value. The more a customer buys wirelessly, the more that customer will then use voice and data. Therefore, this will increase the average revenue per user for the carriers.

Members of the wireless value chain are excited about the opportunities in m-commerce because the devices and services allow them to create a greater affinity with end customers. As m-commerce becomes integrated into everyday purchasing, people's dependency on wireless devices and services could grow exponentially, which would be a boon to the entire industry. That is why the industry is pushing forward the cause of m-commerce, and persistence will eventually make it a reality.

Telemetry and Tracking

Telemetry and tracking refer to applications for automatic measurement and transmission of data from remote sources for control, tracking, and other purposes. The transmitted information could be readings from utility meters at various customer sites or data to track the location of a car or truck. These applications are being adopted in industries where assets such as goods and vehicles need to be managed in real time to improve operational efficiencies and customer service. One of the biggest impacts is expected to be in logistics.

Wireless technologies can provide a flexible platform for information exchange between the central-intelligence unit of a firm and mobile assets, such as physical goods, and people such as field-service personnel and traveling salespeople. They can use the information exchange to meet unforeseen customer needs, improve communication, increase efficient utilization of assets, and instantaneously redeploy if the need arises.

Mobility and time sensitivity are the two main drivers that add value in the wireless space. The value in logistics will come from efficiently managing mobile assets because existing hardwired platforms fail. We term this set of applications "mobile-asset management." Figure 5.6 illustrates a typical network. For example, a trucking company that can track the location and capacity use of its trucks can easily redeploy or reroute its fleet to improve use and customer service. This typical example of a location- and time-sensitive situation is also a perfect opportunity for wireless deployment.

Forrester research and others estimated the total worldwide corporate expenditure associated with managing material and product flows in the vendor-to-customer supply chain to be more than $2 trillion. These expenditures include the entire value chain associated with a product and inbound freight, warehousing, inventory management, outbound freight,

Figure 5.6
A Typical Mobile-Asset-Management Network

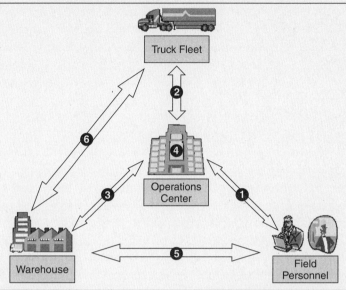

❶ Field Personnel
Wireless Info Exchange
  Job Scheduling
  Job Status
  Customer Info & History
  Job Details
  Location Info
  Database Access
   Technical Info
   Sales Info
   Contact Info
Examples:
  Field-service Personnel
  Field Engineering
  Field Maintenance
  Field Sales

❷ Truck Fleet
Wireless Info Exchange
  Delivery/Pickup Schedules
  Delivery/Pickup Status
  Load Status
  Routing Info
  Performance Info
  Telemetry/Maintenance Info
  Location/Tracking Info

❸ Warehouse
Wireless Info Exchange
  Real-time Inventory
  Status
  Picking/Packing Info

❹ Operations Center
Wireless Info Exchange
  Scheduling
  Tracking
  Fleet Management
  Dispatch
Wireless Info Processing
  Analysis
  Trending
  Reporting
  Access to Corporate d/bs
  Field-staff Support

❺ Warehouse-Field Personnel
Wireless Info Exchange
  Real-time Inventory Status
  Picking/Packing Info
  Equipment-shipping
  Request

❻ Warehouse-Truck Fleet
Wireless Info Exchange
  Docking Information
  Shipping Information

Source: Kapoor, 2000; © 2000 Luminant Worldwide Corporation.

customer service, and administrative and information-systems costs. Administrative and information-systems costs associated with managing the global supply chain average 7 percent to 10 percent of the total expenditure, or $140 billion to $200 billion. Numerous studies, including periodic reports by industry analysts, indicate that enhanced electronic management of information flows between enterprises can reduce administrative costs by at least 20 percent. That would put the cost savings associated with enhanced-value network communications to be around $28 billion.

Telematics, which is the marriage of wireless and automobiles, has garnered considerable consumer attention. The idea is not only to allow access to tracking-oriented data that enhances the driving experience and makes it safer (e.g., mapping and location-specific information), but also to access personal-information-management and communications tools. Safety is currently the main selling point for adoption, although systems like GM's OnStar and Ford's WingCast offer drivers directions, local directory services, and financial information, in addition to emergency services. Eventually, a person could look up the address of a business and receive directions while monitoring traffic conditions and keeping up with e-mail that might include a meeting-cancellation notice. The dealer's repair shop could perform remote diagnostics on cars. Automobile makers not only are excited about creating closer relationships with their customers through these services but also are attracted by the possibility of a recurring revenue stream after a car has been purchased. UBS Warburg expects telematics will be a $47.2 billion industry by 2010.

While mobile-asset management and telematics are two of the most visible growth areas for telemetry and tracking applications, it is not because of the unique value proposition that they offer over landline solutions.

Value Proposition of Telemetry and Tracking Services.   Telemetry and tracking applications inherently deal with remote people, goods, and devices. In such situations, wireless solutions are more cost-effective for data exchange than landline solutions, so this category of applications not only will include extensions of landline applications but also will spur many new applications.

Apart from telematics, telemetry and tracking applications will have their biggest impact in the business space where the emphasis on constantly improving productivity and efficiency will highlight their value. The value of wireless applications in mobile-asset management comes from three main factors:

1. *Context-sensitive information is available anytime and anywhere.* (A trucking company will keep track of its truck locations and their capacity use to optimize customer service and capacity use.)
2. *User has an application-based choice of synchronous or asynchronous information dissemination.* (Automatic meter reading will be synchronous when the technician is always connected to the central database, whereas a traveling salesperson will probably be asynchronous when pulling time-sensitive information as and when required.)
3. *Anytime, anywhere capabilities of wireless make it the most efficient tool for executing communications in the mobile-asset-management industry.* (This is a given because of the inherently vast geographic expanse of this industry.)

The application landscape in wireless has been facilitated by PDA technology, which has made the devices cheaper, smaller, and more robust for industrial applications. Economies of scale, competition, and process innovations have reduced costs making corporations more receptive to wireless solutions such as the following examples.

Package tracking. The shipping industry has long been focused on wireless applications. Traditionally, one of the biggest concerns for shippers was inadequate tracking information once a customer shipped a package. For delivery companies such as United Parcel Service, Federal Express, and McKesson, customer litigation and complaint processing added to the problem. With the primitive paper system, it was extremely costly to reproduce images of delivery receipts, and the shipper occasionally would forget to get the customer's signature. The need for readily available tracking information has made wireless tracking of packages one of the biggest and most successful applications in mobile-asset management. The field–delivery staff is equipped with a wireless handheld device that can scan the barcodes on packages, collect customer signatures, and be constantly synchronized with the central database of the shipping company. Companies such as AvantGo provide solutions for real–time connectivity between the handhelds and company databases. The shippers can access their package information not only via the Web, but also through their PDAs and cell phones. By implementing this system, McKesson reduced its point–of–delivery legal claims by 50 percent and achieved 100 percent reduction in receipt-search and image-manifestation costs.

Automatic vehicle location (AVL).   The AVL solutions can graphically represent a truck fleet on a map. They allow companies to track, manage, and communicate with their mobile assets in real time. By monitoring, the mobile-asset-management solutions provider can deliver improved customer service, optimize the capacity of mobile assets, and provide real-time information to clients about their order status.

In March 2001, Office Depot, Inc., the world's largest supplier of office products, announced its rollout of a wireless mobile-computing transportation and mobile-asset-management system (powered by Aether Systems, Inc., and Symbol Technologies, Inc.) to Office Depot's fleet of more than 2,000 delivery trucks. This real-time delivery and tracking system allows Office Depot to ensure that customers get what they want, when they want it. The company uses Symbol's SPT 1700 Palm O/S handheld computing devices and its Mobile Gateway on-board data-transaction systems for its wireless proof-of-delivery and package-tracking system. Its empowered mobile workforce feeds off the wireless network called Office Depot Signature Tracking and Reporting System (OD STAR). Drivers use handheld devices to reconcile inventory on the truck and complete the transaction by capturing the customer signature.

The AVL solution can help in remote driver-performance tracking by collecting location information as a function of time and distance. It can allow corporations to monitor fuel costs and employees' driving speed, and ensure conformity to company policies. The information can also be used for performance comparisons between employees or different sets of fleet vehicles. In addition, the wireless data-communication link between the vehicle and central control station can track vehicle diagnostic information. The system could be automated such that the central-database intelligence could prompt for vehicular problems before they occur.

Challenges.   The huge geographic distances between utility meters and remote sources in cars are a serious challenge to the omnipresence of wireless connectivity. Network operators such as Sprint PCS, AT&T Wireless, and Verizon have built nationwide networks that provide coverage at least in major cities and on highways. Satellite networks such as the one set up by Globalstar can provide coverage for remote locations. Global position system (GPS) technology can track fleet vehicles. Motient and Aether Systems offer wireless fleet-management services that combine terrestrial and satellite networks. These kinds of effective solutions fill a critical need.

In the mobile-asset-management domain, end-to-end solutions providers are becoming more prevalent, making it easier for companies to implement telemetry and tracking systems. For example, UPS, which holds leadership in package shipping, also provides solutions for supply chain management and critical-parts delivery. The next challenge will be to manage the many partnerships and alliances that can enable a company to leverage its core competency and increase the productivity of its assets. Manugistics provides Enterprise Profit Optimization Solution®, which helps enhance organizational profitability by simultaneously optimizing the supply and demand sides of an organization's business. To be cutting edge, solutions must enable organizations to track their performance. Companies that physically transfer goods in any part of their supply chain cycle must be able to track mobile assets in real time to improve resource use. Companies like Aether Systems that can provide enabling software and services will form the backbone for executing such solutions.

In telematics, interface technology that allows the safe operation of vehicles and interactions with all the applications will be critical to adoption. Solutions will enter the market at different price points. Small, mounted screens will probably sell at a lower price point, whereas heads-up displays will be prevalent in luxury cars. In addition, voice interfaces are attractive because they allow hands-free operation. In the near term, however, user expectations will probably exceed the capabilities of voice interfaces, and that will be a challenge.

Summary

As the geographic reach of remote monitoring increases and the cost comes down, remote monitoring and servicing of assets will become more of a reality. Automobile companies will soon provide remote diagnostics and send customers reminders about maintenance needs. But what if General Electric could do that with washers, dryers, refrigerators, and even lightbulbs? Though the example of a lightbulb may seem extreme, General Electric would be able to structure business service contracts for automatic shipments of lightbulbs to the customer's maintenance department indicating the location of burned-out bulbs. This concept allows consumer-goods companies to structure recurring revenues for what was formerly a single revenue stream at the time of purchase. Even though it may take time to realize this business model with inexpensive goods, it will be a near-term reality for high-priced goods. This is already obvious in the automobile industry.

With mobile-asset management tools, firms will experience productivity and efficiency gains through better management of mobile resources. On average, the time that a product actually gets worked on during manufacture is less than 5 percent. This high proportion of work-in-progress (WIP) time is largely non-value-added for the product, and it holds immense opportunity for productivity improvement. Wireless technologies are central to that goal and have evolved to a level where they are ripe for mobile-asset management.

The very nature of mobile-asset-management operations requires wireless connectivity for efficient communication. As an early adopter of wireless technology, the mobile-asset-management industry has demonstrated the value-added potential. The customer need is clear here. The technology is mature enough for nationwide deployment, and there is a high level of collaboration among the players. The established leadership of service organizations like FedEx and UPS gives them scale to become efficient solutions providers. Companies that leverage such solutions to cut costs, improve their customer service, and optimize their use of resources will benefit in the future.

VERTICAL WIRELESS APPLICATIONS

This section discusses the effect of wireless technologies on applications that are specific to particular industry verticals (Figure 5.7). The two verticals that are likely to spend the most on mobile data are financial services and health care, so this section covers those two industries as well as government services. We also consider the value proposition of bringing wireless to these verticals and other factors that will affect adoption.

Financial Services

Of all the existing and potential wireless applications, m-commerce in general and financial services in particular will likely be the big winners. Such financial services include banking, stock trading, financial and information analysis, and insurance. Wireless communication services have grown exponentially in the past few years, especially in Asia and Europe. As new technologies overcome existing limitations, consumers are using the wireless channel more often for communication as well as for gathering information or conducting transactions over the mobile Internet. Newer technologies and networks will allow a much richer customer experience, including interactive video, graphics, and always-on capability. This new mobile delivery channel offers financial institutions an opportunity to proactively engage their customers with additional services and products.

Figure 5.7
Vertical-Market Revenue Forecast for U.S.
Mobile–Data Market in 2002

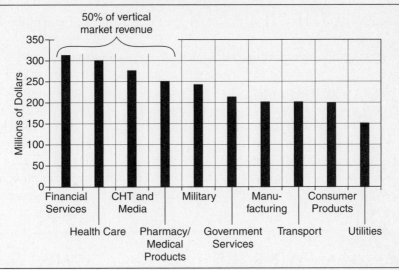

Source: Accenture, 2001.

But despite the ubiquity and convenience of accessing the wireless channel over the past couple years, many companies have been reluctant to fully
embrace this new technology. Because the restricted interface of slimmed-
down devices and slow network speeds can discourage the mobile user from
browsing the Internet, current applications end up stripping out much of
their marketing and navigation material. As a result, mobile users are likely
to carry out transactions for which there is limited context and naviga-
tional overhead. Relative to most other wireless data applications, financial
services are simple to operate, highly focused, and require little navigation
time. That is precisely why consumers have embraced them.

This section first provides a brief overview of the evolution and recent
developments of wireless financial services and takes a look at how segments of the financial-services spectrum will translate into meaningful
applications for the mobile consumer. The players along the wireless value
chain are described, as well as the core competencies that these players
must develop and capitalize on for success. Finally, we suggest how
the wireless financial-services industry may evolve in the next three to
five years.

Value Proposition of Wireless Financial Services

Wireless financial services offer consumers a new level of convenience in a busy world—the avoidance of latency in accessing financial information and greater flexibility in making decisions because they no longer have to be sitting at a PC. Financial services have been the early adopters of wireless applications for several reasons:

- The time and location sensitivity of mobile devices and networks provides significant appeal and value by delivering time-critical information and execution capabilities to the user (e.g., buying or selling a stock when it breaks through a specified limit).
- The consumer has the convenience of performing simple financial and housekeeping transactions, such as bill payments and account transfers, during downtime (e.g., while waiting for a plane or train).
- The mobile device is an efficient means for making payments to retailers and to other creditors.

Thus, the increasing popularity of the mobile Internet coupled with the need for convenience in deciding when and how customers conduct financial transactions presents a compelling lifestyle proposition. Figure 5.8 highlights the results of a pilot mobile-banking study conducted by the Bank of Montreal in which the average user session lasted 3.5 minutes, indicating that most users go online to accomplish specific tasks quickly.

Figure 5.8
Percentage of Customers Using Wireless Banking in Specific Locations

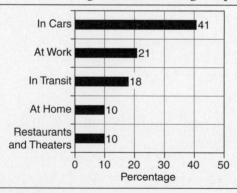

Adapted from Mobilocity.net, 2000.

Market Size

According to a report by Celent Communications, there were 10 million users of wireless financial services in 2000. That number is projected to increase to 150 million by 2004. The leaders in wireless financial services worldwide are Europe and Asia (Figure 5.9), where movement by banks and brokerages into mobile financial services has been aggressive. Only about 10 percent to 15 percent of the estimated $900 million annual market for wireless financial applications emanates from the United States. The main reasons for this poor showing are excessive technical standards, incompatible analog and digital networks, and the plethora of mobile devices (PDAs, cell phones, pagers, etc.) in the United States. Demographics and culture play a big part in adoption rates and profiles as well. Americans are apt to compare the mobile experience with their tethered Internet experience and find it inferior. European and Asian users, on the other hand, are awed by access to financial information over the Internet via their mobile devices, since these areas have relatively low PC Internet penetration. In Japan, more people access the Internet through mobile phones than through PCs.

As was the case with the Internet a few years ago, many new, small companies have assumed pioneering roles in developing and deploying financial services. One financial-services pioneer in the mobile space, MeritaNordbanken, offered mobile bill payment as early as 1992. But larger financial

Figure 5.9
Estimated Number of Users of Wireless
Financial Services around the World

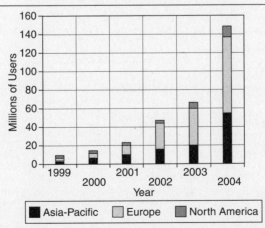

Source: Celent, 2000.

institutions—faced with eroding profit margins, the rising costs of customer service, reduced customer loyalty, and the increasing burden of supporting multiple channels—were slow to adopt these services initially. By 1999, however, over 90 percent of the banks in Europe offered some form of mobile banking. Surveys indicate that only about half of the hundred largest U.S. financial institutions intend to offer wireless services by 2004.

Affluent customers and businesses are more likely to need financial services at the moment, given their varied financial portfolios and the greater likelihood of their owning cell phones and PDAs. This channel also appeals to technically savvy younger people who are on the move, as well as to those with limited access to bank branches.

Despite the obvious attraction, developing successful offerings in this new medium is difficult. It requires access to large amounts of capital, widely accepted technologies, huge databases, fast transaction speeds, and excellent end-to-end security. The services offered today by financial institutions worldwide are largely basic and undifferentiated. Although the capability of accessing information and conducting transactions anytime, anywhere, opens up a wide range of possibilities, few firms have exploited them. The wireless financial offerings available today are thus simply an extension of their Web offerings. Financial institutions are only now reaching a critical point in overcoming some of these challenges and acknowledging the Internet as a mainstream channel rather than an alternative to traditional channels such as branches, ATMs, or customer-service call centers. It is simply a matter of time until they overcome all the challenges in the wireless space as well and offer meaningful services with a broader application and adoption over the long term.

Spectrum of Financial Applications.   Most people still think only of stock trading when they hear the phrase *wireless financial applications*. Although trading is certainly an important element, it is not the most important one. The services that can be extended onto a mobile platform are considerable in every area of financial applications. This section briefly surveys existing and promising financial offerings and the key players in each segment—retail brokerage, retail banking, investment banking, and other financial services (including insurance and real estate).

Retail brokerage.   Retail broking emerged as one of the first killer applications for mobile devices and is probably the most mature of all wireless financial segments. Customers who trade frequently appreciate the timeliness and accessibility of mobile broking because they can react swiftly to changing market conditions. The initial offerings of brokerage applications were information-based services such as real-time stock quotes, stock charts, news clips and alerts, and account information. With the ability to offer secure transactions, however, these applications have evolved to include account management and simple transactions such as stock and option trading.

Retail banking. European banks were quick to offer information-based banking that allowed customers to view account data, check credit-card balances, or access interest-rate information. The rollout of these services was so fast that by 1999 almost 90 percent of European banks offered some form of wireless banking. Although banking transactions don't usually involve as much time sensitivity or urgency as brokerage activities, they are still highly desired applications for over-the-air use according to a study by the Boston Consulting Group in 2000. In North America, the Bank of Montreal, Bank of America, Harris Bank, and Citibank were among the first players to jump-start basic mobile banking. Over the past year or so, banks have been incorporating transactional capabilities such as bill payment, fund transfers, PIN changing, and credit applications. The complexity of services will increase significantly as banks continue their transition to wireless applications.

Investment banking. Investment banks are beginning to explore mobile commerce both as a productivity tool for their employees and as a value-added service for institutional and individual clients. In sales and trading, investment banks are providing just-in-case applications that allow their clients to stay in touch with world markets at all times. Traders can receive news and alerts for rate changes, earnings announcements, and analyst ratings at any time and at any location. In corporate finance and advising, wireless applications will soon provide round-the-clock financial information and advice to key decision makers within client organizations. J.P. Morgan & Co. offers a service called SynDirect Wireless that allows bond issuers to wirelessly contact investors to sell bonds and enables investors to place orders and track their bonds' performance. As bankers and clients use Internet-enabled mobile devices more frequently, the devices will undoubtedly become an attractive channel for service delivery.

Other financial services. Although banks and brokerages have been the first to deliver services to wireless devices, companies in other financial-services sectors such as insurance, mortgage and consumer loans, financial advisory services, and credit cards are entering the market. Because these financial segments are typically research intensive, the main challenge for companies in this space is to offer meaningful services to the user. Financial firms might be able to employ push-based services that alert users about offerings that fit their preferences at the time of need. For example, mortgage and consumer-loan experts might be able to offer customers loan options or credit applications at model homes or car dealerships.

Diversified financial institutions have a tremendous opportunity to provide their clients with rich, tailor-made mobile applications that could serve as a one-stop shop for information and advice. Other institutions could use the medium to become a full-service "mobile concierge," offering integrated financial advice, travel, and credit-card services. Credit-card companies could use m-commerce to cross-sell other financial services or third-party products and services. However, the evolution of such applications will probably occur only after the widespread use of wireless banking and brokerage services.

Figure 5.10 indicates the level of interest of cell-phone users in financial services according to a survey conducted by American Banker and Gallup. Industry experts believe that most consumers still don't have a frame of reference to answer the survey questions, but once they experience wireless financial services, their reactions are usually positive. Hence

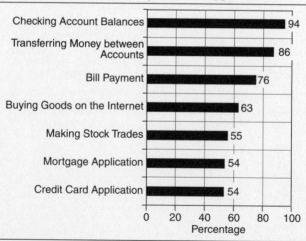

Figure 5.10
Percentage of Cell-Phone Users Indicating
Interest in Specific Financial Applications

Adapted from Mobilocity.net, 2000.

these numbers probably represent a lower boundary on the expected popularity of these applications.

Competitive Landscape. The preceding section discussed financial applications as well as the companies that are playing a major role in those segments. Some of those companies are mapped out across the wireless value chain in Figure 5.11. The next section describes how the offerings of various firms, as well as their cooperative and competitive interactions, are changing the landscape of application and service providers.

Figure 5.11
Players along Application Value Chains

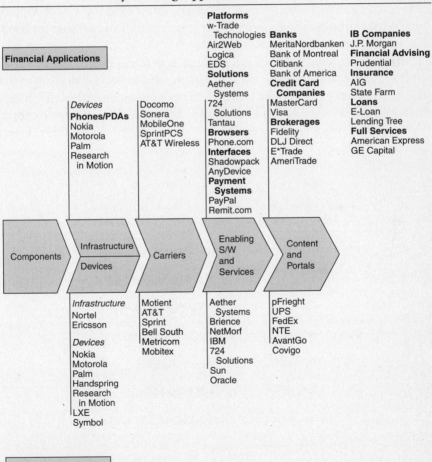

Initial Trends and Observations.   Although the wireless finance industry is still in its infancy, a few key trends have emerged that are likely to take hold and forever alter the competitive landscape. This trend is evident across most other mobile applications as well.

Companies are expanding beyond their traditional industry boundaries. The potential of wireless services is inviting a huge onslaught from nonfinance companies that want to partake in this lucrative sector. To create additional revenues, companies are increasingly cutting across industry and segment boundaries. Obvious new entrants are the mobile-network operators that have an existing relationship with their customers, who will soon also become financial users. NTT DoCoMo, in Japan, charges a 9 percent fee for all goods and services purchased though its I-Mode service. It also offers microbilling services that generate fees ranging from 5 percent to 15 percent of a transaction.

Another example, PayPal, started out a few years ago as a person-to-person payment service via e-mail in the United States. Since then, PayPal has amassed a large consumer and business-customer base that now transacts over the wireless medium as well. PayPal's execution costs are only a few cents per transaction, making them much cheaper than credit-card payments. It has also started offering its customers interest on deposits and insurance-fraud protection, as well as a branded credit card. Such trends promise to change the broader financial industry.

Firms are partnering across the value chain.   Partly in response to the trend outlined previously, as well as to endear themselves to customers by providing a wider range of services, companies all across the value chain are teaming up with each other. L.M. Ericsson and IBM are joining forces to deliver financial solutions over wireless networks. The partnerships between Fidelity and Palm in the United States offer wireless stock trading, and Barclays Bank and BT Celnet offer secure wireless financial transactions in the United Kingdom.

Key Success Factors.   As mentioned, most of the wireless services in the financial space are simply an extension of Web services. It is only a matter of time until activities such as trading and bill payment become commodities. As useful as these services are, they do not fully exploit the anytime, anywhere information and execution of the wireless medium. To extract the maximum benefits from m-commerce, financial institutions need to understand the key strategy and technology drivers of the market. Financial institutions will have to develop the following competencies to be competitive in this space.

Increasing customer loyalty.   Thus far, many companies have ventured into mobile services to enhance their revenues. Instead, firms should view mobile services initially as a cost of doing business. This mind-set will prevent financial institutions from pursuing distracting efforts, such as creating lifestyle portals, or from leaving out services that do not directly add to the top line. They must focus on offering basic services that fulfill immediate needs of their customers.

Differentiating services immediately.   Another important competency that creates customer loyalty is developing services that provide greater value to customers than they can get elsewhere. This approach will gain importance because many of the basic services currently offered will soon become commodities. Companies can do this by offering innovative services as well as device-specific applications. Examples of innovative, value-added features include access to analyst voice recordings or the ability to post to, and view messages from, financial advisers. Financial institutions should also offer services that exploit the strengths of each type of device rather than cater to the least common denominator of devices. For example, mobile phones are better equipped and should therefore be used for alerts or one-touch access to live specialists, whereas PDAs can be targeted for graphical and text-intensive applications.

Alleviating users' concerns about the security of financial applications. The big hurdle facing companies—especially financial firms—that plan to offer m-commerce applications is providing security, privacy, and control of user information. Not surprisingly, nearly 85 percent of customers are worried about the security of wireless transactions. Several vendors offer solutions using biometrics, such as voiceprints, and new technologies, such as elliptical-curve cryptography (ECC), that seem promising and will accelerate the adoption of these services. Customer education regarding mobile-security issues will have to become a crucial component of all marketing activities.

Future Outlook.   Financial institutions that want to surge forward must develop and launch offerings in mobile banking and commerce services as soon as possible to remain competitive, as well as to protect mediation. Few financial institutions will fail to exploit the mobile opportunity over the next several years. Many firms still view mobile data technologies as somewhat immature. Global standards for delivering mobile Internet services will soon be accepted, however, and that will revolutionize the industry. Financial institutions have the wealth, power, and prestige to help implement wireless financial services successfully.

Despite the turmoil in the wireless industry, it is still a matter of when, not if, there will be a deployment of more advanced networks and, hence, more services. Although the recent economic slowdown and the hesitation of mobile operators to rush into launching 3G networks gives players some breathing space, there is no time for them to be complacent and delay the inevitable. The dot-com bust also makes it imperative that financial firms offer even more meaningful services to consumers. Firms will exploit the possibilities of accessing information and conducting transactions in a time-sensitive, location-dependent environment. A Forrester Research survey found that 70 percent of banks and brokerages ranked wireless service as a key component of their overall strategies for the next two years.

Killer financial application. The future belongs not to one or two killer applications but to a suite of them. Here, suite does not refer to a hodgepodge of applications but to a meaningful collection of related personalized applications that are congruent with the offerings of the firm and its partners. Tapping successfully into the financial promise of m-commerce will require companies to understand and address its unique strategic and technological challenges. Firms will progress from simple informational and transactional services to "relationship-building" applications, as shown in Figure 5.12. Financial institutions must address the following issues to develop comprehensive business and technology strategies for financial applications.

Importance of personalization. Financial firms will leverage the advantages of personalization to drive customer loyalty and increase switching costs. Personalization could take many forms such as storing user-driven quote lists or exchange-rate information. Such tools create dependencies and increase the switching costs for the customer. Personalization, however, is the opposite of packaged solutions that some software firms are offering to banks and brokerages for their mobile customers. The solutions offer extremely basic or generalized services that do not capture the level of service to which customers are accustomed. Successful mobile applications will seamlessly integrate basic user-friendliness with that previous experience of service.

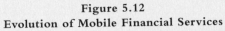

Figure 5.12
Evolution of Mobile Financial Services

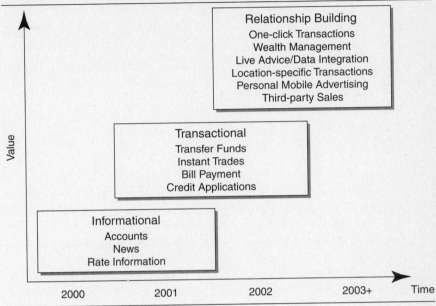

The same argument applies to financial companies' use of middleware applications that attempt to deliver their content to all types of devices. Because they tend to end up satisfying the lowest common denominator of device capabilities, the development of services for each family of devices must continue to be a priority.

Partnering across the value chain.   The emerging trend of companies partnering across the financial value chain will continue where it makes economic and business sense. Financial operators will partner with mobile operators to gain early visibility in this market. Partnerships with other mobile content providers will also remain a necessity. Alliances with technology providers will allow financial firms to remain ahead of emerging technologies and standards. The joint trial between telecommunications giant Motorola and MasterCard International, the leading credit-card network, demonstrates that complex financial transactions using a credit card can be securely carried out with a mobile phone. Such partnerships will draw more traffic to the wireless offering of the financial companies and allow them to exploit brand and billing relationships. Brand names that are associated with trustworthy and reliable fulfillment will translate effectively into the wireless domain.

Open access to the Internet.   At the moment, many mobile-network operators are pushing their own or only their partner's portals to customers, as the Palm VII device can access only a small smattering of sites. An open model will replace this closed model of access, just as happened on the Internet a few years ago, and customers will use their mobile devices to access any site or service. Although firms may give a prominent position on the interface to their partners, they will be unable to curtail their customers' wireless Web reach.

Integration of wireless with other delivery channels.   A wireless m-commerce strategy must be incorporated into an overall strategy that leverages, and is leveraged by, the other channels that institutions offer. Since accessing time-critical information on a mobile device is much quicker than going to a branch or an ATM, firms should encourage customers to view the mobile channel as the primary source of time-sensitive, location-independent information. Financial institutions will therefore position the wireless channel to be the main point of contact with the customer and then transition customers to other points as necessary. Firms can use the wireless channel to selectively drive traffic to other channels for information-heavy content. This will become a major source of cross-selling products and services and also improve the customer experience.

Global outlook.   The pioneering and leadership of Asia and Europe in this industry will continue for the foreseeable future. Those markets will likely achieve criticality for many of the popular brokerage and banking applications within the next two to three years. Until recently, industry experts were predicting that in the United States the Internet was a dress rehearsal for wireless applications. They assumed that American firms would quickly combine Internet business models with European technical and marketing experiences to become the dominant global player in m-commerce and wireless financial applications. The slowdown in the rollout of technology-unifying 3G networks, however, pushes this possibility beyond the realm of the next three to five years. The United States, instead, will probably continue to offer fragmented, yet innovative, financial services to a growing user base.

Summary.   The changes wrought by wireless communications and the Internet are encouraging thinking and sparking new businesses in the financial arena. Nevertheless, only a few big financial institutions have the resources to champion a new technology that must contend with an evolving communications infrastructure and an embryonic user base. That fact, however, doesn't tarnish the market potential for this nascent industry. An increase in users will occur as device and network technologies improve, data-capable devices approach ubiquity, and user-friendly brokerage content becomes commonplace in the wireless channel. Security may also become less of an issue as biometric authentication technology continues to drop in price. That in turn should help financial institutions and consumers feel more comfortable with conducting sensitive transactions over the wireless channel.

Health Care

There are many ways in which wireless technology can and does add value in the enormous health-care sector. The main driver behind the adoption of wireless technology is the desire to reduce the notorious inefficiency and to improve patient care. Wireless technology can add significant value in both areas. Our framework for analyzing the industry, however, reveals some significant obstacles to widespread adoption of wireless technologies in this industry.

Market Size. The health-care industry is enormous, representing one-seventh of U.S. gross domestic product (GDP), with more than $1.5 trillion in expenditures in 1997 and a growth rate of 5 percent a year.

The industry has several constituents, all of which are or will be affected by wireless technology. The market for wireless health care applications includes the following consumers:

- *Doctors.* Wireless handheld devices will deliver various useful applications for prescribing drugs, maintaining patient histories, sending and receiving laboratory tests and results, improving "charge capture," and dictation. Only about 1 percent to 2 percent of the more than 600,000 medical doctors in the United States use PDAs to conduct transactions, though 15 percent to 20 percent of them use PDAs for other purposes, such as schedulers and address books.
- *Patients.* Telemetry systems will allow remote monitoring of patients through wireless monitoring systems.
- *Hospitals.* Wireless LANs will dominate the information-technology infrastructure of hospitals.

- *Insurance companies/HMOs.* Documentation and transfer of information between doctors, patients, and insurers will be digitized and take place in a wireless environment.
- *Pharmacies.* Orders for prescription drugs will be placed wirelessly, improving accuracy and reducing paperwork.
- *Pharmaceutical companies.* Handheld m-commerce applications for sales representatives of pharmaceutical companies will improve efficiency in tracking orders and checking inventory.
- *Government regulators (federal and state).* Wireless applications will streamline the process for complying with Health Care Finance Administration (HCFA) regulations.

In considering the market size in wireless health care, it is important to keep in mind who actually funds most of that care: insurance companies and the federal government (through the HCFA and Medicare). The complicated documentation requirements of those organizations lie behind what many see as the enormous market opportunity for wireless and other technology applications in the industry.

Myriad government regulations require specific types of forms for medical care and drugs covered by Medicare. The HCFA regulations require doctors to classify any type of care into one of five levels, though the five levels vary depending on the stage of the consultation (initial, follow-up, etc.). Failure to properly classify types of treatment can result in more than denial of Medicare coverage. The federal government fined the University of Pennsylvania medical system $20 million for billing at a higher level of service under the HCFA than its backup documentation supported. To avoid such penalties, many health organizations choose always to err on the low side of the HCFA regulations by billing for smaller amounts of service and leaving money on the table. The opportunity to eliminate underbilling is the goal of many companies trying to enter the wireless health care market.

Insurance companies, as private payers, have another set of documentation requirements for doctors and hospitals to ensure that the care given and drugs prescribed conform to policy limitations. The allowable drugs that the policy will cover for any individual is contained in a document called a *formulary*. When doctors prescribe nonformulary drugs, there is generally a dispute between the doctor and the insurance company about cost coverage. Such disputes form a routine part of the practice of medicine in the United States, and the wasted time probably results in billions of dollars of unnecessary transaction costs.

Thus, the potential market size for wireless applications in health care is enormous. Indeed, the sheer size of the industry has drawn more attention from investors than the technology or the benefits that can be derived from wireless in the industry.

Spectrum of Health-care Applications. Numerous applications are already available for point-of-care health-care workers, particularly physicians. Many companies in the wireless area are attempting to address the inefficiencies in handling paperwork related to the myriad regulations and documentation requirements. In fact, wireless PDA applications for physicians that streamline day-to-day activities and reduce the paper burden are easily the most active area of wireless investment and product development in health care. Many of these applications are already viable. The following paragraphs describe some of them (all of which run on either a Palm or Pocket PC-based PDA).

"E-prescribing." This application allows physicians to electronically write, order, and renew prescriptions, as well as review critical information relating to adverse drug effects or drug interactions. There is tremendous value-added in this service. E-prescribing helps ensure formulary compliance by having the formulary for each patient available in real time at the time of prescription. This saves physicians the hassle of having to look in the formularies to confirm coverage. Drugs that are covered are shown on the screen of the PDA. Further, e-prescribing allows doctors to check drug interactions automatically, which will help eliminate a serious area of medical malpractice: prescribing drugs that may have fatal or very harmful interactions with drugs the patient is already taking. E-prescribing has benefits for pharmacies as well, in that prescriptions will be printed out in clear form rather than handwritten, greatly reducing time-consuming callbacks to doctors to clarify instructions.

Charge capture. This is another important added value of wireless applications in health care. Industry studies and HCFA data indicate that practicing physicians are losing more than $25 billion a year in denied or reduced fee-for-service claims. A typical physician with average annual billings of $650,000 is currently losing an estimated $35,000 to $100,000 in annual collected revenue because of claim denials; lost billings average approximately $60,000 per physician. Those lost billings are a direct result of inadequate documentation, invalid codes for procedures or tests, and failure to bill for services rendered outside the office setting. Further, overhead related to claims submission and collection consumes in excess of 40 percent of doctors' revenues.

To further complicate the situation, recent legislation, including the Health Insurance Portability and Accountability Act (HIPAA), has increased the detail and paperwork that the HCFA requires for reimbursement. The charge-capture application does not eliminate such problems, but it represents an opportunity to reduce lost billings significantly. The application allows physicians to more accurately and carefully track the procedures they perform and gives them a suggested HCFA level of care based on the inputs. Using a clear, intelligible format, doctors will be able to enter all the procedures that they followed at the time of care, and the information will be wirelessly transmitted to doctors' record-keeping systems.

Real-time laboratory orders and results.   Another significant function that has not been fully implemented is the use of wireless applications to order laboratory tests and receive and view results on a real-time basis. The technology for this application already exists.

Libraries.   Doctors will be able to wirelessly access databases containing vast amounts of information. They will be able to pull it up almost instantly on their handheld devices, sparing them book- or desk-based research while treating patients.

Regulations and HCFA rules.   Physicians will be able to access and display formularies, drug-use reviews, treatment guidelines, and other rules relevant to their practice areas from their wireless PDAs without the need for book or desk-based research.

The future—telemetry applications.   It is not hard to imagine the day when wireless telemetry will allow wireless remote patient monitoring and patient self-monitoring for many conditions. Thousands of people's pacemakers can now be monitored over phone lines. In the future, telemetry devices should be able to monitor the status of almost every kind of ailment to allow patients under the threat of remission the hope that diseases can be caught early enough to stop them. As wireless devices increasingly monitor health and other advances in biotechnology occur, patients' interactions with their physicians will be fundamentally altered. New understandings of the human genome will identify the proneness of some patients to certain illnesses, and rather than visiting a doctor to see whether a likely disease has developed, patients could be monitored through wireless telemetry devices embedded in their bodies. The image of people carrying wireless monitoring devices in their bodies creates associations with the part-human/part-machine cyborgs of science fiction lore, but advances in technology make this possibility less and less a fantasy.

The future—additional technology changes that will affect wireless health care. Because wireless applications in health care are generally not data intensive, their adoption is not dependent on 3G or other high-bandwidth solutions. More significant for health care will be the widespread adoption of Bluetooth. This technology offers the prospect of physicians' being able to walk into a hospital room and instantly have access on their handheld devices to the heart monitor on the screen in front of them. If they want to do an independent analysis of the data, handhelds will provide that opportunity. The ease of printing and transferring information that Bluetooth promises will certainly facilitate the transition to wireless use throughout the industry. Also, many hospitals in older buildings can be more cheaply outfitted with wireless technology than with wire-line technology.

Key Success Factors. The health-care industry is infamous for its Byzantine nature and staggering inefficiency, and one would think that given those enormous inefficiencies, doctors would be ready to help eliminate the waste. The problem that complicates the situation, however, is the same problem that complicates much of the health-care system: The entities paying for the care are not connected to the point of care. Thus, there is not always a tight link between the people who would be most likely to use the new wireless applications (doctors and other caregivers) and the entities that would benefit most from them financially (insurance companies, through reduced claims).

Doctors are notoriously technology shy, and the inconvenience of disrupting their routine to learn a new technology or application has been a massive barrier to any company trying to enter this space. Further, the benefits to be derived from many of these applications are not easy to quantify for many physicians because the technologies are new. As a result, many wireless health-care companies have had a difficult time convincing doctors that the net benefits are worth paying the typical subscription costs of $100 to $200 a month.

Still, some forces at work in the health-care industry could dramatically accelerate the rate of adoption of wireless technology:

- *Widespread insurance discounting for use of the applications.* Insurance companies might be willing to give significant discounts to doctors

who employ e-prescribing applications because of the reduced inci-
dence of malpractice resulting from improper prescriptions. Some insurers are already helping defray the costs of these services, presumably
with the intention of finding out whether they actually result in fewer
claims against the doctors who use them.

- *Changes in the standard of care required under medical malpractice
  law that will make prescription-management applications a virtual requirement for all physicians.* In the area of medication management
  (prescription services), the standard of minimum care as defined by
  common-law malpractice law could soon include applications that
  check drug interactions and scan relevant databases and client information for possible complications or adverse reactions. If medical malpractice law creates an incentive to adopt these applications, usage
  could become almost universal.
- *Endorsement of the applications by the HCFA.* A gigantic boost in
  adoption would occur if the HCFA endorsed these applications, as this
  approval would achieve a long-sought consistent and predictable manner of communicating with the HCFA.

Summary.   The key driver in wireless adoption is in the cost/benefit category. The potential market is enormous, and the technologies already
largely exist for many applications and functions. The question comes down
to whether insurance companies will create incentives and whether changes
in the standard of care will virtually require wireless technology from a
cost/benefit perspective. Some of the wireless applications that have been
or are being developed promise to alter in fundamental ways how physicians
practice medicine and could result in dramatic cost savings. Companies
such as Allscripts, which is well positioned to ride out the ups and downs
of the market and still be in the game as adoption rates escalate, should be
able to capture a large portion of this value. Companies such as Data Critical, which is exploring medical telemetry devices as well as the physician
applications Allscripts provides, may capture value resulting from major
changes in physicians' interactions with patients. The widespread adoption
of telemetry technology is a long way off, but those companies positioned
to help drive the changes could also capture tremendous value in the future.

Government

Wireless applications are finding a fertile environment for deployment and
development in government public-safety organizations such as police, fire

department, and medical emergency services. The communication platform of these organizations is migrating from old radio- and paper-based systems to new mobile open systems. Public-safety organizations have been early adopters of wireless solutions to support their operations because their mobile workforces have a critical need to access the most-up-to-date databases from anywhere in the field.

Market Size and Applications.   Based on data from the U.S. Bureau of Labor statistics, the market potential for wireless solutions for the government is estimated at around 4 million users and more than $1 billion in revenues by 2003. The existing applications support multiple purposes, such as dispatching, remote data access, field data collection and reporting, on-site inspections and scheduling, and management of personnel and resources.

Wireless solutions for police. Police departments are finding wireless applications are key tools for accessing crime and drivers' databases from the field online. The law-enforcement function—the significant workload of police departments—is driving the development of wireless applications in the public sector because officers in the field need efficient mobile solutions to support quick and broad data access. Traditionally, police officers have relied on a central computer system at headquarters to check criminal and drivers' records, which easily saturated the police communications centers (911). Mobile technologies ease the load on such centers, providing officers with quick response times at their locations, helping them to make rapid decisions on appropriate actions. Public-safety organizations also find wireless applications are a way to get immediate service and dispatch data to their remote workforces.

Other potential users. Traditionally, federal agencies have been slow to adopt wireless technologies other than voice applications because of their high cost and limited coverage and capacity. Other government services that are relying increasingly on mobile solutions are public works, municipal services, health agencies, and courts.

Technology Viability.   The technology for government wireless solutions already exists for many applications, although it is limited by the usual bandwidth considerations. Most of the applications in police work, however, are not extremely data intensive, and therefore bandwidth is not a severely constraining factor. Companies such as Aether Systems are already deploying technologies that enable all the functions described previously. As in the other verticals examined, the limiting factor in government applications does not appear to be technology; instead, it is whether the companies selling the technology and applications can convince consumers (police and fire departments, etc.) that the benefits are worth the investment.

Key Success Factors. The critical driver in this vertical is the same as in the other two. Vertical wireless applications could provide many benefits, both in the performance of public organizations and for the final users (the citizens) of the services. The main problem is helping industries and government entities, which have not required technological sophistication in the past, recognize the advantages the technologies offer. There are several ways that government entities could gain cost efficiency through wireless applications.

Cost of communications. Although deploying equipment and wireless devices requires an initial investment, there would be less overhead in supplying communications support to the mobile workforce. Fewer people would be needed in central headquarters to facilitate the interface/communications with the employees in the field. Wireless could also improve the quality and timing of information, optimizing the resources available in the field. Handling more precise information allows the mobile workforce to allocate its time more efficiently to deliver a better and cheaper service to the community.

Increased security features. Wireless applications for police will not only optimize the cost and quality of their services but also improve the security of police officers by providing information that may reduce the risk in performing dangerous duties.

Crime prevention/awareness. Prospective offenders who perceive the faster response time of police departments derived from wireless technologies may lose incentive to break the rules. Thus, enhanced communications not only improve the quality of the police actions once an offense is committed but also facilitate prevention.

Better services for citizens. Finally, all the improvements in cost and quality will improve the welfare of taxpayers, who will enjoy increased safety and a better response of government organizations to health, fire, or environmental emergencies.

Although these are legitimate areas of cost improvement and efficiency, the difficulty is quantifying them and presenting a viable value proposition to consumers. Companies that are selling and hosting these applications in government services have found it to be a tough sell. Quantifying the value of the offering is customer specific and requires a customized detailing of how the technology investment can save money. Because there is no precedent, that task often proves difficult, if not impossible, except in terms of speculation.

Summary.   Given that traditional communication systems in government organizations support only limited remote online access to central databases, wireless applications that promise efficiency and integration in a safety organization's mobile workforce are likely to have some success in the next few years. Efficiencies in such areas may offset the costs of deploying the technologies and training the workforce. The process will almost certainly take several years, however, given the low level of technological sophistication of the government consumers and the generally slow bureaucratic pace of innovation in the public sector.

Overall in government applications, the limiting factor in growth is once again the cost/benefit proposition to the consumer. The market is large, and the technologies exist to cater to that market, but it is difficult to quantify the benefits to the consumers in a convincing way. Additionally, government consumers are generally slow to recognize the benefits of, and to adopt, new technologies.

Future Trends—Vertical Applications Become Horizontal

Though the wireless application framework has been presented statically with a clear delineation between horizontal and vertical applications, in reality applications are much more dynamic. In particular, the path of some wireless applications will start in verticals and then will migrate across them. Initially, major companies in a particular industry will identify a need for a customized application. The costs of such an application will often be large, but the benefits, which are also larger, will drive adoption. The slow rate of adoption ends up being a function of high costs of adoption and the lack of a compelling value proposition. Over time, as costs come down and adoption increases, the value of the vertical applications will become obvious, and companies will realize that they need to adopt or be left at a competitive disadvantage.

The barriers to horizontal adoption are deeper and relate to issues within the different verticals. The tailored solutions for most industry verticals are often based on proprietary systems and are not easily transported, which will hinder their widespread adoption for the near future. In trying to discern when the bulk of the shift from verticals to horizontals will occur, there are two important factors to consider: standardization and broad functionality. Looking at any technology as it relates to these factors makes it easier to see how industry-specific technologies will begin to move across vertical markets.

Standardization. Standardization of the infrastructure behind the application drives down the costs to the user. At a lower cost, the application addresses a much larger market, and what was once useful in one industry is now worth paying for in another. Figure 5.13 shows that as the cost to the user drops, the addressable market increases and the application migrates into horizontal territory.

The cost of the application drops as the infrastructure standardizes because economies of scope accompany standards. Once a company owns a PC, the marginal cost of adding an additional application is small. The cost of the PC, or underlying infrastructure, is amortized over the benefits received from the numerous applications it can run. Therefore, the benefit no longer needs to be as large as it was for the vertical application because the costs are now much smaller. For the vertical application, the benefits had to cover the cost of not only the application but also the underlying infrastructure.

In wireless, a vast number of standards exist today. On the hardware side, there are many devices, each with different screen sizes and resolutions. On the software side, there are competing operating systems including

Figure 5.13
Migration from Vertical to Horizontal Applications

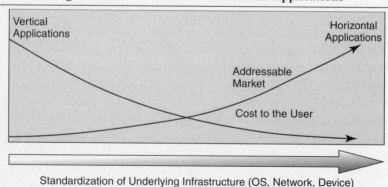

Standardization of Underlying Infrastructure (OS, Network, Device)

Palm OS, RIM OS, Motorola OS, EPOCH, and Windows CE. Even the networks have multiple standards: TDMA, CDMA, iDEN, GSM, and Mobitex. Contrast that with the wired world, where hardware screen sizes are standardized, the operating system has converged on Windows, and the network has conformed to TCP/IP, and it is clear that wireless has a long way to go before achieving standardization. The alphabet soup of standards will hinder progress down the cost curve; consequently, it may also slow the adoption of horizontal applications.

Broad Functionality. The second factor that will influence widespread adoption of applications across industries is broad functionality. An application created for a vertical likely has some functionality that is specific to that vertical and some functionality that is useful to many industries. Before a vertical application starts its migration, a modified version must be created that removes the industry-specific functionality. Not every vertical application has enough common functionality to drive demand in the broad market. The process is more akin to natural selection. Whereas it is possible to discover a horizontal application for businesses, it is more likely that a vertical application will be modified to target a larger market.

One example is the spreadsheet. Conceived from accounting research, large accounting organizations used such applications to process accounting information on mainframes. It wasn't until the advent of the PC that VisiCalc was created to address the large market for spreadsheets.

Crossing the Chasm and Competition in the Value Chain. Geoffrey Moore, in his book *Inside the Tornado,* explains that in an early market period, margins are typically high and solutions tend to be custom. Product leadership is key during this phase, since innovators and early adopters are attracted to leading products and applications. The foundation for growing a customer base is built in this early cycle, and as Sun-Tzu (the author of *The Art of War*) states, "Opportunities multiply as they are seized." The market for mobile data has seen adoption by many innovators and early adopters. Many early winners in the value chain have been either enabling-software and services companies or solutions providers that have cobbled together leading-edge solutions for specific industries or a narrow set of horizontal applications such as messaging. Moore also writes in *Inside the Tornado* that as the early majority is adopting a product, margins start decreasing. Solutions are still somewhat customized, but operational excellence becomes key as well as product leadership. As the product moves to the late majority, low margins can be expected, and products tend to be standardized. At that point, operational excellence and customer intimacy play a bigger role. Dell Computer is an excellent example in the now-mature PC industry.

In much the same way, the wireless value chain will see a change in competition as the market matures and applications become more standardized—either as extensions of already existing wired horizontal applications or modifications of applications that were previously isolated to a vertical. This will put increasing pressure for operational excellence on wireless carriers, device makers, and solutions providers. Carriers will have to use their allocated bandwidth more effectively; device makers will see deteriorating margins that they can combat only with continuous incremental innovations; and solutions providers will have to create standard core-product platforms that they can modify to fit the needs of customers.

Customer intimacy will play a larger and larger role, particularly in the case of *consumer* adoption of wireless applications. The phenomenal success of I-mode in Japan is a tantalizing example of strong branding and widespread consumer adoption of mobile data. This chapter concludes with a discussion of I-Mode and the technological, cultural, and business challenges that will factor into the adoption of similar services and applications in the United States.

I-Mode: Killer Application in Japan

After the deregulation of the Japanese telecommunication industry in 1992, the telecommunications giant NTT spun off DoCoMo, maintaining two-thirds ownership. To date, DoCoMo's greatest success has been I-Mode (information mode), a wireless data service.

Since its entry into the market, I-Mode has experienced phenomenal growth, the number of subscribers overtaking Nifty, the Fujitsu-owned competitor, within a year of its launch in February 1999. Subscribers now exceed 20 million. In comparison, Nifty won its 3.5 million customers over 15 years. New customers continue to come in at the rate of 50,000 to 70,000 new ones every day. I-Mode users represent more than half of the wireless Internet users worldwide according to Eurotechnology.com. An additional 5 million Japanese use WAP phones. Users of the I-Mode service access the Internet an average of 10 times a day according to DoCoMo.

I-Mode now commands upward of 70 percent market share (Figure 5.14). Two other players round out the wireless data market in Japan. KDDI markets a service called EZWeb, based on WAP protocols. The 68 Kbs packet-based service gives KDDI superior voice quality and supports

Figure 5.14
Japanese Mobile Interactive–Services Market in 2000

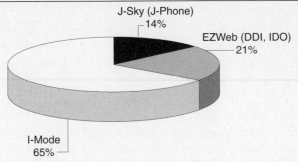

Source: Ministry of Posts and Telecommunication, June 2000.

higher–speed data transfer rates than I–Mode's 9.6 Kbs offering, though voice quality and speed have not compromised I–Mode's strong market position. Japan Telecom's J–Phone also offers its J–SkyWalker service, based on its own protocol, called Mobile Markup Language.

DoCoMo's significant market power has helped it maintain its dominant position by influencing the development of both phones and content. DoCoMo works with phone manufacturers to design I–Mode phones that

---

The I–Mode Concept

- Adapted Netscape's business model with a low entrance threshold including low fees. AOL's model: proprietary portal.
- Focuses on fresh, interesting, entertaining content, not technology.
- Uses strong I–Mode branding, not technology specific, open to future technologies.
- Includes content provided by alliance partners and other voluntary sites.
- Sells information, transactions, and entertainment in small, convenient, inexpensive packets.
- Uses successful micropayment system through NTT DoCoMo phone bill.
- Easily creates I–Mode Web sites on existing Internet.
- Accelerated introduction of 3G to Japan, bringing 200 times the current bandwidth.

are user-friendly and light and that boast the latest in technological advances. In January 2000 DoCoMo introduced phones with color screens capable of 256-bit color graphics that can display animated GIF files just like Web browsers. In addition, the extensive market penetration of I-Mode makes the I-Mode application a must for content developers.

Business Model

DoCoMo's emphasis on developing a compelling business model and using technology to support that business model significantly affected I-Mode's success. When it came to technology, the operator had little choice: Since the WAP option was not available, DoCoMo had to implement HTML-based technology. That helped to broaden the applications available on I-Mode. The initial hurdle that the I-Mode team faced was to convince management that DoCoMo should target I-Mode to consumers rather than to PC and Internet-friendly business users. Once focused on consumers, developers selected services they thought would be useful to people on the go—bank balances, restaurant reviews, and related information were available at the touch of a button. To encourage use, the developers concentrated on developing user-friendly software. I-Mode technology made mobile surfing and access easy through a customer-focused interface and a continuous Internet connection whenever the phone is on.

DoCoMo realized that cost was a major factor that had limited the adoption of the wired Internet but recognized the potential for widespread acceptance and demand for Internet services. To attract this market, it developed a sophisticated micropayment system, charging users according to the amount of data downloaded and not the time online.

I-Mode: The Essentials

- More than 80 percent of the world's wireless Internet users are in Japan.
- I-Mode's brand is not fixed to a single technology.
- I-Mode makes DoCoMo Japan's largest Internet Service Provider.
- It is a benchmark for m-commerce and micropayment platforms.
- The technology uses packet-switched (Internet protocol, always on, no dial-in) overlay over circuit-switched digital voice mobile.
- I-Mode uses cHTML (subset of HTML), not WAP.

The packet-switching technology facilitated that charging structure. To expand content, DoCoMo does not charge content providers like Disney anything (except for bill-collection services). It operates a billing system that records the customer's traffic and subscription costs (along with any charges made by content providers) all on one bill. DoCoMo then collects revenue, including its 9 percent fee on charged content, and distributes what is due to the content providers.

The average I-Mode customer generates revenue of $17 per month, composed of the following charges:

Subscription fees: $3

Traffic costs: $12 ($0.003 per data packet of 128 bytes)

Commission: $2 (9 percent of amount content providers charge for downloading applications or services)

SERVICES

A competitive advantage of I-Mode is the service and content available at the user's fingertips with relative ease. Transactions fall into four categories:

1. *M-commerce*. Banking, books and CDs, trading, airline and concert tickets. Sony's online store now also takes orders via I-Mode. The stockbroker DLJ Direct receives 30 percent of its transactions in Japan over I-Mode. Japan Airlines and Nippon Travel get 10,000 reservations per month over I-Mode.
2. *Database access*. Telephone and restaurant directories.
3. *Weather, news, and stock information*.
4. *Entertainment*. Games, karaoke, and club events.

A survey by Information Communications, an NTT subsidiary, shows that the sites that help the user explore I-Mode are now becoming the most popular. I-Mode designates 10 to 20 official I-Mode sites from the thousands of applications it receives each month. Many of the most popular applications are among the 16,000 or so unofficial sites. For example, one popular site helps the user trick the system to send and receive longer text messages than DoCoMo allows. Some other popular sites on I-Mode include:

- *Yamaha Corporation*. Maintains a site enabling users to download hit songs to use as dial tones.

- *Olympus.* Has launched a camera designed to transmit digital photos when connected to an I–Mode phone.
- *DoCoMo.* Launched a global positioning system that tells users where they are and gives directions to a destination.

Although 95 percent of I–Mode users purchase content or use premium sites primarily for entertainment (various cartoon sites are especially popular), 43 percent of I–Mode traffic is e-mail messages, despite a 250-characters-per-message limit, underscoring the importance of the traditional network killer app. A survey by InfoCom Research found that I–Mode phone users spend 34.2 percent of their total use time making and receiving calls (an average of 3.67 calls per day); 41.8 percent send e-mail (an average of 9.08 e-mail messages sent and received per day); and 24 percent surf I–Mode sites. Only 26.2 percent use I–Mode at work or school (Figure 5.15).

Factors Driving I–Mode's Success

Mobile data requires the integration of the programming environment, content, transport, and the end-user terminal. No carrier outside Japan has executed end-to-end service to the same extent as DoCoMo. I–Mode destroyed one great wireless data myth—that you need a lot of bandwidth for a successful wireless operation. The following elements have contributed to I–Mode's accomplishments:

- *Market power.* The company leveraged its channel dominance to get handset developers such as Sony, Sharp, Kyocera, and even Nokia to

Figure 5.15
Use of I-Mode Services

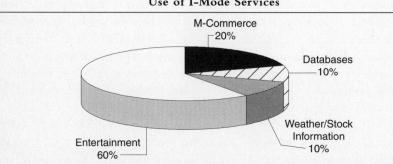

Success Factors

- Content is compelling and attractive, with frequent updates to encourage multiple accesses per day.
- Micropayment via NTT phone bill attracts partners and makes m-commerce easy for the consumer.
- Market is focused on entertainment, not technology.
- DoCoMo has a large market share.
- Japanese people love gadgets, and Japanese youth have a high rate of technology adoption.
- Japanese people walk and take trains, giving them more time to access I-Mode content. In the United States, people primarily drive cars for transportation and cannot use the wireless Internet while driving.
- Packet switching eliminates wait time for access and connection-based fees.

---

do its bidding. Thereby I-Mode was able to provide phones that were technologically advanced, appealing to consumers who wanted cutting-edge technology. At industry shows in the past several years in Japan, close to 40 new I-Mode devices were on display, resembling everything from a traditional cell phone to a cosmic egg to a TV-like palm device. Sony is rolling out the Cybershot, a camera that will allow consumers to transmit digital images to color I-Mode cell phones from PCs through Sony's i-Jump network service. Other companies are offering photo-printing services that work with I-Mode phones. DoCoMo, Oki Electric, NTT Data, Mizuho Financial Group, Microsoft, and others are collaborating on the first secure-payment system for I-Mode.

- *Consumer focus.* DoCoMo recognized the tremendous opportunity to connect consumers to the Internet when landline access was limited. After seeing the potential, DoCoMo's concentration on connecting with young consumers, early adopters of mobile technologies, tapped a lucrative market. In addition, it realized that an application capitalizing on the large amount of idle time that the Japanese spend commuting could be very successful.
- *Brand development.* In its marketing, DoCoMo did not refer to established interactive mediums such as the Web. Instead, it focused on services that are available uniquely on I-Mode, such as the ability to

send messages to friends, which created strong brand awareness among consumers.

- *User interface.* To create a better consumer experience, DoCoMo developed a friendly and intuitive user interface. For example, train schedules are retrievable in two clicks. Packet-switching technology made mobile surfing and access easy, since the customer is connected whenever the phone is on and it takes only one button to enter the I–Mode services. Compact HTML is flexible enough to accommodate multibyte kanji characters and other graphical elements, further improving the user interface. Because only 13 percent of Japanese have access to the Internet through a home computer, they were more accepting of Internet access on a small phone screen.

- *Content quality.* The development team focused on including content that would be valuable to individuals on the go. I–Mode was also attractive to content developers since, unlike WAP, it allows site designers to write programs in a stripped-down version of HTML. That further encouraged the development of content and the creation of valuable unofficial I–Mode sites. The media director of DoCoMo, T. Natsuno, says quality of content has been the key to I–Mode's success. He emphasizes that content should change, encourage repeat visits (e.g., games), and have an easily recognizable benefit. To help establish this quality content at the start of the service, I–Mode signed up 67 application alliance partners (AAPs), which are similar to online content partners and are part of the I–Mode on-screen real estate. I–Mode now has several thousand content partners, including many thousands of unofficial offerings (independently established I–Mode-compatible sites). DoCoMo recently allied with Sony to jointly develop PlayStation and I–Mode technologies, further strengthening its strong content position.

- *Economical positioning.* DoCoMo took advantage of the high cost of installing and maintaining a landline connection by developing an economical cost structure. A new telephone line connection costs $600 (72,000 yen) in Japan before usage charges; by contrast, I–Mode costs $28 for the connection, and monthly bills average $17. For the wireless version, the cost is linked to data downloaded and not to time online, which allows users to explore I–Mode without incurring high expenses. The company built a packet-data overlay on its PDC network to facilitate the charging structure.

- *Existing customer base.* As a preexisting provider of mobile voice services to the Japanese market, NTT DoCoMo had an established

---

I-Mode Service Classics

- iBanking—mobile banking.
- iTrade—credit cards, securities, share trading, insurance.
- iTravel—hotel, car, and airline reservations, directions.
- iTicket—event tickets, apartment rental, employment postings.
- iGourmet—restaurants, recipes.
- iMode mail—e-mail, 250-character limit, 50-message memory.
- iNews—news and information.
- iTown—town information.
- iEntertainment—mobile karaoke, games, cartoons.
- iTool—dictionary, telephone directory.
- iAnime—animated cartoons, pals, and pets for download onto the mobile screen.
- iMelody—ringing.

---

customer base. At the launch of I-Mode, all but the most basic phone came equipped with I-Mode, thereby removing the impact of switching costs. That is particularly important in the Japanese market, where mobile phones are often perceived as a fashion accessory and regularly updated.

Future of I-Mode

As part of a strategy to transport I-Mode outside Japan, DoCoMo has made many strategic overseas investments and alliances in North and South America, Europe, and Asia, most notably with AOL. DoCoMo has a strategic partnership with AT&T. NTT DoCoMo and AT&T Wireless plan to jointly develop the U.S. mobile multimedia market by leveraging the nationwide network infrastructure of AT&T Wireless and the I-Mode-based mobile Internet technology and related business know-how. Additionally, an NTT subsidiary, NTTCommunications, acquired the U.S. network-services provider Verio, which hosts more than 400,000 Web sites, in a move to promote the development of I-Mode-enabled Web sites. NTT is under domestic pressure to expand broadband access in Japan, which lags not only behind Europe and the United States, but also behind Korea and Taiwan.

DoCoMo put in place a value chain that will serve the operator well when 3G services come online and starts to gain customer acceptance. It includes $7.6 billion to build the world's first Wireless-CDMA network, which is due to open for service in April. Initially the 3G service will run at 386 Kbs, rising to 2 Mbs by 2003. That means that 3G services will be launched in Japan approximately two years earlier than in the United States, giving DoCoMo a strong technological lead.

WIRELESS MARKET IN THE UNITED STATES

Because of all this momentum, tremendous growth was projected early for information services for cell phones.

- Gartner Group projected that by 2004, 95 percent of new mobile phones will be WAP-enabled.
- A Strategis Group survey found 34 percent of wireless users were interested in a wireless portal service. The study predicted that the number of wireless portal users would grow to nearly 183.7 million worldwide in the five years following 2000.
- An AOL/Roper Starch Worldwide study in 2000 found: "More than half of Internet users said they would be interested in using small, non-PC Internet devices to go online from anywhere."

Yet all is not rosy for mobile-phone services. Concerns over privacy, security, and the usability limitations of current Web-browsing phones may limit the rapid adoption of services in the United States.

- Forrester Research found that 72 percent of U.S. households have no interest in receiving data like news, weather, and sports scores on their wireless phones and that nearly 75 percent say they are not comfortable with the concept of mobile e-commerce.
- Allied Business Intelligence (ABI) found that less than 5 percent of a sample that included both cell-phone users and nonusers say the cell phone would be a good Internet access tool, whereas 40 percent think it would not be.

Since Sprint's introduction of PCS phone services in 1994, the U.S. wireless industry has evolved from a niche player that offered expensive voice services on clunky equipment to a nearly ubiquitous presence in corporate and consumer America. At the same time, non-voice-based information services, including mobile commerce, have proliferated on wireless phones, though they have yet to achieve their market potential. For example, Sprint customers can send gifts using the recipient's e-mail address. Most new cell phones have the ability to receive e-mail and other short messages and to act as pagers. The newest models add limited Web-browsing ability and even e-commerce capabilities. In fact, more than half (58 percent) of all cell phones bought at retail in Q4 2000 were Net ready—a 10-fold jump from the same period a year before, according to the NPD Group. Despite these inroads, however, U.S. wireless phone capabilities have continued to lag considerably behind overseas goods and services.

Unlike the Japanese, the American market remains highly fragmented, with service providers, hardware manufacturers, and content developers vying for consumers. The competitive environment has kept costs to consumers down and impeded the development of a consistent technological standard.

U.S. Consumers

The Wireless Commerce Monitor data shows that information services provided through a wireless device are still on the relatively flat part of the early adoption curve in the United States, with overall use of wireless information services by less than 10 percent of wireless phone users. At the same time, industry beliefs suggest that large-scale opportunities exist in the wireless information arena. Topping most predictions for areas of growth are traffic/directions and e-mail/text messaging.

However, ConStat Research has illustrated that although users in the United States are willing to receive e-mail and short text messages on their traditional wireless handsets, most are absolutely unwilling to peck out even the shortest of messages using a numeric keypad. Voice-recognition systems may provide a partial solution to this problem, but it is questionable whether these systems will adequately replicate these functions.

Young Consumers.   Children and young adults ages 10 to 24 may be the fastest growing U.S. market for wireless voice and data services over the next several years, according to surveys by Cahners In-Stat Group. Young wireless subscribers will jump from 11 million in 2001 to more than 30 million in 2004, and the number of users will rise from nearly 24 million to 43 million. That means that by 2004, half of U.S. youths will own a wireless phone and nearly three out of four will use one.

Although this group represents a high credit risk to carriers, youth actually have significant spending power, as 10-to-17-year-olds alone spend $50 billion annually, In-Stat estimates. Other sources estimate that youth between 12 and 19 spent as much as $105 billion of their own money. Even lacking credit histories, these consumers are lucrative targets for wireless carriers.

Non-college-attending young adults ages 18 to 24 could be the largest segment of the youth wireless market. This group would probably embrace wireless services enthusiastically because its members enter the job market early and have significant disposable income. InStat surveys suggest that the wireless Internet may lure this segment most easily with content such as shopping, news, sports, entertainment, education, and opinion polls.

Carriers in the United States hope American youths will take to wireless services as enthusiastically as their counterparts in Japan, where 60 percent to 70 percent of teens use wireless e-mail. According to the U.S. Census Bureau, there are approximately 60 million people in this country between the ages of 10 and 24, making it an ideal segment to target for wireless services, even though several cultural and environmental differences exist between Japan and the United States. According to a nationwide survey compiled in December 2000, a cell phone was the number one item on American teens' wish lists. It is the hottest coming-of-age badge among today's teens. According to a recent national study by Teenage Research Unlimited, 6 million teens in the United States own one. Cellular companies are hoping to connect with Generation Y by offering a colorful assortment of phones that provide both flash and function.

Companies such as the start-up wireless carrier Talking Drum are hoping to cash in. It markets Kode, a wireless communication network oriented toward youth culture. "We're really kind of pushing the envelope on technology, on fashion and music, and the kids pick up on it like that. So that's why we build Kode around youth culture and communications." Although these phones provide Internet access, voice functions remain the most popular—especially group chat functions that allow as many as five users to talk at once. Talking Drum launched Kode in November in Sacramento, California, targeting 30,000 of the city's teenagers and hoping to attract 2 percent of them as subscribers by the end of the year.

Another company targeting the youth market is Cybiko, a handheld-device manufacturer that aims to fill the gap between Palm handhelds and GameBoy. The Cybiko looks like a walkie-talkie with a small keyboard, performs organizer functions, and allows users to communicate with other Cybikos within 300 feet. Users can download games from the Web at no charge and purchase an MP3 player that fits into the device's expansion slot. In an interview with LocalBusiness.com, the founder of Cybiko, Don Wisniewski, commented: "We have a very fickle group to market to. They're not only interested in technology and efficiency, but they are also into fashion."

Network Access

Network infrastructure in the United States has differed from that in other countries, affecting the development of wireless services. Current wireless networks are either 1G (analog) or 2G (digital, such as PCS). They typically support data access at 9.6 Kbps, but some support 19.2 Kbps. Since wired modem access averages above 28.8 Kbps, and Web sites are becoming more and more graphics intensive, some content modification is necessary for wireless devices. Other modifications are necessary because of the small screen size. The next generation of wireless networks will deliver increased bandwidth, though it is unclear exactly how fast they will get and by when. Some network vendors are targeting so-called 2.5G technologies such as GPRS and enhanced data rates for GSM evolution (EDGE), which can increase maximum bandwidth to 384 Kbps and will serve wireless devices large enough to support video transmissions. DoCoMo is preparing to offer similar video services in Japan over its I-Mode phones. Others are waiting for 3G, which promises speeds up to 2 Mbps.

Choosing a Standard

The fragmented market structure has precipitated competing standards. In the United States, a battle over the transmission protocols used in cell-phone telephony is being waged among code-division multiple access (CDMA), time-division multiple access (TDMA), and global system for mobile communications (GSM), which predominates in the rest of the world. All sorts of standards for fixed wireless networking also contend for supremacy. The two most important standards in the near future for the wireless marketplace are WAP and I-Mode.

WAP versus I–Mode

- I–Mode uses a modified version of HTML (cHTML). Thus it is easy and straightforward to build Web sites for it. WAP uses its own language, so barriers to creation of WAP Web sites are higher.

- I–Mode is always on; there is no need for dial–up, and no fees are associated with connection time. WAP uses circuit switching (dial–up). Users must wait to dial up and are charged per minute of connection time.

- WAP services are limited to lines of text and simple monochrome graphics. I–Mode already allows color, GIF animation and Java–enabled games, software, and security.

WAP Problems. Critics are quick to point out WAP's most glaring fault: By trying to turn the phone (an audio device) into a browser (a visual device), WAP goes against the very nature of the device, which is to deliver audio information. People are not used to watching their phones, and thus using WAP requires a behavior change. Some critics have gone so far as to state that WAP solves a problem nobody cared about: how to turn an audio phone into a visual browser. Even Phone.com, one of the inventors of WAP, has said it expects to eventually move away from the technology.

A related problem is reducing rich, multimedia content designed for large PC screens to fit the small windows on most wireless devices. Some critics call this the "Honey, I Shrunk the Web" syndrome. It is a given that not all Web content is appropriate for delivery to wireless devices. Despite Macromedia's recent introduction of pocket Flash, most multimedia–intense sites will be left out of the wireless revolution.

Of more concern is the growing tendency of vendors to tweak the WAP standard just enough to compromise interoperability. Other concerns revolve around security. Gartner's Vice President, John Pescatore, believes that as mobile phones become smarter, attacks through software updates and simple scripting will increase because wireless vendors have taken short-cuts that leave systems vulnerable. Since wireless phones and PDAs are single–user devices, they typically do not implement the same file–access security as other computing platforms. In addition, the limited computing resources available on wireless platforms make tight security or antivirus measures difficult. Of course, security involves more than just protection against viruses. Ensuring secure, private transactions is essential for developing m-commerce. Baltimore Technologies sells a wireless device to gateway data-transfer technology called wireless-transport security layer (WTLS) that guarantees authentication and the integrity and confidentiality of data.

Another problem with WAP is uneven support for the evolving standard. Some critics claim that phone manufacturers, who are releasing new models and microbrowsers on an almost monthly basis, do not even support WAP the same way in different iterations of the same phone. For example, several versions of the Nokia 7110 microbrowser are available, each version supporting WML code differently. This inconsistency makes for a less-than-optimal user experience and makes service developers' lives difficult as well. The complicated process of signing up for a new WAP service on a phone further impedes usability.

A final concern is that the initial version of WAP, at least as implemented in Europe, is not always on. European users endure a dial-up delay because WAP is a circuit-switched protocol and thus requires establishing an Internet session. As a final insult, Europeans must pay connect charges to use WAP features. Leave the phone on by accident, and a 16-hour mistake could cost $250.

I-Mode: Threat to WAP Standard?   I-Mode's entry into the American market opens the standards competition further. Given the limitations and criticisms of WAP, some form of accommodation or convergence with the I-Mode standard seems likely. A major factor that could limit I-Mode's expansion is its proprietary technology. WAP is an open standard that any manufacturer can adopt. DoCoMo, on the other hand, controls I-Mode, at least so far. If the two standards do not converge, it might be tough for DoCoMo to make a go of it in the United States. The short-term future in Europe and the United States appears to be WAP. Hardly a day goes by without another WAP device being announced. But the cost of the service, combined with the inconvenience of completing a dial-up may lead consumers to demand sweeping changes that could open the door for I-Mode.

Transferring I-Mode to the United States.   Wireless Internet on a phone platform has yet to catch on in the United States. Although I-Mode has many advantages over WAP, several of its features are unlikely to be accepted in this country. It is still questionable whether Americans would be willing to type on such a small keypad for e-mail and Internet access. A voice-recognition phone is a possible solution, but a better answer might be a stylus-operated system, which would avoid issues associated with consumer technology adoption. In fact, PDAs have been widely accepted in the United States, and wireless Internet on the Palm now makes up 1 percent of wireless access worldwide.

For I-Mode to succeed in the United States, an alteration in content is also necessary. American consumers have, on average, less downtime for viewing content than their Japanese counterparts. Meanwhile, high-graphic game devices such as the GameBoy already exist to fill single-user game needs. Thus, multiple-player games should be targeted heavily to interaction-thirsty teens and may prove the killer app in the United States for I-Mode. As in Japan, entertainment content can function as the gateway to other mobile Internet content. Over time, as users grow used to the medium, they will demand other, more complex content. Also over time, the user group profile will expand from specific groups, such as youngsters and businesspeople, to include a large part of the population. When the homogeneity of the users decreases, so will the homogeneity of the content.

Pricing must be approached differently in the United States. Wireless carriers have discovered that American consumers prefer transparent, flat-rate billing plans. Analysts of the American mobile Internet market have questioned whether it will be possible to charge users for content. Among other things, they claim that the users have been spoiled by the free content on the fixed Internet and will therefore be reluctant to pay on the mobile Internet. Although that is true, users would probably be willing to pay for certain premium services if specific fundamental requirements were fulfilled. The most important of these would be a convenient micropayment system. The second requirement would be to keep all charges so small that users would not hesitate to pay. If users perceive payment as a hassle, they will not bother to buy the content.

Components of the Japanese billing systems do have value in the realm of online shopping. For example, a teen could buy a book over a wireless phone without a credit card and simply pay for the item as part of the monthly phone bill. This service is also likely to appeal to business travelers, who normally pay for expenses in advance and seek reimbursement later. Using the micropayment system, travelers could pay for airline, hotel, and car rentals and provide the employer with the itemized charges on their monthly phone bill.

The service also needs to offer competitive family plans, similar to the Family Plan and Family Talk programs offered by AT&T and Sprint, respectively. Most parents in the United States purchase wireless phones for their teens as a security measure as well as to have unlimited access to their child. DoCoMo must satisfy these needs in a competitive service plan. In addition, DoCoMo may consider integrating other security features into its devices (e.g., audible alarms).

In addition to the flat-rate system, I-Mode should have optional services that users can charge to prepaid calling cards. This would allow teens to make purchases that parents might not be willing to pay for under the flat-rate plan. These optional services could include music downloads, premium games, and live-concert access.

Marketing should focus on the image-motivated consumer, differentiating I-Mode from other business-focused wireless Internet providers in the United States. This might be best accomplished by cross-promotions with other popular teenage items (e.g., color-coordinated phones, nail polish, and hair colors). Most important from a marketing perspective is the need for I-Mode to develop a brand name and customer base. Established services such as WAP will always have some advantages because they have been in existence for a long time. An emerging service must put forth more effort and resources to reach the market with a product and establish a customer relationship.

I-Mode should enter the market as soon as possible to gain useful experience about the characteristics of the medium and its users. However,

---

Recommendations

Applications: Focus on multiuser interface gaming, e-mail with attachment capability, music, movie, and online shopping applications. Form alliances with already popular content providers and retailers.

Launch: Consider launching first in western states, which have the fastest growing population of young adults and high first adopter rates.

Pricing: Implement tiered flat-rate system. Create add-on plans/calling cards for premium content.

Product: Develop phones with larger screens and keypads or stylus/ voice recognition functionality. Consider accessory devices such as fold-out keypads. Promote compatibility with PDAs and PCs. Consider adding personal security features such as audible alarms.

Promotion: Give complimentary phones to early subscribers. Develop competitive family plans. Focus on image-based advertising targeted toward young consumers. Cross-promote with cosmetic/clothing companies.

I–Mode should launch on a small scale until it has fully tested the concept. As soon as there is evidence of its becoming successful, it can move forward on a larger scale. Release of I–Mode services should be staggered, focusing first on the western states, which have the highest growth in the young-adult segments and also high adoption rates of new technology. Early promotions should include free phones to reduce switching costs.

CONCLUSION

This chapter discussed a framework for applications providing detail on both horizontal and vertical application areas. Many applications will start in verticals as customized applications for a particular industry before crossing industries horizontally. This trend will surely happen, much as it did in the PC industry. However, many wireless applications will end up being simple extensions of applications that already exist on PCs. This is especially true with knowledge and communications applications. The question is whether taking the desktop user experience and simply shrinking it for the smaller displays on wireless devices will really work. For some applications, maybe it will, but for many it won't. Application developers will need to be cognizant of how wireless access to applications can complement both the desktop experience and interaction with an application, instead of viewing it as a replacement.

Security is a concern across all applications, but especially for m-commerce and applications that will pass corporate data. Since the industry wants wireless devices and applications to become a prominent part of their customers' lives, it is working constantly to improve security technologies. Thus, these issues will likely decrease over time.

New business models will emerge as the technologies get cheaper and more ubiquitous. Telemetry applications may allow makers of goods to sign people up for service contracts that include remote monitoring and diagnostics. This is already happening in the automobile industry at companies such as GM and Ford. Producers of goods will be attracted to this business model because it is an opportunity to gain recurring revenues from a transaction that previously included only the revenue stream at the time of purchase. It will first occur with costly goods such as automobiles or home appliances but could eventually extend to cheaper goods, such as lightbulbs.

Finally, I–Mode is a phenomenal consumer success in Japan, but some adjustments will be necessary to achieve similar success in the United States. Although many widely used applications in Japan, such as e-mail, will also be popular in the United States, application design must reflect that U.S.

wireless-device consumers have less downtime than Japanese users, many of whom have lengthy train commutes. Billing for the use of applications and content will be a critical issue in adoption, and micropayments and simpler billing plans will be helpful in making I-Mode a success.

References

Adhikari, Richard. "Wireless Banking Erupts" (February 6, 2001).

Bear Stearns. "Wireless Primer." *Bear Stearns Equity Research* (February 2000).

Boston Consulting Group. "Mobile Commerce: Winning the On-Air Customer" (2000).

———. "The Next Wave: Wireless Financial Services" (2000).

Briggs, Bill. "Getting Around with Handhelds." *Health Data Management* (March 3, 2001).

Celent Communications. "Wireless Financial Services: A Global Overview" (August 2000).

Coster, Paul. "Out of Thin Air." *J.P. Morgan Securities* (September 29, 2000).

Fisher, Josh, and Rosemary Wang. *The Cure Is in Hand: Bringing Information Technology to Patient Care.* WR Hambrecht & Co., 2000.

Freudenheim, Milt. "Digital Doctoring." *New York Times* (January 8, 2001).

Greenberg, Paul. "Wireless Banking Poised to Go Mainstream" (January 3, 2000).

Gulati, Ranjay, and Alex Panas. "Brave New World of Wireless Web." Kellogg School working paper (2001).

J.D. Edwards and Symbium Corporation. "Value Networks and the Digital Economy: An Evolutionary Opportunity" (May 15, 2000).

Kapoor, Madhur. *Wireless in Logistics: Exploring Opportunities for Improved Logistics Functions Provided by Wireless Technologies.* Luminant Worldwide Corporation, 2000.

Kiesnoski, Kenneth. "Wireless Banking: Momentum Builds with Banks" (February 2000).

Lewis, Leo. "Room bkd 4u @ Hldy In—CU L8R." *The Independent* (February 4, 2001).

McGarvey, Robert. "Wireless Craze." *Upside Today* (January 31, 2000).

"Mobile Financial Services: Strategies for Success." Mobilocity.net (July, 2000).

NPD Group. "NPD Reports Almost Half of Cellular Phones Sold at Retail Are Internet-Ready" (August 3, 2000).

Smith, Brad. "U.S. Drives the Telematics Show." *Wireless Week* (March 23, 2001).

Tanikawa, Miki. "Japan Paves the Way in Wireless Stock Trading" (January 29, 2001).

"Wireless Financial Applications: Products and Services That Make Sense" (1999).

Zehren, Charles. "Advertisers Set Sights on Wireless Hand-Helds to Target Their Message." *Newsday* (October 19, 2000).

SECTION III

EMERGING TECHNOLOGIES

CHAPTER 6

RECENT TRENDS IN NANOTECHNOLOGY

Nanotechnology will make us healthy and wealthy. . . . In a few decades this emerging manufacturing technology will let us inexpensively arrange atoms and molecules in most of the ways permitted by physical law. It will let us make supercomputers that fit on the head of a pin and fleets of medical nanorobots smaller than a human cell able to eliminate cancer, infections, clogged arteries, and even old age. People will look back on this era with the same feelings we have toward medieval times—when technology was primitive and almost everyone lived in poverty and died young.

—Ralph Merkle, Principal Fellow, Zyvex

While some of the earlier chapters have discussed former breakthrough technologies, this chapter presents a perspective on a new breakthrough technology, *nanotechnology,* which will disrupt and enhance the business world in the years to come. The ability to manipulate individual molecules and atoms will create countless product and process opportunities in the microelectronic and biotechnological fields. Nanotechnology will help create smaller, stronger, and more precise products, as well as more effective delivery systems. It will radically affect industries in both the near and long term.

The nineteenth century saw an industrial revolution led by an array of inventions. Each creation addressed the shortcomings of its predecessor, fulfilled an unmet need, or developed an entirely new solution. The key contributor to this revolution was technological innovation. The conversion of energy—from heat to steam to movement—spawned many applications, such as the spinning jenny, the steam train, and the combustion engine. The application of that breakthrough became the driving force for improvements in existing infrastructure and the creation of new domains. With rapid progress, however, the development curve eventually reached a plateau, and only marginal improvements could be achieved for mechanical devices.

Then another technological innovation appeared. The ability to store and to communicate information and knowledge electronically with bits and bytes led to the information-technology revolution of the twentieth century. The era redefined our working parameters for distance and timing, as demonstrated with applications like the Internet. A by-product of the underlying technology was the incredible growth of intellectual capital. Although information technology continues to advance, and the industry pushes forward at a rapid rate, the incremental benefits from it will eventually decrease. As in the past, we will reach a plateau on the development curve of improvements to our existing technology and infrastructure. The information-technology age will eventually be displaced.

A new model that fuses the breakthroughs from the two preceding revolutions will accomplish just that displacement. Nanotechnology will apply knowledge and information to the transformation of material or energy. Previous advances focused on using materials to produce energy, which then transported knowledge and information—this is a reactive approach. In the future, we will use our knowledge of molecular structure and energy to produce new materials in a specific and desired state—a truly proactive approach.

SETTING THE STAGE

Technical Background

Nanotechnology designs and manufactures devices from atoms. By definition, devices with minimum feature sizes of 1,000 nanometers (one micron) or less are considered products of nanotechnology, although much of the work focuses on feature sizes smaller than 100nm. The field of nanotechnology encompasses many disciplines, such as computer science, physics, chemistry, and biology. Its aim is to manipulate individual molecules and atoms. Achieving this goal has been a major hurdle, and it has produced substantial skepticism about the feasibility of nanotechnology. Recent theoretical and laboratory progress, however, has been extremely encouraging. There is now considerable evidence that individual molecules and atoms can be manipulated to build systems at the microscopic scale.

Ralph Merkle, a pioneer in the field, noted that objects take on particular characteristics depending on how their atoms are arranged. By rearranging the atoms in coal, we can make diamonds. By rearranging the atoms in sand and a few other trace elements, we can make computer chips. By re-arranging the atoms in dirt, water, and air, we can make grass. Quoting the Web site for Zyvex Inc., where Ralph Merkle is a Principal Fellow:

> Today's manufacturing methods are very crude at the molecular level. Cast-ing, grinding, milling, and even lithography move atoms in great, thun-dering, statistical herds. It's like trying to make things out of LEGO blocks with boxing gloves on your hands. You can push the LEGO blocks into great heaps and pile them up, but you can't really snap them together. In the future, nanotechnology will let us take off the boxing gloves. We'll be able to snap together the fundamental building blocks of nature easily, in-expensively, and in almost any arrangement that we desire. This will . . . let us fabricate an entire new generation of products that are cleaner, stronger, lighter, and more precise.

Two of the most important enablers for widespread use and develop-ment of nanotechnology are:

1. The ability to position essentially every atom in the right place.
2. The ability to keep manufacturing costs from greatly exceeding the costs of required raw materials and energy.

For the first ability, technologists are working on nanomachines with precise positioning and assembly capability at the molecular level. This would allow us to arrange atoms and molecules as desired, much like LEGO blocks. For the second ability, the consensus is that if trillions of nano-machines are needed to make things on a scale useful to us, the cost will be prohibitive unless the devices can self-replicate. When these two chal-lenges are overcome, the possibilities will multiply.

Timing

Although it may not be commonly known, nanotechnology has been around for many years. During the 1940s, von Neumann discussed the pos-sibility of self-replicating manufacturing systems that would lower costs. These systems would be able to both manufacture useful products and repli-cate themselves. In 1959, the transcript of a speech by Richard Feynman called "There Is Plenty of Room at the Bottom" provided the first writ-ten description of the subject. In this speech, Feynman stated: "The prin-ciples of physics, as far as I can see, do not speak against the possibility of maneuvering things atom by atom. We need to apply at the molecular scale the concept that has demonstrated its effectiveness at the macroscopic scale: making parts go where we want by putting them where we want!"

Despite the insights of these inspiring pathfinders, no tangible results or advancements appeared until the 1990s. The late development reflected a series of barriers that prevented major progress or made the need for such progress less urgent. The barriers included the absence of tools to operate and manipulate at the nanoscale, as well as a general lack of knowledge in this area. Sufficient room to optimize existing technology was another important barrier, since the need for new tools was not pressing. The microprocessor industry exemplifies the situation. The ever-evolving miniaturization process of microprocessors seemed to have reached an end every six months; however, only a few months after the roadblock had been identified, there would be new improvements using updated techniques, tools, and methodology. Thus, the incremental advances circumvented the need for progress in nanotechnology because there was no sense of urgency for it.

Nevertheless, the paradigm has begun to change since the late 1990s. The ultimate roadblock might well be on the immediate horizon and, consequently, a look outside the box and into radically new techniques will be necessary. The tools and the budget to explore these new realms have now become available, helping to speed developments. Nanotechnology will be much more than an incremental improvement; it will be a deep structural improvement, allowing for far-reaching developments.

Enabling Technologies

The development of additional enabling technologies will further aid nanotechnology and will result in the emergence of a cluster of related activities. Following are a few initial developments that will complement the value addition of nanotechnology in business applications:

- *Nanoscale microscopes*. Further improvement in observation techniques will provide an impetus for nanotechnology research.
- *Micromanipulation techniques*. Tools and aids to manipulate objects at the nanotechnology level will be necessary—initial work has begun on exponential assembly, which involves using miniature robotic assembly units to help create nanotechnology manufacturing architectures.
- *Nanoassemblers*. The assembler of nanolevel products to achieve molecular manufacturing will be developed (the current definition of an *assembler* envisages the construction and synthesis of an unprecedented array of desirable materials).

- *Computational nanotechnology.* Simulation techniques will expedite the development of this new technology, and computational nanotechnology will be to nanotechnology what bioinformatics is to the human genome sequence.

This limited list of enabling advances in related technologies will be complementary to the development of nanotechnology. Numerous enabling developments will be necessary for nanotechnology applications in specific industries.

FRAMEWORKS AND ANALYSIS

The past may not repeat itself, but it sure does rhyme.

—Mark Twain

This section addresses why nanotechnology will have a tremendous impact on industries, how large this impact will be, which industries will be affected, what the opportunities are, what the implications of this technology are, and how firms can position themselves to leverage advances in nanotechnology. We do not have to be caught unawares by the proliferation of technology in general, and by nanotechnology in particular. In looking ahead, we have the benefit of the lessons of hindsight. Reviewing the historical impact of prior technological advances can help us evaluate the future effects of this new and revolutionary technology.

We first present a preliminary industrywide approach to the consequences of nanotechnology and identify the areas in which value creation will occur. Next, three theoretical models are used to analyze firm-specific issues. Finally, all the issues are incorporated into a single practical framework that shows how firms can best leverage nanotechnology.

The Evolving Value Chain.   This section addresses the ambiguity that encompasses nanotechnology. Nathan Rosenberg's framework aids in understanding the uncertainty that accompanies technological progress. This approach helps to identify the sources of ambiguity, which are also the sources of the value creation that will occur as a consequence of the new technology.

Five Ambiguities.   A common feature of technological progress is that it is "characterized by a high degree of uncertainty," according to Rosenberg.

He presents five dimensions of uncertainty that surround the emergence of
new and important technological innovations. Although this approach provides valuable insights, there are a few caveats. First, Rosenberg's analysis
is best interpreted within the context of an entire industry. It is not immediately or easily transferable to a firm-specific situation. Second, the
framework is easy to apply in retrospect but complex to use in forecasting
industry evolution (see Figure 6.1):

1. *Primitive technological capabilities.* The newborn technology is not
   a fully formed animal. What it will grow up to be is often ambiguous; it is unclear, at its birth, what the implications of the technology will be and where they will manifest themselves. ENIAC, the
   first computer ever built, was scarcely an indication of the PC revolution that followed. Similarly, it is difficult to forecast a full host
   of capabilities of nanotechnology. A few that we can anticipate today
   are applications that manipulate atoms, drug-delivery systems, and
   nanophotolithography.
2. *Complementary searches.* The birth of a technology gives rise to
   searches for complementary and/or enabling technologies that broaden

Figure 6.1
Evolving Value Chain

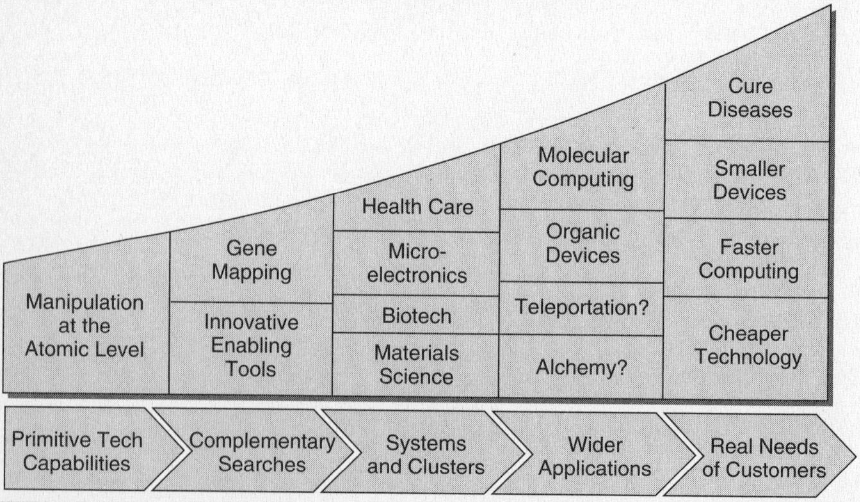

Source: Rosenberg, 1996.

the initial impact of the core technology. Fiber-optic technology was made possible by the invention of cables that could carry light pulses, although the laser had been invented many years before. The search for fiber-optic cable was a complementary search. Similarly, using nanotechnology in the semiconductor industry may not be possible until the enabling photolithographic tools are invented.

3. *Clusters.* Often an entire system of complementary inventions follows from the core technology, just as the telephone, the facsimile, and the Internet were created around basic telephone cable. It appears that nanotechnology will prompt the formation of clusters in at least two major industries: biotechnology and microelectronics.

4. *Specific problems/wider application.* Not uncommonly, the invention is made for a particular purpose and developed in a particular context, but something comes along that allows for its use in a different context. The steam engine is a classic example. By definition, it is impossible to accurately predict wider applications of progress in nanotechnology. Some of the more remote applications introduced later in the chapter may be examples.

5. *Evaluating real needs of customers.* Finally, it is impossible to ignore customer preferences in dictating the proliferation of new technologies. Even though, in a technological sense, the Concorde was a success, its tremendous economic failure illustrates how essential it is to have a connection between what is technologically feasible and what customers desire. Examples of customer needs that drive the science of nanotechnology are faster, smaller, and cheaper computers in the microelectronics industry or improved drug-delivery systems in the biotechnology industry.

The evolution of nanotechnology will progress through the preceding ambiguities. Rosenberg's analysis allows us to arm ourselves with knowledge of the sources of both uncertainty and value creation, and it is in this revelation that his analysis has most value.

Models of Innovation

Phases of Innovation.   According to James Utterback, there are two forms of innovation: process and product (a concept also attributed to William Abernathy). He maps each of these as three phases of industry evolution: fluid, transitional, and specific (Figure 6.2). The model is straightforward: Product innovation is characterized by major product development; process

Figure 6.2
Rate of Innovation

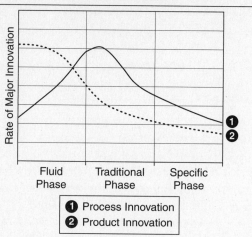

Source: Utterback, 1994.

innovation is characterized by incremental development in process capabilities. The fluid phase occurs in the early stages of an industry's development. The rate of product change is rapid, high technical uncertainty prevails, and competition is generally fierce. The specific phase is characterized by industry consolidation and a shift of focus to process innovation as price competition becomes the primary basis for rivalry. The transitional phase, as the name implies, is the intermediary stage between the fluid and the specific. Industries follow a predictable pattern of evolution from the first stage to the last.

Utterback's model provides a framework to map the impact nanotechnology will have on different industries and specifically which industries will first receive potentially disruptive threats from this new technology. In addition, nanotechnology is neither a product innovation, nor a process innovation. It is both.

Firm Capabilities. The Henderson-Clark model presents an explanation for why some firms can leverage innovations, whereas others cannot. The essence of their argument involves distinguishing between two kinds of knowledge: component knowledge and linkage knowledge. The former describes the information a company may possess in a particular product area; the latter describes the company's knowledge base relating to its product. It shows how the product interacts with other products, as well as the synergies that can be created.

Different innovations hold different implications depending on the type of knowledge a firm possesses. For example, a firm that is weak in the linkage knowledge sphere will be at a disadvantage when it comes to benefiting from an incremental process innovation. This framework is particularly relevant to the puzzle of why incumbent firms face so much difficulty in dealing with minute changes in existing technologies. The Henderson-Clark model can be used to outline the capabilities an individual firm must assemble to leverage nanotechnology (see Figure 6.3).

Disruptive Technologies.   Bower and Christensen developed a framework for grappling with disruptive technologies. They claim that some of the deliberate strategic choices firms make, such as staying close to customers, are the root causes for failure in embracing technological innovations. The Bower-Christensen approach can be simplified into four fundamental questions. We will pose the questions and, to explain them, simultaneously illustrate how nanotechnology will affect the photolithographic–equipment manufacturing industry:

1. *Is the technology disruptive or sustaining?* The first step is to determine that the technology is indeed disruptive to the firm's existing business. Nanotechnology will be disruptive to manufacturers of photolithographic equipment, who will have to migrate to manufacturing nanolithographic equipment that is capable of producing structures smaller than 100nm.
2. *What is its strategic significance?* Why should a photolithographic-equipment manufacturer react? The answer to this question lies in the value creation to the end user. Since nanolithography will result in improved speed and accuracy of building nanolevel structures, it

Figure 6.3
Henderson-Clark Model

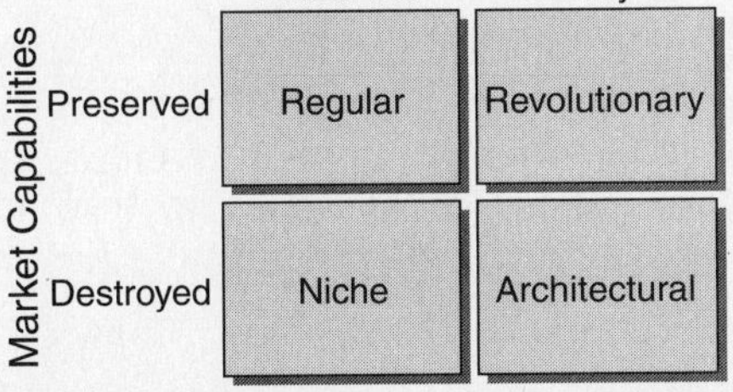

will eventually result in significantly more powerful microprocessors. There is clear evidence of value creation from the improved process.

3. *What is the initial market?* How can the photolithographic-equipment manufacturer capture the value it creates? Since the technology creates value for computer users, chip manufacturers would pay for the improved tools. The initial market would be large chip manufacturers.

4. *What can the company do?* The firm should create an independent organization to develop the technology. Bower-Christensen would advise the photolithographic-equipment manufacturer to create a separate division to build and sell nanolithographic equipment.

A PRACTICAL ROAD MAP

Some of the frameworks and analytical tools just described apply to industries at large, and others can be applied to firms. How does a firm make the right decisions if it believes nanotechnology will have an impact on the industry in which it operates? How does it apply the frameworks specifically to make strategic decisions? The following interpretations of the models in the context of nanotechnology offer a road map to the corporate reader for navigating through this strange new technology.

Extent of Disruption

The adoption of new technologies is usually characterized by an S-curve, as was described in Chapter 3. This S-curve describes the life cycle of a firm that is creating or marketing a new technology. The beginning of the curve represents the "ferment" stage when no one really understands what is happening. It is characterized by the appearance of an enormous number of new business models or approaches. Eventually, when a company finds out what works, the era of implementation starts. This is called the golden era, in which the company experiences significant growth. Maturity—the top of the curve—is attained when the company is strong and very good at what it does. At this point, should technology change again, the company might be in trouble. Different kinds of people and skills are needed at different stages of technology life cycles, making it difficult for an established firm to move from one generation of technology to another.

Nanotechnology is in the ferment stage, or the early phase of the S-curve. It is therefore likely that strong incumbents either have never heard of nanotechnology or do not possess the right skills (or do not want to use the necessary resources) to start investigating the impact of this new technology on their businesses. As analyzed in previous sections, nanotechnology will be a disruptive technology: It will affect existing business processes and create new ones. To the extent that incumbents fail to prepare for the takeoff of nanotechnology, the disruptive effect will be exponential.

Knowing the sources of competitive advantage, or core competencies (branding, sales force, IT, etc.), is a critical first step in the management of a disruptive technology. No matter how disruptive the new technology wave, some existing sources of competitive advantages or assets will be critical in the next S-curve. Inevitably, though, some current competitive advantages that sustain the company will become obsolete.

The second step is to establish some distance from the current consumers. Disruptive technologies create problems for established firms because the management rule "focus on your consumer" leads them to miss new opportunities. The rational, analytical investment processes are focused—for all the right reasons—on current customers and markets. The processes are designed to weed out proposed products and technologies that do not address customer needs or that have negative net present value (NPV). The bottom line is that disruptive technologies look financially unattractive to established companies. The potential revenues from discernible markets are small, and it is difficult to project market size over the long term. Any rational resource-allocation process in companies serving established markets will go upmarket rather than downmarket.

All these characteristics, in fact, increase the disruptive potential of nanotechnology. Incumbents will most likely not prepare for the upcoming revolution. This dramatically increases the potential for their displacement. New companies with a relatively small R&D budget, betting on a narrow application segment, may gain a technological competitive advantage that, with some time and consumer education, will be translated into a real customer need. At that point, it will be too late for the incumbents to react. The only way to keep the customer will be to buy either the technology or the company—if it is still possible. That is a risky step.

Different types of technological innovations affect performance trajectories in different ways. *Sustaining technologies* maintain the rate of improvement, giving customers something more or better in the attributes they already value. Although nanotechnology could drastically improve certain existing processes, its real impact will most likely be as a *disruptive technology*. It will introduce a package of attributes different from those that customers have historically valued and that often perform worse along one or two dimensions of particular importance to those customers at a certain time.

Process and Product

There will be two types of nanotechnology innovations. *Process innovations* will be applications to improve existing processes—to make them faster, more efficient, more accurate, more precise, and perhaps more cost-effective. Such innovations can range from lithographic tools in the microelectronics industry to drug-delivery systems in health care. *Product innovations* will arise from the application of nanotechnology to create revolutionary new products. It is hardly surprising that these will be more difficult to predict.

Nanotechnology process innovations will appear primarily in industries in the specific phase. As industries mature, and cost efficiencies becomes the focus of production, process innovations become more important relative to product innovation. Nanotechnology product innovations will appear in industries in the early stages of their development, or the fluid phase, for similar reasons. Although we can make certain predictions about the impacts of nanotechnology on different industries and where they will appear, we cannot predict their timing (see Figure 6.4).

Figure 6.4
Impact on Different Industries

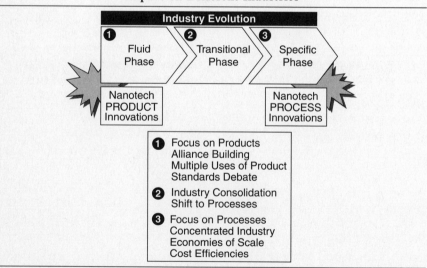

Source: Henderson and Clark, 1999.

Risks and Opportunities in Specific-Phase Industries

The risks posed by nanotechnology as a disruptive force are significant in specific-phase industries. Incumbents will have to incorporate process improvements to remain cost competitive. Likewise, process improvements offer great opportunities to established firms. Product innovations, on the other hand, are a substantially less attractive opportunity. Firms in mature industries will have to develop their knowledge of linkages to fully benefit from incremental process improvements and to prevent their established organizational structure from hindering the adoption of technological progress (see Figure 6.5).

Risks and Opportunities in Fluid-Phase Industries

Firms in the fluid-phase industries face a different risk-opportunity profile. They are positioned to benefit from the potential opportunities of disruptive technologies and product innovations, and they also benefit from the absence of an organizational heritage that can act as a burden. Product innovations pose a risk to these firms, however, since at this early stage of the industry, it is unclear which products will become industry standards. Finally, developing a linkage knowledge base is an opportunity for future process innovations, but firms have less to fear from its absence (see Figure 6.6).

Figure 6.5
Firms in Mature, Specific-Phase Industries

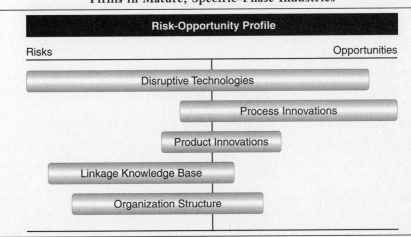

Figure 6.6
Firms in Early, Fluid-Phase Industries

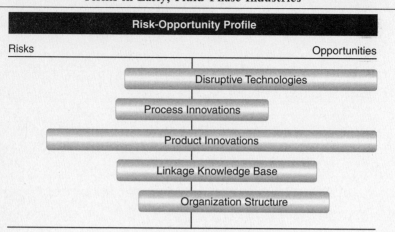

Capabilities to Build and Deploy

Extending the Henderson-Clark argument, it is apparent that firms in the specific phase must focus on fostering linkage knowledge and firms in the fluid phase must focus on building component knowledge.

Fortunately, this is not a revelation. Competitive forces often prompt firms in the specific phase to focus on process innovations. The Henderson-Clark argument, however, carries an implication for the allocation of research and development budgets. A specific-phase firm operating under a defensive strategy must expend its R&D dollars to explore the ways in which its manufacturing inputs and components and finished products relate. A thorough understanding of these linkages can enable it to discern opportunities to apply the emerging discipline of nanotechnology. A firm might improve operations processes by following a cost-minimization strategy. Alternatively, it might follow a product-differentiation strategy by improving product features.

On the other hand, a fluid-phase firm following a first-to-market and volume strategy might devote its R&D budget to increasing component knowledge as opposed to linkage knowledge. It is important to note that R&D refers not only to a determination of what is technologically feasible but also to an analysis of customer requirements. Value capture occurs at the intersection of technical feasibility and customer desirability.

The precise capabilities that a firm must build are dictated by the phase in which it finds itself, but it must also consider a second input—strategy. A specific-phase firm in a defensible position may be able to devote a higher proportion of its R&D budget toward building component knowledge and attempt to further both process and product innovation. The reverse, however, is rarely true. A fluid-phase firm is rarely in a sufficiently defensible position to spend budget funds on expanding linkage knowledge.

APPLICATIONS

The following framework (Figure 6.7) attempts to identify the areas where the new technologies will arise. Process innovations relying on nanotechnology will be dominant in mature industries, whereas new-product innovations incorporating nanotechnology will essentially see the light in industries in their early development stage.

The rationale behind this segmentation is that mature industries rely on current core competencies and installed customer bases, but new applications in these industries must stay closer to the current product line and are therefore labeled process innovations. New-product applications, on the other hand, will emanate from new companies, potentially spun off from mature players. These new companies will focus on the new technology, without having to please an installed customer base. They are likely to experiment with more radical ideas and products, and thus product innovations are classified in the early stage of industry development.

Figure 6.7
Application Localizer

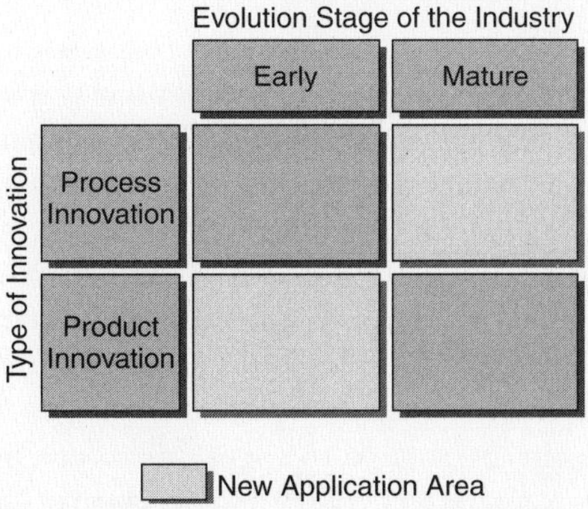

New Application Area

Microelectronics

The idea of mechanical computing devices is not new. In fact, the first known computing device did not use electronics at all. The difference engine, created by Charles Babbage in 1822, was solely mechanical. The device, which required close to two thousand parts, served the single function of fixing entries for tables on the steam engine. The purely mechanical computing device gave way to electronics in the twentieth century, driving into obsolescence the machinery Babbage created. Today, the idea of returning to Babbage's concept at first seems comical, but the emergence of nanotechnology provides new motivation for studies of mechanical computers. Nanotechnology will lead to microscopic computer systems at the molecular and, eventually, the atomic scale. At present, we do not know how to design electronic components of that size, although if Moore's law (see Chapter 1) prevails, and smaller, faster devices are required, a nanocomputer constructed by solely molecular mechanical nanodevices may be on the horizon.

Even if an abrupt shift from electronics back to pure mechanics is doubtful, the arrival of nanotechnology will lead to a strong combination of the two in the near future. Carbon nanotubes, discovered in 1991 by Sumio Iijima of NEC Corporation, are an exciting example. These tubular structures impart mechanical and electronic properties that become an exotic variation of common graphite. A short list of their attributes includes super strength combined with low weight, stability, flexibility, good heat conduction, large surface area, and intriguing electronic properties. Today's nanotechnology has already proven able to create material many times stronger and lighter than steel. The following microelectronic applications could emerge from these advances in both the short and long term.

Plastics.   Nanotechnology will most likely have its first significant industry impact in the area of materials science. Through process innovation, it will create stronger and lighter plastics from nanoclay. The nanomaterials are layered, often chemically modified, clays consisting of nanometer-thick platelets up to 1,000nm in diameter. Implementation will lead to improvements in staple products such as countertops, auto parts, toys, and nylon-packing applications. Though experts estimate that the current market demand for such products is only $10 million, they predict that the global market will expand to $500 million by 2010.

Several companies have already entered this space. Nanocor, a subsidiary of Amcol International, has patented technology and development agreements with Bayer, Eastman Chemicals, and Toyota. The five-year-old group plans to produce 20,000 tons of nanoclay this year for packaging applications and auto parts. Another group, RTP Company, focuses on plastic components for film and sheet applications. Others, such as Dow Chemical and Magna International, are developing production technology for automotive applications. Even if these innovations do not lead to new products, they will change the standards of existing ones.

Nanomemory Computers. According to Moore's Law, computer-chip sizes decrease exponentially with time. This trend indicates that atomically precise computers will arrive by about 2010 to 2015. Nanotechnology will be required to work at this scale. In the near future, devices with nanoscale computer memory will provide orders-of-magnitude improvements in RAM density along with picosecond switching speeds.

Faster computer processors and increased memory storage improve the product. Although the major players still primarily seek improvements through electronic innovation, they are aware of nanotechnology. Players such as David Tomanek's group at Michigan State University have a patent pending on the design of Nano-memory, a computer that will be 1,000 times smaller than our standard today yet hold the same amount of memory. The design employs nanotubes that literally change the state of the computer's on and off functions. Although this device or a different prototype may not emerge in the next 10 years, the trend is clear. A day will arrive when a standard personal computer will have enough storage to literally keep track of every conversation a person has ever had from birth to death, and the individual will be able to access the information quicker than the blink of an eye.

Batteries and Cell Phones. The emergence of nanotubes could have a significant impact on the global $2.8 billion battery market. They will create ion storage for batteries, improving the performance of rechargeable batteries through changes in the molecular electrochemical behavior. Since this technology has already been created, it should have an immediate impact on cell phones and computer batteries. In addition, innovations for batteries in electric cars will significantly cut down on the hours it takes to recharge. In fact, nanotechnology could make recharging quicker than refueling. A high-performance capacitor could store an electrical charge when two conductors are placed close together with an insulating layer. Such devices could be instantly recharged with large amounts of electrical energy, which could then be drawn off slowly by a motor.

The introduction of nanotechnology to computer and cell-phone batteries will happen soon. Tokyo-based Ulvac recently announced it had found a way to "grow" nanotubes in specific arrays and positions that will allow manufacturers of lithium batteries and computer displays to start using nanotubes within the next year.

Fuel Cells.   If electric cars do not emerge, many people believe that nanotechnology will enable environmentally improved and efficient fuel cells to power automobiles and other motor-driven devices in the future. Many fuel cells operate by oxidation involving hydrogen, oxygen, and a catalyst—hydrogen is introduced at the anode of the fuel cell, and oxygen at the cathode. Nanotubes may be able to absorb hydrogen in fuel tanks, compressing hydrogen more densely than is possible today. This will lead to increased power and efficiency, as more hydrogen fuel cells can be added.

In 2001, companies including NEC and Sony announced work on fuel-cell battery technology using nanotechnology. Though revenues for this technology are small today, analysts predict that the market will grow to $14 to $17 billion for distributed generation in North America in 2010 and $40 to $50 billion worldwide. Ballard Power, a leader in this industry, has a market capitalization of close to $4 billion yet had revenues of only $55 million in 2000. As an enabler, nanotechnology should have a strong impact on the portable-power industry.

Other Potential Applications.   Flat-screen TVs and optical-switch improvements are also areas of potential microelectronic applications. Today's television sets are so large because three electron guns are firing electrons from the back. Molecule-sized nanotubes could emit the electrons with the precision of one nanotube per pixel, resulting in a television with the depth of a framed print. Also, it would use far less power than present-day electron guns, in which silicon does the electron emitting.

The boom in optical telecommunications, spurred by the explosive growth of the Internet, has been provoking the growth of micromirrors and microlenses to bounce a laser beam around on the surface of a chip for routing optical signals. This process eliminates the need to switch from photons to electrons for routing data signals and thereby reduces transmission time. As innovative as optical switches sound, nanotechnology can miniaturize these switches, making them more effective and efficient. In addition, there is room to make intelligent photons that carry their own destination information with them, thereby making optical switches redundant.

The information-technology age saw precision farming, which used global-positioning systems (GPS) and geographic-information systems (GIS) to create yield maps for harvesting. The $800 billion U.S. food industry targeted several products for improvements. Genetic engineering eliminated some of the potential problems. The first generation of products resulting from genetic engineering has focused on making plants (seeds) stronger and more robust without much change in functionality or the nature of the product.

The advent of nanotechnology will bring second-generation products that alter the very structure and function of those products to make them more useful and convenient. For example, in addition to making cotton more robust and pest resistant, nanotechnology will make it possible to grow colored cotton or wrinkle-free cotton right from the seed. These changes will not be limited to cotton but will be applied across multiple agricultural products, enhancing their nutritional and commercial value. Moreover, nanotechnology will allow us to grow these products artificially on a large scale that could compete with traditional agriculture.

Health Care and Biotechnology

Diseases are caused largely by damage at the molecular and cellular level. Today's surgical tools are, at that scale, large and crude. From the viewpoint of a cell, even a fine scalpel is a blunt instrument better suited to tear and injure than to heal and cure. Modern surgery works only because cells have a remarkable ability to regroup, cleanse their dead, and heal over the injury.

Nanotechnology should let us economically build a broad range of complex molecular tools much smaller than a human cell and constructed with the accuracy and precision of drug molecules. Such tools will let medicine intervene in a sophisticated and controlled way at the cellular and molecular level: They could remove obstructions in the circulatory system, kill cancer cells, or take over the function of subcellular organelles. Just as today we have the artificial heart, so in the future we could have the artificial mitochondrion.

Equally dramatic, nanotechnology will provide new instruments to examine tissue in unprecedented detail. Sensors smaller than a cell could allow an inside and exquisitely precise look at ongoing function. Tissue that was either chemically fixed or flash frozen could literally be analyzed down to the molecular level, giving a completely detailed snapshot of cellular, subcellular, and molecular activities.

Nanotechnology will also enable genetic medicine with a far-reaching impact on the health care industry and how pharmaceutical companies conduct business.

Inside versus Outside.   Today's medicine attempts to find a weapon that works against a given health threat. Tomorrow's medicine, enabled by nanotechnology, will largely replace the current approach and reveal the actual cause and biomedical pathways of disease. An ability to understand the causes and work "inside" the human body versus "outside" will lead to a new form of medicine that will succeed through the genetic prevention of disease rather than treatment of the disease itself. The health-care industry and subsequent applications will move toward understanding the human genome and its relation to diseases and consequently provide customized medication.

"Pharmacogenomics."   In the near term, pharmacogenomics will develop precise drugs that treat specific genetic sets of patients. At present, $8 billion worth of prescribed medicines do not work on all patients or need to be discontinued because of adverse side effects. Instead of a one-size-fits-all approach, wherein one drug is meant for everyone, precise drugs will be configured for distinctive gene types, leading to custom treatments that are more effective and have fewer side effects. Herceptin, developed by Genentech, which targets the 25 percent to 30 percent of breast-cancer patients who have a gene called HER2, is already on the market. In the future, a doctor will meet a patient and prescribe or even configure the exact treatment needed for a particular gene type.

Cancer Cures.   About 1.2 million cases of cancer were diagnosed in this country in 2001, but 60 percent of those cases had no therapy. After several years of research, there are over 350 biotech cancer therapies in clinical trials, 57 of those in final-phase 3. Most of those therapies work with viruses or proteins. For example, tumor necrosis therapy (TNT), from Techniclone, uses a genetic smart bomb, which is injected into the bloodstream and finds its way to the tumor, delivering precise radiation treatment to the inside of the tumor, killing it from the inside and leaving the surrounding issue intact. Nanotechnology promises to provide scalability and cost-effectiveness for these solutions by helping the production of smart bombs.

Artificial Red Blood Cells and Mitochondria.   Once scientists can manipulate at the molecular level, they will be able to provide metabolic support in the event of impaired circulation by providing artificial red blood cells. Not only could these cells be produced externally, but genetic enhancements to the immune system would allow for immediate recognition of tissue damage or blood clotting, resulting in restored blood flow at an appropriate level. An alternate possibility is a nanotechnology-enabled artificial device that releases oxygen at a constant rate to maintain metabolism and keep tissues healthy.

Biomachinery for Drug Delivery. In the classic 1966 science-fiction film *Fantastic Voyage*, a submarine and its crew are shrunk to microscopic size and travel through the bloodstream of a scientist to remove a clot in his brain with an onboard laser. Nanotechnology holds the promise of making an adaptation of this concept a reality: Miniaturization techniques will enable innovative drug-delivery systems to serve as doctors inside a human body and provide effective medical treatment by enhancing the immune system or supplanting corrective-surgery methods.

CONCLUSION

Nanotechnology is more than an enabling technology; it is a revolutionary technology that will have a great impact not only on early-stage industries but also on mature industries. Early-stage industries will see product innovations, and mature industries will see process innovations in the form of nanotechnology applications. Developing internal capabilities for relevant process innovations in nanotechnology should appear on the agenda of companies in mature industries. On the other hand, companies in early-stage industries should direct resources toward product innovations. It is important to keep in mind that these are guidelines rather than rules. Other strategic options, such as external technology acquisitions and outsourcing of research and development, are also available.

The science of nanotechnology exists on the frontiers of technological innovation. Many of the applications considered in this chapter will become reality only in a mid-to-long-term time frame. However, two principal decisions are necessary in the short term. The first is which developments to choose among the nanotechnology-enabling products and services. The second involves the allocation of resources and must take into consideration any implications that nanotechnology will have for a company's future processes and products. These decisions may alter the business model.

Nanotechnology will change the existing paradigm of thinking and have more profound effects than any previous technology. It will touch every facet of the economy and have a wide-ranging impact across all industries. Some industries, such as health care and electronics, will feel the effects earlier than the others because of the short product cycles and the need for innovation.

In typical industries, value is created when new technology is matched to customer needs. Common questions in evaluating a project are: Does the customer want it? How big will the market be? Is this a positive net-present-value project? However, those are not the appropriate questions for evaluating nanotechnology initiatives—nanotechnology is an object of "causal ambiguity." The existing customer may reject nanotechnology for its discontinuous or radical nature. Initially, the market might not capture a sizable chunk, and the opportunity cost of capital might not favor the nanotechnology initiatives. Thus, it is imperative that organizations understand its strategic significance by estimating the initial performance level of the technology. Once the exponential benefits are identified, the organization should locate the initial market and consider the potential of developing the technology independent of its current operations.

References

Bauschlicher, Charles W., Jr., Alessandra Ricca, and Ralph Merkle. "Chemical Storage of Data." *Nanotechnology* (March 1997).

Bauschlicher, Charles W., Jr., and M. Rosi. "Differentiating between Hydrogen and Fluorine on a Diamond Surface." Submitted to *Theor. Chem. Acta.*

Brown, Eric. "A Better Optical Switch." *MIT Technology Review* (2001).

Brown, Kathryn. "Hugs Biotech Trees." *MIT Technology Review* (2001).

Christensen, Clayton, and Joseph Bower. "Disruptive Technologies: Catching the Wave." In John Seely Brown (ed.) *Seeing Differently: Insights on Innovation.* Harvard Business Review Book, 1997.

Drexler, K. Eric. *Journal of the British Interplanetary Society* (1992).

———. *Nanosystems: Molecular Machinery, Manufacturing, and Computation.* New York: Wiley, 1992.

Drexler, K. Eric, Chris Peterson, and Gayle Pergami. *Unbounding the Future.* New York: Morrow, 1991.

Hyman, Anthony. *Charles Babbage: Pioneer of the Computer.* Princeton, NJ: Princeton University Press, 1982.

Iijima, Sumio. "Helical Microtubules of Graphitic Carbon." *Nature* (November 7, 1991).

Kurzweil, Ray. "The Story of the 21st Century." *MIT Technology Review* (2000).

Leo, Alan. "Wiring Up Nanoelectronics." *MIT Technology Review* (2001).

Merkle, Ralph C. "Nanotechnology" http://www.zyvex.com/nano.

_____. "Nanotechnology and Medicine." In *Advances in Anti-Aging Medicine,* vol. 1, Ronald M. Klatz (ed.). Liebert Press, 1996.

_____. "Two Types of Mechanical Reversible Logic." *Nanotechnology* (1993).

Merkle, Ralph C., and Drexler, K. Eric. "Helical Logic." *Nanotechnology* (1996).

Moore, Geoffrey. *Crossing the Chasm.* New York: HarperBusiness, 2d ed., 1999.

NanoInk, Incorporated. Presentation at Digital Frontier Conference, Kellogg Graduate School of Management, Northwestern University (2001).

"Nanotubes Show Promise from TVs to Velcro." *MSU Media Communications: News Releases* (February 18, 2000).

National Nanotechnology Initiative. "The Initiative and Its Implementation Plan." National Science and Technology Council, Committee on Technology, Subcomittee on Nanoscale Science, Engineering and Technology, 2000.

Oliver, Richard W. *The Coming Biotech Age.* New York: McGraw Hill, 2000.

Piner, Richard D., et al. " 'Dip-pen' Nanolithography." *Science* (1999).

Rosenberg, Nathan. "Uncertainty and Technology Change." In Landau, Taylor, and Wright (eds.). *The Mosaic of Economic Growth.* Stanford: Stanford University Press, 1996.

Shapiro, Carl, and Hal Varian. *Information Rules.* Boston: Harvard Business School Press, 1998.

Smalley, Richard. "Wires of Wonder." *MIT Technology Review* (2001).

Taylor, R., and Walton, D. R. M. "The Chemistry of Fullerenes." *Nature* (June 24, 1993).

Thayer, Ann M. "Firms Find a New Field of Dreams." *Chemical & Engineering News* (October 16, 2000).

Utterback, James. *Mastering the Dynamics of Innovation.* Boston: Harvard Business School Press, 1994.

Voss, David. "Nanomedicine Nears the Clinic." *MIT Technology Review* (2000).

Wang, Linda. "Live Wires." *MIT Technology Review* (2000).

CHAPTER 7

PEER-TO-PEER COMPUTING

In the public eye, peer-to-peer (P2P) computing has become almost synonymous with Napster, but it really goes beyond Napster and music sharing to include a broad sharing of resources and information through the direct linking of systems within networks. The underlying technology will change the way the growing number of participants in the wired world share information, content, and resources. The question that remains, however, is whether a viable business model exists underneath all the hype. Even in today's relatively unfriendly technology market, over a hundred companies occupy the P2P computing space. Although many companies and individuals have entered this space, only a few contenders appear to have a sustainable business model. By examining the existing models, we can develop a framework indicating who will be the ultimate winners.

HISTORY OF NETWORK COMPUTING

The emergence of peer-to-peer computing signifies a revolution in connectivity that will be as profound to the Internet of the future as Mosaic was to the Web of the past.

—Patrick Gelsinger, Vice President and
Chief Technology Officer, Intel Corporation

Back in the 1960s, when the Internet was conceived, it was a P2P system. The Advanced Research Projects Agency (ARPA), of the Department of Defense, created ARPANET, which was the precursor of the Internet. The agency's goal was to develop a host-to-host protocol that would improve and increase computer-research productivity through resource sharing over a common network. The University of California, Los Angeles, and the Stanford Research Institute were the first two hosts, with independent computing sites

284

and equal status on the network, and ARPANET connected these universities as computing peers. After ARPANET was up and running, the researchers and developers realized that assisting human communication was the network's most important contribution.

Early killer apps of the network provided a fundamental symmetry that made it radical in relation to other network structures. FTP and Telnet were client/server applications. While an FTP client sent and received files from a file server, a Telnet client logged into a computer server. The applications were client/server, but the usage patterns were symmetrical. The first e-mail program for a distributed network was released in 1971, and Telnet appeared in 1974. By 1983, ARPA research had developed the TCP/IP protocol (Transaction Control Protocol/Internet Protocol), to which it converted all the interconnected research networks of ARPANET, and the "Internet" became official. It had 500 hosts.

In 1984, the Domain Name System (DNS) was established as a solution to a file-sharing problem. DNS blends P2P networking with a hierarchical model of information ownership, and it was developed to distribute the data sharing across the P2P Internet. Also in 1984, Mosaic, the first graphical Web browser, was released and took the Internet by storm. The Internet now comprised over three million hosts.

The explosion of the World Wide Web caused the Internet to become more and more restricted and pushed development toward the client/server model. This structure has plagued the Internet with firewalls and thus with extreme partition. There is a need to return the Internet to its initial design to effectively serve its original purposes of sharing and cooperating. Figure 7.1 diagrams this evolution of networks.

Figure 7.1
Development of Networks

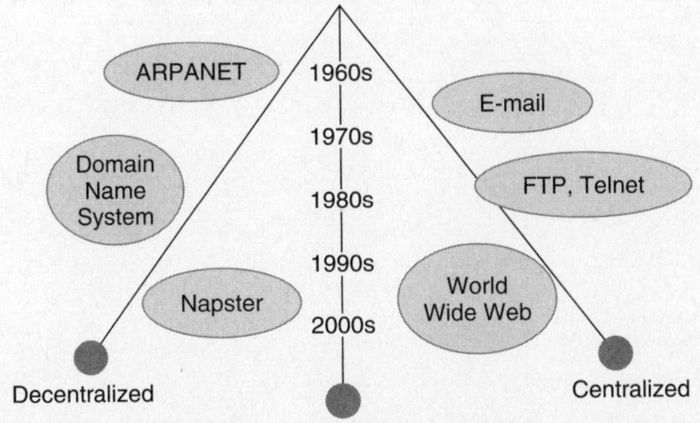

CURRENT SCENE

With the development of networks, information has multiplied and become a critical resource. Within this sea of information, we have some that others may want. There is no reason for us not to provide it to them, but we have no system that allows us to find one another effectively. Napster overcame the challenge for music. By allowing its users to find the content they were looking for anywhere in the world, Napster greatly increased the content available to all.

Most of the technical requirements to handle this type of file-sharing community are already available. Today's file-sharing software has only marginal use outside the music industry, but that will change. P2P computing allows people and companies to significantly decrease the complexity and expense of networking. It is not difficult to create Napster- or Gnutella-like programs that are specific for other communities, such as business to business (B2B). XML will be a major enabler for interoperability among networks.

P2P technology is already giving rise to new ways of networking and collaborating directly with peers and avoiding the complexities of centralization. It is not hard to imagine the value of a private collaborative network. The idea of sharing spaces with peers and working together without redundancy on a project is fundamental in any industry. Security, however, is a serious concern even in traditional networks that depend on centralized servers, and P2P networks exacerbate the problem.

"The old days [i.e., the current Internet] were all about centralization and control, almost Soviet style," says Miko Matsumura, the CEO and co-founder of Kalepa Networks, a 3-year-old start-up that intends to link P2P networks and create a sort of alternative Internet. "In this new topology, everyone brings his or her own resources. The new network will be built on top of the old network, like Rome was built in different layers."

One recognized application using aggregated resources is the SETI@home project. Launched May 17, 1999, at the University of California, Berkeley, the project set out to help find extraterrestrial life beyond our solar system. Radio-frequency signals received from outer space are distributed among the participating computers in the network to enable an unprecedented number-crunching application, as those computers use the minute gaps in their processing time to analyze chunks of the signals for a repeated pattern that would indicate an intelligent source. To date, over 2.8 million users in more than 226 countries have contributed nearly 583,000 years of computing to the cause. This computing rate of 25 teraflops more than doubles the speed of IBM's ASCII White, the fastest supercomputer in the world.

The power behind this direct two-way exchange of information and the vast pool of underused resources represent a wealth of opportunities waiting to be exploited. Pioneering individuals and firms have organized, planned, and are already off and running in search of the pot of gold that awaits them. Before declaring any winners, it is imperative to consider what lies beneath the P2P technology, understand the sources of value, consider the landscape as it exists today, identify the technology enablers, and address the barriers that still need to be overcome.

P2P MODEL

Clay Shirky, from the Accelerator Group, indicates that two questions test whether we have a P2P network:

1. Does it allow for variable connectivity and temporary network addresses?
2. Does it give the nodes at the edges of the network significant autonomy?

If the answer to both questions is yes, the application qualifies as peer to peer.

P2P computing allows for the sharing of resources and information through the direct linking of systems within a network. Since the Internet is the most extensive computing network available, P2P computing can take advantage of that existing infrastructure to connect peers. In a typical Internet client/server interaction, the computer at the edge of the network acts as a client while central servers store information. In the P2P system, an additional software layer enables the computers at the edge of the network to act as clients and/or servers depending on the need. Now the computer is able to respond to a request for information or computing resources from another peer computer. This deviation from the classic client/server system has led to common network topologies: pure P2P and hybrid P2P. Each offers advantages and is coexisting with the current Internet topology.

Pure P2P Network Topology

Figures 7.2 and 7.3 illustrate the change from a client/server topology to a pure P2P topology. Pure P2P models, as illustrated in Figure 7.3, do not use any central servers to direct or control interactions between peers. Individuals or companies in the network bypass central exchanges to relay

Figure 7.2
Client/Server Topology

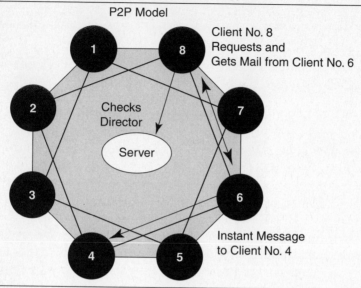

P2P Model

Client No. 8
Requests and
Gets Mail from Client No. 6

Checks Director

Server

Instant Message to Client No. 4

Figure 7.3
Pure P2P Network Topology

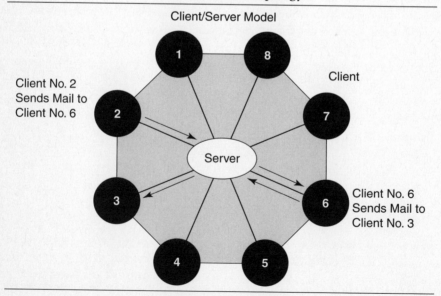

Client/Server Model

Client No. 2
Sends Mail to
Client No. 6

Client

Server

Client No. 6
Sends Mail to
Client No. 3

information directly with one another. Without the central server, peers poll adjacent peers in search of the desired information or resource. Those peers will, in turn, poll other adjacent peers, quickly resulting in an exponentially growing tree. Gnutella-type applications have become one of the most common applications under this network structure.

Hybrid P2P Network Topology

Unlike the pure P2P model, hybrid P2P models, such as Napster, incorporate some traces of the client/server relationship. Central servers within the network fulfill two primary functions. First, they act as central directories where either connected users or indexed content can be mapped to the current IP address. Second, the servers act as a traffic cop and direct traffic among the peers. The hybrid form of P2P computing is a compromise between the pure P2P networks of the ARPANET structure and the client-server structure. The alternative topology, shown in Figure 7.4, reflects the additional role of the server in this case.

Whether the model incorporates the pure P2P or the hybrid form, the key is that, unlike the client-server hierarchical approach, the peers share the resource or information. Clay Shirky has indicated that complete decentralization is not the goal; instead, it is that the application can provide

Figure 7.4
Hybrid P2P Network Topology

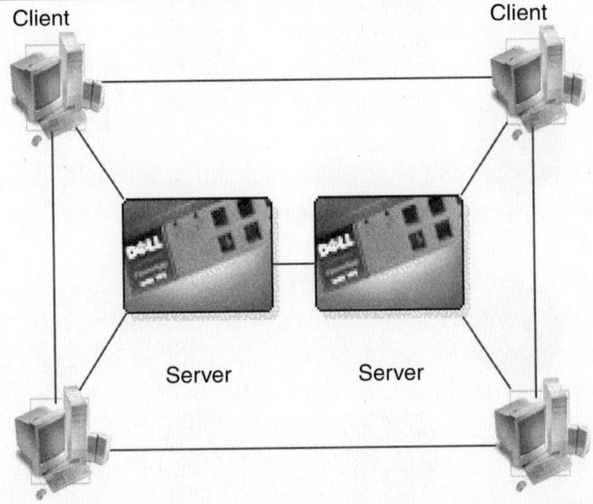

just enough decentralization. Both topologies are the basis for several applications in the market today.

TODAY'S P2P PLAYERS

Even though the lack of emerging standards for the peer platforms would seem to indicate that P2P technology is still in its infancy, a host of players have already suited up and taken the field. This section provides an assessment of the major players within the primary P2P categories of content indexing and file sharing, instant messaging, and distributed computing. Many of today's players are based on a single functional capability.

Content Indexing and File Sharing

Napster is the ultimate example of P2P file sharing. Users open up their hard drives to anyone who is registered on the system in exchange for the same access to others' files. This concept is extremely powerful in that it opens truly millions of doors to valuable information.

Content indexing and file sharing go hand in hand, for content indexing is the essential first step in file sharing. Since data is scattered throughout a network, an efficient search engine and indexing system must be available to find the critical information and organize it. This is similar to the search method used by Napster or another search engine. Several companies are jumping into the general file-sharing business space, including Aimster and Mangosoft.

Many of the original players in the content-indexing and file-sharing space are related to sharing music since that is the killer application that brought P2P computing to the forefront. In addition to music, other players in this space allow for sharing programs, videos, images, and documents.

Napster.   Napster is now well known as the grandfather of P2P computing in the media, even though it was not even the first P2P music-sharing application. The first was Scour, but Napster became the most popular. Napster focused exclusively on sharing music files and subsequently reached an agreement with Bertelsmann to establish a subscription-based system to compensate the record companies for copyrighted material. Its long-term business model is under question because of the great degree of change that it is facing. Napster used a hybrid P2P architecture in which several of its own servers maintained the index of music files available on peers' computers.

Business model: subscription based

Topology: hybrid P2P

Gnutella. Gnutella is software that was developed as a protocol by Null-soft engineers. The program was placed on America Online (AOL) servers for a short time and soon removed because AOL-Time Warner saw its possibilities as a conflict of interest with the media industry. Gnutella can be used to share any type of file. As Gnutella's code was released and is now open source, no single entity owns the rights to it, which has resulted in many Gnutella look-alikes. In addition, Gnutella's architecture is pure peer to peer; rather than relying on central servers to index content, it uses the other clients within a user's "horizon" to complete an extensive search. This decentralized architecture is challenging not only to shut down but also to manage.

Business model: none

Topology: pure P2P

Scour. Scour was the first P2P music-sharing program. Under the threat of looming lawsuits, Scour closed shop during the last quarter of 2000. CenterSpan Communications bought the rights to Scour.

Business model: N/A

Topology: hybrid P2P

Aimster. Aimster is not all that different from Napster. Like Napster, the software is geared toward the consumer market. Rather than allowing sharing of information with everyone on a network, the available network is limited to a smaller set of "buddies." These people have mutual access to files on a designated location on their hard drive. Aimster latches onto the user's instant-messaging (IM) service and uses the buddies within that system as the community for file sharing. Aimster allows the user to conduct natural-language searches of peer systems, permitting the exchange of files and information within a core group of a community.

Business model: portal partnership

Topology: hybrid P2P

iMesh.   iMesh is a general file-sharing program that has attracted more than 2 million users. The system is similar to Napster's in that there is a central server, but it allows for file sharing beyond music files. In addition, iMesh developed a technology that allows it to identify and remove copyrighted files. This may prove to be a valuable functionality in the software as copyright owners push to preserve their intellectual property rights.

    Business model: advertising

    Topology: hybrid P2P

Mangosoft.   Mangosoft is geared toward the commercial market and provides a means to share and modify files in a team environment. It is a multi-user, Internet-based, file-sharing system whose product, Mangomind, is a secure way for multiple users to access, share, and store files.

    Business model: software licensing

    Topology: hybrid P2P

Instant Messaging

Instant messaging was one of the first P2P applications. The launch of ICQ in 1996 meant that for the first time individual users could directly address intermittently connected personal computers; any two users on the system could directly communicate with one another. The development enabled future P2P applications, since many users are still connected using intermittent Internet addresses (i.e., the IP address is different each time the user connects). As the ICQ Web site states: "You can chat; send messages, files, and URLs; play games; or just hang out with your fellow 'netters' while still surfing the Net." Instant-messaging applications for the consumer market have proliferated and use different standards, so to communicate, users must use the same application. The applications are relatively small and run in the background of a user's computer. Many of these systems are hybrid P2P systems in that servers act as critical brokers in facilitating communication.

ICQ.   ICQ was the first instant-messaging system that addressed intermittently connected personal computers. The application allows for instant messaging and also includes other modes of communication such as voice, message board, data conferencing, and file transfer. The information regarding users is stored on central servers that maintain the database and check for users on the network. It is best for group chat and file transfers among instant-messaging applications. ICQ is attempting to develop a platform that it can use to build P2P applications, since it has developed the infrastructure.

Business model: free software

Topology: hybrid P2P

America Online Instant Messenger. AOL's Instant Messenger, AIM, has jumped up as one of the leading instant-messaging services because of AOL's presence on the Internet. It handles basic one-on-one chat effectively and adds additional capabilities. AIM targets the novice computer user, but because of the large number of America Online members, it controls a major portion of the instant-messaging market.

Business model: free software, subscriptions from America Online users

Topology: hybrid P2P

Windows Messenger. Microsoft's new Windows Messenger, included with the new Windows XP operating system, is the company's effort to bundle instant messaging with what it hopes will remain the world's ubiquitous operating system. It allows users to page cell phones, send pictures and music, and complete free voice and video calls to another PC on the Internet. Windows Messenger also makes it possible to call from a computer to a telephone just as easily, using the PC-to-phone service provider that the user selects. It is a direct challenge to AOL's Instant Messenger, currently the market leader. Increasingly, AOL and Microsoft are going after the same customer.

Business model: free software, free subscription required

Topology: hybrid P2P

Distributed Computing

The overwhelming response to SETI@home's distributed computing initiative has led both nonprofit organizations and profiteers alike to explore alternative applications. Other firms and institutions with processing-intensive applications have already made use of the supercomputer power embedded in the network. Cancer and AIDS research, earthquake simulation, and particle physics research are just a few of the fields that have benefited from this raw processing horsepower.

Popular Power. Popular Power is one such broker that has entered the market by offering users $5 per month to capitalize on their underused CPU cycles. This aggregated processing power is then auctioned off to bioengineers, mathematicians, and others in need of a computation community.

> Business model: transaction fees
> Topology: hybrid P2P

Entropia. Entropia has also entered this space, focusing primarily on non-profit applications such as FightAIDS@home. By marketing with the slogan "Activate your PC's power to save the environment," Entropia has created the image of performing tasks for the good of humankind.

> Business model: transaction fees
> Topology: hybrid P2P

Envive. Envive is one of the leading providers of Web-application performance-management solutions. P2P Web testing provides real-world Web site-performance testing. Instead of using servers that are located within ISPs to simulate users, P2P Web testing uses actual PCs that are connected to the Internet, which is a more accurate method. It incorporates all the inherent delays and upsets that are normally present on the network into the test.

> Business model: transaction fees
> Topology: hybrid P2P

As of February 2001, more than 110 companies were relying on the P2P structure as the heart of their business. About 35 of these companies are competing in the file-sharing arena; 15 companies are in cycle sharing; and the remainder are spread out as combinations of these categories or are in smaller niche areas.

Up to this point, we have considered the functionality behind P2P computing and some of the participants in the field, but we have not looked into the value proposition that it brings.

VALUE DRIVERS: COMPUTING AT THE EDGE OF THE NETWORK

The direct link to peers enabled by bypassing larger networks produces value from several sources. Shifting from the client/server architecture to the peer connections makes better use of the available resources. The change in network architecture takes computing power, which in the current Internet architecture resides on servers, and moves it to the edge of the network. This is not a new concept, as networks were originally built on a P2P architecture. With the growth of the World Wide Web, the network architecture evolved into a hub-and-spoke model that placed servers at the core of the network and individual PCs at the edges. The model developed into a system in which knowledge and information transfer was mostly a one-way street. When someone surfing the World Wide Web requests information, a server retrieves it. However, the PC user is not sending back much information that increases the knowledge base of the network. The PCs connected to the Internet are restricted simply to being clients that receive information. This model works well when users need content and information stored in a central location but is not as efficient when the information is needed at the edges of the network.

The value drivers that individuals and corporations are capitalizing on with P2P systems are described in the following section.

Distributed Parallel Processing

Move over supercomputer, here comes grid computing. Creating a network of directly connected peers now enables processing resources to be aggregated and used at a large scale. While processor speeds on even home PCs are surging, only a fraction of the processing power is actually used. Peer computing now allows complex and time-consuming processing applications to be distributed and processed at the end nodes. Math-intensive operations that were once impossible without a supercomputer are now feasible at a more economical level.

Distributed Content Storage

Like distributed parallel processing where resources are underused, distributed content storage takes advantage of underused storage resources among all participants in a peer network. Since even within a large corporation, the use of hard-drive storage is only about 50 percent, terabytes of storage capacity go underused. Although dropping prices per unit of storage negates this value proposition, the real value lies in the aggregation of the available capacity on a larger scale within a corporation.

In addition, edge services act as caching mechanisms as they move data closer to the point of consumption. A global company that gives online training to its employees through the Web can store the video on local clients, which act essentially as local database servers. Because the streaming goes over the local area network (LAN) instead of the wide area network (WAN), the company saves time; it also saves money by eliminating the need for local storage on servers.

Direct Communication/ Information Distribution

The majority of Internet applications are structured such that information is pulled from the business to the consumer (B2C). Though this arrangement obviously produces valuable applications, it doesn't enable the end user to share anything meaningful with others on the network. Content sharing is at the heart of what has brought recognition to peer computing. Previously, making content available to the public was a tedious process that most users were unwilling to undertake. They needed to obtain a fixed IP address from an ISP and wade through the technicalities of setting up a Web site. Now users can download a free interface, install it, and within minutes share their content with peers on the network.

P2P networks need to operate outside the DNS system with nearly complete autonomy. Therefore, collaboration through P2P technology takes advantage of resources such as storage, human presence, and content at the edge of the Internet. These new platforms will fully embrace existing systems. Current collaboration platforms through client/server arrangements are not flexible in that a collaborative team needs to adapt to it and its applications. Through P2P computing, a collaboration environment will leverage the strength of existing assets of applications and computing. Companies will be able to adapt their databases stored through their Enterprise Resource Planning (ERP) systems and share information with partners in a seamless and secure environment without relying on a third party.

Dynamic, Distributed Search

Unlike Napster, in which a directory of each node's content is stored on a central server, Gnutella applications have been based on searching the content on the peer's storage device. Typically, a handful of adjacent peers are polled in search of the desired content. Each of these peers in turn polls a handful of other adjacent peers. The exponential growth of this search quickly returns the results from potentially thousands of peers.

To be a viable source of value, a software interface is essential to match the desired content with the available content residing among peers on the network. The Napster model and other search engines using the server-based directory are very effective in mapping the content available on the network and are limited only in the time between mapping updates. To be advantageous, the pure P2P application would benefit most in cases in which the real-time updates are needed when searching the network.

SECRET OF SUCCESS

Though P2P computing is not completely revolutionary, technological advances have enabled it to progress to where it is today and will further propel it into the future. Increasing bandwidth, hybrid centralized/decentralized models, scalability, and the sheer growth in the number of participants have enhanced the P2P offering.

Bandwidth Availability

Widespread use of broadband enables P2P computing because it facilitates communication between the nodes at the edge of the network. "Last mile" bottlenecks limit the speed of data transfer on the network. This becomes even more critical in P2P networking, since a majority of the communication occurs over the last mile. The rollout of broadband makes P2P computing much more powerful. Although the increase of broadband has not lived up to expectations, its steady growth improves the prospects for the success of P2P computing.

P2P applications are changing the assumption that end users want only to download from the Internet and never upload. The Web was the killer application of the Internet, and it is made up mostly of clients, not servers. New P2P players face great challenges sparked by the rise of asymmetrical network connections such as cable modems and Asymmetric Digital Subscriber Line (ADSL). Until this asymmetry is resolved, digital subscriber line (DSL) providers have an advantage in the race to enable P2P networking because of their relatively symmetrical technologies.

Hybrid Centralized/Decentralized Models

Napster struck oil by integrating the benefits of the direct P2P connection with the centralized directory search to efficiently pair up the seeker and provider of content. P2P success stories will properly balance this blend of centralization and autonomy to facilitate people's tasks in a more efficient manner or allow them to complete new functions that are not even out there today. As noted, the goal is to be just decentralized enough.

Network Externalities

As the number of participants grows, the available shared resources (content, storage, or processing) increase as well. The increase in available resources then attracts new participants, and the cycle continues. Napster managed to build a database of more than 50 million addresses. Virtually any song from any genre was available because of the enormous number of participants.

Napster changed the economics of the music industry because the marginal cost of downloading a song is virtually zero. By creating one more copy of a song in the network, a user increased the chances that the next user who searched for that song would find it. Therefore, accidentally, value was created in the network. Designing systems that create value automatically will be key for succeeding in the P2P space.

Scalability

By using the resources of the end user, peer networks benefit from the scalability inherent in the network. In the corporate environment, instead of fighting the bureaucratic channels to obtain additional storage and processing capacity for the servers as the users grow in numbers, each new user brings the incremental resources to grow the network.

CHALLENGES

Even as technological advances are ushering in peer computing, critics maintain that issues of security and data integrity pose threats to its usefulness and growth. Also, bandwidth not only contributes to P2P penetration, but potentially poses a barrier by increasing traffic flow across the network. Finally, the rush to establish industrywide de facto standards is resulting in applications flooding the market and a lack of interoperability.

Security

Security and authentication are two crucial factors that will determine the success or failure of P2P networks. It is predictable that P2P networks will become the killer application for virtual private networks. It is hard to imagine those networks without state-of-the-art security systems. Some players in the P2P space have already created maverick forms of security. These include one pass phrase per account, one asymmetrical key per account, and one asymmetrical key pair per identity for signature/verification, and another asymmetrical key for encrypting/decrypting symmetrical keys. There is little doubt that the latest technological advances that allow for increasing security will be key for these applications.

Bandwidth Limitations

Transferring client-server traffic to P2P connections can be likened to moving traffic from highways to residential streets. The move may alleviate the traffic on the highways and provide potentially more efficient routes, but the residential network is not designed to handle the traffic. As the growth and penetration of broadband continues, it will alleviate the congestion in the last mile of the network and facilitate efficient P2P computing.

Interoperability

Because of the rapid proliferation of P2P computing technologies, several such technologies are available. Although that situation provides many choices for the consumer, the lack of standardization also prevents computers with either different computing systems or software platforms from communicating with one another.

CURRENT APPLICATIONS AND VALUE DRIVERS

The main applications for P2P computing include file sharing, instant messaging, and distributed computing. These individual functions are evaluated along with the crucial value drivers. Table 7.1 contains a summary.

Table 7.1
Value Drivers

Application	Critical Value Drivers
File Sharing	• Distributed Content Storage • Dynamic, Distributed Search
Instant Messaging	• Direct Communication/ Information Distribution
Distributed Computing	• Distributed Parallel Processing • Direct Communication/ Information Distribution

File Sharing

The current killer application for P2P computing has certain key value drivers. The success of file sharing depends on both distributed content storage and dynamic search capabilities. Initially, the information must be indexed in a way that makes it accessible and understandable. Then a powerful search capability is required to find the data. This can be implemented through a system in which the information either resides on central servers or is created dynamically by each user who logs on. The ability to distribute content storage prevents overburdening any individual node and optimizes storage usage.

Instant Messaging

Instant messaging is another popular function in P2P computing. The critical value driver in instant messaging is direct communication/information distribution. To find another user on the network, the instant-messaging system must allow users to directly access intermittently connected computers that have changing IP addresses. This capability allows the program to connect any two or more users and allows them to communicate directly.

Distributed Computing

The key value driver of distributed computing is parallel processing. The ability to take a large task, break it into manageable pieces, and then send it out to individuals is at the heart of distributed computing. The value of direct communication further enhances this proposition by enabling direct connectivity with the nodes.

Viable Business Models

The question that still remains, however, is how value will be captured and who will capture it. Even Forrester Research has stated that although millions of consumers and dozens of companies are jumping on the bandwagon, profitable business models remain elusive. Is the end result a networked world in which consumers are simply sharing and receiving content for free?

For the application to represent a viable business model, it must accomplish one or more of the following three propositions for the end user:

1. *Revenues must be generated above and beyond the costs to produce them.* These revenues can fall into several models:

   —*Transaction.* Fees collected on the basis of an occurrence.
   —*Subscription.* A fixed fee for the content or service over a predetermined period.
   —*Information selling.* Includes the selling of consumer-behavior information.
   —*Advertising.* Banner advertisements or other kinds of advertising placement.
   —*Software licensing.* License fees for applications.
   —*Solutions providing.* Bundling of service and support with applications to suit the particular needs of an organization.

   Increasing revenues cannot be confused with market share. It is imperative that these revenues not be obtained "at any cost," but that the costs be low enough to net a profit.

2. *A cost savings must be realized that outweighs the implementation costs.* Companies will look to P2P computing not only to enhance their revenues but to reduce costs. Large corporations may be attracted to enterprise solutions that will actually enable them to operate at a lower cost. Once again, the gain must exceed the cost of implementing the solution.

3. *Better information must be received to enable better decision making.* Though better decisions will ultimately lead to increased revenues or reduced costs, it is often difficult to justify a project when the financial gains are not easily quantifiable up front. For that reason, this third option may not target immediate cost savings or revenue gains but rather may improve the overall decision-making capabilities within the corporation. Expedient, reliable

information previously unavailable may now be delivered right to the desktop.

Future Applications

The current network requires and allows minimal interaction between clients. Figure 7.5 illustrates the lack of communication between peers. The focus, as discussed, is on the interaction between the client and the server. Information has to be manually transferred between the clients with no direct means of communication.

P2P applications will allow clients to interact in ways that do not erect barriers between them. Clients will be able to peer through the firewall and share information and resources. These applications will bring together in a unique way the functional capabilities already offered in the market. The appropriate set of functionalities from Figure 7.6 will come together to create a potential killer application.

Collaboration in Project Management

Application. ERP providers such as SAP, JD Edwards, and Peoplesoft are adding online collaboration networks through which different parties can participate in a given project with different levels of access. Other firms, such as Bidcom and Cephren, provide the same service mainly for

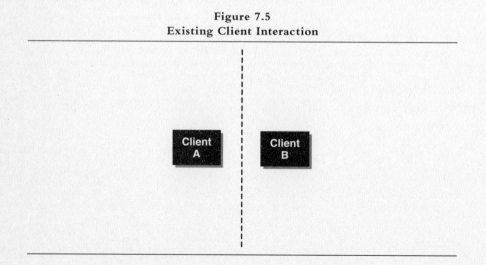

Figure 7.5
Existing Client Interaction

Figure 7.6
P2P-Enabled Client Interactions

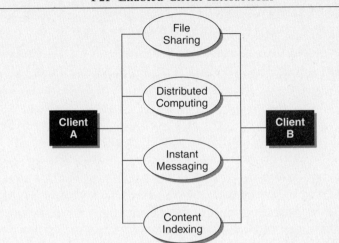

the construction industry. They have been providing these services mostly through hosting, not through P2P applications. These application service providers rent the service and keep the project information on their servers, usually in huge data centers.

Collaboration will evolve in an unimaginable way through P2P computing because of the symmetry of the participants in the network, as well as the economics of not using an administrator. Imagine a group of engineers working on the same drawing. Each engineer does not need to have his or her own drawing, so the drawing can be stored in pieces on computers on the network. Solution providers allow for files to be in bits and pieces, so instead of a 3 gigabyte file on somebody's hard drive, there can be a (3 gigabyte)/n file stored on each computer on the network, with n being the number of computers on the network.

Alternatively, imagine an engineer checking an architect's drawings. The file needs to be in only one space in the network. It does not matter where on the network the file is stored. The engineer can have access to it from his computer, and his changes or comments will be automatically saved on the other team member's computer. Since the engineer does not have the file, all he is sending is information about the changes that need to be made. His computer is not processing that information; the computer that has the file is doing it.

P2P computing fits perfectly with the collaborative feature of the Internet, as shown in the latest project from Ray Ozzie, the inventor of Lotus Notes. Ozzie is working on a product that will allow small teams to share information and collaborate on tasks and projects. His company, Groove Networks, is being watched with great interest.

For collaboration to succeed as a P2P application, several users on a team must have access to the same documents. Beyond that, the ability to modify the documents and update the shared versions at all locations is necessary. Finally, since project groups must work closely together to implement a project, direct communication between users is a key capability. On the basis of these requirements, the critical value drivers for collaboration are distributed content storage and direct communication. Distributed content storage will allow the essential information to be stored at the location where it is used the most. A requirement for partial content storage is that all users must be online at all times to assure access to the necessary information.

Business Model. We can expect vendors to charge subscription and monthly fees for their platform service. As in the traditional software industries, there are significant development costs. Whoever comes out with a flexible, easy-to-use collaboration platform will enjoy a first-mover advantage in a new market willing to pay dearly for significant cost reductions in day-to-day team-project management.

Knowledge Management

Application. As the economy develops toward a more information-driven system, the ability to manage knowledge within the enterprise is going to become even more critical. The power of using P2P computing for knowledge management is enormous, since it makes vast amounts of knowledge available to everyone. For reasons of security and intellectual-property protection, however, users are highly unlikely to open up and share knowledge with any stranger on the network.

Although it does not appear likely that we will be able to peer into the computers of total strangers on the Internet, the possibility of implementation on a smaller scale is nonetheless attractive. Even within a corporation, imagine the time that is spent reworking problems that were solved previously. In many cases, issues come up repeatedly, but because of personnel turnover and lack of appropriate social networks, those same problems are worked on again from scratch.

Another part of knowledge management that P2P computing can facilitate is automatic backups. Since P2P computing can use unused resources on computers such as storage, a knowledge-management system can include the capability of taking information that resides on a user's hard drive and backing it up to another user's hard drive. That eliminates the need for expensive central storage while maintaining enterprise-critical data.

Business Model. Two approaches potentially offer viable business models in the knowledge-management space. These are software licensing and solutions providing. The first, licensing, is straightforward in that a vendor would provide a software program allowing a company to index, store, and retrieve information. This is the first area of focus for companies interested in the market. As additional competitors enter the market, however, this space will become commoditized. Those vendors who understand the functions of the company will be able to add more value as solutions providers and generate higher revenues. In addition, a vendor might be able to use the transaction model on a megabyte-per-megabyte-of-data basis to generate revenue.

Enterprise Processing

Application. Distributed computing has tremendous potential because the price of supercomputers is high and a great number of unused computing assets are available. Many of the entrants in the market are developing applications that target general computer users on the Internet. The business model generally involves enticing users by paying them some nominal amount or asking them to donate computing power to nonprofits. The emphasis of these companies on the general public presents some challenges. These include the reliability of computing resources, payment of individual users, and the security issues that companies may have with sending their information outside the firewall.

Using the computing resources within the enterprise offers tremendous opportunity. Corporate IT managers will likely be loathe to give up control and allow computing resources outside the company to become critical, but those same resources are available within the enterprise. Great computing power remains unused inside corporations. P2P distributed-computing companies that focus within the enterprise have incredible resources.

In addition to providing the processing power to handle major computing, these software providers must provide solutions. Combining desktop computers to form a supercomputer will provide only part of the solution needed to gain traction in corporate environments. The providers must combine a killer application with the computing power. That means gaining a deep understanding of the end users' market and needs. Rather than just being computing experts, they will need to develop a vertical focus and be industry experts as well. The opportunities for enterprise processing lie in financial services, biotechnology, and general research and development within the semiconductor, aerospace, and defense fields.

Business Model. The aggregators of computing power who seek to serve the enterprise market must focus on securing a transaction-based revenue stream or becoming a solutions provider. The transaction-based system is the first step and is attractive for customers whose tasks are not critical. These customers would be willing to let their processing be done outside their firewalls and pay a per-usage charge. However, the majority of major corporations would like to maintain control over their processing. In these cases, P2P computing vendors will need to propose an enticing value proposition that will allow them to get their foot in the door. That entails becoming a solutions provider and understanding the inner workings of a customer's business and the intricacies of P2P computing.

Games

Application. Games are just not that much fun when played alone. Developers initially resolved this problem by building intelligence into the game, thereby setting up the "man versus machine" situation. Although that provided some form of competition, the human element and varied opponents were still missing. P2P computing brings an abundance of opportunities into the games world. To be effective, two criteria must be established.

To engage in multiperson game playing through the Internet, it is first necessary to find potential partners. For some time, online game players have used host servers to find opponents for Monopoly, chess, and other games. Although using a directory service through a server is an effective way of pairing these aficionados, the Gnutella technology could also be used. Instead of the players' registering in a directory, the game software could have an interface that would poll for peers out on the Internet to find others with the same interface.

Additionally, larger software developers could create a suite of game possibilities so that, depending on mood, a user could play any one of several possible games online. Consider a sports-games developer such as EASports.

A Gnutella-type interface could be included on all software applications such that an enthusiast could connect and find other players thirsting for some competition in basketball, football, baseball, golf, and other sports. Whether the competition is matched up through a server directory or through the Gnutella search, the key is to link those individuals seeking to engage in competition in the same game.

The second essential ingredient for success is where P2P computing really delivers something new. Even though the client-server relationship enables locating other game players, it still requires the information to flow through the server. That may be fine for games in which response time is not critical, but for arcade-style applications, in which the actions of one player must be immediately fed back to the other, the client-server doesn't suffice. P2P computing provides the direct connection to engage in the action-packed games that thrill seekers are looking for.

Business Model. The transaction-revenue model in which game players pay a fixed fee per occurrence is a possible revenue source but probably not the best. The subscription plan would increase overall revenues more because the smorgasbord mentality of game players would lead these enthusiasts to devour more than they would have otherwise. The increase in revenue would outweigh the increase in cost because of the greater demand (see Table 7.2).

Another area of opportunity is on the software-development side. Competition for the killer-application game has been stiff for a while, but now the focus will change to game applications that make the most of the P2P connections. Games that involve several individuals competing simultaneously with near real-time interactions will ultimately succeed.

FUTURE LANDSCAPE

In the past several years, there has been talk about the death of the personal computer. The popular prediction was that the intelligence would lie at the heart of the network, within servers, and the users would connect to the network using simple terminals. P2P computing will be a strong opposing force to this trend. Instead of using a "dumb" machine to connect into a powerful network supported by servers, the terminals of the future will be smart and provide the computing horsepower.

Servers within the system will not be eliminated either, for two reasons. First, companies will not walk away from their investments in servers. Second, servers will play an integral role in the P2P topology. PCs

Table 7.2
Potential Business Models

Peer-to-Peer Applications	Transaction	Information Selling	Advertising	Subscription	Solution Provider	Software Licensing
Collaboration in Project Management						
Knowledge Management						
Enterprise Processing						
Games						

	Weak		Moderate		Strong

and servers will work together to take advantage of their appropriate strengths.

Rather than users' receiving information from a network, there will be true two-way communication, and the computers at the edge of the network will play a critical role. This will require more computing resources in the networked computers. The resources will be used for many applications, including collaboration, knowledge management, games, and enterprise processing. As P2P computing continues to develop, we will see further integration of the different functions into more sophisticated applications. This includes the integration of instant messaging and file sharing into the collaboration application, which is already occurring. This trend will continue as more of the functions come together to create killer applications.

The ability to build a network around individual PCs dramatically changes the network architecture. Instead of relying on central server farms that are vulnerable to going down, the network is more stable by being spread throughout the system. In addition, the incremental investment to expand a network is dramatically reduced. Rather than buying a new server to expand the network, firms can simply add another PC to the system.

Building relationships will drive the future development of P2P computing; the technology will be an enabler. To build a P2P network, traditional walls of separation must be torn down. This applies in both the corporate setting and the home-user environment.

Corporate Setting. Even within corporate divisions, the traditional mode of operation is to divide the business into departments and maintain autonomy and information within those silos. The influence of P2P computing will help tear down these divisions. The information that is available in one part of the corporation will be readily accessible to all. That presents some management challenges in implementing P2P systems. Managers unfamiliar with the technology behind peer-to-peer systems may be reluctant to embrace what may appear to be radical changes. Although adoption may initially be difficult, tremendous returns await companies taking advantage of the benefits of P2P computing.

Home-User Setting

Only a small percentage of home users have taken on the challenge of building their own Web sites to share their treasured images with family and friends. The increasing number of digital cameras, coupled with higher-resolution images, has created a strong demand for ways of sharing these memories. Forrester Research has projected that P2P computing offers a much easier solution to this once formidable and intimidating task. Users can now place their digital images and other content in a directory and make it available to those to whom they want to give access.

By 2005, 35 percent of all online households will be using P2P technologies for personal sharing (Figure 7.7). Though a potential market of nearly 24 million users is certainly worth writing home about, shared utilities do not present credible business models. Essentially, the functionality could be built directly into the operating system and simply provide one more compelling reason to purchase the OS upgrade. The real winners in the home-user domain are the consumers themselves. Although the development in the games frontier may create coveted revenues, most other applications will enhance the consumer's computing experience without making billionaires out of the solutions providers.

Figure 7.7
Personal Sharing Projections through 2005 (Forrester Research)

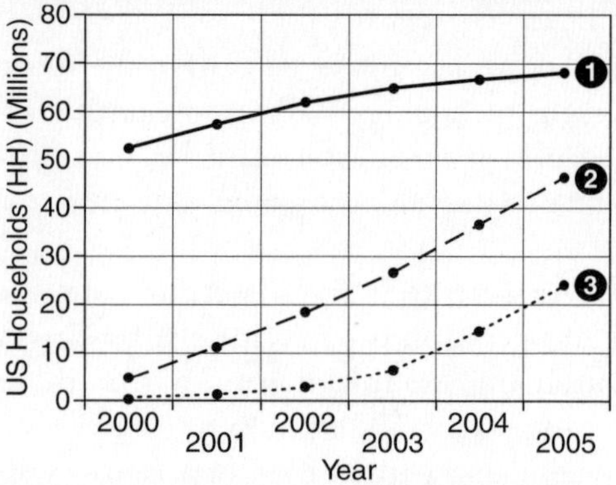

	2000	2001	2002	2003	2004	2005
❶ Total online PC HH (millions)	53.2	58.7	61.8	64.2	66.7	68.6
❷ Total broadband HH (millions)	5.0	11.0	18.9	27.7	37.0	46.7
❸ Personal P2P HH (millions)*	0.6	1.1	3.0	8.5	14.8	23.9
P2P as % of online HH	1%	2%	5%	13%	22%	35%
P2P as % of broadband HH	2%	8%	12%	25%	33%	43%

Note: Personal P2P services include sharing user-created photographs and calendars.
Source: Forrester Research.

CONCLUSION

Though it is not certain who will discover the pot of gold, P2P computing will change the way we communicate and share information today. Whether it becomes a revolution, as Patrick Gelsinger, of Intel, predicted, or simply merges the centralized model of today with the decentralized model of yesterday, we all stand to gain from the functionality it brings.

References

Boyd, Jade. "Load Testing Uses Distributed PCs." *InternetWeek* (November 13, 2000).

Greenfeld, Karl Taro. "Meet the Napster." *Time* (October 2, 2000).

Karel, Bruce, et al. "P2P's Pervasive Future." *Forrester Report* (January 2001).

Kutler, Jeffrey. "Rocking the Buy Side." *Institutional Investor International* (November 2000).

Mahowald, Robert. "Peer-to-Peer Computing: A Primer." *IDC Report* (January 2001).

Mahowald, Robert, and Mark Levitt. "Deja-Vu All Over Again: Collaborative Applications Meet Peer-to-Peer Computing." *IDC Report* (December 2000).

McAfee, Andrew. "The Napsterization of B2B." *Harvard Business Review* (November–December 2000).

McDougall, Paul. "Envive Taps Peer-to-Peer to Test Web Sites." *Information Week* (December 4, 2000).

Minkoff, Jerry. "Napster-style Programs May Revolutionize Financial Services." *Web Finance* (January 2001).

Oram, Andy. *Peer-to-Peer: Harnessing the Power of Disruptive Technology.* Sebastopol, CA: O'Reilly & Associates, 2001.

Scannell, Ed. "P2P Takes on B2B." *InfoWorld* (November 27, 2000).

Shirky, Clay. "Lessons from Napster." Presentation at O'Reilly Peer-to-Peer, San Francisco. (2001).

Walsh, Mark. "Napster Wannabes See Big Bucks on Wall Street." *Crain's New York Business* (October 2000).

CHAPTER 8

A FRAMEWORK FOR THE BIOTECHNOLOGY INDUSTRY

The biotechnology industry is in transition. In the past several years, it has moved from infancy into a stage of rapid growth. Success stories such as those of Amgen, Genentech, and Biogen have given validity to the industry, its technology and products, and its viability. The industry has received public attention for such accomplishments as mapping the human genome and developing cloning technology, feats previously only in the realm of science-fiction authors.

Tremendous opportunity has come from the success of early biotech firms and the promise of their technological breakthroughs. Many new companies entered the industry, hoping to strike it rich during the biotech gold rush. Having seen the high failure rate of early biotechs, many of these firms tried to reduce their exposure to risk either by specializing in a single aspect of product development, such as research, or by developing tools for product-development firms. Many firms that hoped to capitalize on the technology by selling services have found, however, that the returns they had envisioned are not materializing. They have learned that product development and commercialization, while risky, is the most profitable and highly valued activity of the biotech industry. As a result, many biotech firms are forward integrating in the hope of leveraging their current competencies and expanding into product development.

This chapter examines how biotech firms are repositioning themselves to better capitalize on the value they are creating. It begins with a historical overview of the pharmaceutical industry and the drug-discovery process. Then the evolution of the horizontal business model is described, along with the shortcomings of that approach. An analysis of the hybrid business model next provides a framework for biotechnology companies that are considering forward integration. Finally, there are predictions for the structure of the industry in its next stage, maturity.

HISTORY OF THE PHARMACEUTICAL INDUSTRY

Many large pharmaceutical companies evolved from chemical companies. These companies had established core competencies in chemistry, manufacturing, marketing, and sales. Over time, they migrated their core competencies into pharmaceuticals and built additional capabilities in biological research, development, and clinical trials.

This vertically integrated structure was adopted not only by pharmaceutical and chemical companies but also by companies in industries such as automobiles, steel, and even computers. However, unlike these other industries, large, vertically integrated pharmaceutical companies have continued to prosper as a result of the dynamics of drug discovery.

TRADITIONAL DRUG DISCOVERY

Having evolved from chemical companies, large pharmaceuticals had expertise in chemistry and thus developed their drugs using small-molecule

---

Case Study: Pfizer

As one of the largest and most successful pharmaceutical companies in the world, Pfizer illustrates many of the characteristics of large pharmaceutical firms. It was founded in New York City in 1849, as a specialty-chemical company. The first medicine that it marketed was an antiparasitic that could be swallowed. Pfizer expanded its product line to include many chemicals and medicines. Interestingly, Pfizer's first blockbuster product was citric acid, which is needed for industrial applications and food products. Using a fermentation process it developed in 1919, Pfizer was the first company to mass-produce citric acid.

In 1944, Pfizer's expertise in fermentation allowed it to become the first company to mass-produce penicillin, and it became the world's largest producer. In 1950, after a hundred years of business, Pfizer introduced the first pharmaceutical that it had discovered in its own laboratories—the antibiotic Terramycin. In 1971, Pfizer formally established its Central Research Division to bring efficiency and organization to the development of pharmaceuticals.

Source: www.pfizer.com.

methods. Most small-molecule drug-development efforts use a screening approach, a methodology that begins with samples of organic material, such as plants collected from the Amazon rain forest. These materials often contain unique chemical species of unknown efficacy. In the past, screening such materials for efficacy against specific targets was time-consuming and laborious, but the technique of combinatorial chemistry has greatly enhanced this drug-discovery process.

After researchers have identified a new chemical as being active against a target disease, further development leading to commercialization is a notoriously long, arduous, and expensive process. Typically, developing a drug requires 10 years and an investment of $500 million to $750 million. Further, for every drug or treatment that gains Food and Drug Administration (FDA) approval, 5,000 to 10,000 compounds and combinations are tested. Of these, 250 make it to the clinical-test phase, and only 5 ever reach Phase 3. On average, only one of these gains approval, and this in turn is no guarantee of commercial success.

Drug-Development Value Chain

The drug-development value chain can be broken down into five stages: target discovery, lead discovery, clinical trials, manufacturing, and marketing, sales, and distribution (Table 8.1). These stages are often categorized and discussed as research (R), development (D), and commercialization (C).

$$R \to D \to C$$

Each step along the drug-development value chain has an inherent risk and return associated with performing those activities. The value of a product increases as it moves from one stage to the next. At each successive stage, the likelihood of success increases, but the loss associated with failure increases as well.

Target Discovery

The first stage of the drug value chain is target discovery. The goal of this process is to identify a target, or a physiological phenomenon, implicated in a disease that a drug can neutralize. Historically, this process was a bottleneck in the drug-development value chain because the screening approach took so long to identify new targets. Since it was a bottleneck, pharmaceutical companies often created copycat drugs that used the same

Table 8.1
Drug-Development Value Chain

	Stage	Activity	Core Competency
C	Marketing, sales, distribution.	Targeting, educating, and distributing the product to the appropriate consumer.	Marketing capabilities, distribution channels, sales force and support, and relationships with doctors and payers.
C	Manufacturing.	Manufacturing process of the drug is developed and implemented.	Process science and engineering and FDA interaction.
D	Clinical trials and regulatory approval.	Leads are tested in human models for efficacy and safety. The ideal end result is FDA approval.	Clinical expertise, trial design, and FDA interaction.
R/D	Lead discovery and development.	Potential therapeutics are identified to remedy the target. Preclinical trials in animal models.	Scientific expertise, intellectual property, and R&D operations.
R	Target discovery.	Targets are identified for therapeutic development.	Scientific expertise, intellectual property, and research and development operations.

biological target. The result was a significant number of competing drugs developed for similar indications.

Lead Discovery and Development

With a specific target in mind, researchers use several methods to develop a substance, or *lead,* that regulates the target's activity in causing disease. Before lead molecules can be moved into the next phase of clinical testing in humans, researchers typically conduct in vivo preclinical trials in which molecules are tested in animals for efficacy and safety at effective dosage.

Clinical Trials and Regulatory Approval

The third stage is clinical trials, in which lead molecules are tested in human models for efficacy and safety. The ideal end result is FDA approval, which is required to commercialize a drug. This step accounts for a major portion of the time and expense involved in bringing a drug to market. Designing and completing clinical trials, together with the FDA review process, historically has required 5 to 10 years and has accounted for 80 percent of the total cost of developing a drug. To gain FDA approval, new drugs must successfully complete three phases of clinical trials, as shown in Table 8.2.

After Phase 2 trials, the drug has demonstrated safety and efficacy. Once the product passes through this stage, its value jumps significantly as the prospects for commercialization increase. This phase can be seen as the tipping point in the value chain. According to Mike Gallatin, Vice President and Scientific Director at ICOS, the Phase 2 clinical trial is the "sweet spot." At this point, a small company can partner with a pharmaceutical company to avoid the hefty registration fees associated with Phase 3 trials. By bringing a product through Phase 2, a company can get full value for it because the likelihood of reaching the market is high. After clinical trials are complete, the company submits a New Drug Application to the FDA. Following its review, the FDA Advisory Panel submits a recommendation for or against approval, and the FDA renders its decision.

Manufacturing

Manufacturing can be performed in house or outsourced to other companies. This step in the value chain is highly regulated, and companies are required to follow stringent guidelines to enforce quality and uniformity in the products. In the event that a company fails to meet FDA requirements,

Table 8.2
Clinical-Trial Process

Objective	Scale
Does it hurt healthy people?	20–50 healthy human subjects.
Does it seem to help sick people?	100–300 patients with the condition.
Does it have statistically demonstrable efficacy within acceptable safety parameters?	500–5000 patients with the condition.

Source: Harry Arader, 2001.

**Current Trend: FDA and the Prescription
Drug User Fee Act**

Prior to 1992, it took an average of 30 months for the FDA to approve a
new drug. During that year, the Prescription Drug User Fee Act (PDUFA)
was enacted. PDUFA provided the FDA with increasing levels of resources
for the review of human-drug applications. Fees that the FDA collected
from drug and biologics firms from 1993 to 1997 were to be used to reduce the time required to evaluate certain human-drug applications without compromising review quality.

This legislation reduced the average time it takes for drug approval to
12 months, and to as few as 6 months for breakthrough drugs. Since then,
the number of drugs approved per year has increased by 40 percent, and the
total development time has been shortened by 20 percent. The original act
expired September 30, 1997, but the FDA Modernization Act of 1997
amended and extended PDUFA through September 30, 2002.

Source: www.fda.org.

---

it can incur significant costs and lost revenue. Depending on the therapeutic product, manufacturing capacity can be a bottleneck.

Marketing, Sales, and Distribution

Commercializing a drug requires considerable infrastructure to educate,
sell, and provide support to health care providers, health insurers, and end
users. The infrastructure generally takes a sizable investment and results in
a significant fixed-cost base. This is the stage at which a firm decides
whether to build a consumer brand name for its company. Deciding whether
and how to invest in this stage of the value chain represents one of the fore-
most challenges for biotechnology firms in determining business strategy.

EMERGENCE OF THE
BIOTECHNOLOGY INDUSTRY

The advent of biotechnology stemmed from the belief that, with advanced
understanding of biological processes, researchers could manufacture

molecules that are highly specific to the targeted biological pathway. Such drugs would presumably be safer and cause fewer side effects.

When recombinant DNA technology was discovered in the 1970s, it became a disruptive force for the entire pharmaceutical industry. The technology allowed companies to mass-produce human proteins for the first time by growing the proteins in *E. coli* bacteria. Instead of screening compounds and then searching for the active targets of those compounds, biotechnology now identifies disease targets first and then searches for ways to manipulate those targets. Technologies developed to perform this include genomics, bioinformatics, and molecular genetics.

Recombinant DNA changed the philosophy for developing drugs from the traditional process of trial and error with small molecules to a process that begins with understanding the disease pathway and then finds the proteins to modify the disease biology. Targeted proteins held the promise of more specific drugs that had fewer side effects (see Table 8.3).

Many of the initial biotechnology companies (Amgen, Genentech, and Chiron) emulated the structure of the large, vertically integrated pharmaceutical companies. That strategy was driven by four main factors. First, it was the known and established business model of the drug-development industry. Second, this model allowed companies to retain control so that they could continue to develop drugs differently—from disease to drug, rather than from compound to disease to drug. Third, no pharmaceutical company had the technology or manufacturing prowess to manufacture the proteins. The biotechnology companies had the most knowledge about the processes, so it made more sense for them to develop these capabilities.

Table 8.3
Traditional versus Biotechnology Drug-Development Approach

Traditional	*Biotechnology*
Diseases characterized by symptoms and chemistry.	Diseases more finely characterized by genetic analysis.
Discovery becoming more expensive and slower.	Discovery faster with targets and high throughput screening.
Trials require drugs to be safe for all.	Patient profiling allows better interpretation of trial data.
Some therapies not effective for some patients.	Therapies tailored to individual through genetic information.

Source: Applied Biosystems presentation, 2001.

Case Study: Genentech

In 1976, 29-year-old Silicon Valley venture capitalist Robert Swanson approached Herbert Boyer, a professor of biochemistry and biophysics at the University of California, San Francisco, about forming a business for drug development. Boyer had been conducting groundbreaking research with recombinant DNA, and Swanson believed that his research could provide a new way to create commercially viable human therapeutics.

Initially, Boyer was reluctant to create Genentech because the academic research community saw working in industry as selling out. Swanson, however, convinced him that together they could create a company whose research was as good as that being conducted in university laboratories and that he would be proud to be a part of it. They called their company Genentech and chose to focus on creating pharmaceuticals that addressed significant unmet medical needs. In doing so, they launched the biotech industry.

The following year, Genentech produced the first human protein, and in 1982 the first recombinant DNA drug was introduced to the market in a joint venture between Genentech and Eli Lilly. Since then, Genentech has developed eight drugs to treat cancer, heart disease, and diseases requiring growth hormones.

Source: www.gene.com.

Finally, biotechnology products had not been proven efficacious or cost-effective. The market value of the products was uncertain, so the pharmaceutical and biotechnology companies had difficulty agreeing on appropriate partnering arrangements.

EVOLUTION OF BUSINESS MODELS IN THE COMPUTER INDUSTRY

Biotechnology companies that started during the early 1980s primarily evolved into fully integrated biopharmaceutical companies. That trend is similar to what happened in the computer industry, where vertically integrated companies like IBM and DEC dominated early on (Figure 8.1). According to David Yoffie (1997), a Harvard Business School professor, "This model was viable in the era of the mainframe because proprietary, closed products created a one-stop shop for the customer, which in turn generated

Figure 8.1
Vertically Integrated Companies

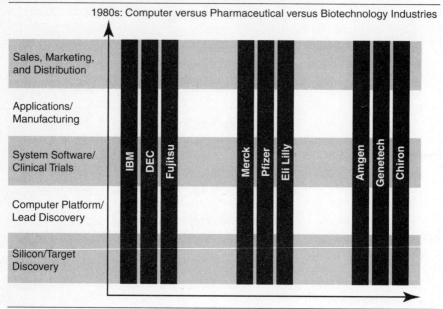

1980s: Computer versus Pharmaceutical versus Biotechnology Industries

Adapted from Yoffie, 1997.

very high margins for the dominant players." These margins could then be reinvested into the entire value chain, which allowed the company to remain competitive. To be successful, companies had to be large and have access to sufficient resources. To sustain this model, they had to establish and maintain a large market share.

As the computer industry evolved, it began to decouple. Specialized core competencies and economies of scale allowed companies to become dominant at horizontal layers such as microprocessors and operating systems. The horizontal model emerged in the computer industry as firms such as Microsoft and Intel came to power (Figure 8.2).

SHIFTING INDUSTRY

In the early 1990s, the biotechnology industry reached a critical mass of product-development companies, and new companies began to implement horizontal business models. These companies specialized in a particular stage of the value chain and used economies of scale to create profit by selling their services. Companies following this strategy established

Figure 8.2
Horizontal Business Model

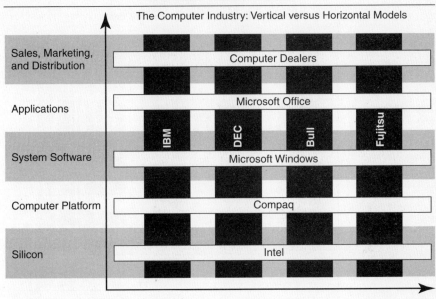

The Computer Industry: Vertical versus Horizontal Models

Sales, Marketing, and Distribution	Computer Dealers
Applications	Microsoft Office
System Software	Microsoft Windows
Computer Platform	Compaq
Silicon	Intel

IBM   DEC   Bull   Fujitsu

Adapted from Yoffie, 1997.

platform technologies and services that could be used across multiple drug-technology silos (Figure 8.3).

This shift toward horizontal models occurred because of certain dynamics in the industry and the emergence of three disruptive technologies. Three key characteristics of the industry were the inefficiency of research, the difficulty of successfully commercializing drug products, and the strength of intellectual-property protection. The three disruptive technologies were computing power, genomics, and the Internet. The fundamental change resulting from these disruptive technologies occurred as companies realized that the drug-development industry was not product driven but information driven. In essence, companies recognized that those firms that control the information created in the early research and development stages can control the downstream products and therefore the downstream profits.

Dynamic 1: Inefficient Research Programs

As discussed, drug-development companies were originally vertically integrated and developed products around in-house expertise. Before the

Figure 8.3
Platform Technologies

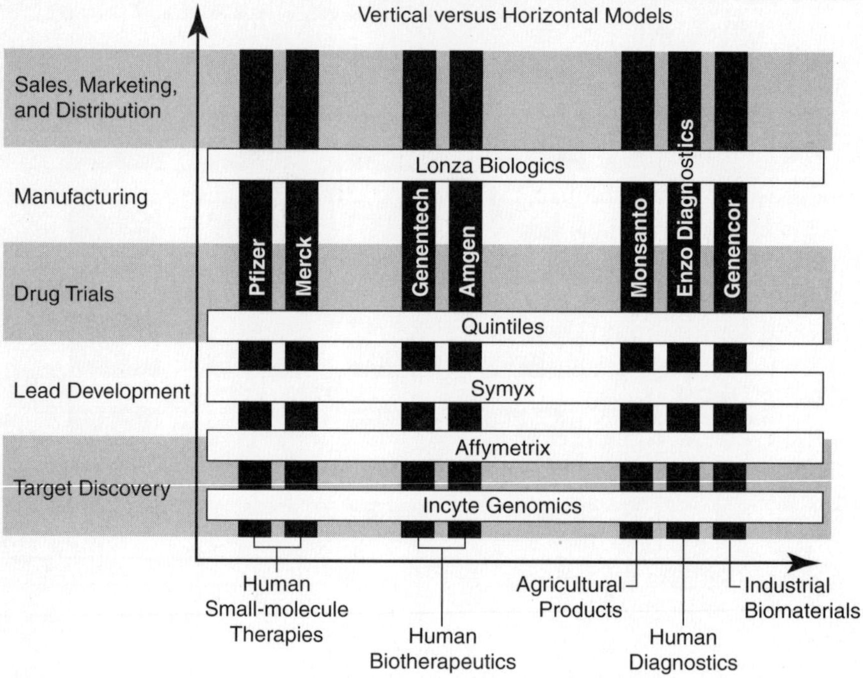

Vertical versus Horizontal Models

appearance of computers and the Internet, several aspects of the industry made this organizational structure ideal. Information exchange between collaborators—other companies, government agencies, and academic institutions—was slow, uncertain, and costly. Thus, in accordance with ideas first expressed in Ronald Coase's 1937 article, "Nature of the Firm," companies organized vertically to optimize the sharing and transfer of knowledge (value) across different functional areas within the company. Maintaining excellence in vertical models, however, is often difficult. Human and capital resources are limited, and companies are forced to make trade-offs in some value-chain activities. It is extremely difficult to maintain a core competency in research, development, and commercialization.

Trade-offs lead to two problems. First, because of the diverse competencies required, firms tend to allocate inadequate capital or human resources to compete effectively in any one area. Thus, they spread their resources too thinly and fail to establish a competitive advantage in any area of the value chain. Second, trade-offs leave the firm vulnerable to competitors who make fewer, different, or ultimately better choices. More focused companies could innovate more quickly and produce services and products more efficiently than larger diverse companies.

Dynamic 2: Risk of Product-Based Strategies

Motivated by the economic incentive of profits from potential blockbuster drugs, early biotech companies performed all the activities required to develop and sell biotherapeutics. On average, however, only 1 in 10 of these early biotech firms was able to bring a product to market. During the 1970s and 1980s, investors focused only on the tremendous upside potential of biotechnology, but in the early 1990s investors became less willing to sink money into the black hole of drug discovery. This gave rise to a deconstruction of the industry and created the opportunity for more nimble, horizontally oriented platform companies to enter the arena. They could compete effectively by specializing in one aspect of the drug-discovery value chain.

Discovering targets for larger companies or specializing in one link on the value chain was less risky, required less capital, and generated more immediate results (Table 8.4).

Dynamic 3: Strong Intellectual-Property Laws

During the 1990s, there was a correlation between the emergence of horizontal business models and the sharp increase in patents issued in the biotech industry. Most likely, the availability of patent protection drove the emergence of these companies (Figure 8.4).

Biotech firms in the United States understand that protection of intellectual property through enforceable patent rights is critical to success. Biotechnology is an information-driven science, and the industry thrives when researchers share thoughts and data. Since developing biotherapeutics

Table 8.4
Tools Are a Good Business

	Gold Rush	*Biotechnology Revolution*
Tools	Picks and shovels	Protein and DNA sequencers
Time	1849	1979
Risk/reward	Find gold!	Make the right drug!

Source: Applied Biosystems presentation, 2001.

Figure 8.4
Trend in Biotech Patents Issued

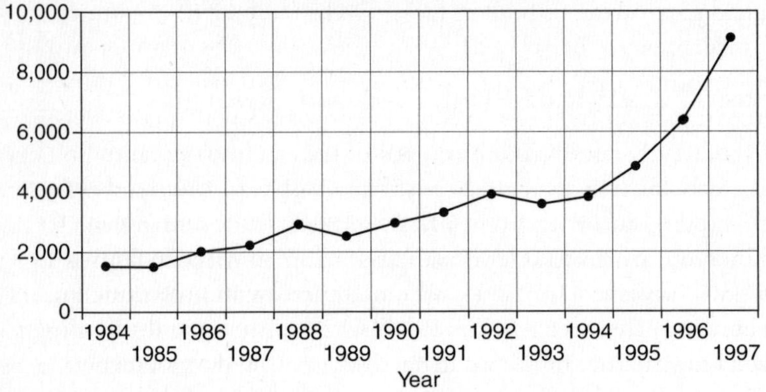

Source: Biotechnology Industry Organization.

and platform technologies is capital intensive, however, companies may be reluctant to innovate or share information unless there is a law to protect their discoveries. Biotechnology companies create and protect value as a direct function of their intellectual property. The preceding dynamics coincided with the following three disruptive technologies to drive the emergence of horizontal business models.

Technology 1: Genomics

Genomics-technology development also led to a quicker and more accurate method of identifying drug targets and drug leads. Advances in DNA-sequencing technology and the development of microarray technology have driven the emergence of genomics. To begin with, the commercialization of automated DNA sequencers significantly enhanced the collection of raw DNA sequence information. Using instruments such as the ABI 377 sequencers (produced by Applied Biosystems), laboratories could easily collect sequence information within hours on 32, 68, and eventually 96 samples at a time. More recently, the advent of capillary-based automated sequencers has further improved the quality and throughput of sequencing. This technology, combined with advances in fluorescent chemistry, has encouraged the emergence of specialized, high-throughput-sequencing laboratories that now sequence hundreds of thousands of DNA samples a week. The level of sequencing throughput has created an explosion of DNA information and allowed the first draft of the human genome to be finished years ahead of expectations.

In addition to sequencing technology, microarray technology has also had a profound impact on genomics. Microarrays consist of pieces of DNA attached to a substrate such as glass. In the mid-1990s, commercialization of this technology began with companies such as Synteni (acquired by Incyte Genomics in 1997) and Affymetrix. The density of DNA strands on microarrays is on the order of tens of thousands per square centimeter and will soon reach hundreds of thousands. This technology allows scientists to collect data such as expression profiles on tens of thousands of genes in a single experiment, with tremendous savings of time and money. Companies like Zyomyx are now commercializing microarray technology for proteins, which will achieve a similar exponential increase in proteomic information.

The disruptive technologies in DNA sequencing and microarrays have altered the structure of the value network in drug development. Using these advances, companies can specialize in specific areas of the value chain, such as target discovery, and execute faster, better, and more cheaply than by focusing on the entire vertical drug-development process. This has led to a dramatic change in the landscape. A decade ago, the vertical companies

---

Case Study: Incyte Genomics

Incyte Genomics, formed in 1991, was one of the first biotech companies to use high-throughput, computer-aided gene sequencing to identify genes and their corresponding proteins. Today, Incyte is one of the leading providers of genomic technologies designed for research in the molecular basis of disease. It sells subscriptions to its genomic databases, genomic data-management software, microarray-based gene-expression services, related reagents, and services to pharmaceutical and biotechnology companies. They use this information in all the phases of drug research and development, including gene discovery, disease pathways, new disease targets, and the discovery and correlation of gene-sequence variation to disease.

Unlike other platform companies, Incyte has not chosen to forward integrate and use its technology to develop drugs. Instead, Incyte negotiates royalty rights to the targets that are identified from its database and eventually used to develop drugs. Given the lengthy time of drug development, Incyte has yet to see any money from these royalties. However, Incyte believes that by concentrating on its core competency of gene sequencing and letting the pharmaceutical companies develop and sell drugs, it will maximize its risk-return ratio.

Source: www.incyte.com.

were developing therapeutics from approximately 500 targets. Now the number of targets has grown to 5,000. This has shifted the focus of early research to target validation and lead-molecule development. Some are claiming that therapeutic targets are now commodities, but patent protection is still allowing genomic companies like Celera and Incyte Genomics to capture the value of the targets they have identified.

Technology 2: Affordable Computing Power

The second disruptive force was the tremendous advance that occurred simultaneously in the high-tech industry. It enabled researchers to handle the vast raw-data collection that was now possible with the DNA sequencing and microarray technologies. At this convergence of computer technology and biotechnology, a whole new field of bioinformatics appeared. The exponential increase in raw genomic data created the need for sophisticated algorithms and computer software to make sense of the data. Companies like Incyte Genomics soon had more software engineers on the payroll than traditional scientists. Again, bioinformatics promoted the rise of platform companies that used large computer systems to perform such functions as massive parallel assays and genomewide sequence analysis. These companies could focus and create expertise in bioinformatics much faster, better, and more cheaply than a fully integrated drug-development company. Thus, they created value that vertical companies would buy.

Furthermore, the exponential increase in computer-processing power had a significant impact on bioinformatics. In the formative days of the industry, researchers used very expensive supercomputers that were affordable only to a few companies. Although the necessary computing tools are still a significant investment, they are much more broadly available and affordable. In perhaps the most notable example, Celera has assembled the world's most powerful supercomputer outside the defense industry. The system consists of 1,200 interconnected Compaq Alpha processors that can perform more than 250 billion sequence comparisons per hour for more than 300,000 genomic fragments per day. It feeds Celera's database at a rate of 15 to 20 gigabytes per day. In addition, Incyte Genomics has assembled one of the five largest Linux farms in the world, and the largest outside the financial-services industry.

These technological innovations have altered the very nature of the biotech industry. According to Randy Scott, Chairman of Incyte Genomics, the industry has seen an application to biology of principles similar to Moore's law for the growing power and decreasing costs of electronic hardware and information processing. Whether it is DNA sequencing, microarray-expression analysis, or single-nucleotide polymorphism (SNP) analysis, the cost has come down dramatically.

Technology 3: Internet Communication

The biotechnology industry is organizing itself as a network of companies that create and exchange information. As an industry becomes information driven, the arguments for vertically integrating become less compelling. Information, compared with products such as automobiles, can be easily manipulated, stored, and exchanged among companies. The emergence of the Internet has allowed information sharing to become more efficient and has made it possible for smaller, horizontal companies to thrive in the industry. Coase suggests that when market transactions become more efficient than the costs of maintaining a fully integrated firm, the industry will decouple. Large companies will no longer need to generate expertise

---

Case Study: The SNP Consortium

The Single Nucleotide Polymorphism (SNP) Consortium is an excellent example of individual companies leveraging the power of the networked economy and working together to accelerate the growth of their own industry. Eleven large life-sciences and technology companies, one bioinformatics company, four research centers, and one nonprofit foundation established the consortium. Its goal was to code the 300,000 SNPs in the human body and to create a publicly available database for drug discovery.

The purpose of the consortium was to provide a common road map for the human genome. This road map now serves as a research tool for every organization that conducts genomic research. According to consortium president Arthur Holden, the members viewed the map as a "precompetitive research tool." By collaborating, the members were able to create the map more quickly while sharing financial risk and reducing the duplication of effort.

This consortium illustrates both the power of shared information and the utility of networks. The organizations realized that a common backbone was necessary to advance their companies and the industry. Now that the infrastructure is established, each member can easily interact with other members of the consortium. Thus, the utility of the network for all members has increased exponentially.

at every level in the value chain. Rather, smaller and more specialized companies can add value within the network of the larger firms.

SHORTCOMINGS OF THE HORIZONTAL MODEL

Horizontal companies have been successful in generating immediate revenue; for several reasons, however, the profits have not been as large as anticipated.

Stiff Competition and Rapid Technological Changes

Companies that seek to make extraordinary profits through advanced technology have difficulty maintaining their competitive advantage. First, new entrants emerge with similar products and steal customers. Second, existing technology improves, increasing competition and eroding margins. Third, with numerous companies and academic institutions pouring significant resources into research, technology in this industry advances extremely quickly. A firm's technological source of competitive advantage could easily become obsolete within a few years or even months.

To prevent the loss of market share, companies that sell technology must continually invest in research and development. This investment may ensure the sustainability of a company, but it does not ensure its profitability. For example, in 2000, Incyte Genomics invested 105 percent of revenues in research and development. Although that has sustained Incyte's industry leadership, the level of expenditure prohibits its profitability.

Long Product-Development Cycle

Horizontal companies sometimes anticipate compensation through royalties generated by sales of the drug. Since sales may not be recognized for 7 to 10 years, this places a large strain on their financial position. Further, as few drug candidates are actually brought to market, major potential revenue for horizontal companies may never be realized.

Principal-Agent Problem

Another reason biotechnology companies have had difficulty negotiating for what they perceive as fair value from prospective buyers is that they disagree with their negotiator about the likelihood of the drug's success and therefore its value. Biotech companies systematically overestimate their products' likelihood of success. They do so largely because they have invested a tremendous amount of time, effort, and money into their development. Similarly, biotech companies often underestimate the difficulty and importance of a sales force in making a drug successful, while large companies systematically overestimate the effectiveness of their sales force. Because an efficient capital market is lacking, the biotech companies often lose this argument about value. As a result, the bargaining zones between the seller and the buyer don't always overlap. This disagreement is a form of the "principal-agent problem."

What's more, biotech companies have more information than their negotiating partner does, and as the seller, they do not have the incentive to fully disclose all the risks associated with their product. Realizing that likelihood, the more risk-adverse pharmaceutical companies systematically underestimate the likelihood of success. This is the "lemon problem." The bidders knowingly bid low because there is a chance they will be stuck with a lemon—a product that has no value.

Inefficient Capital Markets

Perhaps the most significant reason that horizontal business strategy has not worked is the inefficient capital market within the drug-development industry. The efficient capital-market theory states that market prices are correct on average. In the market for biopharmaceutical products, however, that is seldom the case because there is limited competition for those products.

Globally, only about 20 pharmaceutical companies are in a position to buy biotechnology products. Within each therapeutic area, the competition may include only one or two companies. Thus, the pharmaceutical companies can underbid, knowing that the biotechs do not have other sources of capital, and the biotech companies are left with few choices. Further, large pharmaceutical companies require new drug candidates to have potential sales of at least $700 million, which means that many drug candidates have no interested bidders.

EMERGENCE OF THE HYBRID MODEL

The failure of the horizontal biotechnology model has led to a hybrid business model. A hybrid model results from a platform (horizontal) company attempting to forward integrate and develop its own drug candidates.

Platform-based companies are beginning to develop drugs to capture more of the value created by their technology. Forward-integration strategies include in-house product development, collaboration and licensing, and mergers and acquisitions.

Figure 8.5 provides a schematic representation of Millennium Pharmaceutical's migration from a platform strategy based on target discovery to a hybrid strategy that incorporates aspects of the vertical value chain.

Although the hybrid strategy may sound like a panacea, the approach has potential pitfalls. The first is that it is extremely expensive. Maintaining a technology lead alone is difficult and expensive; developing a drug at the same time significantly increases the expense and complexity of a company's operations.

The second pitfall is that this strategy stretches a company's focus. A hybrid company must be conscious of its core competency and expend its managerial, financial, and human resources to maintain it. To do that while

Figure 8.5
Millennium's Hybrid Strategy

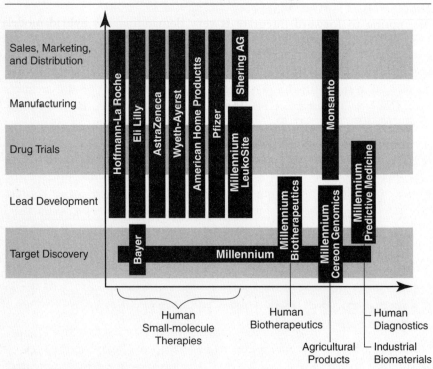

Case Study: PPD, Inc.

PPD is another example of a platform company that has adopted a hybrid business model. PPD began as a contract research organization (CRO) that performed contract Phase 1 through Phase 3 clinical trials for drug-development companies. Today, it offers data-management tools and consulting services in addition to contract research. It has also forward integrated into contract sales and marketing services and has backward integrated into target- and lead-identification services.

By offering customers drug-development solutions, PPD believes that it can offer them more value. In effect, it lessens the extremely high fixed costs and risks associated with drug development. It also believes that this strategy will allow it to capture more value. Currently, PPD is working for, or partnering with, such firms as Affymetrix, Oracle, Bristol-Myers Squibb, Axys, and Eli Lilly.

---

attempting to forward integrate is very demanding. As hybrid models emerge, the key challenge companies face is how to forward integrate (the same challenge that start-up product-development companies face). The following is a strategy for evaluating options of forward integration.

STRATEGY FOR SUCCESSFUL FORWARD INTEGRATION

Since many small biotechnology companies have their own products to develop, these companies all face issues of what to do when their initial products look promising enough to warrant further development. Many of the firms must deal with this question in the near future, since the industry is maturing and more drug candidates are being developed.

The Strategic Decision Matrix (Table 8.5) is a conceptual framework to help executives and management teams of small biotech companies reach informed decisions about the strategic future of their company and its key products. The framework describes three major sets of variables directed at a company's internal capabilities that management should consider as the product passes through the drug-development value chain. These variables are related to the biotech company, its product and portfolio, and important external factors to which all companies are subject.

Table 8.5
The Strategic Decision Matrix—Strategies for Forward Integration

Capabilities	Definition	Licensing	Partnering	Control Capability in House
		Company Variables		
Technical core competencies	What is my competitive advantage (technology platform, understanding a disease pathway)? Where on the value chain is competitive advantage?	My research produces platform technologies that are narrowly focused, or my products are ready to generate immediate revenues.	I want to retain partial control and add more value by going further downstream.	I have a blockbuster drug or true disruptive technology.
Management core competencies	Does our present team have a broad range of managerial skills that support our future product development? How comfortable are we with risk?	My team is narrowly focused in research with no development or commercialization expertise. We are risk adverse.	My team is strong in research, and we have some skills in development and commercialization but need help. We are willing to assume risk under the proper circumstances.	My team does not have all capabilities now, but we are going to develop them. We have decided as a team to "bet the ranch" on our company.
Stage of company life cycle	Is my core competency validated? How much of the value chain do I occupy?	My technologies or products are not appreciated or understood. By licensing, I can increase their efficacy.	My technology and product is credible, but we are too busy and too small to fully develop it.	We are on the edge of explosive growth and are going to do it on our own.
Cash	Amount of cash on hand.	I need an immediate cash infusion.	Some cash would be nice, but I really need added technical and managerial competencies.	Cash is no problem, given the nature of my blockbuster drug or disruptive technology.
		Product and Portfolio Variables		
Therapeutic focus of company	Is my company clearly focused on a single therapeutic area? Or are we developing a broad range of technologies and biologics?	I have multiple areas of interest and would just as soon license out my drugs.	While I have broad interest, I would like to develop deeper penetration in a single therapeutic focus, for example, oncology.	I am a single-product, highly focused, value-driven company, and I am sure my product is a blockbuster.

Table 8.5 *(Continued)*

Capabilities	Definition	Licensing	Partnering	Control Capability in House
Therapeutic market	What is the size and nature of the market for my drug or technology?	It is difficult to reach my target audience without a large, highly developed marketing and sales force that I can rely on.	I want to help educate and develop the sales force, yet I do not have the infrastructure to do so on my own.	The market is large with a high demand for my product or technology. The distribution is concentrated, and it is easy to reach customers.
Company Pipeline	What is the development history and future of my company? How robust and diversified is my portfolio?	I have a lot of candidates in the pipeline and really enjoy exploring different areas.	Though I have broad interest, I would like to develop deeper penetration in a single therapeutic focus, for example, oncology.	I'll use the profits and the infrastructure I've created to develop or acquire other areas of interest in the future.

External Variables

Capabilities	Definition	Licensing	Partnering	Control Capability in House
Access to capital markets	Can I get external funding from investors?	I am a long way from a quality revenue stream if I choose to develop my products further, and I don't want to further dilute my equity.	I want the credibility of a major partner, and additional cash would be nice.	I have ready access to all the capital I need.
Number of bidders for product	What is the demand from other companies for my product?	There is a "feeding frenzy" of companies interested in my product or technology; I will get exceptional value for it.	There are many bidders for my product, and I will get a fair value, but I want to maintain some control.	There are not many bidders for my product because it is not appreciated or understood. To receive an acceptable return, I will need to develop it myself.
Competitors	What is the likelihood of delivering my product to market effectively?	There is strong competition with abundant resources. I'll never make it on my own.	With a little help we can be successful in the market.	I've got a "category killer" or a killer app.

We have identified three basic options for the further development of the company's product. The executive team could consider licensing the product to another company, partnering with another company, or building in-house capabilities for bringing the product to market. By building in-house capabilities, a company can choose to develop these activities internally, including mergers and acquisitions, or control contractual arrangements with another organization. Thus, the ultimate decision involves a matrix matching these two broad areas: analysis of internal capabilities and options for the further development of the product. At the end of this process, the executives must weigh their decision in light of the added value to their company. Decisions may be different depending on the individual product or technology. A truly disruptive technology or blockbuster drug might drive the executive team to develop pure in-house capabilities that

---

Case Study: Geron versus ICOS

Geron and ICOS are companies that have decided to forward integrate but have considered the variables in the Strategic Decision Matrix and have chosen differing business strategies.

Geron is a biotech company that has three proprietary platform technologies and has adopted the strategy of complete forward integration. As it develops its technologies and products, it is trying to do as little partnering as possible. According to Geron's CEO Thomas Okarma: "When you partner with pharmas, you are really selling assets. The only time you should partner is when you cannot access capital from the markets."

Geron has high risk tolerance in both its strategy and its technology. Geron is developing products based on its controversial stem-cell research and has also purchased the rights to the cloning technology that developed DAHLi. Therefore, partnering is difficult because of the controversial, cutting-edge technology that they are developing.

George Rathman, an original founder of Amgen, created ICOS Corporation in 1989. ICOS is one of the few biotech companies established in the 1980s that have survived to launch their first product. To stay alive during the 13 years it took to bring its product to market, ICOS chose to colicense all the products it was developing. According to Mike Gallatin, the vice president and scientific director, this decision was based on the need to reduce risk. Because of the low probability of success but high financial return associated with drug development, he says, "I would rather have a 50 percent stake in two products than a 100 percent stake in one."

will leverage its value rather than to pursue a licensing or partnership agreement. The ideal option will maximize the value of their company and leave it with the most independence yet increase its attractiveness to both investors and potential acquirers.

A popular decision is for the company to license its product to a larger company for development. This creates an immediate revenue stream and credibility in the marketplace. Often a company must license its initial products at a lower value than perceived to raise capital for future development, validate its technology, and learn skills from its partner.

As the company grows and develops new candidates, it is more likely to forward integrate. According to Geron's CEO, Thomas Okarma, the way to build a company is to "vertically integrate by first renting activities (licensing) to create cash flow, and when you reach critical size, then make (build) in-house capabilities."

On the other hand, when a company has a true disruptive technology or blockbuster drug, it may be wise to skip the licensing stage altogether, obtain financing, and build an independent sales and distribution network.

FUTURE OF THE BIOTECHNOLOGY INDUSTRY

Over the past 20 years, the biotechnology and pharmaceutical industries have evolved as a result of technology advances. This evolution resulted in changes in company strategy and structure. Initially, companies such as Amgen and Genentech sought to emulate the vertically integrated pharmaceutical companies. In the early 1990s, firms such as Incyte Genomics and Applied Biosystems sold tools and information to emulate the horizontal business model so successfully implemented by Intel and Microsoft in the PC industry. By the start of the 2000s, the poor profits in the horizontal models caused firms such as Millennium Pharmaceuticals to employ a hybrid strategy, in which they used the revenues from the technology to fuel their own drug-development programs.

It is likely that product companies will continue to capture the most value from the drug-development process. Although it is risky, such companies have the most sustainable business model once a drug is introduced. Opportunities will also probably continue to exist for horizontal business models as companies identify innovative approaches that create efficiencies and cost savings for drug-development companies. These companies, however, will not be able to achieve extraordinary profits like Microsoft and Intel.

From these two views, the following trends appear.

Continued Forward Integration

Companies seeking to develop drug candidates, whether hybrid companies or product start-ups, are indicating that they will build in-house capabilities for all stages of the value chain. Companies that are active in research and development have a stated objective of commercializing their products because they gain increased value and profitability further down the value chain. The most value is created when a company demonstrates that a product shows safety and efficacy. Biotech companies typically start with a core capability in research and then acquire competencies in development. Thus, companies forward integrate to gain and control the rewards garnered downstream from commercialization. This trend toward forward integration will continue for three reasons:

1. Many biotech companies have products in development. This suggests that these companies are looking to build their marketing and sales infrastructure. Many companies will do this.
2. Since the critical inflection point for a drug's value is achieved after the drug passes Phase 2 clinical trials, most biotech companies will seek to bring their product to that point before seeking licensing or partnering arrangements. The forward integration to this stage will occur because inefficiencies in negotiating with large pharmaceuticals before this stage are likely to remain.
3. Biotech companies have been validated by the investment community and are therefore able to obtain funding from the capital markets. These companies now have the resources to build infrastructure and bring products to market on their own.

Though the stated objective of the biotech companies is to bring products to market, most companies will not achieve this on their own. Once past Phase 2, they will license their drug candidate or collaborate with other firms to bring the product to market. The stated objective of being able to bring a product to market simply increases the option value and improves a biotech company's position in negotiations with potential partners. George Rathman, the chairman and former president and CEO of Hyseq, concurs: "You need to get a joint venture because the pay-off reduces thereafter." The way to accomplish this is by having positive clinical data. Rathman further elaborated on this concept by saying that when negotiating a partnership, "you have to pose a credible threat of forward integration" to get fair value for a product.

Increased Mergers between Biotechnology Companies

There will be more mergers and acquisitions in the industry. The M&A activity will continue between pharmaceutical and biotech companies but will be most prominent between biotech companies. This trend is predictable for two main reasons. First, the biotech companies that choose not to partner with pharmaceutical firms will need to merge to achieve economies of scale in the value chain, particularly in clinical trials, manufacturing, and marketing and sales. Companies need to bring more than one product to market to achieve economies of scale. Second, by obtaining the acquired competencies, they will be able to make deals that they could not accomplish previously. These M&A activities will increase the option value for biotech companies and allow them to enter into negotiations and deals not possible or even considered earlier.

Increased Global Partnerships

As biotechnology has been transformed into an information-driven industry, the boundaries for new companies have expanded. Regardless of location,

---

Case Study: Gilead-NextStar

The merger between Gilead Sciences and NextStar is an excellent example of both the value of embedded options in capital investments and the increasing trend toward globalization. In 1999, Gilead purchased NextStar, a biotechnology company based in Cambridge, England. The NextStar acquisition helped Gilead to round out its portfolio of infectious-disease and cancer products, as well as a new liposomal drug-delivery platform.

Because NextStar had a sales presence in Europe and Australia, embedded in the purchase was the option for Gilead to expand its products into these new markets. The value of this option was not lost on Gilead's CEO, John Martin: "We not only gain a new drug-delivery platform of proven liposomal technology but the international resources to fully realize the commercial potential of future products in our combined pipeline."

This international presence has led to further opportunities. In January 2001, Gilead entered into an exclusive partnership with Cubist Pharmaceuticals whereby Gilead will market Cubist's infectious-disease products in 16 European countries in exchange for licensing and royalty fees.

Source: www.gilead.com.

companies can share the same information, such as genomic databases, to add value to the drug-development process.

The trend toward globalization of biotechnology will increase as opportunities for mergers and acquisitions are centered around coordinating activities on a global scale. For example, venture capital can be raised in Japan or Israel, while managerial talent can be supplied from the United States and Germany. Target and lead development and pharmacology and toxicology tests can be outsourced and performed in India. The potential drug can then be licensed to a large pharmaceutical company that can shepherd it through clinical trials and market it around the world. Thus, each stage of the drug-discovery chain is optimized globally.

Continued Existence of Horizontal Models

There are compelling reasons for companies to continue competing in horizontal spaces on the value chain. First, product companies cannot effectively bring a product to market and be technology leaders. They will continue to outsource and buy technology from horizontal companies, which will be the source of innovation within the industry.

Second, although platform companies have not generated sustainable profits, they generate immediate revenue and have the potential to provide an effective resource and financial base for becoming a hybrid company. Millennium Pharmaceuticals started as a target-validation platform company but now has adopted a hybrid strategy to bring drug candidates to market and achieve maximum value.

Finally, the shortcomings associated with the horizontal model are changing. More and more biopharmaceutical products are entering the market, and biotechnology companies are establishing themselves as successful organizations with solid business models. It follows that the market for their products and the likelihood of reaching an agreeable valuation with pharmaceutical companies will improve, as is seen in the valuations of such companies as Millennium and Amgen. The market is realizing the value they are creating and bidding their valuation up accordingly.

Continued Evolution of Virtual Corporations

The existence of niche horizontal companies creates the potential for virtual vertical companies to evolve. Virtual corporations control the activities of many smaller firms and synthesize the information obtained in a central location. Evidence of this trend is seen in larger firms, such as Pfizer and Pharmacia, which may evolve into virtual corporations and organize networks of the best firms around them. The information network of the biotechnology industry will allow this scenario to happen because companies can combine, cooperate, and disassemble more easily and quickly than in the past.

A notable difference between the biotechnology industry and other industries is the ability of smaller companies to more easily sustain themselves. In the microelectronics, personal computer, and Internet industries, smaller companies are often swallowed or worked around by larger companies. However, smaller companies in the drug-development industries show more staying power and can remain independent because of the regulated nature and complexity of the industry, as well as the protection of patents.

Because of the complexity of the landscape, the ability to synthesize information and orchestrate technologies to provide solutions will be an important source of value creation. Tremendous opportunity exists for virtual companies that are brokers in high-quality networks and can control a network hub. Large pharmaceutical companies may be the best candidates to pursue a virtual strategy. First, they have established consumer-brand equity. Second, the large pharmaceutical firms are maintaining their ability to shepherd products through clinical trials. Finally, they are developing the expertise to manage a large network of companies as they attempt to participate in "plug and play" with the best available companies for particular projects.

CONCLUSION

As the biotechnology industry has matured since its inception in the late 1970s, one fact has remained constant—the biology creates the profits. Those companies that create safe and effective drug therapies capture the most value and are the most successful. Throughout the past 20 years, firms have employed strategies for capturing profits. Some models, however, did not achieve a level of extraordinary profitability. This reaffirmation that the largest financial gains come from developing products will drive horizontal platform companies to develop drug candidates.

References

Arader, Harry. Northwestern University TechVenture Lecture (March 6, 2001).

Barron, David P. *Business and Its Environment.* 2d ed. Englewood Cliffs, NJ: Prentice Hall, 1996.

Bernstein, Karen. "The Deal-Maker." *BioCentury* (December 12, 1994).

_____. "Post-Industrial." *BioCentury* (June 26, 2000).

Bernstein, Karen, et al. "Big Thinkers II." *BioCentury* (June 15, 1998).

Bernstein, Karen, and Michael Schuppenhauer. "Back to Fundamentals." *BioCentury* (January 8, 2001).

Calkins, Kathryn. "Millennium's Product Plays." *BioCentury* (October 15, 1999).

Coase, Ronald. "The Nature of the Firm." *Economica* (1937). Reprinted in Coase, Ronald. *The Firm, the Market, and the Law.* Chicago: University of Chicago Press, 1988.

Davidow, William H., and Michael S. Malone. *The Virtual Corporation.* New York: HarperCollins Press, 1992.

Eisenberg, D.M. "Medical Malpractice Implications of Alternative Medicine." *JAMA* (November 11, 1998).

Feldbaum, Carl. "Primer: Genome and Genetic Research, Patent Protection and 21st Century Medicine." *BIO, Issues & Policies* (July 2000).

Garber, Ken. "Homestead 2000: The Genome." *Signals Magazine* (March 3, 2000).

Heron, Elaine, and David Greeting. Applied Biosystems Presentation (March 14, 2001).

Kelly, Kevin. *New Rules for the New Economy.* New York: Viking Press, 1998.

National Bioethics Advisory Committee. "Research Involving Human Biological Materials: Ethical Issues and Policy." *Guidance,* Vol. I, *Report and Recommendations of the National Bioethics Advisory Commission,* August 1999.

Naude, Alice. "Focus Report: Pharmaceuticals/Drug Discovery 99: Contract Research Organizations Grow from the Core." *Chemical Market Reporter* (August 16, 1999).

Rogoski, Richard R. "Firms Meet Biotech, CRO Software Needs." *Business Journal* (March 24, 2000).

Rohde, Laura. "Smart Cards to Contain Biometric Data" (February 9, 2000). http://www.cnn.com/2000/TECH/computing/02/09/biometrics.card.idg.

Rosen, Ben. "Keynote Address at the 1999 Biotechnology Industry Organization Conference" (May 18, 1999).

Sawhney, Mohan. "Net Economy Boundaries: Use 'Em and Lose 'Em." *Business 2.0* (July 11, 2000).

_____. "Seeing Ahead by Looking Back: Lessons from Network Evolution and Implications for the Internet" (February 2001).

Scott, Randy. "Incyte Genomics Chairman Predicts New Phase of Genomics-driven Discovery as Science Harnesses Knowledge of Gene Transcripts and Proteins." *Incyte Genomics Press Release* (2000).

_____. "Testimony of Randall Scott." *Subcommittee on courts and Intellectual Property. Committee of the Judiciary, House of Representatives* (July 13, 2000).

SNP Consortium. http://snp.cshl.org.

U.S. Food and Drug Administration. *Prescription Drug User Fees* (February 13, 2001).

U.S. Patent and Trademark Office. *Technology Profile Report, Patent Examining Technology Center, Groups 1630–1650, Biotechnology 1/1977–1/1998,* April 1999.

U.S. Patent and Trademark Office. "Utility Examination Guidelines." *Federal Register* (January 5, 2001).

Van Brunt, J. "Pharma's New Vision." *Signals Magazine* (June 1, 2000).

Waxes, Stephan Beckert. "Poetic about Telematics." *Executive Insights: Strategis Group.*

Werth, B. *The Billion Dollar Molecule.* New York: Touchstone, 1994.

Wolk, Marianne, and Bryan Candace. "Wireless Data—The Next Internet Frontier." *Robertson Stephens Technology Research* (January 25, 2000).

Yoffie, David. "Chess and Competing in the Age of Digital Convergence." *Competing in the Age of Digital Convergence.* Boston: Harvard Business School Publishing, 1997.

Index

Abernathy, William, 267
Adleman, Leonard, 24
Advanced Research Projects Agency (ARPA/
ARPANET), 284–285, 289
Advanced Television Enhancement Forum
(ATVEF), 175, 176, 189
Advertisers/advertising:
interactive television, 166–167, 177–178
location-based services and:
pull, 117–119
push, 115–117
Aether Systems, 214, 235
Affymetrix, 324, 331
Aimster, 290, 291
AirFlash (U.S.), 124
Airline industry, 12–13
Albuquerque, 39
Alcatel, 49, 55, 62, 140
Allen, Paul, 175
Alliances/partnerships/mergers:
biotechnology, 337–338
global, 337–338
interactive television, 173, 176, 186
network externalities through, 186
semiconductor industry, 9
across value chain, 227
wireless, 227
Alltel, 107
Amcol International, 276–277
America Online (AOL), 84, 85, 127, 163,
188
Instant Messenger, 293
television, 173, 177
Time Warner, 157, 173
Ameritech, 57
Amgen, 312, 334
Apple Computer, 137
Applied Biosystems, 324, 335
ARPANET, 284–285, 289

Artificial intelligence, 21
Asymmetric Digital Subscriber Line (ADSL),
297
AT&T, 46, 57, 172, 174, 190, 199, 214, 247,
254
ATVEF. See Advanced Television
Enhancement Forum (ATVEF)
Automated synchronization, 143
Automatic vehicle location (AVL), 214
Automobile industry, 145, 256
Aytar, Ozgur, 93, 99

Baca, Jim, 39
Ballard, Nigel, 141
Ballard Power, 278
Baltimore Technologies, 253
Bandwidth:
abundance (case study), 18, 27
applications hungry for, 39, 73
as commodity that can be traded, 76
peer-to-peer computing and, 297, 299
value shifts and, 17
Banking, 221
Bass Hotels, Inc., 206
Batteries and cell phones (nanotechnology),
277–278
Becker's theory of allocation of time, 11
Biomachinery for drug delivery
(nanotechnology), 281
Biometric access-security system (BASS)
authentication and authorization service,
146
Biotechnology industry, 23–24, 312–339
case studies:
Genentech, 319
Geron vs. ICOS, 334
Gilead-NextStar, 337
Incyte Genomics, 325
Pfizer, 313

Biotechnology industry *(Continued)*
  PPD, Inc., 331
  SNP Consortium, 327
  current trend: FDA and Prescription Drug
    User Fee Act (PDUFA), 317
  emergence of, 317–319
  evolution of business models (compared to
    computer industry), 319–320
  future of, 335–339
    continued evolution of virtual
      corporations, 338–339
    continued existence of horizontal
      models, 338
    continued forward integration, 336
    increased global partnerships, 337–338
    increased mergers between biotechnology
      companies, 337
  history of pharmaceutical industry, 313
  horizontal model, shortcomings of, 328–329
    inefficient capital markets, 329
    long product-development cycle, 328
    principal-agent problem, 328–329
    stiff competition and rapid technological
      changes, 328
  hybrid model, 329–331
  platform technologies, vertical *vs.*
    horizontal models, 322
  shifting industry, 320–328
    disruptive technologies, 321
    dynamic 1: inefficient research
      programs, 321–322
    dynamic 2: risk of product-based
      strategies, 323
    dynamic 3: strong intellectual-property
      laws, 323–324
    technology 1: genomics, 324–326
    technology 2: affordable computing
      power, 326–327
    technology 3: Internet communication,
      327–328
  Strategic Decision Matrix, 331, 332–333
  strategy for successful forward integration,
    331–335
  traditional drug discovery, 313–317
    vs. biotechnology drug-development
      approach, 318
    clinical trials and regulatory approval,
      315–316
    drug-development value chain, 314–317
    five stages, 314
    lead discovery and development, 315
    manufacturing, 316–317
    marketing/sales/distribution, 317
    overview table, 315
    target discovery, 314–315

vertically integrated companies (computer
    vs. pharmaceuticals *vs.* biotechnology
    industries), 320
Blackberry, 82, 201, 202, 203
Bluetooth, 129–150
  advantages, 131
  alternative technologies (substitutes *vs.*
    complements), 131–138
    access device, 135–138
    IEEE.802.11b in a competitive battle,
      132, 138
    LAN technologies, comparison of (table
      overview), 136
    relationship between 3G and local-area
      networks, 132–134
    WLAN technologies, 134–135
  applications/market segments, 130,
    142–147
    ad hoc connectivity, 143–144
    automated synchronization, 143
    automotive and industry applications,
      145
    company profiles and product rollout,
      146–147
    home networking, 130, 144
    interactive office, 130, 144–145
    mobile e-business, 145
    wireless personal-area networks
      (WPAN), 144
  future outlook for, 148–150
  impediments (obstacles *vs.* opportunities),
    139–142
    cost, 140
    interoperability, 140
    network externalities, 141–142
    security, 140–141
    standardization, 139–140
  PC industry and, 27–28, 30
  products/application rollout (graph), 147
  promise of, 129–131
  SIG, 146, 149
  value chain (wireless), 80, 205, 208–209
Boeing, 12, 13
Bowen, Debra, 188
Bower-Christensen framework, 269–270
Boyer, Herbert, 319
British Telecom, 96, 224
Broadcom, 146
Brown, Shona, 3–4

CableLabs, 189
Cable providers (iTV), 171
Cambridge, 108, 140, 146
Cancer cures (nanotechnology), 280
Carr, Harry, 74

CDMA (code-division multiple access), 88,
    91–92, 93, 108, 239, 248, 251
Celera, 326
Cell-Loc Inc., 101, 102, 108, 118
CellPoint, 124
Cell sites in commercial use in the United
    States (graph), 81
Cellular. *See* Wireless
Cellular Telephone Industry Association
    (CTIA), 89
Charge capture, 231–232
Child tracking, 122
cHTML, 252
Ciena, 47, 49, 50, 52, 61, 62
Cisco Systems, 55, 72, 73, 137
ClearWorks Communications, 67, 70
CLECs (competitive local-exchange carriers),
    45, 57, 68
Client/server topology, 288
CMOS transistor gate oxide limits, 6–7
Coase, Ronald, 322, 327
Columbitech, 95
Communications:
    analog, 91
    biotechnology industry and Internet,
        327–328
    convergence with computing/entertainment
        (interactive television), 158
    direct (P2P), 296
    wireless applications, 201–204, 236
Company profiles and product rollout,
    146–147
CompuServe, 85
Computer industry:
    biotechnology industry and affordable
        computing power, 326–327
    convergence with communication/
        entertainment (interactive television),
        158
    evolution of business models, 319–320,
        321
    history of PC, 14–15
    new disruptive paradigms, 22–25
        DNA computing, 23–24
        nanotubes, 8, 22, 24–25, 277
        quantum computing, 23
    predictions about death of PC, 27–28, 307
    utility of increased computing power,
        14–22
        proponents of high utility, 20–22
        proponents of low utility, 15–20
Content providers and advertisers, 177–178
Context indexing and file sharing, 290–292
Corvis, 47, 49
Crime prevention/awareness, 236

CT Motion's M-Coupon application, 117
Customer relationship management (CRM),
    199
Customization (iTV), 178
Cybiko, 251

Daniel Island Media Company (DIMC) of
    Charleston, South Carolina, 46, 65, 66,
    70
DEC, 34, 319
Dell Computer, 137, 240
Dertouzos, Michael, 16–17, 19, 20, 21, 30
Device-to-device (D2D) model, 19
Dexheimer, John, 41
diAx, 108, 128
Digital satellite providers (iTV), 171
Digital subscriber line (DSL), 297
Diminishing returns, law of, 11–12
Direct communication/information
    distribution (P2P), 296
Directory services, 117–119, 125
DirecTV, 173, 175
DishNetwork, 173
Distributed computing, 293–294, 300
Distributed content storage, 295–296
Distributed parallel processing, 295
Distributed processing units (DPUs), 17
DNA computing, 8, 22, 23–24
DoCoMo. *See* I-Mode; NTT DoCoMo
Domain Name System (DNS), 285
Dopants, maximum limit to use of, 7
Drug development/discovery. *See*
    Biotechnology industry
Dynamic, distributed search, 296–297
Dzubek, Frank, 38–39

E-911 services. *See* Emergency services
EDGE (enhanced data rates for GSM
    evolution), 251
Edwards, Morris, 73
Electronic program guide (EPG), 158, 168,
    174, 175, 177, 190
Eli Lilly, 319, 331
Emergency services, 103, 114–115, 125
Enterprise processing, 302, 305–306, 308
Enterprise Profit Optimization Solution,
    215
Entertainment (I-Mode), 243. *See also*
    Interactive television (iTV)
Entropia, 294
Enviro21, 19
Envive, 294
E-prescribing, 231
Ericsson, 84, 85, 96, 97, 121, 137, 146, 224
Exponentials (nonlinear growth), 32–34

FDA and the Prescription Drug User Fee Act
    (PDUFA), 317
FDMA (frequency-division multiple access),
    91
Federal Express, 213, 216
Feynman, Richard, 263–264
FiberPath, 68
Fiber to the home (FTTH), 45, 46, 62, 75.
    See also Optical networking, last mile
    (fiber to the home: FTTH)
File sharing (P2P), 290–292, 300
Financial services (wireless applications),
    216–229
  competitive landscape, 223
  customer loyalty, 225
  future outlook, 225–228
  global outlook, 228
  initial trends and observations, 224
  integration of wireless with other delivery
      channels, 228
  investment banking, 221
  key success factors, 224–225
  open access to Internet, 228
  partnering across value chain, 227
  retail banking, 221
  retail brokerage, 220–221
  security concerns, 225
  service differentiation, 225
Five Forces model, 26
Fleet management, 120–121, 214
Formulary, 230
Fuel cells (nanotechnology), 278

Galileo, 33
Gallatin, Mike, 316, 334
Games, 306–307, 308
Geiling, Greg, 46–47
Gelsinger, Patrick, 284, 310
Gemstar, 174, 190
Genentech, 280, 312, 319
Genomics, 324–326
Geron, 334, 335
Gilead-NextStar (biotechnology industry case
    study), 337
Global Crossing, 46, 50, 51
Global partnerships, 337–338
Globalstar, 214
Global system for mobile communication
    (GSM) standard, 87–88, 91–92, 96–97,
    201, 203, 239, 251
Gnutella, 291, 296, 306–307
Go2 Services, 118, 127
Government:
  health care and, 230, 232
  location-based services and, 103

optical networking and, 75
wireless applications, 234–237
  better services for citizens, 236–237
  cost of communications, 236
  crime prevention/awareness, 236
  increased security features, 236
  key success factors, 236
  market size and applications, 235
  technology viability, 235–236
GPRS (general packet-radio service), 92,
    251
GPS (global positioning system), 104–105,
    214
Groove Networks, 304
Grove, Andy, 11, 25, 33
Growth:
  across time horizons, 29
  nonlinear, 32–34
GSM (global system for mobile
    communication) standard, 87–88, 91–92,
    96–97, 201, 203, 239, 251
Gulati, Ranjay, 197, 257

Health care, 229–234, 279–281
  biotechnology and:
    artificial red blood cells and
        mitochondria, 280–281
    biomachinery for drug delivery, 281
    cancer cures, 280
    inside vs. outside human body, 280
    pharmacogenomics, 280
  wireless applications:
    charge capture, 231–232
    e-prescribing, 231
    future, 232–233
    key success factors, 233–234
    libraries, 232
    market size, 229–231
    real-time laboratory orders/results, 232
    regulations and HCFA rules, 232
    remote patient monitoring, 232–233
    telemetry applications, 232–233
Health Insurance Portability and
    Accountability Act (HIPAA), 232
Henderson-Clark model, 268–269, 274
Hewlett-Packard (HP), 137, 146, 149
Home networking (Bluetooth), 144
HomeRF, 131, 133, 135, 136, 137
Horizontal business model, 320, 322,
    328–329, 335, 338
Horizontal/vertical wireless applications, 197.
    See also Wireless application(s)
Howard, Michael, 47
HTML, 199, 208, 246, 252
Hughes Electronics, 173

Hutcheson, Dan, 3, 8, 11
Hutchison Telecommunications, 96, 119

IBM, 7–8, 34, 146, 224, 286, 319
ICOS Corporation, 316, 334
ICQ, 292–293
IEEE 802.11b, 131, 132, 133, 135, 136, 137,
    141
IEEE 802.14.1, 148
Iijima, Sumio, 276
iMesh, 292
I-Mode, 240–248. *See also* NTT DoCoMo
  business model, 242–243
  charges, 92, 224, 243
  future of, 247–248
  overview of concept/essentials, 241, 242
  services, 82, 92, 205, 243–244, 247
  success factors, 244–247, 256–257
    brand development, 245–246
    consumer focus, 245
    content quality, 246
    economical positioning, 246
    existing customer base, 246–247
    market power, 244–245
    user interface, 246
  United States, transferring to, 253–254
  WAP standard and, 251, 253
  wireless generations (2.5G/3G), 93, 101
Incyte Genomics, 325, 326, 328, 335
Infrared (LAN technology), 136
Infrasearch, 19
Infrastructure providers (MSOs) (iTV),
    170–176
Innovation, 267–278
Instant messaging (IM), 99, 292–293, 300
Institute of Electrical and Electronic
    Engineers (IEEE):
  IEEE 802.11b, 131, 132, 133, 135, 136,
    137, 141
  IEEE 802.14.1, 148
Intel:
  Bluetooth, 146, 149
  growth across three time horizons, 29–30
  horizontal business model, 320, 335
  Microsoft and, 15, 22, 26, 30
  Moore's law, 8, 9, 10
  peer-to-peer (P2P) technology, 17
  Pentium 4 chip, 15, 22
  potential strategy for, 25–31
    scenario 1: Moore of the same, 25–26
    scenario 2: vicious circle, 26–27
    scenario 3: business will use less
        processing power, 27
    scenario 4 and others: the PC is dead,
        27–28

strategic posture, 30
wireless standards and, 137
Intellectual property laws, 190, 323–324
Intelligent optical network, 48, 75–76
Interactive conferences, 145
Interactive office, 144–145
Interactive television (iTV), 155–191
  adoption forecasts (S-curve), 162–163
  alliances/partnerships, 173, 176, 186
  assumptions, continuum of, 156
  cable providers, 171
  challenges, 162, 188–190
  consumer benefits and value creation, 180,
      183
  consumer-centric approach to
      functionality, 179–182
  content providers and advertisers, 177–178
  control of consumer interface, 173
  convenience and productivity, 179–181
  convergence of computing/
      communication/entertainment, 158
  cross-media enhancements, 183–184
  current state of, 164–178
  customer-service skills, 172
  customization, 178
  data enhancement broadcasting services,
      174–176
  defining, 158
  digital satellite providers, 171
  enhanced entertainment, 181–182
  evolution of, 158–163
  future of, 178–190
  hardware providers (set-top box
      manufacturers and PVRs), 176–177
  history of, 155–157
  impact on players' landscape, 185–188
  incumbents, 164–165
  industry patterns, expected, 187
  infrastructure providers (MSOs), 170–176
  intellectual property, 190
  manufacturing capabilities, 177
  migration to network model, 182–185
  mobility enhancements, 184–185
  models for (three):
    Internet model, 159–160, 161, 169
    MSO model (multiple service operators),
        159, 160, 168
    PVR model (personal video recorder),
        159, 163, 168, 169
  peer-to-peer networking, 185, 186
  privacy, 188
  revenue models, 165–170, 178
    access (subscription and pay-per-view),
        166
    advertising, 166–167

Interactive television (iTV) *(Continued)*
  hardware purchase, 167
  Internet model, 169
  MSO model, 168
  program licensing, 167
  PVR revenue model, 168
  T-commerce (television-based e-
    commerce), 167–168
 service offerings by model, 161
 social interaction, 182
 software providers, 173–174
 standards, need for, 176, 177, 178,
    188–189
 telecommunications companies, 171–172
 value, 164–165, 185–188
International Technology Road Map for
  Semiconductors (ITRS), 6, 10
International Telecommunications Union
  (ITU) specification for the third
  generation, 93
Internet:
 communication, and biotechnology
    industry, 327–328
 model (interactive television), 159–160,
    161, 169, 178
 precursor (ARPANET), 284–285, 289
 TCP/IP protocol (Transaction Control
    Protocol/Internet Protocol), 285
 World Wide Web, 285, 296
Interoperability, 140, 299
Investment banking, 221

Japan. *See* I-Mode; NTT DoCoMo
JDS-Uniphase, 53

Kalepa Networks, 286
Kiosks, walk-up, 145
Knowledge applications (wireless), 197–201
 challenges, 199–200
 typical system architecture, 200
 value proposition, 198–199
Knowledge management (peer-to-peer),
    304–305, 308
Kotler, Philip, 72
Kurzweil, Ray, 20, 21, 22, 32, 34

LAN (local area network) technologies,
    132–134, 135, 136, 145. *See also*
    Wireless local area networks (WLANs)
Lang, Larry, 39
Last Mile. *See* Optical networking, last mile
    (fiber to the home: FTTH)
Level 3 (company), 46, 50, 57
Liberate (iTV), 173
Lithography, 7, 28

Location-based services (LBS), 101–129, 205
 application(s):
    analysis of, 114
    categories, 111
    child or pet tracking, 122
    emergency services, 114–115
    fleet management, 120–121
    navigation, 119–120
    pull advertising and directory services,
      117–119
    push advertising, 115–117
    social uses/entertainment, 123–124
    tracking, 120
    traffic monitoring, 122–123
 application developers, 127
 business models, 110–114
 equipment manufacturers and location-
    technology providers, 127
 evolution of, 125
 government's role, 103
 industry components, 103–110
 location-based service providers, 127
 market attractiveness, analysis of, 115
 market size, analysis of, 113
 outlook for, 124–126
 overview, 102–103, 105, 106, 111
 privacy/security issues, 110, 119
 profit drivers (three), 111
 survey of customer interest in, 112
 technology, 104
    carrier model, 108
    cost structures, 109–110
    device-dependent location, 106–107
    GPS (global positioning system),
      104–105
    multiple standards, 107
    network-dependent location, 107
    network triangulation, 106
    third-party model, 108–109
    time of arrival (TOA) method, 107
    two dimensions, 104, 106
 value chain (diagram), 104
 value migration (long-term future),
    127–129
 value position, analysis of strength of,
    112
 wireless carriers, 127
Long-haul. *See* Optical networking, long-
    haul segment
Lucent, 45, 52–53, 55, 62, 146
LuxN, 43

Mangosoft, 290, 292
Manugistics, 215
Martin, John, 337

MasterCard International, 227
Matsumura, Miko, 286
MCI WorldCom, 57
McKesson, 213
M-commerce:
 I-Mode, 243
 wireless application, 204–210
  challenges, 206–208
  security providers, 208
  transaction enablers, 206–208
  translation/integration, 208
  value proposition, 205–206
Mergers. See Alliances/partnerships/mergers
Merkle, Ralph, 261, 262–263
Metro-area networks, 54–62
 end customer, 56–57
 model of, 56
 network operator, 57–59
 solutions provider/equipment
  manufacturer, 59–62
 telecom vendor and infrastructure
  investment, 55
 value chain, 56–62
Metro-market winners, 45–46
Metro optical networks (MONs), 45
Microelectronics (nanotechnology
 application), 276–279
Micromanipulation techniques, 264
Microsoft:
 Bluetooth and, 141, 146, 149
 broadband wireless, 98
 horizontal business model, 320, 335
 Intel/semiconductor industry and, 15, 22,
  26, 30
 interactive television, 157, 163, 173, 174,
  175, 188
 secure payment system for I-Mode, 245
 Windows/Office platform (reaction as key
  indicator of change), 31
Middleware, 173
Millennium Pharmaceuticals, 330, 335, 338
Mitochondria, 280–281
Mitsubishi, 176
Mixed Signals, 174, 175, 176
MMS (multimedia messaging service), 100
Mobile e-business, 145
Mobitex, 239
Moore, Geoffrey (Inside the Tornado), 239
Moore, Gordon, 3–6
Moore's Law, 3–16, 31–35, 276
 biology and, 326–327
 costs of, 9–14
 first ten years (hitting physical limits?),
  6–9
 history of, 3–6

illustrated by Intel architecture, 4
 market dynamics, 9–12
 perils of prediction and, 31–35
 Second Law, 9
 seeing ahead by looking back, 12–14
 solutions, 15–16
 technological challenges, 6–7
 technological solutions, 7–9
MoreCom, 173
Motient, 214
Motorola, 9, 84, 85, 97, 137, 146, 176, 227,
 239
MSO (multiple service operators) model
 (iTV), 159, 160, 168, 170–176, 178
Multimedia messaging service (MMS), 100
Mumford, Greg, 52
Myhrvold, 22, 26

Nanocor, 276–277
Nanotechnology, 8, 22, 24–25, 261–282
 ambiguities, 265–267
  clusters, 267
  complementary searches, 266–267
  evaluating real needs of customers, 267
  primitive technological capabilities, 266
  specific problems/wider application,
   267
 applications, 275–281
 enabling technologies, 264–265
  computational nanotechnology, 265
  micromanipulation techniques, 264
  nanoassemblers, 264
  nanoscale microscopes, 264
 evolving value chain, 265
 frameworks and analysis, 265–270
 health care applications, 279–281
  artificial red blood cells and
   mitochondria, 280–281
  biomachinery for drug delivery, 281
  cancer cures, 280
  inside vs. outside human body, 280
  pharmacogenomics, 280
 microelectronics applications, 276–279
  batteries and cell phones, 277–278
  fuel cells, 278
  miscellaneous, 278–279
  nanomemory computers, 277
  plastics, 276–277
 models of innovation, 267–270
  disruptive technologies, 269–270
  firm capabilities, 268–269
  phases of innovation, 267–278
 nanotubes as solution to Moore's law, 8,
  22, 24–25, 277
 practical roadmap, 270–275

Nanotechnology *(Continued)*
  capabilities to build and deploy,
    274–275
  extent of disruption, 270–271
  process innovations, 272
  product innovations, 272
  risks and opportunities in fluid-phase
    industries, 273
  risks and opportunities in specific-phase
    industries, 273
  S-curve phase of, 270–271
  technical background, 262–263
  timing, 263–264
Napster, 284, 289, 290–291, 296, 297, 298
Natsuno, T., 246
Navigation, 119–120
NEC, 97, 278
Netbatch, 17
Network(s)/networking:
  computing (history of), 284–285
  externalities, 141–142, 186, 298
  home, 130, 144
  intelligent optical, 48, 75–76
  local-area (LAN), 132–134, 135, 136, 145
    (see also Wireless local area networks
    (WLANs))
  metro-area, 45–46, 54–62
  metro optical (MONs), 45
  operator, 42, 57–59, 65–67
  optical *(see* Optical networking)
  P2P topology *(see* Peer-to-peer (P2P)
    computing)
  passive optical (PONs), 63
  personal area (PAN), 129, 133, 137
  provider, 50–51
  standards (IEEE 802.11b), 131, 132, 133,
    135, 136, 137, 141
  triangulation (location-based services), 106
  wide-area (WANs), 46 *(see also* Optical
    networking, long-haul segment)
  wireless carriers, 82
  wireless local area (WLANs), 95, 101, 133,
    134–135, 137, 149
  wireless personal-area (WPAN), 144
Network-dependent location, 107
Network model (interactive television):
  migration to, 182–185
  peer-to-peer networking, 185, 186
  value in the networked landscape, 185–188
Network 21, 19
Newtonian physics, 33
Nextel, 107
Niemela, Jennifer, 62
911 services. *See* Emergency services
Nokia, 83, 84, 85, 97, 100, 137, 146, 253

Nonlinear growth, 32–34
Nortel, 47, 49, 50, 52, 55, 61, 62, 72, 73,
    118
NTT DoCoMo. *See also* I-Mode:
  GPS-based mobile personal-navigation
    service (DokoNavi), 120
  market capitalization, 93

Office Depot, Inc., 214
Okarma, Thomas, 334, 335
Olympus, 244
OmniSky, 202, 203
One 2 One, 96
OnStar, 212
Open-source standards, 74
OpenTV, 157, 161, 173
Optical networking, 38–77
  components manufacturer, 42–43
  components of value chain, 42–43
  end customer, 42
  future of, 72–76
    consolidation, 73–74
    consumer access, 74–75
    government's role, 75
    intelligent optical network, 75–76
    migration to fiber, 74
    move to open-source standards, 74
    optical-hardware development and
      upgrades, 73
  growth/trajectory of, 76
  last mile (fiber to the home: FTTH), 46,
    62–72
    end customer, 65
    network operator, 65–67
    normative framework conclusions,
      68–70
    solutions provider/equipment
      manufacturer, 67–68
    time-scaled value capture, 70–72
    value chain, 64–68
    winners, 46
  long-haul segment, 44, 46–55
    end customer, 49–50
    network provider, 50–51
    systems provider, 52–53
    value chain, 49
    winners, 44
  metro-area networks, 45–46, 54–62
    end customer, 56–57
    model of (figure), 56
    network operator, 57–59
    solutions provider/equipment
      manufacturer, 59–62
    telecom vendor and infrastructure
      investment, 55

value chain, 56–62
winners, 45–46
network operator, 42
normative framework, 44–46, 68–70
solutions provider, 42
technology of, 40–41
value analysis, 41–46
Optical Solutions, Inc., 46, 67, 68, 69, 70
Orange Telecom, 96, 124, 128
Oxygen, Project, 16, 19
Ozzie, Ray, 304

Pace Micro, 176
Package tracking, 213
Palm, 16, 84, 98, 184, 203, 224, 239
Panas, Alex, 197, 257
PANs (personal area networks), 129, 133,
    137, 144
Parikh, Dave, 185
Partnerships. See Alliances/partnerships/
    mergers
Partovi, Naser, 40, 73
Passive optical networks (PONs), 63
PayPal, 205, 224
Peer-to-peer (P2P) computing, 17, 99,
    284–310
  bandwidth availability/limitations, 297,
    299
  business models, viable, 301–302
  challenges, 298–299
  collaboration in project management,
    302–304, 308
  context indexing, 290–292
  corporate setting, 309
  current scene, 286–287
  direct communication/information
    distribution, 296
  distributed computing, 293–294, 300
  distributed content storage, 295–296
  distributed parallel processing, 295
  dynamic, distributed search, 296–297
  enterprise processing, 305–306, 308
  file sharing, 290–292, 300
  future applications/landscape, 302–309
  games, 306–307, 308
  history of network computing, 284–285
  home-user setting, 309
  hybrid centralized/decentralized models,
    298
  instant messaging (IM), 99, 292–293, 300
  interoperability, 299
  knowledge management, 304–305, 308
  models, 287–290
    hybrid P2P network topology, 289–290
    pure P2P network topology, 287–289

network externalities, 298
scalability, 298
security, 299
success factors, 297–298
today's players, 290–294
value drivers, 295–297, 299–300
Personal area networks (PANs), 129, 133,
    137, 144
Personal computer. See Computer industry
Personalization (financial applications), 226
Personal video recorder (PVR) model (iTV),
    159, 163, 168, 169, 177, 178
Pescatore, John, 252
Pet tracking, 122
Pfizer, 313, 338–339
Pharmaceutical industry, history of, 313. See
    also Biotechnology industry
Pharmacia, 339
Pharmacogenomics (nanotechnology), 280
Philips, 177
Phone.com, 252
Pinckney, Bob, 65–66
Plastics (nanotechnology), 276–277
Ponder, Daryl, 67, 68
Popular Power, 294
Porter's five-forces analysis, 25
PPD, Inc. (biotechnology industry case
    study), 331
Prediction:
  Moore's Law and the perception of time,
    34–35
  nonlinear growth, 32–34
  over-/under- (in S-curve type
    developments), 33
  perils of, 31–35
  seeing ahead by looking back, 12–14
Prescription Drug User Fee Act (PDUFA),
    317
Preston, Claire, 93
Principal-agent problem, 328–329
Privacy/security issues:
  Bluetooth, 140–141
  financial applications (wireless), 225
  interactive television, 188
  location-based services, 110, 119
  peer-to-peer, 299
  wireless, 208, 225, 236, 256
Productivity, and diminishing returns, 14
Program licensing (iTV), 167
Project management collaboration, 302–304,
    308
Project Oxygen (MIT's Media Lab), 16, 19
Psion, 146
PVR (personal video recorder) model (iTV),
    159, 163, 168, 169, 177, 178

Quantum computing, 8, 22, 23
Qube, 156–157
Qu-bits, 23
Queue killer, ultimate, 145
Qwest, 46, 50, 51

Raab, Carolyn, 74
Rabin, Bill, 47
Rathman, George, 334, 336
"Raw" architecture proposed by Project
    Oxygen, 19, 31
Rayleigh's law, 7
Real-options-based outlook (semiconductor
    industry), 25, 28–30
RealPort, 147–148
Real-time laboratory orders/results, 232
Registry Magic, 146
Remit.com, 205
Replay TV, 168, 175
RespondTV, 174, 175, 176
RIM (Research-in Motion), 82, 201, 202,
    203, 239
Rosenberg, Nathan, 265–267
Rye Telephone Company, 44, 46, 66, 69,
    70

Satellite providers (iTV), 171
Sawhney, Mohanbir, 185
Scott, Randy, 326
S-curve, 32–33, 162–163, 270–273
Secure socket layer (SSL), 208
Security issues. See Privacy/security issues
Semiconductor technology, 3–35
  change, key indicators of, 31
  costs of Moore's Law and market dynamics,
      9–14
    market dynamics, 9–12
    Moore's Second Law, 9
    seeing ahead by looking back, 12–14
  first ten years (hitting physical limits?),
      6–9
    technological challenges, 6–7
    technological solutions, 7–9
  history of Moore's Law, 3–6
  perils of prediction, 31–35
    Moore's Law and perception of time,
        34–35
    nonlinear growth, 32–34
  potential strategy for Intel and the
      semiconductor industry, 25–31
    real options, 28–30
    scenario 1: Moore of the same, 25–26
    scenario 2: vicious circle, 26–27
    scenario 3: business will use less
        processing power, 27

scenario 4 and others: the PC is dead,
    27–28
ten years out: new (disruptive) paradigms,
    22–25
  DNA computing, 23–24
  nanotubes, 24–25
  quantum computing, 23
utility of increased computing power,
    14–22
  proponents of high utility of computing
      power, 20–22
  proponents of low utility of computing
      power, 15–20
Seti@home, 17, 286, 293
Shipley, Dave, 44, 66–67
Shirky, Clay, 287
Shopping channels, enhanced, 167
Short-message service (SMS), 99, 100, 196,
    201, 203, 204
Siemens, 97, 119
SignalSoft Corporation, 101, 119
Silicon. See also Semiconductor technology:
  alternatives to, 8
  beauty of, 6–7
  knowledge based built around, 25
  switching layers, 8
Single-nucleotide polymorphism (SNP)
    Consortium (case study), 327
SnapTrack, 108
Software:
  interactive television, 173–174
  wireless applications, 82–83
Solow, Robert, 14
Sonera, 205
SONET network, 45, 48, 55, 56, 57
Sony, 98, 137, 176, 177, 245, 246, 278
SourceMedia, 173
Speech technology, 27
Spotcast, 116
Sprint, 46, 57, 61, 94, 103, 107, 214, 249,
    254
Standard(s)/standardization:
  Bluetooth, 139–140
  GSM (global system for mobile
      communication), 87–88, 91–92,
      96–97, 201, 203, 239, 251
  I-Mode, 251–256
  interactive television, 176, 177, 178,
      188–189
  networking (IEEE 802.11b), 131, 132,
      133, 135, 136, 137, 141
  open-source, 74
  wireless applications, 238–239
Starcer, Jeff, 66
Strategic Decision Matrix, 331, 332–333

Sun-Tzu, 239
Swanson, Robert, 319
Sycamore, 47, 49
Synchronization, automated, 143
Synteni, 324

Talking Drum, 250
T-commerce (television-based e-commerce),
    167–168
TCP/IP protocol (Transaction Control
    Protocol/Internet Protocol), 285
TDMA (time-division multiple access), 88,
    91–92, 239, 251
Technology(ies):
    challenges/solutions (Moore's law), 6–9
    disruptive, 271–272, 321
    emerging (see Biotechnology industry;
        Nanotechnology; Peer-to-peer (P2P)
        computing)
    enabling/infrastructure (see Optical
        networking; Semiconductor
        technology; Wireless)
    product life cycle, 14
    sustaining vs. disruptive, 271–272
Telecommunications companies (iTV),
    171–172
Telematics, 212
Telemetry and tracking (wireless application),
    210–216, 232–233
    automatic vehicle location (AVL), 214
    challenges, 214–215
    health care (remote patient monitoring),
        232–233
    package tracking, 213
    value proposition, 212–214
Teletext model, 155–156
Television. See Interactive television (iTV)
Texas Instruments, 9, 67, 140
Theory-of-constraints (TOC) view, 20–21
3COM, 84, 137, 146, 147
3G. See Wireless generations
Three-in-one phone, 144
Time:
    Becker's theory of allocation of, 11
    growth across, 29–30
    Moore's law and perception of, 34–35
    pacing of technology, 3–4
    real-time laboratory orders/results, 232
Time-division multiple access (TDMA), 88,
    91–92, 239, 251
Time of arrival (TOA) method, 107
Time-scaled value capture, 70–72
Times Three (L-Tokens application), 125
Time Warner, 157, 173
TiVo, 163, 168, 173, 174, 175, 177

Tomanek, David, 277
Tracking, 120, 122. See also Telemetry and
    tracking (wireless application)
Traffic monitoring (LBS), 122–123
Transaction enablers, 206–208
Transistor, 10
Transmeta, 16

UBS Warburg, 212
Ulvac, Tokyo-based, 278
Universal mobile-telecommunications system
    (UMTS), 93, 96
Universal remote, 144
UPS, 213, 215, 216
Utterback, James, 267–268

Verizon, 83, 101, 107, 214
Video on demand (VOD), 165
Virtual corporations, 338–339
Virtual mall (iTV), 167–168
Vodafone, 96, 101
Voice application (wireless), 99
Vulcan Ventures, 175

WAP (wireless application protocol), 98, 119,
    208, 240, 246
    vs. I-Mode, 251, 252, 253
    location-based technology, 119
    problems, 252–253
Warner Communications' Qube, 156–157
Webraska, 102, 117, 118
WebTV, 173, 174, 175
Western Wireless, 107
Wherify Wireless Location Services, 123
Wide-area networks (WANs), 46. See also
    Optical networking, long-haul segment
Willamette architecture, 5
Williams, 46, 50, 52, 57
Windows Messenger, 293
WingCast, 212
Wink Communications, 174, 175
Wired-equivalent privacy (WEP), 141
Wireless, 79–150, 193–257. See also
    Location-based services (LBS)
    carrier perspective on revenue trends,
        89–90
    competing networks (three), 93
    data landscape, 132
    defined, 79
    local technologies, 135
    market growth by geographic region,
        86–87
    market growth by technology, 87–89
    United States market, 248–256
        choosing a standard, 251–256

Wireless *(Continued)*
  network access, 251
  recommendations, 255
  young consumers, 249–251
Wireless application(s), 193–257
  argument for, 190–196
  framework, 196
  future trends (vertical applications become
      horizontal), 237–240
    broad functionality, 239
    crossing chasm/competition in value
        chain, 239–240
    standardization, 238–239
  horizontal, 196–216
    automatic vehicle location (AVL), 214
    communications, 201–204
    knowledge applications, 197–201
    M-commerce, 204–210
    package tracking, 213
    telemetry and tracking, 210–216
  killer application in Japan (*see* I-Mode)
  summary (horizontal and vertical), 197
  vertical, 216–240
    financial services, 216–229
    government, 234–237
    health care, 229–234
Wireless-application-protocol (WAP), 84
Wireless generations, 91–101
  1G: analog communication, 91
  2G: today's wireless, 91–92
  2.5G: the bridging technology, 92
  3G: future of wireless, 91, 93–101
    data rates, 94
    defined, 93
    financing threats, 95–98
    outlook, 100–101
    possible killer applications, 98–100
    relationship with local-area networks,
        91–93, 95

Wireless local area networks (WLANs), 95,
    101, 133, 134–135, 137, 149
Wireless Markup Language (WML), 199, 208
Wireless personal-area networks (WPAN),
    144
Wireless value chain:
  cell sites in commercial use in the United
      States (graph), 81
  defined, 79, 80–85
  diagram, 80
  elements, 80–83
  equipment:
    components, 80–81
    devices, 81–82
    wireless infrastructure, 81
  future trend: crossing chasm/competition
      in, 239–240
  networks—wireless carriers, 82
  players, 83–84
  software and services:
    carrier and enterprise-class solutions,
        82–83
    content and portals, 83
    enabling software and services, 82
  value creation, 84–85
Wisniewski, Don, 251
WML (Wireless Markup Language), 199, 208
Wong, Richard, 53
Word processing, 13–14, 20
WorldCom, 46, 52
WorldGate, 174, 175
World Wide Web, 285, 296

xDSL, newest DSL development, 64
Xircom, 147–148

Yahoo!, 84, 124, 127, 180
Yamaha Corporation, 243
Yoffie, David, 319